Elements
of
Personnel
Management

Elements of Personnel Management

Revised Second Edition

K.J. PRATT MSc, FCIS, AIPM
Principal Lecturer, Danbury Park Management Centre,
Anglia Higher Education College

S.G. BENNETT MSc, FCIS, MInstM, MInstAM (Dip)
Head of External Relations,
Anglia Higher Education College

CHAPMAN AND HALL

LONDON • NEW YORK • TOKYO • MELBOURNE • MADRAS

UK	Chapman and Hall, 2–6 Boundary Row, London SE1 8HN
USA	Chapman and Hall, 29 West 35th Street, New York NY10001
JAPAN	Chapman and Hall Japan, Thomson Publishing Japan, Hirakawacho Nemoto Building, 7F, 1-7-11 Hirakawa-cho, Chiyoda-ku, Tokyo 102
AUSTRALIA	Chapman and Hall Australia, Thomas Nelson Australia, 480 La Trobe Street, PO Box 4725, Melbourne 3000
INDIA	Chapman and Hall India, R. Seshadri, 32 Second Main Road, CIT East, Madras 600 035

First edition 1985
Second edition 1989
Reprinted 1990

© 1990

Typeset in Plantin 10/11 by Best-set Typesetter Ltd, Hong Kong

Printed in Great Britain at the University Press, Cambridge

ISBN 0 412 383802 (HB)

British Library Cataloguing in Publication Data

Pratt, K.J. (Kenneth J)
    Elements of personnel management.—Rev
    2nd ed.
    1. Personnel management
    I. Title II. Bennet, S.G. (Stephen G.)
    658.3

    ISBN 0-412-38380 2

Contents

Preface

Like its predecessor, this book is an introduction to the theory and practice of personnel management. It contains the elements of the subject in what we hope is sufficient detail, while remaining concise and easy to refer to. We have updated the employment legislation and added sections on topical matters and other areas reflecting our experience of professional examinations. It is designed primarily for those who are studying Personnel Management as part of a professional course such as those referred to below. It should also be useful as a primer for undergraduates and for those engaged upon various management and business courses such as the DMS or BTEC Higher Level Awards.

A book of this length can only provide a general overview of the subject. For those wishing to pursue a particular topic in more detail it does, however, provide valuable references and further recommended reading. These, together with the sample examination questions, are considered to be a particularly beneficial feature of the book.

We should like to thank the various publishers and other organisations who kindly consented to the reproduction of certain passages, diagrams, etc. Also, our thanks and acknowledgement to the following professional bodies for permission to use sample examination questions:

Institute of Chartered Secretaries and Administrators (ICSA)
Institute of Personnel Management (IPM)
Chartered Association of Certified Accountants (CACA)
Chartered Institute of Bankers (CIB)
Chartered Building Societies Institute (CBSI)
Institute of Administrative Management (IAM)

KJP SGB

Note: Throughout this book we have used 'he', 'him', 'his' etc when making reference to staff. This is primarily to avoid clumsy sentences and readers are requested to read 'she', 'her', 'hers' etc into all these references.

Preface to revised second edition

This revised edition reflects changes in employment law, personnel theory and practice, as well as examination questions where appropriate. We have tried to incorporate the considerable number of changes without major disruption to the structure and substantive content of the second edition.

KJP SGB (1989)

Part 1
The personnel
function

1
The role of the personnel function

A BRIEF HISTORY

Although aspects of personnel management can be traced back as far as the ancient Egyptians, its more recent history finds its source in the industrial revolution of the late eighteenth and early nineteenth centuries. The period was one of tremendous prosperity for the middle classes, though this prosperity was not generally shared with the employees manning the ever more numerous factories. Wages were low, conditions were poor, management was often harsh and feudal in style. Workers frequently found themselves in competition with the inmates of workhouses and gaols. For example, many of Telford's canals were dug by prison labour. Serfdom still existed in Scottish colleries and to find children under seven years of age working down mines was not unusual. In the silk industry, the workforce was almost totally composed of children under sixteen years.

Workers were often beaten — though usually only up to their fourteenth birthday. For other misdemeanours, e.g. singing, workers could be fined two or three days' wages.

Frequently, employers' attitudes reflected religious beliefs — often those of the Quakers — and for this reason, despite its severity, the period was one of paternalism. Eventually as a result of the efforts of a few reformers and the total squalor of working conditions, Parliament intervened with the introduction of the Factories Act 1833.

Although the Act was applicable only to the textile industry and dealt with children's working conditions, it also established the Factories Inspectorate and paved the way for a series of further statutes, chiefly in 1867 and 1878. These extended the earlier regulations and rights of the Inspectorate to other industries. Even so, the standard working week was still 60 hours and the minimum age for employment in a factory remained at 12 until 1918.

The second half of the nineteenth century also saw increasing interest in trade unionsim. Despite stringent and repressive government controls, increasing membership of the movement strengthened demands for improved conditions. The union voice was further strengthened by the election of trade union sponsored Members of Parliament in 1885.

In addition to trade union demands, the pioneering work of Quaker employers, such as the Rowntrees and the Cadburys, foreign competition, and a growing awareness of the effects of environmental conditions on worker performance, combined to stimulate interest in employee welfare. The first full-time industrial welfare-worker is reputed to have been appointed at the Rowntree factory in 1896. Other employers rapidly followed Rowntree's example, and in 1913 the inaugural meeting of the Welfare Workers' Association was held. In 1946, after several changes of name, this association became the Institute of Personnel Management.

World War I brought new problems for industry. The war effort required that optimum use be made of all resources. In the factories women replaced men conscripted into the armed forces. As a part of the war effort, long hours — up to 90 hours a week — were worked in conditions that by present day standards would be considered wholly unnacceptable. It soon became clear that output was not increasing in proportion to the increased effort. In 1915 the Health of Munition Workers Committee was established to investigate the effect of working conditions on output and worker health. In its reports, the Committee published much useful information that was applied in the munitions factories, but only minimally elsewhere. In 1916 the Ministry of Munitions set up an Industrial Welfare Department under Seebohm Rowntree with the job of encouraging the introduction of welfare practice into factories. During the same year, the Home Secretary was authorized to require the appointment of factory welfare officers, and by the end of the war it is estimated that around 1000 were so employed.

Between the wars, the period was initially one of deep economic depression. Many of the welfare workers recently recruited soon lost their jobs. Nevertheless, in 1918 the Industrial Welfare Society (now the Industrial Society) was established together with the Industrial Fatigue Research Board. These were joined in 1921 by the National Institute of Industrial Psychology. As the country emerged from the depression, the earlier paternalism was replaced by a more scientific style of management, influenced to a considerable degree by the work of Taylor, Gilbreth and Gantt.

World War II demonstrated that sometimes lessons have to be repeated before they are learnt. Working hours were increased and the emphasis was again on maximum production with little consideration for either the physical or mental well-being of workers. Absenteeism and sickness soon began to take their toll of production. Ernest Bevin, as Minister of Labour, attacked the problem, building on experience gained as General Secretary of the Transport and General Workers' Union. By a series of Ministerial orders he introduced new disputes and dismissal procedures; required the provision of welfare and training facilities; and established a guaranteed minimum wage. The powers of Factories Inspectors were extended to include medical and welfare services and a Factory and Welfare Department of the Ministry of

Labour set up to improve the health, safety and welfare of men and women at work. Demand for personnel staff increased continuously, and by the end of the war around 5500 personnel and welfare officers were employed in factories. Government measures and research had clearly established the importance of the personnel function.

Instead of the anticipated slump, the post-war years brought 30 years of full employment and economic boom. This, together with changing technology and social attitudes, meant new difficulties for management. Shop floor control took over from the formerly highly centralized union executive committees. Governments of all complexions increasingly involved themselves in daily life both at and away from work. Indeed, despite the 'liberalizing' approach of much current government policy, there is now hardly any aspect of the employer/employee relationship that is left unaffected by direct or indirect government control.

RISE AND FALL

Reflecting the general socio-economic climate, the personnel function during the 1960s and most of the 1970s experienced an apparently endless increase in attention, authority and senior management support. Membership of the IPM increased almost fivefold between 1959 and 1979. Personnel management made its mark in almost every area of public and private industry. Surveys of organizations employing personnel specialists showed a 25% increase between 1972 and 1978 [1]. However, with economic decline, major shifts in international trade and a change of government in 1979, the trend began to reverse as industry became pre-occupied with slimming its workforce, reducing unit costs and meeting the challenges of recession.

The personnel management function was not immune from such influences and unemployment among personnel specialists increased. The first signs of economic recovery in the mid-1980s arrested this trend, but made no significant contribution to the regrowth of the profession [2]. Instead it became evident that the use of consultants was gaining popularity even in areas central to the majority of personnel functions, e.g., recruitment, selection, training and management development.

The fears of many for the future were identified in the Cassels Report on personnel work in the Civil Service which argued for the devolution of personnel management to operational unit managers [3], and Mackay and Torrington's study which indicated that about 87% of the organizations investigated had transferred, or were in the process of transferring, at least some personnel management responsibilities to line managers [2].

PERSONNEL MANAGEMENT – A DEFINITION

The Institute of Personnel Management (IPM), in its 1980 Code of

Professional Practice in Personnel Management, published the following definition:

> Personnel Management is that part of management concerned with people at work and with their relationships within an enterprise. Its aim is to bring together and develop into an effective organisation the men and women who make up an enterprise and, having regard for the well-being of the individual and of working groups, to enable them to make their best contribution to its success.

FUNCTIONS OF PERSONNEL MANAGEMENT

While no longer a wholly satisfactory description of personnel management in the late 1980s, the definition is nevertheless a useful starting point to examine its role in the organizational context. In its 1987 Code of Conduct, the IPM stated the detailed areas in which personnel managers are expected to have understanding:

☐ *Resourcing:* Organization structure, job analysis, patterns of work, human resource planning, recruitment and selection, equal opportunity, disciplinary, redundancy and termination procedures.
☐ *Rewards and benefits:* Job evaluation, pay structures, rewarding performance, strategies for employee motivation, contracts, conditions of employment and pensions and benefits.
☐ *Employee relations:* Employee involvement and communications, morale and climate at work, employment law, representative structures, relationships with trade unions and negotiations.
☐ *Training and development:* Continuous development of all employees, needs analysis, performance review and appraisal, design and implementation of training programmes and career planning coaching.
☐ *Working environment:* Health, safety and welfare and working conditions, internal and external to the organization.

One of the main responsibilities of personnel management is the formulation and implementation of policy in all of the above areas. The term 'policy' is used regularly, but what is a policy and what are the principles on which it should be based?

PERSONNEL POLICY

A policy may be described as:

> A course of action recommended or adopted by an organization.

It should provide a framework that sets patterns of behaviour for the organization and the individuals within it. People want to know how the organization is going to behave towards them and what it expects from them.

Why have policies?

Various influences lead to policy decisions and formulation. These may include:

1 Recognition of some inadequacy or weakness in operations owing to a particular incident or through regular review, e.g., increase in accidents, high staff turnover.
2 The need to set priorities where resources are limited or where a choice exists.
3 External influences, such as legislation, social standards or accepted practice. These might affect policies on equal opportunities or fringe benefits, for example.
4 Pressures from the workforce for guidelines on their behaviour and relationships with the organization.

What form should a policy take?

This will depend upon the area in question and the circumstances of the organization. Many managers consider that any policy worth its salt should be in writing. This is probably fair comment provided it does not lead to inflexibility or present a mass of pious documents which are filed away and never consulted.

Most policy statements will consist of two parts:

(a) A statement of principles upon which the policy is based.
(b) Procedures/regulations to guide actions.

Certain principles are widely accepted in respect of policy formulation. These include:

1 Making policy that deals with 'real' matters as a guide to action rather than for show.
2 Ensuring that there is a fair degree of acceptance by both management and the workforce before policy is made.
3 Policies should be well publicized and understood by all those affected.
4 Policy should be acted upon, monitored and up-dated where necessary.
5 Personnel policy, in particular, will be based upon certain stated principles regarding the employment relationship such as equity, opportunity, reward, etc. [14].

From these principles more detailed 'working' policies will be prepared to cover the various areas of the personnel function.

An example of a Training Policy is given below to illustrate the format of a typical policy statement.

Training policy

Principles and objectives

1 The company will provide opportunity, facilities and financial resources to enable employees to acquire and develop the skills and knowledge required to perform their duties effectively and develop their potential for future opportunities and demands.
2 The company will not discrminate on the grounds of race, sex or marital status in the provision of tranining opportunities.
3 The needs of the organization, workgroups and individuals will be recognized when training requirements are assessed.

Procedures and administration

1 The Personnel and Training Department will be responsible for the development and review of training plans, programmes and preparation of training budgets.
2 All managers are responsible for the training and development of their subordinates within the framework of the Training Policy and with advice from the Training Manager.
3 Departmental training plans and budgets will be prepared annually, based upon the needs of the individual and departmental requirements, together with the demands and resources of the company as a whole.
4 Employees who wish to receive training or pursue further educations will be encouraged to do so. (See Further Education Scheme for details of educational release).
5 The training needs of individuals will normally be assessed as part of the annual Staff Appraisal Scheme. Any other requests for training should be made initially to the appropriate manager, who will endeavour to accommodate this within the departmental plans. Any difficulties in providing the necessary training will be investigated by the Personnel Department, who will endeavour to satisfy requirements or provide alternatives.
6 All new staff will be provided with induction training, and provision will be made for appropriate instruction and training in health and safety matters.

THE PERSONNEL ROLE

The definition above offers few surprises, describing very clearly those responsibilities constituting the personnel function in many organizations. However, in another sense it is perhaps misleading in as much as it suggests that there is a consensus regarding the detailed responsibilities and role of the function. This is simply not so. For very obvious reasons, detailed responsibilities vary from organization to organization. More important, however, is the disagreement about whether a discrete, cohesive personnel function can or should exist.

Extracts from elsewhere in the Code of Practice demonstrate several elements of disagreement:

the management of people forms part of every manager's job

and later:

the personnel manager has 'a special involvement in the livelihood of people, their working conditions, security of employment, reward and development. He is also a privileged recipient and guardian of personal information and confidences.

A PART OF EVERY MANAGER'S JOB

The first problem has to do with *responsibility* for personnel management. The statement above suggests that it is the responsibility of *all* managers. Indeed, management has been defined as:

deciding what has to be done, and then getting other people to do it.

If this is so, then personnel management must surely be an intrinsic part of every manager's job and the personnel specialist potentially superfluous. Empirically, the personnel manager is apparently considered by many organizations to be far from superfluous. How then may this paradoxical situation be reconciled?

Line and staff

Before dealing with the problem, it is necessary to outline two organizational terms: line and staff. Line managers are those with overall authority and responsibility for the performance of their department or unit. Staff managers, on the other hand, are specialists providing line managers with service or advice. Typically a production manager would be considered to occupy a line management post, whereas a personnel manager would be considered staff, along with other specialists, including for example the company legal adviser or the company accountant. It must, however, be noted that the division between line and staff will vary, depending on the type of organization concerned: also that whereas a staff manager has no formal authority over any line manager or line manager's staff, within his own department the staff manager will normally have full line managerial authority and accountability.

Although the staff manager has specialist expertise, he has not the formal authority to insist that such and such be carried out. The final decision must always rest with the line manager since ultimately he will be held to account for the results achieved by his department. Should the specialist fail to persuade the line manager of the validity of a proposed course of action, all he can do is to refer the matter upwards to his superior who may at a more senior level be able to arrange the implementation of his proposal.

A line responsibility, a staff function

How can these terms assist in resolving the paradox? Pigors and Myers [5] very succinctly summarize the role of the personnel function:

> Personnel administration is a line management responsibility, but a staff function.

The personnel specialist exists therefore to give to other managers advice and guidance on personnel policy and its application. If and how that advice is implemented is a line management matter. Such an arrangement obviously offers endless opportunity for frustration and conflict. The problem is not however peculiar to the personnel manager/line manager relationship, but tends to occur whenever the work of line managers and specialists of any kind overlap. In theory the line and staff management structure adopted by many organisations should offer an ideal combination of specialist expertise and clarity of authority and responsibility. In practice, it provokes frustration and conflict. Why?

Line and staff conflict

To the line manager, the specialist will often represent a threat to his security and status. Typically the staff man will be younger, better educated and with different attitudes, styles of behaviour and vocabulary. For a line manager, particularly an older man who has worked his way up from the shop floor, such a combination may be wholly unacceptable. He may feel threatened by the younger man's apparent technical expertise, particularly in areas where the line manager is not thoroughly acquainted with recent developments. He may doubt the younger man's worth, his ideas often being largely based on academic theories rather than line management expertise. The jargon shorthand of which all specialists are fond may present a further barrier to the relationship.

The role and position of the specialist is often a source of resentment, irrespective of any personal characteristics. The specialist, sometimes because of his location, is considered (often quite justifiably) to have the ear of senior management and is thus somebody to be handled with greater circumspection than normally justified by his status. His effect on the line manager's job is often to require the provision of apparently unimportant or obvious data which subsequently leads to requests for explanations and further data; such activities consuming time that in the opinion of the line manager should be devoted to getting on with the job. Specialists may wish to further interfere with the achievement of line objectives by introducing 'unnecessary' or 'irrelevant' considerations e.g. job satisfaction, when what is more important to the line manager is profitability, operating within his budget or meeting delivery deadlines.

The nature of the specialism may also affect the situation. Although generally the reason for the existence of staff functions is to improve organizational efficiency and effectiveness, some are more overtly geared to improving or assessing the efficiency of line management. Thus, for example, organization and methods or internal audit staff will often be received with something less than warmth. Specialisms of the O & M or work-study type by their nature imply that work is not being managed as efficiencly as it might: and audit staff in their role of organizational policemen normally unsettle even the most assured and innocent of line managers.

Other specialisms, e.g. personnel management, may produce adverse reaction for a combination of reasons. In many ways, with increasing legislation, the personnel specialist is forced to act as a policeman, or if not as a policeman, then to insist rather than advise that certain policies and courses of action be adopted. In this way the personnel specialist intrudes to an increasing degree into the special relationship that should exist between a manager and his staff [6]. With some justification, the line manager may thus consider that his authority is being reduced or even usurped. One other factor must also be taken into account: the extent to which the theoretical basis of a specialism is acceptable to line management. Although some specialisms, often those that are engineering based, will be readily accepted, and others, e.g., data processing, may be the subject of quiet admiration [7], areas such as personnel management will often be dismissed as not warranting specialist skills, or, with its emphasis on behavioural theories, be met with open derision [8].

The conflict is not, however, totally one-sided. The specialist may become equally embittered. Inevitably he is likely to be frustrated by his lack of authority, particularly in instances where line managers do not request or refuse to accept his advice. In many cases he will be aware of the other man's scepticism or antipathy, while at the same time being deprived an opportunity to prove his case. In other instances he may be frustrated by the line manager's inability to grasp his argument, with the result that his attitude reveals doubts as to the other man's ability. If his services are requested, it will often be as a last desperate measure to save an already irreversible situation, the results of which will be attributed to him. How may such problems be overcome?

Resolution of conflict

In general, there are no easy or short-term solutions. Senior management can give a lead by creating an environment that actively encourages co-operation. Clearly if an example is set at senior level, it is likely to be followed elsewhere. 'Police work' should be deprecated and specialists reminded that their role is to strengthen line management. In some organizations, specialists are encouraged to treat line management always as clients: to be given the best possible advice and then allowed to accept or reject it. To re-inforce such an arrangement, line department budgets are charged with the cost of specialist time used. Such a method is obviously not appropriate to all staff functions.

Another possibility is to consider the use of staff rotation schemes. Specialists are required to spend a period gaining experience of line management, and vice versa. Again this may not be appropriate in all cases, but will generally be possible to some degree. In this way both line manager and specialist gain an insight into each other's problems and potential [9]. By placing specialists on the staff of line managers, many of the problems mentioned above may perhaps be overcome. The specialist will have the opportunity to become more fully involved in the operation of the line department and his advice may therefore have more day-to-day relevance, or be couched in terms more acceptable to his line colleagues. His role may still be to improve the efficiency of the line management team, but his contribution will now be made as a member of that team working from within, rather than being imposed from outside.

To a very large extent, the success or otherwise of the specialist will be determined by his personality and approach whatever his organizational position. We have already suggested that he should see line management as clients; free to choose their own course of action. Common objectives should be emphasized and problems tackled as a joint venture.

A contingency approach

Legge [8], Akinmayowa [7] and others emphasize the need for a 'contingency' approach, both in relation to the manner in which personnel policy is developed and implemented. They argue for the design and implementation of policy that matches, or is contingent upon specified organizational requirements and circumstances. Before rushing to introduce the latest personnel technique, personnel specialists should re-assess their proposals in the light of the problems confronting the enterprise and its constituent parts. In order to be convincing, they must become more objective, relevant and reliable in recommendations, matching the scientific approach used in other functions to reduce the chance of failure and so promote credibility.

The advisory role in practice

In practice, although the personnel specialist may not have formal authority, nevertheless once he has achieved the respect and acceptance of his management colleagues, his role may extend very much further than implied by his advisory status. Line managers are frequently overloaded with responsibilities directly geared to the achievement of their particular functional goals. Technology at all levels and in all specialisms is increasingly complex, and operational problems are further confounded by the composition of a multiplicity of statutory regulations. Under such circumstances, it is little wonder that line managers are often only too happy to pass to personnel specialists apparently 'peripheral' aspects of their work. This transfer of unwanted tasks has in part given rise to the 'trashcan' description of personnel management, which is discussed below.

A SPECIAL INVOLVEMENT IN THE LIVELIHOOD OF PEOPLE

As described earlier, modern personnel management finds its roots largely in a reaction to the squalid working conditions of the late eighteenth and early nineteenth centuries. For very many years its preoccupation was with employee welfare. Generally, this arose not out of any ulterior motive, but out of a sincere concern. Although attitudes have largely changed, the old welfare image is one that personnel managers have often found difficult or been reluctant to shake off.

Regrettably this led on occasions to personnel staff being seen as existing solely to represent employee interests, or in less extreme cases, to occupy a 'man in the middle' position seeking to balance the conflicting demands of management and employees a 'custodian of the corporate conscience'. A typical view is expressed by F.O. Hoffman [10] who refers to 'an identity crisis' in the personnel function that will only be overcome when personnel staff abandon such roles, concentrating instead on aiding the achievement of organizational goals.

For the personnel manager to adopt the role of spokesman for the labour force is clearly an abdication of his management status. However, because of the way in which personnel management developed in this country, it is hardly surprising that the personnel specialist is often seen in this way.

What such an assessment ignores, however, is the changing set of circumstances within which the employer/employee relationship now exists. The growth of trade unionism demanded radical change of direction. More recently the balance has shifted even further as statute increasingly strengthens the status and rights of workers. Although the personnel manager may still have a welfare function, it is a very different type of welfare to that earlier dispensed, and in proportion to his overall responsibilities represents a relatively minor part.

His function today must be clearly synchronized with those of other managers, i.e., to plan, organize, motivate and control, in order that organizational objectives may be efficiently and effectively achieved; and it is in the last of these functions, control, that the nature of the new welfare role may be identified.

With his knowledge of the behavioural sciences, it is the personnel specialist's role to examine the human resource implications of management action or inaction. Reference has already been made to statute's effect on the employer/employee relationship: this, too, must be monitored and controlled. None of this is meant to imply that other managers are ignorant or unconcerned with such things; rather than because of their concern for other matters there may be a need for a 'Devil's Advocate' casting a fresh eye over circumstances that through familiarity or proximity are no longer apparent to line management. It is this sense that the personnel manager may perhaps be reasonably described as 'custodian of the corporate conscience'.

Douglas McGregor [11] has suggested that:

> The helping role and the role of the policeman are absolutely incompatible roles. To place an individual in the latter is to destroy the possibility of his occupying the former one succesfully.

Clearly this is the direction in which personnel management as a staff function is heading. If the two roles are incompatible, as McGregor suggests, this is perhaps in part an explanation of the dilemma in which personnel management finds itself.

What the long-term consequences of this are likely to be are obviously impossible to forecast with any accuracy. It is already apparent, however, that statutory controls in particular are demanding not only that personnel staff be actively involved in the formulation of corporate policy, but also that such policy be implemented in a manner prescribed rather than recommended by the personnel specialist.

The corporate 'trashcan'

Several writers have put forward the argument that personnel management as a cohesive function simply does not exist. Drucker [12] for example suggests that 'personnel administration . . . is largely a collection of incidental techniques without much internal cohesion', and goes on to discuss whether personnel management as a specialist function is 'bankrupt'. McFarland [13] has described as the 'trashcan hypothesis' the personnel department's propensity for collecting various apparently unconnected tasks. To what extent is this description justified?

An examination of the detailed responsibilities of even a limited number of personnel departments soon reveals that the description has some substance. Whether or not this should surprise us is, however, another matter. Personnel management has, after all, evolved from two principal disparate sources: the early welfare officer and the more recent control orientated labour manager. The essential skill of the personnel specialist is his ability to understand and deal with people, in an equitable fashion, often in trying or difficult circumstances. It is therefore hardly surprising that he acts as a magnet for other tasks differing in nature, but requiring the same basic skills.

Other explanations have to do with the extent to which there exists a satisfactory body of knowledge to provide a professional basis, and indeed the extent to which personnel management may accurately be described 'a profession'. Even among practitioners there appears often to be a lack of agreement about the content and purpose of the function. Twenty years on, Drucker's question appears more relevant than ever: 'Is personnel management bankrupt?' [12].

A crisis of confidence

The answer now, as then, must surely be an unequivocal 'No'. However, like the rest of the economy, it is certainly experiencing straitened times and a major re-appraisal of traditional roles and attitudes.

As a profession it has, it would appear, persistently suffered a lack of confidence and something of an identity crisis. In 1978 a leading article [15] in the IPM Journal *Personnel Management* called for, among other things, a more united profession 'competent and organized to handle all aspects of personnel management'. In 1979 in the same journal, under the heading 'Thirty More Years in the Fourth Division?' [16], personnel managers were urged to terminate their passive acceptance of a role as agents implementing already determined management policy and, instead, set about influencing the content of such policy.

In 1982, yet again *Personnel Management* posed the question, 'Personnel management in the UK – a case for urgent treatment?' [17], while in 1987, Lesley Mackay considered the profession's future in an article entitled 'Personnel: changes disguising decline' [18]. Nevertheless, given the statistics referred to earlier, its apparently poor image in the minds of other managers [19], together with trends in government and industrial policy, any unease is surely wholly reasonable.

An examination of the history of the 1960s and 1970s reveals, we would argue, that many of the nation's pre-occupations, productivity, strikes, participation, prices and incomes policies etc., emphasized the importance of the personnel role and reinforced it with statutory provisions. Current economic and industrial policies have changed this situation dramatically.

Current government policy appears to turn its back on traditional machinery and methods for achieving industrial consensus. Instead, financial control and, in particular, the control of money supply is the all-determining factor. Such national policies are inevitably reflected at company level

Such a view relegates industrial relations and personnel issues to a subsidiary role on the periphery of the economic systems, whereas previously it had been seen as a, if not *the*, major influence on industrial performance. [20]

Given that the conditions prevailing before 1979 seem unlikely to return, at least in the short-term, the future for the personnel specialist appears a little bleak. However, evidence suggests that the situation may be more favourable than might have been anticipated.

A change of role?

In a survey of 382 personnel directors conducted by Heidrick and Struggles in 1981 [21], most appeared optimistic about their role in the immediate future and anticipated greater future involvement and influence over matters affecting business performance. This role included the identification of future top management personnel speedy response to new technology, employee participation and motivation, and the reduction of labour costs. In a smaller study, Beaumont [22] showed that, although half the companies studied had cut back on personnel activity on the basis that, in crude terms, recession was an effective motivator, the other half claimed that it provided a good opportunity to develop policies and practices designed to encourage participation, communication and productivity.

In 1982, in one of a series of articles giving senior managers' views on the personnel role, Sir Derek Ezra [23] expressed the view that the future would demand personnel skills of a very high order that would touch every part of the business and so draw the personnel function more and more into the general management of the business. It was now time for its traditionally reactive role to be abandoned in favour of a more positive stance. The task of the personnel function in future would be to move from the status quo and to provide managers and employees in general with the means for personal and co-operative achievement, permitting the full development of a highly skilled and contained workforce committed to the success of the enterprise.

Pursuing a similar theme, Professor John Hunt [24] argued that the function's future must focus on:

☐ the process of developing, sustaining and reinforcing the corporate culture — with all the advantages of modern media, advertising and public relations
☐ the resourcing of highly qualified talent, both managerial and technical
☐ the exiting of talent that has had its turn in employment as well as those whose talent never matured
☐ the rewarding of people with intrinsic and extrinsic rewards relevant to the task and to the individual.

Such roles as envisaged by Sir Derek and Professor Hunt were very different from those often occupied in the early 1980s; and indeed, to some, they must have seemed an abandonment of everything professional personnel management represented.

Whether, indeed, any real abandonment of professional standards was necessary appears to us unlikely. Rather, what is often referred to with unease is the conflict between the 'corporate conscience' role and the need for personnel managers to slot into a more conventional, but no less professional, managerial function. It is the conflict typified between effecting a complex redundancy programme and anxiety about what happens to those made redundant. In any case, the evidence appears to suggest that personnel managers in general would prefer to shed the conscience role and to demonstrate technical competence to their peers and superiors [25]. Such competence, however, is most amply demonstrated when the organization is assisted in effectively and smoothly meeting its manpower problems. In so doing there are, of course, many choices of approach and attitude that may be adopted. It is, therefore, in no sense necessary to throw overboard some of the more valuable traditions on which the profession is founded.

It is in meeting, or failing to meet, the challenge of role change that, in our opinion, personnel specialists will determine their own future. That the profession is very clearly making the move from traditional personnel management to a Human Resource Management role geared directly to strategic business concerns is, we believe, a major step forward in re-establishing credibility and influence [26]. Indeed, David Guest [20] suggests that where the transition is made and the function's credibility established as a mainstream management activity, personnel managers are busier than ever before. Their contribution is more central to the organization and more obviously recognized as changes forced by the recession require changes in the workforce. By maintaining peaceful industrial relations, obtaining low wage settlements and managing redundancy programmes, personnel specialists have made their most visible contribution to business performance to date. In organizations past the workforce slimming stage or where recession has not been so severe, opportunities again exist through productivity improvement and improved manpower planning for the personnel manager to occupy a major role in building a basis for future corporate success. Although changes in the profession's attitudes are important, it seems unlikely that these alone can resolve the 'identity crisis'. More potent factors, however, are apparent; some have already been mentioned. All may be summarized in one word: change. Statute constantly modifies the employer/employee relationship. Technology changes daily. Long-established patterns of international trade are turned upside down, apparently overnight. Worker attitudes and aspirations are in a constant state of flux. Increasing corporate size and multi-nationalization have contributed to an ever more complex management task as well as heightening individual feelings of anonymity. In response to such trends, management in all disciplines and at all levels has become more specialist and professionalized.

Such changes all have consequences for people at work. The likely attitude of workers to change is at best unpredictable, and often overtly hostile. Nevertheless, management has a responsibility not only to respond to change, but indeed to act as an agent thereof. In doing so it must obviously have a full understanding of the possible social and technological consequences. Clearly, this is an area where the personnel specialist has a potentially major role to play.

REFERENCES

1. Brown, W. (Ed) (1981). *The Changing Contours of British Industrial Relations*. Blackwell.
2. Mackay, L. and Torrington, D. (1986). *The Changing Nature of Personnel Management*. IPM.
3. Cassels, J.S. (1983). *Review of Personnel Work in the Civil Service. Report to the Prime Minister*. HMSO.
4. IPM (1987). *The IPM Code of Conduct*. IPM.
5. Pigors, P. and Myers, C.A. (1973). *Personnel Administration: A Point of View and a Method*. McGraw-Hill.
6. Legge, K. (1978). *Power, Innovation and Problem Solving in Personnel Management*. McGraw-Hill.
7. Akinmayowa, J.T. (1980). 'Relationship of personnel managers to others', *Personnel Review*, Vol. 9, No. 4, Autumn.
8. Legge, K. (1978). Op. cit.
9. Brewster, C.J. and Connock, S. (1980). *Industrial Relations Training for Managers*. Kogan Page.
10. Hoffman, F.O. (1978). 'Identity crisis in the personnel function', *Personnel Journal*, March, pp. 126–132 and 162.
11. McGregor, D. (1960). *The Human Side of Enterprise*. McGraw-Hill.
12. Drucker, P. (1968). *The Practice of Management*. Pan.
13. McFarland, D.E. (1968). *Personnel Management Theory and Practice*. Macmillan.

14. Rothwell, S. (1984). 'Integrating the elements of a company employment policy', *Personnel Management*, November.
15. Johnston, N.M. (1978). 'Planners come of age', *Personnel Management*, Nov, p. 5.
16. IPM (1979). 'Thirty more years in the fourth division?' *Personnel Management*, January, p. 3.
17. Thurley, K. (1982). 'Personnel management in the UK — a case for urgent treatment?', *Personnel Management*, August, pp. 24–29.
18. Mackay, L. (1987). 'Personnel: changes disguising decline', *Personnel Review*, Vol. 16, No. 5.
19. Tyson, S. (1979). 'The study of personnel management as an occupation, using Repertory Grid', *Personnel Review*, Vol. 8, No. 3, Summer, pp. 34–39.
20. Guest, D. (1982). 'Has the recession really hit personnel management?', *Personnel Management*, October, pp. 36–39.
21. Heidrick and Struggles (1981). *Chief Personnel Executives in the United Kingdom 1981*. Heidrick and Struggles.
22. Beaumont, R. (1982). *Employment Relations during the Recession*. Industrial Relations Resource Centre, Cambridge.
23. Ezra, Sir Derek (1982). 'How I see the personnel function', *Personnel Management*, July.
24. Hunt, J.W. (1984). 'The shifting focus of the personnel function' *Personnel Management*, February, pp. 14–18.
25. Watson, T. (1977). *The Personnel Managers*. Routledge & Kegan Paul.
26. Hendry, C. and Pettigrew, A. (1986). 'The practice of strategic human resource management', *Personnel Review*, Vol. 15, No. 5.

2
The organization and control of the personnel function

ORGANIZATION OF THE PERSONNEL DEPARTMENT

In many small organizations, a full-time personnel specialist does not exist: personnel matters are dealt with as part of some other officer's job or by line managers as part of their day-to-day duties. As an organization grows, the need for a more formalized style of personnel management usually becomes apparent.

A study carried out in 1983 [1] suggested that the strongest single influence upon whether establishments had personnel specialists was the number of people employed at the workplace. Where 100 or more people were employed it appeared normal practice to have a member of staff concentrating on personnel. With 200 or more employees it was normal for a personnel specialist to exist.

Even within the same industry the structure of the personnel department naturally varies from organization to organization, its overall shape being largely determined by four factors:

☐ the number of employees
☐ the extent to which staff are dispersed or concentrated in one workplace
☐ the degree to which management functions are centralized or decentralized
☐ the extent to which matters of personnel policy are imposed from outside the organization, e.g., by nationally negotiated agreements.

Although various bases have been suggested, e.g., dividing the personnel department into sections each dealing with a specific type of employee; most departments are principally organized on a functional basis, as illustrated in outline in Fig. 2.1. In very large organizations with semi-autonomous divisions or subsidiaries, some further division of the personnel function often occurs, as for example in Fig. 2.2. In this case a further level has developed. The head office specialists plan, develop, co-ordinate and advise on personnel policy and procedures

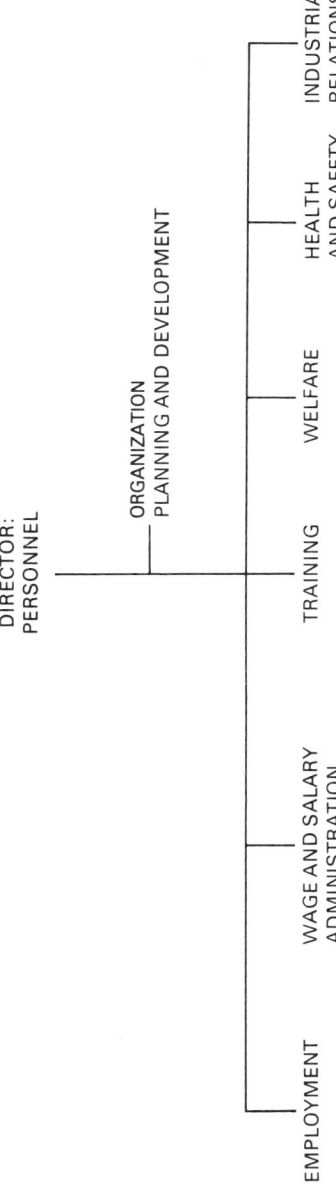

Fig. 2.1 Personnel department organized on functional basis

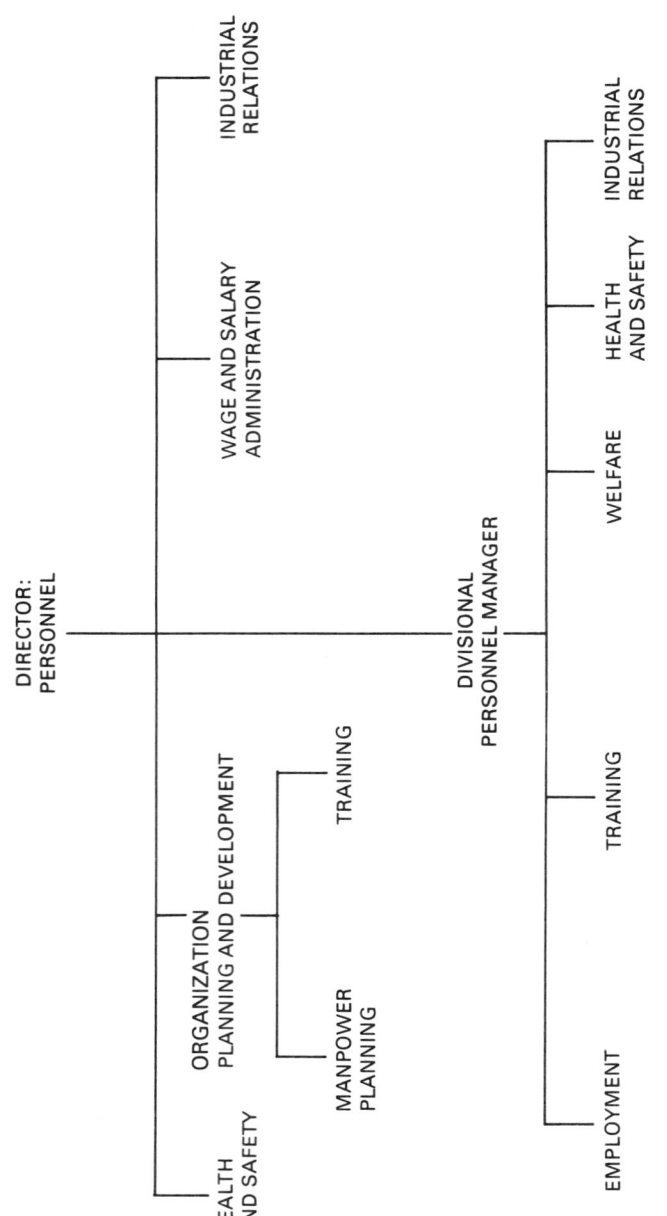

Fig. 2.2 Personnel department structure in an organization with semi-autonomous divisions

throughout the organization, while leaving detailed day-to-day management of the function to divisional personnel managers. Their relationship with divisional personnel management is staff or advisory in nature, each divisional personnel manager having line responsibility to his divisional chief executive. In addition to their advisory duties, the head office staff may also carry out certain major functions that affect the entire organization, such as the negotiations of national wage agreements. In respect of such matters, the responsibility of the divisional manager is to interpret and apply such agreements, negotiating only such modifications as are necessary because of special local circumstances.

Both at head office and divisional level, in addition to personnel specialists, there will of course be employed clerical staff dealing with correspondence, maintenance of records and statistical analysis. Each section of the personnel department will have an appropriate structure that once again, will be determined by the criteria outlined above.

RECORDS AND STATISTICS

Without accurate information, effective performance of the managerial function is rendered impossible, whatever the discipline concerned. Personnel management is no exception. Although the expertise of the personnel specialist may very well be based on knowledge of the behavioural sciences, it is only when such knowledge is applied to actual situations and problems that it becomes meaningful. Up-to-date records and statistics provide the facts necessary for rational, informed decision making.

Personnel records serve several purposes:

☐ they are a store of data about employees past and present
☐ they record action taken in respect of individual employees
☐ they guide future action
☐ they provide a basis for statistical analysis
☐ they satisfy statutory requirements

In order to serve such purposes, records should be up-to-date, accurate, capable of easy reference and adequate. By 'adequate', we mean that all relevant information should be collected together in order that management obtains a complete picture of employees collectively or as individuals. It is not our intention to discuss here detailed points of form or record design. It must nevertheless be borne in mind that effective design will, to a very considerable degree, determine both the adequacy and use made of the records system. Records commonly maintained are discussed below.

Individual employee records

The basis of most personnel record systems is the individual employee card. This will summarize all information known about each employee. Typically this might include:

- [ ] name
- [ ] address
- [ ] employee number
- [ ] sex
- [ ] date of birth
- [ ] marital status
- [ ] details of children/wife
- [ ] date commenced employment
- [ ] details of past and present posts
- [ ] past and present wage or salary
- [ ] reasons for changes of post
- [ ] employee grade
- [ ] holiday entitlement
- [ ] retirement date
- [ ] qualifications
- [ ] courses attended
- [ ] registered disabled number
- [ ] date of termination of employment
- [ ] reason for termination

Various additional items might be included, or some omitted. Some companies include a recent photograph; others, particularly those with computerized personnel records systems, integrate sickness and absence records.

Medical records

In companies with their own medical staff or a company doctor to whom employees may be referred, individual medical records may be kept. Some organizations require that all employees have a medical before commencing employment; others require regular check-ups. Under certain circumstances, statute may require medical examinations, e.g., minors employed in factories. An analysis of records may be useful, too, in the identification of health hazards. Whatever the reason, all visits by employees to company medical staff or advisers should be recorded. Such records may be stored separately, but generally they are integrated with individual personnel records. For this reason, in particular, personnel records staff must be made clearly aware of their position of trust and the total confidentiality of records in their care.

Accident records

It is essential that full and accurate records be kept of all accidents, however minor. Details may be required for statutory or insurance purposes. Details may also help to identify particular hazards or training needs on an individual or occupational group basis.

Absence records

Although absence is normally primarily the responsibility of the appropriate line manager, the personnel department is usually charged with maintaining a centralized record and high-lighting any outstanding cases. The department is also frequently responsible for Statutory Sick Pay provisions (See Chapter 23). Often each manager submits a weekly summary of absences analysed by individual and cause. Self-certification returns will also be made by employees absent from work through sickness. The practical application of such information is considered in Chapter 24.

Training records

Training records are required both for internal control and, where they exist, Industrial Training Board purposes. Training Boards may require records to be available for inspection and submission at regular intervals, and details should therefore be kept both on a collective and individual basis. Again, these are normally integrated with employees individual records.

Earnings records

The law requires that records shall be kept of each individual's earnings, tax and national insurance contributions. These may be maintained in a form prescribed by the Inland Revenue, or in some other form with their approval. Such records may be kept separately and transferred to employee files at the end of each year, or where a computer exists may be integrated with individual employee records.

Termination records

Details should be kept of all terminations whatever their cause as a basis for the calculation and investigation of labour turnover. Turnover is discussed in detail later. Information normally required will include reasons for leaving, age, sex and length of service.

In each of the above cases, information will normally be stored in two forms: on an individual basis and on a collective basis, e.g., by department, division, company, etc. On an individual basis, the collected information will provide an overall pen-picture of the employee concerned, which will obviously be useful when dealing with individual matters. For purposes of policy formulation and control, however, collective data with opportunities for the identification of trends will probably prove more valuable. Any records systems introduced must therefore have the capacity to satisfy both sets of requirements.

REFERENCE TO RECORDS

If records are to be of any value they must be capable of easy reference. A wide range of both general and specialist systems are available. Increasingly, however, with growing emphasis on personnel as a control function, manual records systems are proving inadequate for purposes of rapid analysis and summary of data. This, together with the decreasing costs of computerization through the use of micro-processors, is causing greater attention to be given to the use of computerized records systems even by comparatively small organiz-ations.

COMPUTERS AND THE PERSONNEL FUNCTION

The capabilities of computers are by now surely well known. Huge quantities of data may be absorbed, analysed, manipulated and reproduced at fantastic speeds. Such characteristics have encouraged many organizations to use computers for some years for various personnel activities, in particular the processing of wages and salaries and personnel record keeping.

However, in personnel as in other areas of management, increasing attention is currently being given to the advantages of management information systems (MIS). Although technically highly complex, the principle of MIS is very simple.

In most organizations, there exist a collection of free-standing, compartmentalized record systems, frequently manually maintained. Each typically provides detail of specific aspects of organizational activity. What none really gives is an overall picture, nor is it often easy to interrelate information held in one system to that in another. An MIS seeks to draw together the full range of available information into one integrated database, which then provides an overall picture or has the capability selectively to interrelate and report on particular aspects of activity. Although theoretically feasible using manual systems, it is only with computerization that such integrated systems become practicable. With such systems, it is therefore possible to obtain accurate, current information about aspects of an employee, or summarize data about all employees at the press of a button.

In addition to tasks of storing, processing and reproducing data, the analytical ability of MIS can relieve personnel staff of boring, routine tasks, e.g., standard letters or government returns, while offering management more accurate and rapid data with which to plan, organize and control. Not only can current data be manipulated, but projections and simulations may be developed as a basis for manpower planning, job evaluation, radical policy changes or in the course of wage negotiations. A further advantage is the ability to exploit the exception principle to the full: bringing selectively to management's attention matters that require action.

Examples of the application of MIS to a range of organizations of varying size may be found in 'Computers in Personnel' [2], a collection of papers presented at a joint Institute of Manpower Studies/Institute of Personnel Management Conference in 1982. Another well documented application is MANIS [3], British rail's manpower information systems which has the capability to interrelate some 110 separate sets of records in respect of all or any of British Rail's 170 000 staff.

Benefits claimed for such systems include:

☐ greater control and thus efficiency derived from the rapid availability of high quality and up-to-date information
☐ an improvement in confidentiality (though some would dispute this)
☐ a reduction in record-keeping and other administrative costs
☐ improved compliance with statutory rules
☐ a release of personnel department time from clerical routine to focussing on policy formulation and implementation
☐ a stimulus to more creative problem-solving through model-building capability

A by-product would also appear to be that by providing up-to-date statistics more quickly, the personnel department's credibility with other managers is enhanced, and the function is also more likely to be involved in mainstream organizational policy matters [4]. A word of warning must, however, be introduced. Computerized systems, to be effective, must be carefully planned and implemented. Not only are the costs of failure considerable, but also there is a high risk of too much data causing 'mental indigestion'. Data is only the raw material that needs to be processed in order to provide information. If that data is to be useful, management must, at an early stage, determine what it requires for planning and decision-making purposes, and thus what is essential and what is merely unwanted detail.

It should also be noted that however sophisticated the computer system, it is not usually practicable to store all collected data in computer-acceptable form. Some data, e.g., reports, letters, etc., will still have to be retained in conventional form. To store such information a simplified manual system is usually appropriate.

THE DATA PROTECTION ACT 1984

Earlier it was noted that one of the claimed advantages of computerization is improved confidentiality. This is a claim with which not everybody would concur. In response to concern about the confidentiality and possible misuse of computer records, the Data Protection Act was introduced in 1984. Although dealing with computer records generally, certain aspects are of particular concern to personnel managers. These are summarized below.

Data

The Act defined 'data' as:

> information recorded in a form in which it can be processed by equipment operating automatically in response to instructions given for that purpose

or, in simple terms, information kept on a computer. Manual records are thus excluded from the Act.

Personal data

It is only 'personal data' that the Act protects. Personal data is:

> data consisting of information which relates to a living individual who can be identified from the information, or from that and other information, including any expression of opinion about the individual but not any indication of the intentions of the data user in respect of that individual

(The 'data user' in this context is, of course, normally the employer.) In consequence of this definition for example the content of a computerized appraisal would appear to be 'personal data', whereas any proposed action following that appraisal would not.

Exemptions

Certain types of personal data are exempt. The principal of these so far as the personnel department is concerned are accountancy and payroll records, but only so long as they are used exclusively for paying remuneration or pensions. Detail held for statistical or research purposes is also exempt, so long as the results do not identify individuals.

Data protection principles

The manner in which personal data is stored is subject to eight principles that form the core of the Act:

☐ Personal data must be obtained and processed fairly and lawfully, i.e., it must not be used or obtained in a misleading fashion. Generally this seems to imply the knowledge of the employee concerned.

☐ Personal data must be held for specified and lawful purposes. When registering (see below), such purposes have to be recorded. This of course requires not only a description of current use, but also some thought as to how records may be used in the future.

☐ Personal data shall not be used or disclosed in a manner incompatible with the specified purposes.

☐ Personal data shall be adequate, relevant and not excessive in relation to the specified purposes.

☐ Personal data shall be accurate and up to date. It should be noted here that accuracy refers to fact rather than opinion. Nevertheless it will be necessary to ensure that at regular intervals employee records are updated. This revision may well have implications for the retention of computerized files on ex-employees, where updating will often be impossible.

☐ Personal data shall not be kept for longer than necessary.

☐ An employee shall be entitled at reasonable intervals and without undue delay or expense to be informed by his employer whether personal data is held about himself, and if so:
to have access to such data (usually within 40 days) and, where appropriate to have the data corrected or, where appropriate, removed.

☐ Appropriate security measures shall be taken against unauthorized access to alteration, disclosure or destruction of personal data and against accidental loss or destruction.

Registration and enforcement

Responsibility for supervising the Act's implementation is that of the Data Protection Registrar. Employers holding personal data as described above are obliged to register with him and provide various details, but in particular, the purposes for which data is held, a description of the data, sources of the data, to whom the data will be disclosed.

Employees who suffer loss through inaccuracy, loss or disclosure of data or who require the rectification or erasure of records have access to the Courts, who may award damages or require action to be taken.

Practical implications

For the personnel manager the practical implications of this would appear to be the need for:

☐ regular staff training on the Act and its practical implications.

☐ a regular review of personal data held: its accuracy, currency,

provision for its maintenance and the need to hold it on computer.
☐ a scrutiny of procedures to ensure that records can be produced in an intelligible form within 40 days.
☐ a regular review of data security safeguards.
☐ consideration to be given to the development, preferably with employees, of a stated and publicized policy on the retention and protection of personal data.

In relation to this final point, several employers, often in co-operation with trade unions, have already developed such policies and procedures. That developed by IBM, which is supported by guidelines and examples, is detailed in Fig. 2.3.

MEASURING PERSONNEL DEPARTMENT PERFORMANCE

In response to the need for tighter cost control, reduced manpower, improved productivity and other factors discussed in the previous chapter, increasing attention has been given to the development of measures of personnel department performance. As in other control systems, it is intended that these shall:

☐ measure comparative performance
☐ highlight problem areas
☐ provoke corrective action
☐ provide feedback on action taken
☐ focus attention on areas of maximum importance

A range of measures have been devised that naturally enough resemble those used in more general financial control and in the assessment of production and marketing departments.

Granada TV Rental [5], for example, in 1982 introduced an 'objective measurement system' to encompass four major personnel areas of activity: recruitment, remuneration, employee relations, training and development. In relation to each area ten to twelve ratios were determined.

Examples dealing with training included training costs per capita, training budget as a proportion of total personnel expenditure, trainee days per company trainer, etc. Examples of other measures (some more established than others) include:

Recruitment   Cost per filled post
                Job offers made to offers accepted
                Time taken to fill posts
                Voluntary terminations of employment within x months after recruitment

IBM internal programme
for the protection of personal data

Main principles and practices

1 Purpose definition The purpose(s) of any file or application that makes use of personal data should be clearly defined and shown to be in support of valid IBM business needs.

2 Collection and use limitation Only the personal data that is needed for the defined purpose(s) of an application or file may be collected. It should be collected by fair and lawful means and from reliable sources. It should be correct, complete and kept up-to-date, and be used and retained on the active file only to the extent necessary for the defined purpose(s) of the application on file.

3 Access and communication limitation Within one IBM company, personal data should be made available only to data users/recipients with a well defined need-to-know. Communication of personal data outside the IBM company that holds that data should be avoided insofar as possible. Such data should be anonymised or aggregated whenever feasible in order to avoid identification of the data subject.

To data users/recipients outside IBM, personal data should be communicated only:
when required for legal reasons, or
when required for valid business reasons when legally permitted, or
when requested by the data subject concerned.

Accountability and data security

The person responsible for an application or file that makes use of personal data must be identified. All information containing personal data must be carefully classified and protected against unauthorised or accidental disclosure, modification or destruction.

Data subject involvement

IBM honours justified requests from data subjects to have data related to them corrected, completed or updated. Insofar as compatible with its valid business interests and applicable legal requirements. IBM also honours data subjects' requests for information about data related to them that is collected, stored and used by IBM, about the sources of that data and about data users/recipients outside the company to whom such data is communicated.

Fig. 2.3 IBM policy for personal data protection (reproduced from Bell, D.,
Personnel Management, *June, 1984).*

Training	Test results before and after training Cost of in-house training compared with external training courses.
Wages and salaries	Company rates compared with competitors' rates Cost of bonus schemes compared with on-job-performance Ability to retain and recruit staff Number of pay anomalies and queries
Welfare	Cost of welfare facilities per employee Cost of welfare benefits as a proportion of total personnel expenditure.
Industrial relations	Numbers of grievances per x employees Number of strikes Days lost through strikes Numbers of formal disciplinary procedures Cost of operating joint consultative machinery
Health and safety	Severity and frequency of accidents Days lost through accidents Cost per accident/day lost Number of prohibition/improvement notices issued by the inspectorate
Absenteeism and labour turnover	Days lost through absenteeism Labour turnover Skill wastage rates Cost of labour turnover

All of these, in addition to other aspects of the areas described, may be quantified, and in that form may be readily acceptable to senior management. Nevertheless, such measures however calculated must be treated with caution. Although a proposal to take the personnel department 'on trust' without attempting to measure its activities objectively seems unlikely to be acceptable in the current climate there are dangers in placing too much emphasis on the precise measurement of a department whose activities are frequently incapable of precise definition or demonstrating cause and effect.

As Alan Fowler [5] points out, it is first necessary to determine whether efficiency, effectiveness, or both are to be measured. There is a danger in emphasizing efficiency and thus cost without considering the effectiveness with which a task is carried out. The contrary is also true. In making comparisons with earlier data, or data derived from outside the organization, there is inevitably the risk of failing to compare like with like or to allow for factors outside the personnel function's control. Indeed, since most of the areas in which personnel performance is likely to be measured fall to some degree under the influence of other functional or line managers, the objective and precise measurement of exclusively personnel activity will frequently be impossible. One group of American researchers indeed have concluded that direct measures of overall effectiveness and efficiency are simply 'unmeasurable' [6].

As an alternative, they suggest peer rating by user departments. As a method of assessing performance, this has much to recommend it, since if users are not committed to a service then it must raise questions as to its value. Nevertheless, given organizational politics and in-fighting for resources, together with the body of evidence dealing with the personnel/line manager relationship, the validity of such assessments might reasonably be open to question. How then may performance be measured?

Several writers dismissing demands for objective measurement recommend a more qualitative or subjective approach. Armstrong [7] suggests that the successful personnel manager is one who can persuade top management and his management colleagues that he is providing them with a good service and encourage them to accept that they are likely to benefit from its extension.

Fowler [5] lists key questions that he believes readily indicate efficiency and effectiveness:

- [ ] Are the personnel manager and key staff expertly knowledgeable?
- [ ] Is the department's advisory role interpreted positively, i.e., pro-active rather than purely passive or reactive?
- [ ] Are the personnel department's initiatives relevant?
- [ ] Are personnel policies properly monitored?
- [ ] Is the department willing to delegate to user departments?
- [ ] Does the personnel function understand and support organizational objectives?

Such measures clearly will not satisfy those who demand that management must constantly demonstrate that its efforts make sense quantitatively — in objective, cold, hard-cash terms. Indeed it would be foolish for any personnel manager to consider it unnecessary to at least attempt to prove that his department justified its existence. Nevertheless it may be, at least for the moment, that subjective criteria, however deficient, may be the best measures available.

REFERENCES

1. Daniel, W.W. and Millward, N. (1983). *Workplace Industrial Relations in Britain*. Heinemann.
2. IPM/IMS. (1982). *Computers in Personnel*. Institute of Personnel

Management/Institute of Manpower Studies.
3. For a full account of MANIS see: Bowran, R. (1982). 'Computers in personnel', *Personnel Management*, July, pp. 46–49.
4. IPM. (1983). 'Ability to deliver the goods quickly has boosted standing of personnel department', *Personnel Management*, September, pp. 19–20.
5. Fowler, A. (1983). 'Proving the personnel department earns its salt', *Personnel Management*, May, pp.26–29.
6. Mushkin, S.J. and Sutter, F.H. (1979). *Personnel Management and Productivity in City Government*. Lexington Books.
7. Armstrong, M. (1984). *A Handbook of Personnel Management Practice*. Kogan Page.
8. Fowler, A. (1984). *A Handbook of Personnel Management Practice*. Kogan Page.

PART 1: FURTHER RECOMMENDED READING

Thomason, G. (1981). *A Textbook of Personnel Management*. IPM.
Legg, K. (1978). *Power, Innovation and Problem Solving in Personnel Management*. McGraw-Hill.
IPM/IMS (1982). *Computers in Personnel*. IPM/IMS.
Tyson, S. and Fell, A. (1986). *Evaluating the Personnel Function*. Hutchinson.
Pearson, S. and Coulthard, D. (1987). *Personnel Procedures and Records*. Gower.
Torrington, D. and Hall, L. (1987). *Personnel Management. A New Approach*. Prentice-Hall.
Evans, A. and Korn, A. (1988). *How to Comply with the Data Protection Act*. Gower.

PART 1: SAMPLE EXAMINATION QUESTIONS

What is the role and function of a personnel department within a typical building society?   CBSI

Compare and contrast the functions of the personnel and production departments in a large manufacturing company.   CACA

Personnel Management has traditionally been regarded as a 'staff' rather than a 'line' function. Comment on the validity of this view, and illustrate your answer by reference to the role of the Personnel Manager.   CBSI

In 1979, Peter Drucker wrote that 'Personnel managers everywhere complain that they are "not listened to", "not supported", "have not been truly accepted" by their management colleagues'. Discuss the possible reasons for this state of affairs, and indicate what the personnel function might do in order to remedy the situation.   ICSA

How and why does the personnel role differ in different organizations?   ICSA

How has the profession of personnel management altered in the last ten years?
                                                                          IPM

In what ways has the personnel function lost influence in organizations in the last four to five years?   IPM

To what extent can the personnel manager make a measurable contribution to the profitability of the organization?   ICSA

Imagine that you have just been appointed as personnel manager for an organization that has hitherto not enjoyed the benefits of a separate personnel function. The organization employs around 400 people and you can vizualise it as one of the following:

A small government department employing unionized (mainly female) clerical staff.

Administrative headquarters of an insurance company or building society, employing non-unionized and predominantly male executives.

An electronics manufacturing unit employing 200 research staff (non-unionized) and 200 assembly personnel (unionized).

You have permission to engage up to four staff for your new department. How many would you recruit? How would you organize them and your department, and why? What would be the objectives that you would try to set for the personnel function?   ICSA

(a) Why is it recommended that an organization's Personnel policy be written down?
(b) Which principles should lie behind such a Personnel policy?
(c) What should be included in the contents of a Personnel policy?
(d) Which sources will have to be drawn on in the initial compilation of the policy?   CBSI

Apart from the potential to make administrative procedures more efficient, what are the implications of growing computerization for the work of personnel officers?   IPM

Is small beautiful? What are the implications of your answer to this question for the organization of personnel departments?   IPM

What are the differences between personnel management and human resource management? Which do you prefer, and why?   IPM

How does work on organization structure differ between that done by personnel specialists in corporate personnel departments and that done by personnel specialists in operating units?   IPM

What personnel records are needed in a typical organization? How can the cost-effectiveness of collecting and maintaining such records be justified? Given the increasing use of computers in organizations, what methods should be used to guarantee the confidentiality of personnel information?   ICSA

Why does the role of personnel management differ so much between organizations? To what extent do you envisage any trend towards convergence in the way that the personnel function operates, or do you believe that diversity will continue? Give your reasons for holding either of these views.   ICSA

Nearly 20 years ago, Crichton said that personnel management often entailed 'collecting together such odd jobs from management as they are prepared to give up'. To what extent has the position changed?   ICSA

The Institute of Personnel Management recently organized an essay competition under the title 'Excellence in Personnel Management'. What, in your view, are the components of 'excellence' in the personnel function? How might such 'excellence' be achieved and sustained?   ICSA

Part 2
Behavioural aspects

3
Human relations and work groups

In subsequent chapters of this book, we describe and examine various techniques, practice and law that together constitute the personnel management function. Although such things may sometimes appear very straightforward, the difference in practice between mere performance and truly effective action is often determined, as in many disciplines, by knowledge not only of what should be done, but also why. Before dealing with more practical matters therefore, in this chapter we attempt to outline some of the behavioural science theory on which modern personnel management is largely based.

Acceptance of behavioural theory as a basis for management action is a fairly recent phenomenon.

With the development of mass production methods in the late eighteenth century, workers were largely seen as components of or extensions to machines. Management attitudes being typified by the 'Lancashire Labour Laws' reproduced in Fig. 3.1. This perception of the role of the worker was further emphasized by the work of F.W. Taylor and other Scientific Management protagonists including H.L. Gantt and Frank and Lilian Gilbreth. Taylor's [1] theory of greater productivity was based on scientific analysis of work and the scientific selection and training of workers, replacing management by rule of thumb with management based on science. He argued that management and workers had a common interest in increasing organizational prosperity, prosperity that could be shared by all. In return for his share, a worker would submit to being set up like a machine to produce in pre-determined fashion pre-determined units of output.

Scientific management dominated the industrial scene until the early 1940s and was typified by highly repetitive, simplified, short-duration tasks of the kind that may still be seen in many mass-production factories. Around the beginning of the Second World War attention began to concentrate on studies conducted 20 years earlier by the so called Human Relations school of management. The theories of this school, although still geared to productivity were qualitatively very different from those of Taylor, in as much as they emphasized the sociological and psychological aspects of work. The basis for a great deal of this thoery was a series of studies conducted by Elton Mayo and

LANCASHIRE LABOUR LAWS 1852

The following 'Rules and Conditions' appeared on the office notice board of a Burnley cotton mill in 1852:

1 Godliness, cleanliness and punctuality are the necessities of a good business.

2 This firm has reduced the hours of work, and the clerical staff will now only have to be present between the hours of 7 am and 6 pm on weekdays.

3 Daily prayers will be held each morning in the main office. The clerical staff will be present.

4 Clothing must be of a sober nature. The clerical staff will not disport themselves in raiment of bright colours, nor will they wear hose, unless in good repair.

5 Overshoes and top-coats may not be worn in the office, but neck scarves and headwear may be worn in inclement weather.

6 A stove is provided for the benefit of the clerical staff. Coal and wood must be kept in the locker. It is recommended that each member of the clerical staff bring 4 pounds of coal each day during cold weather.

7 No member of the clerical staff may leave the room without permission from Mr Rogers. The calls of nature are permitted, and clerical staff may use the garden below the second gate. This area must be kept in good order.

8 No talking is allowed during business hours.

9 The craving of tobacco, wines or spirits is a human weakness, and, as such, is forbidden to all members of the clerical staff.

10 Now that the hours of business have been drastically reduced, the partaking of food is allowed between 11.30 am and noon, but work will not, on any account, cease.

11 Members of the clerical staff will provide their own pens. A new sharpener is available, on application to Mr Rogers.

12 Mr Rogers will nominate a senior clerk to be responsible for the cleanliness of the main office and the private office, and all boys and juniors will report to him 40 minutes before prayers, and will remain after closing hours for similar work. Brushes, brooms, scrubbers and soap are provided by the owners.

13 The new increased weekly wages are as hereunder detailed:
Junior boys (up to 11 years) 1s 4d. Boys (to 14 years) 2s 1d. Juniors 4s 8d. Junior clerks 8s 7d. Clerks 10s 9d. Senior clerks (after 15 years with owners) 21s.

The owners recognize the generosity of the new Labour Laws, but will expect a great rise in output of work to compensate for these near Utopian conditions.

Fig. 3.1

colleagues from the Harvard Business School — the Hawthorne experiments.

ELTON MAYO — THE HAWTHORNE STUDIES

The Hawthorne studies [2] were conducted from 1924 to 1932 at the Hawthorne works of the Western Electric Company in Chicago. The company was, for the time, an enlightened employer paying above average wages, with good working conditions and welfare facilities. Nevertheless, management was concerned about a growing sense of dissatisfaction that appeared to be pervading the workforce. They approached the problem in accordance with the scientific management principles then in vogue. Two groups of workers were selected; one to act as a test group; the other a control group. The consultants began by increasing the level of lighting in the test group's work area, arguing that if lighting was improved, output should similarly improve. The control group's lighting was not changed. As anticipated, the output of the test group did indeed rise, but so did that of the control group. The test group's lighting was reduced: but again output rose in both groups. In some confusion, the scientific experts requested Mayo's assistance. Mayo, an Australian carrying out research at Harvard, was a psychologist. Nevertheless, he viewed individual workers in the same mechanistic way as Taylor.

The telephone relay study

Mayo's first study was carried out in a section of the factory that produced telephone relays; each relay consisting of around 40 parts. Relays were assembled by teams of girls who were paid in accordance with output on a group incentive scheme basis. For payment purposes, workers were divided into groups of about 100. The number of relays produced was counted mechanically.

For the purposes of his study, Mayo selected two girls, segregated them from the rest of the work force and asked them to select four others to join them. Before transferring them to a special work area, the output of each girl was recorded without her knowledge. Before the experiment, each girl produced around 2400 relays in a 48-hour week, including Saturdays, and with no rest pauses.

The six girls were transferred to their special work area and left alone for 5 weeks to adjust to their new surroundings. With them was a member of Mayo's team who was to observe the behaviour and output of the group and provide feedback. At the end of the 5-week period, Mayo began to make changes.

A group incentive scheme was introduced involving only the experimental group: output rose. Two 5-minute rest periods, one in the morning, and one in the afternoon were introduced: output rose. Rest periods were increased to 10 minutes each: output rose. Six 5-minute rest periods were introduced: output faltered slightly, the girls claiming that the frequent pauses broke their natural work rhythms. Two longer rest periods were introduced, the first with a free hot meal provided: output rose. The girls were sent home at 4.30 pm each day: output rose. They were sent home at 4.00 pm each day: output remained the same. During the next two periods, all improvements were gradually withdrawn, until the group was again working a six day, 48-hour week, with no meals and no rest periods: output rose to a record average output of 3000 relays per girl per week and remained at this level when rest periods were subsequently re-introduced. In total, the study lasted 5 years. During this period, regular medical examinations showed no signs of fatigue, and absenteeism fell by 80%.

On the basis of these results it became clear to Mayo that the physical environment was not all-important as he had previously supposed. His explanation was that:

☐ the group felt important: management cared about them
☐ the style of supervision was more friendly than the style to which the group was accustomed
☐ the girls had been allowed considerable freedom to organize and control their own work
☐ as a group, they had developed close friendships.

His findings caused him to qualify and later abandon his earlier 'rabble hypothesis'. This hypothesis stated that:

☐ natural society consists of a horde of unorganized individuals
☐ every individual acts in a manner calculated to secure his self-preservation or self-interest
☐ every individual thinks logically, to the best of his ability, and in the service of this aim

A new hypothesis was necessary. His conclusion was that productivity and work satisfaction are to a very large extent dependent on the social relationships between workers and between workers and their supervisor.

The bank wiring room

In a later study, Mayo attempted to learn more about the nature of such social relationships and the extent to which groups exercized control over individual workers. In order to achieve this, he observed the behaviour of 14 men in a part of the works known as the bank wiring room. Their task was to wire and solder the circuitry of certain telephone exchange equipment. Nine wiremen attached wires to terminals: three men soldered the wires to terminals, the two remaining inspected the finished product.

Although the workers were paid according to output, it soon became apparent that the group never produced more or less than 6000 units per day. Although this was not an unacceptable level of output, it was obvious that the group could have produced more and thus earned more if it wished. It appeared that it did not wish to increase its output; rather a group norm had been established to which all were required to adhere. If a worker produced too much, he was a 'rate-buster'; too little and he was a 'chiseller'.

Such norms related not only to output. Other aspects of behaviour were also subject to a group code of conduct. Aspects of dress were included; inspectors being required, for example, to wear a coat, waistcoat and tie as an indication of status. However, members with formal authority or status were required not to 'act officious or take advantage of their authority position'. Inspectors were expected not to behave like inspectors.

Group members deviating from norms were brought back into line by a variety of means, including sarcasm and ridicule, being 'sent to Coventry', or the use of force — 'binging' — a punch on the upper arm.

Although one cohesive group when dealing with management and other outsiders, the group in fact consisted of two distinct cliques, the status of the clique at the front of the room being higher than that at the back. Each clique assigned to its members roles and status. Although forbidden by management, wiremen and soldermen often exchanged jobs. However, status considerations required that such an exchange should only be instigated by a wireman. Individual output varied considerably. However, dexterity tests did not reveal any correlation with output. Instead, it became apparent that output was linked to status, the high status clique consistently producing more than the low status clique. Despite the existence of a formal management structure, the studies showed that the group had appointed its own natural leaders and that these were more influential than their official counterparts. The official group chief was accepted as a 'facilitator', communicating information to and from management, while at the same time adhering to group norms. The foreman was considered totally separate from the group.

A foundation for further research

It should be borne in mind that the Hawthorne experiments were conducted in an era when 'scientific management' was a popular concept in the search for industrial efficiency. Unwittingly, the Hawthorne experiments precipitated the active involvement of psychologists and sociologists in industrial affairs. By endeavouring to measure the effects of changes of working conditions upon productive efficiency, they stumbled upon other factors that proved to be of greater importance. Despite criticisms of the methodology employed, Mayo's findings laid the foundation stone of the Human Relations Movement, prompting a great deal of further research into such things as leadership, group dynamics, job satisfaction and motivation.

INFORMAL WORK GROUPS

One of the most important observations made during Mayo's Hawthorne studies had to do with the existence of informal work groups. For many years, work people have been formed into groups by management in order to achieve tasks as efficiently and economically as possible. Various group incentives have been devized with a view to increasing production. Generally, however, the groups have only been considered in their formal structure as illustrated in job descriptions or organization charts. In *Management and the Worker*, Roethlisberger and Dickson [2] state that:

> Many of the actually existing patterns of human interaction have no representation in the formal organization at all. . . . This fact is frequently forgotten when talking or thinking about industrial situations in general.

Management simply cannot afford to ignore the existence and importance of informal work groups. Numerous studies have, for example, shown the economic consequences of informal control on output despite the existence of incentive schemes. Other studies have demonstrated the dangers of disregarding informal structures.

The Longwall coal-cutting experiment

One of the best known series of such studies is that which was conducted by Dr Eric Trist and K.W. Bamforth [3] of the Tavistock Institute of Human Relations. Their report, published in 1951, demonstrated the disastrous consequences of introducing technological change without considering human relations aspects.

Their studies were conducted in the coalfields of North-West Durham. Traditionally coal was mined by small teams of between 2 and 8 men, known locally as 'marrow groups'. Each group worked a small section of the coalface, cutting and loading coal and propping up the roof. Payment was based on group output and was shared equally. Groups were self-selected and formed small tight-knit communities: if a group member was injured or killed, his family was often cared for by the other group members. The dangers inherent in mining together with the emotional pressures of working underground in darkness stimulated a high degree of interdependence within the groups.

For technical reasons it was decided to modify the working arrangements. A mechanical coal-cutter was introduced. The small marrow groups were disbanded and replaced by three shifts of 40 to 50 men working a coalface up to 200 yards long. Each shift specialized in either coal-cutting, loading or propping the roof.

The new system proved disastrous. Spread along the coal face individuals were both physically and emotionally isolated. Previously high morale disintegrated. Disciplinary problems occurred. Inter-shift tension, conflict and absenteeism rapidly increased. Pilfering — something previously unknown — became commonplace. Productivity deteriorated.

These results were later compared with those achieved by a modified working arrangement called the 'Composite longwall method'. Although still employing the new technology, this restored the use of self-selected groups again responsible for all three tasks. Although the groups were bigger than before, productivity rose, fewer accidents occurred and absenteeism was 40% lower than in any other longwall group.

What these studies clearly showed is that changes in work organization must take account not only of technical considerations, but also the likely social and psychological effects. In particular account must be taken of the extent to which the revised method seems likely to disrupt established work groups. Even the most perfect formal structure may thus be rendered meaningless if it ignores the informal. Acceptance of Trist's theory, supported by subsequent research [4], has radically changed the traditional approach to job organization and design. This is discussed in more detail later (see Job Design, Chapter 5).

WHAT IS A GROUP AND WHY DOES IT OCCUR?

Schein [5] defines a group as 'any number of people who (a) interact with one another, (b) are psychologically aware of one another and (c) perceive themselves to be a group'. A group may, of course, occur anywhere, in any aspect of life. Similarly it may be formally created or naturally evolve. What we are principally concerned with here is informal groups in the workplace; why they occur, their functions, and their implications for management.

Whenever people work together, a social group is likely to evolve. As we shall see later it is generally accepted that man has a certain basic psychological needs. Group membership offers opportunities for their satisfaction. It satisfies social needs for friendship and communication as well as security, supportive and status needs. However, because of the individual's reliance on the group, the group can obviously strongly influence the individual's behaviour.

EFFECTS OF GROUP MEMBERSHIP

Group norms

Perhaps the most commonly observed aspect of group behaviour is the establishment of group standards or norms. It appears that often such standards start life as a compromise between individual members' attitudes and ideas, eventually hardening to become an established norm. Once such a norm is established, deviation is frowned upon; deviants being subjected to group pressure until conforming again, or being forced from the group. The means of exercising such pressure vary considerably; deviants being 'sent to Coventry', subjected to derision, or in some cases subjected to violence. Generally, the more attractive a group is to members, the more likely they are to conform and the greater the pressure the group can apply without losing a member.

Norms appear to encompass all aspects of group life. In his studies at Hawthorne, Mayo observed that workers had developed their own patois or slang. Although such language may very well aid communication within the group, it also sets the group apart from others, reinforcing its solidarity. He also identified group customs dealing with clothing appropriate to members occupying certain positions. Standards of behaviour and attitude dealing not only with work activity, but also life away from work commonly exist. However, the most frequently researched example of group norms has to do with group control of productivity.

Group control and productivity

F.W. Taylor in his scientific management studies referred to the problem of 'soldiering', i.e., workers artificially controlling output. What does not appear to have been obvious to him, however, was that such control was group based. This was subsequently identified by Mayo in his bank wiring room studies. Although paid on an incentive scheme that would have allowed considerably higher earnings, the group had determined a maximum level of output beyond which it refused to go. The explanation was that a higher level of output and thus higher earnings would encourage management to reduce the rate paid for the job.

Several researchers have chosen to observe from within the working group. Roy [6], for example, worked for a period as a drill operator in a machine shop, recording both his own behaviour and that of his workmates. He describes the complex systems devised to mislead management while at the same time ensuring that wages did not fall below an acceptable level; such ploys again being largely based on a fear of rate-cutting.

Positive and negative group control

It would be a mistake to assume that group control is always directed against organizational interests. Both in the UK and elsewhere, the armed forces have demonstrated their firm belief in the development of cohesive groups as the most efficient way of getting the job done. The increasing number of companies experimenting with quality circles (see Chapter 5) indicates a similar conviction. Studies carried out by the University of Michigan Institute for Social Research suggest that labour turnover and absenteeism are lower among members of cohesive groups and that their productivity is generally higher.

Such points cannot however be taken for granted, since by reason of its cohesiveness a group may control conformity to group norms, whether they be in sympathy or conflict with those of management. Even at national level examples of group uniformity can be identified that lead to behaviour supporting or detracting from 'corporate' performance. Janis [7], for example in his book *Groupthink* examines four political disasters occurring under four different US Presidents. In each case, profound errors of judgement were made by a small, cohesive group that did not allow conflict or deviation, and that did not accept, believe or communicate information that proved proposed decisions to be wrong but conflicted with group norms.

GROUP COHESIVENESS

Generally the degree of control that a group may exercise will be determined by the sense of belonging or cohesiveness created and enjoyed by its members. What are the factors that contribute to cohesiveness?

Among the more important are:

1 Group size — if a group becomes too large it simply divides into several smaller groups. For example, in the bank wiring room experiment, a group of 14 men informally divided itself into two smaller groups: one at the back of the room, one at the front

2 Group stability — if membership is frequently changing, members will not have the opportunity to get to know each other and so develop cohesively. Research by Katz [8] suggests that stable groups tend to be high producing groups.

3 Physical proximity — unless communication, in whatever form, is possible, the social interaction necessary to stimulate cohesiveness is unlikely to occur.

4 Compatibility — employees who vary widely in terms of age, skill, social status, etc., are unlikely to achieve easy cohesiveness.

5 Work structure — workers carrying out the same or similar tasks will tend to experience the same problems and thus offer each other support based on their shared experience. Equally, the way in which work is structured may also affect the situation. For example, in the Volvo experiment, described later, management wished groups to form and so re-arranged the traditional mass production work lines so providing opportunities for communication and group decision making.

6 Leadership — the style of leadership adopted may affect the cohesiveness of a group in two ways. Generally it has been demonstrated that a democratic style that allows group members opportunities for participation will not only increase cohesiveness, but will also aid the integration of group and corporate goals. At the same time, an autocratic style may have a very similar effect, the manager concerned being seen as a threat to the group. Indeed, any external threat to a group's continued existence or authority is likely to encourage cohesiveness.

WORKING GROUPS — IMPLICATIONS FOR MANAGEMENT

As we have seen, the extent to which a group can control the behaviour of its members is largely determined by its cohesiveness. A cohesive group may use its power to support or militate against corporate objectives. It has been shown that labour turnover, absenteeism, job satisfaction and productivity may all be improved by the formation of cohesive work groups. But equally in other instances, such groups have been shown to create resistance to change; harnessing their power to the frustration of management aims. How may we ensure both the cohesiveness *and* contribution of such groups?

We may start by creating an environment within which groups are likely to form. Trist and Bamforth's coalmining experiments, for example, showed how certain work arrangements positively hinder group formation whereas others encourage it. Groups should not be too large and should be constituted of members whose characteristics complement those of their colleagues. This implies management care in the selection and allocation of staff. Work may be structured in a manner encouraging co-operation rather than conflict. Generally such consideration will aid cohesiveness. But how may it be ensured that this is applied to the achievement of corporate goals? Here the formula for success is more elusive.

At least one clue is provided by Mayo's telephone relay room experiment. The style of leadership was one to which the group was unaccustomed, but to which it nevertheless responded. It involved a high degree of group participation in decision making, the superior demonstrating at the same time his real interest in the group members. This democratic or participative style has been shown by several studies to be associated both with cohesiveness and the integration of corporate and group objectives. Rensis Likert [9] has emphasized the importance of the manager's attitude towards the group. He suggests that a manager must set high standards both for himself and his subordinates, demonstrating 'with contagious enthusiasm' his belief in the group's ability to succeed. Such participation is particularly important in dealing with change. In such an instance, management must bear in mind not only the initial difficulties of group resistance, but also the long-term consequences for group structures.

Other frequently quoted solutions include integrating informal leaders into the formal management structure and encouraging inter-group competition. However, such solutions, although solving one set of problems may create others. At first sight the integration of formal and informal leadership appears to be a wholly logical step. However, it is, perhaps, built on false assumptions. It is assumed, for example, that it is the informal leader who develops and controls group attitudes and behaviour. Although this may be so, it is perhaps rather more likely that since the group determines who shall lead it, a leader will probably be selected who is known to be in sympathy with determined group attitudes; the group thus determining at least initially the behaviour of the leader, rather than vice-versa. It assumes that once an individual has emerged as informal leader, he will continue to occupy that role. Empirically this is not so: rather what tends to occur is that leaders emerge according to the situation in which the group finds itself. Thus one individual may lead in times of conflict; another in more settled circumstances. In addition, the relationships between group and leader will in very few cases remain constant following the leader's 'legitimization'; indeed the formalization of the informal leader may lead to overt resentment and ostracism of a 'poacher turned gamekeeper'.

Inter-group competition

The encouragement of inter-group competition may very well have the required effect. However, as a group increases in cohesiveness, its relationship with other groups tends to change. The nature of such change was first demonstrated by Sherif [10] in a study of competition between two groups of boys. More recent studies have confirmed his findings.

Each group tends to see others as 'the enemy'. This may be manifested in hostility or a lack of co-operation and communication. Stereotyped and distorted images of the behaviour of others tend to develop; examples of behaviour being seized upon whenever they appear to support pre-conceived notions, but otherwise ignored. Each group becomes increasingly structured in its behaviour and organization, demanding greater loyalty from its members. Although such behaviour may be productive, the negative aspects of non-co-operation and non-communication may become an organizational liability. Management must therefore ensure that negative aspects of competition are prevented or at least limited, while encouraging positive aspects. In practice, this may be achieved by encouraging inter-group communication and interaction, emphasizing common difficulties and objectives or planning organization and work structures so as to promote co-operation rather than conflict.

REFERENCES

1. Taylor, F.S. (1911). *The Principles of Scientific Management*. Harper and Row.
2. Roethlisberger, F.J. and Dickson, W.J. (1939). *Management and the Worker*. Harvard University Press.
3. Trist, E.L. and Bamforth, K.W. (1951). 'Some social and psychological consequences of the longwall method of coal getting'. *Human Relations*, No. 4, pp. 1–38.
4. See for example: Engelstad, P.H. (1972). 'Socio-technical approach to problems of process control' in Davis, L.E. and Taylor, J.C. (Eds), *Design of Jobs*. Penguin.
5. Schein, E.H. (1970). *Organisational Psychology*. Prentice Hall.
5. Roy, D. (1955). 'Efficiency and the fix'. *American Journal of Sociology*, Vol. 60, pp. 255–266.
7. Janis, I. (1972). *Groupthink*. Houghton Mifflin.
8. Katz, R. (1982). 'The effects of group longevity on project communication and performance'. *Administrative Science Quarterly*, Vol. 27, No. 1, pp. 81–104.
9. Likert, R. (1961). *New Patterns of Management*. McGraw Hill.
10. Sherif, M. (1961). *Inter-Group Conflict and Co-operation: The Robbers Cave Experiment*. University Book Exchange.

4
Motivation and job satisfaction

In order to ensure that the most effective use is made of manpower, it is obviously essential that management not only understands how people behave, but also why. The complexity of individual motives and attitudes clearly renders any sweeping generalization valueless. Nevertheless, several social scientists have put forward theories that seek to throw at least a little light on the problem. In a book of this length we can do little more than acquaint the reader with some of the more commonly accepted of such theories. This is, however, an area to which both practising managers and examiners are giving increasing attention, and it is therefore particularly important in this case that students make use of the recommended reading list that will be found on page 94.

The reader will note in this, and indeed the previous chapter, that some of the references quoted are by now a little 'elderly'. We make no apology for this. As David Guest [1] suggested recently, although considerable investigation into the area continues, there is little recent work that threatens to eclipse many of the earlier studies. This is a view with which we would concur.

A. H. MASLOW — THE HIERARCHY OF NEEDS

One of the most commonly accepted theories is Maslow's 'hierarchy of needs' [2]. The theory rests on the basic assumption that individuals are in a constant state of motivation, never achieving a state of satisfaction except for a very short time. Man is therefore motivated by constantly unsatisfied and changing needs. Maslow arranges human needs in a 'hierarchy of potency' (see Fig. 4.1); the resulting order being:

☐ physiological needs
☐ safety needs
☐ love needs
☐ esteem needs
☐ the need for self-actualization

51

Physiological needs

The most basic human instinct is survival. It follows therefore that man's most basic needs are those that arise from that instinct, i.e., food, drink, sleep. If such needs are unsatisfied, then questions of esteem or self-actualization, etc., simply do not arise. However, immediately physiological needs are satisfied, then the other 'higher' needs emerge.

Fig. 4.1 The hierarchy of needs

Safety needs

His physiological needs satisfied, the individual turns his attention to safety or security needs. These include protection from the elements, shelter, clothing, etc. For modern man, physical security is perhaps not the problem it once was. Instead, in an industrial society, security needs take on the form of job security.

Love needs

When both physiological and safety needs are adequately satisfied, then love or belonging needs emerge. Such needs include not only the need to give and receive love and affection, but also to associate with and be accepted by others in an atmosphere of friendship.

Esteem needs

By esteem is meant both self-esteem and the esteem of others. Maslow divides such needs into two groups:

☐ needs relating to self-esteem, e.g., confidence, independence and freedom
☐ needs relating to reputation or prestige, e.g., recognition, attention, importance and appreciation.

Obviously there is a degree of overlap between esteem and love needs. However, although esteem needs may be satisfied by social relationships, they may equally be satisfied by status symbols, such as being in charge of others, a certain sized desk, a carpet on the floor, a company car, etc.

Self-actualization needs

The final and highest group of needs are self-actualization or growth. Self-actualization refers to the need to achieve one's potential, 'to become everything that one is capable of becoming'. The extent to which such needs are capable of satisfaction in the workplace is clearly dependent on the nature of an individual's task; the prospect of self-actualization being obviously greater for the professional, skilled or managerial employee.

It should be noted that Maslow does not assume that the order of needs will always be the same. However, he does suggest that the pattern is appropriate in most cases. Nor does he argue that a need must be totally satisfied before another assumes greater potency. Man, he suggests, is never completely satisfied in respect of any need, but a reasonable amount of satisfaction must exist before his attention passes to a hierarchically higher, but lower priority, need. An average individual, he suggests [3], might be 85% satisfied in his physiological needs, 70% in his safety needs, 50% in his love needs, 40% in his esteem needs and 10% in his self-actualization needs.

Maslow's theory obviously has much to offer in assisting management in the motivation of staff. For example, a company indulging in vast expenditure on glossy magazine style premises may very well be disappointed by employee response if it has not taken care to establish a fair and secure remuneration policy. Status, according to Maslow, is unimportant to the average worker until the more potent physiological, security and love needs are satisfied. Similarly, the potency of money as a motivator seems likely to decline sharply once an individual has satisfied his more basic needs and starts to seek love, esteem and self-fulfilment. Management must therefore seek to provide job opportunities for the satisfaction of such needs, or accept that the energies of staff may be applied to their satisfaction outside the workplace.

Criticisms of the theory

Maslow's theory is widely accepted and has provided the basis for much subsequent research. However, this has not always fully confirmed the theory.

Several studies, although confirming the existence of a hierarchy, have cast doubt on both the order and constituents of Maslow's hierarchy. Alderfer [4], for example, identifies three rather than five needs:

☐   the concern for existence (including pay and security,
☐   relatedness (all social aspects of work)
☐   growth (job content and personal development)

Other studies deny the existence of any hierarchy [5]. Generally those studies that have confirmed the theory have concentrated on the lower physiological and security needs. What does not appear to exist is confirmation of the theory as a whole. This is probably so for several reasons.

To begin with, Maslow fails to define the needs in measurable operational terms. Similarly he fails to provide any sort of time scale. Any subsequent attempt to prove the theory is likely, therefore, to vary in its basis and thus be of doubtful value. A proper test of the theory would, in any case, require persons totally unsatisfied to be given the opportunity to satisfy all needs. To set up such an experiment would be notoriously difficult, if indeed possible at all. Although Maslow acknowledges that his theory is not capable of universal application, critics have suggested that individual need patterns are so varied as to render any generalization worthless. Blackler and Williams [6], for example, suggest that the theory reflects only that section of American society with which Maslow came into contact. The theory's ease of application to the industrial scene has also been questioned. If motivation is to be geared to employee need patterns, how can this be achieved when, according to Maslow, such needs are in a constantly shifting state? Is the theory indeed relevant to industry? Maslow apparently considers satisfaction to be a worthwhile outcome: however, other research suggests no certain correlation between satisfaction and job performance.

FREDERICK HERZBERG: THE MOTIVATION—HYGIENE THEORY

Among the researchers to develop Maslow's theory was Frederick Herzberg. In his motivation—hygiene theory [7] he divides factors affecting the individual into two groups: motivators and hygiene factors.

Herzberg together with Mausner and Snyderman carried out critical incident interviews with 200 engineers and accountants in the Pittsburgh area of the USA. (The research has since been replicated many times with different occupations.) Each individual was asked to decribe events at work that had made him feel 'exceptionally good' or 'exceptionally bad'. Having identified such events, the researchers attempted to discover why each worker felt as he did. On the basis of that information, Herzberg developed his two groups of factors. He concluded that the elements in a job that produced satisfaction were:

☐ achievement
☐ recognition
☐ work itself
☐ responsibility
☐ advancement

These he called 'satisfiers' or 'motivators'. Factors involved in job dissatisfaction included:

☐ company policy and administration
☐ supervision
☐ salary
☐ inter-personal relationships
☐ working conditions

These he called 'hygiene' or 'maintenance' factors. Using a medical or engineering analogy, he considers that they can be the cause of dissatisfaction if not maintained to an appropriate standard.

Herzberg concludes that motivation and increased job satisfaction may only be achieved via the motivators. The existence of adequate hygiene factors will prevent job dissatisfaction; their absence will promote dissatisfaction. However, hygiene factors can never motivate nor stimulate job satisfaction. Job satisfaction and job dissatisfaction, according to Herzberg, are therefore totally separate on two distinct continuums (see Fig. 4.2).

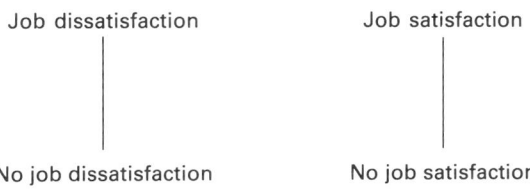

Fig. 4.2 Herzberg's two separate continuums of job satisfaction and dissatisfaction

The implications for management are clear. If all management seeks is an acquiescent labour force, then adequate provision of hygiene factors will probably be enough. If however motivation to greater productivity is sought, then opportunities for personal growth via the motivators must exist.

Criticisms of the theory

Many studies duplicating Herzberg's methodology have confirmed his findings. However, researchers using other methods have often failed to do so. This has led to suggestions that the theory is 'method bound'. It is argued that the two-factor theory is a natural consequence of

Herzberg's two-question approach, and that it is a predictable human trait to attribute to ourselves circumstances that make us feel good while reserving blame for others when circumstances are less favourable [8]. Further, that since answers to questions were assessed and categorized by members of Herzberg's team, the results are inevitably biased. Certainly other studies in which workers categorized their own responses tend to have produced a rather different picture [9].

Others question the general relevance of a theory based on interviews with a small group of specialist professional staff, a theory apparently unsupported by behavioural criteria, e.g., turnover, absenteeism, etc. There is evidence to suggest that Herzberg's motivators are closely linked to organizational status, being often scarcely relevant at shop-floor level, but increasing in potency as one rises through the organizational hierarchy. This view is supported by a survey conducted by Whitehill [10] that examines evidence produced by surveys of production workers in the US car industry. His findings suggest that management has perhaps over-reacted to Herzberg's theory and has concentrated too much on motivators. Recent studies, he argues, show that at least at shop-floor level, 'there are more workers concerned about fundamental conditions of their *work environment* than there are those worried about intrinsic elements of the job itself'. 'There is', suggests Professor Whitehill, 'a good chance that managers have been talked into serving champagne and caviar while ignoring the muffled pleas of workers for more meat and potatoes'.

The most widespred criticism, however, has to do with Herzberg's insistence that the two groups of factors are entirely separate. Today, it is generally accepted that the two groups cannot be considered mutually exclusive. Rather, that motivators may be sources of dissatisfaction, just as hygiene factors may be strongly motivating for certain individuals.

Herzberg's theory has, it appears, been widely and variously criticised. However, few of his critics dismiss the theory out of hand. Instead most agree that although perhaps over-emphasizing the importance of certain factors, Herzberg nevertheless has directed both research and management attention to a greater awareness of the possibilities of intrinsic motivation.

V. H. VROOM — EXPECTANCY THEORY

Several relatively recent theories suggest that motivation is a function of an individual's expectancy of achieving an objective that has value for him. Such theories use two principal variables: 'valence' and 'expectancy'. What do these terms mean?

Valence is the measure of an individual's desire for certain results. It may be positive, i.e., an outcome is desired; zero, i.e., the outcome is neither desired nor unattractive; negative, i.e., the outcome is unattractive. *Expectancy* is an individual's assessment of the likelihood that a particular act will or will not lead to certain outcomes.

Stated very simply, Vroom's [11] theory is that motivation is a product of valence multiplied by expectancy, i.e.:

Motivation = Valency × expectancy

Thus for example, an outcome may have a high valency for an individual. If, however, he has no expectancy of achieving that outcome, then it will have no motivating force. For motivation to occur there must exist both positive valency and expectancy.

THE PORTER AND LAWLER MODEL

Drawing upon the work of Vroom together with several earlier writers, Porter and Lawler [12] have developed a more detailed model of motivation based on expectancy theory (Fig. 4.3). Their theory is that the amount of effort an individual will expend in pursuit of a reward will be determined by:

1 his expectancy that his effort will achieve the task
2 his expectancy that he will be rewarded as a result of achieving the task
3 the value the reward has for him

In addition to effort, the level of performance will also be determined by an individual's ability and role perception. Role perception describes the behaviour that an individual believes necessary to achieve effective job performance. Performance accomplishment is satisfied by both intrinsic and extrinsic rewards. From these rewards, the individual derives satisfaction, the degree of satisfaction being determined by what the individual perceives to be an equitable reward for his accomplishment, compared with the rewards received. The level of satisfaction derived naturally determines the value of the reward, and so the cycle begins again.

Expectancy theories, such as those of Vroom and Porter and Lawler, may be described as a major step forward in understanding factors determining employee motivation. In response the amount of research into the area has grown considerably. An excellent summary of such work is provided by Campbell and Pritchard [13].

In particular, such theories highlight the importance of individual perceptions and attitudes. It is not enough that a particular outcome satisfies a need. What is important is that employees see effort linked to performance and performance linked to outcomes or rewards that have value for them.

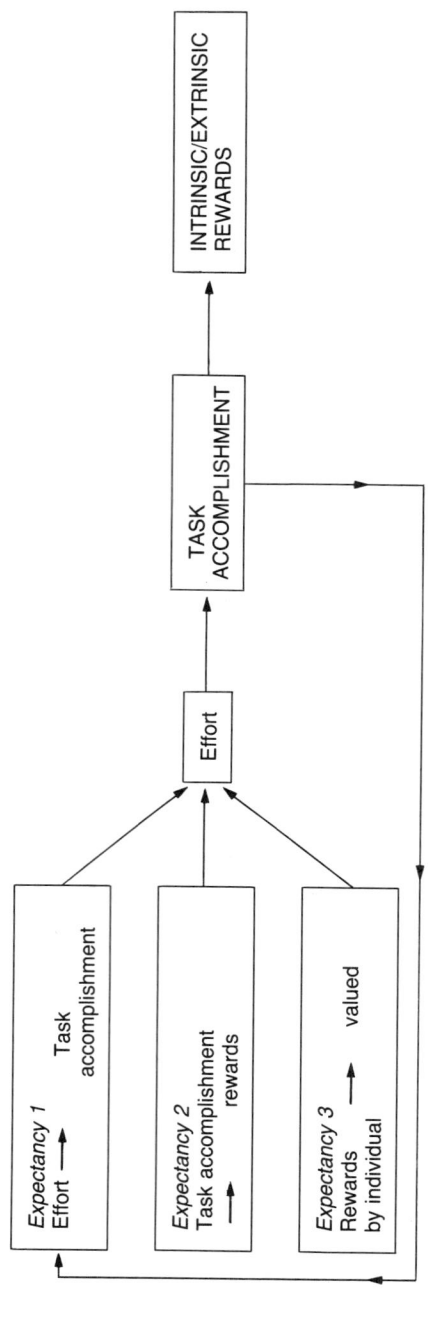

Fig. 4.3 A simplified model of LAWLER and PORTER'S Expectancy Theory

EQUITY THEORY

At first sight a very different explanation of employee behaviour is proposed by John Adams [14] and other equity theorists. It should be noted, however, that Lawler [15] and others argue that equity and expectancy theory though essentially different may be used to explain other conclusions [16].

Equity theory is based on the idea that individual workers seek what they perceive to be an equitable return for their efforts. In particular, Adams suggests that an individual consciously or sub-consciously determines a ratio between what he puts into his job and what resulting outputs accrue to him in the form of pay, intrinsic reward, status, fringe benefits, etc. This ratio, again consciously or sub-consciously, is compared with those of other employees and equity or inequity perceived.

Where equity appears to exist, the individual is content. Where inequity is evident he takes steps to achieve equity. The greater the inequity, the greater the resulting dissatisfaction, and the greater is the motivation to achieve equity.

Certain predicted effects of perceived inequity on quantity and quality of performance are indicated. Differentiation is made between workers paid on a time basis and those on piece rates. The reason is that a piece rate worker increases his pay as he increases his output, whereas a worker on time rates is normally paid irrespective of output. The predicted consequences of perceived inequity are as shown in Table 4.1.

Table 4.1 Predicted consequences of perceived inequity

Inequity	Predicted consequences
Underpayment	
Hourly paid worker	Reduced quality and/or quantity
Piece rate worker	Reduced quality and increased quantity
Overpayment	
Hourly paid worker	Increased quality and/or quantity
Piece rate worker	Reduced quantity and increased quality

Although certain aspects of the theory appear potentially naive, independent tests have generally supported Adams' hypothesis.

In practical terms, the significance of the theory would appear to be that in determining reward packages, organizations must develop and maintain systems that present a picture of equity on an individual to individual and worker group to worker group basis. Further, that since employees act on the basis of their perceptions and beliefs, whatever system is adopted must be one that is understood and accepted as fair by all concerned.

FRUSTRATION

In our discussion of motivation, we have assumed so far that an individual motivated towards satisfaction of a need, job satisfaction or some other form of reward always achieves his objective. Realistically, we know that this is not always so. All of us at some time or another set ourselves objectives that we are unable to achieve. In such circumstances, one is said to be 'frustrated'. What are the consequences of frustration?

In 1939, Dollard et al. [17] suggested that:

aggression is always a consequence of frustration. More specifically, the proposition is that the occurrence of aggressive behaviour always pre-supposes the existence of frustration and, contrariwise, that the existence of frustration always leads to some form of aggression.

Today, although it is accepted that frustration may indeed manifest itself in aggression, it is acknowledged that this will not always be the case. The response to frustration may be negative or positive. Typically, negative response results in one of four types of behaviour:

☐ aggression — hostility or anger
☐ regression — childish behaviour
☐ fixation — rigid dedication to established practice or ideas even if outmoded
☐ resignation — giving-up or withdrawing

Reaction to frustration is, however, not always negative. Rather, an individual may respond in an adaptive fashion, by trying to find some other means of achieving his goal or replacing it with some other objective, more easily attained but equally acceptable.

Frustration — a problem for management

What is the significance of frustration in the work place? Very simply, frustration is a factor that has been shown to contribute to many of the day-to-day problems that face management. Poor quality and quantity of work, accidents, absenteeism, labour turnover, disciplinary problems, fatigue, sickness and industrial disputes have all been shown to be likely consequences of a frustrated workforce. In particular, attention has been given to the role of frustration as a cause of or major factor in the promotion of strikes.

An examination of striker behaviour often reveals examples of the classic reactions to frustration described above. It would obviously be ridiculous to suggest that all strikes are a reaction to frustration. However, the theory does at least provide a starting point for explaining why comparatively highly paid mass-production workers, e.g., in the motor industry, appear to have a propensity for striking over what appear to be matters of only minor significance. The various means that may be adopted by management to avoid such situations will be discussed later.

JOB SATISFACTION

In our examination of Herzberg's motivation—hygiene theory, reference was made to 'job satisfaction'. Although most people would claim to understand the meaning of the expression, and indeed could probably say whether or not they find their chosen job satisfying or otherwise, its definition is nevertheless elusory. On occasions, job satisfaction has been used synonymously with, amongst other things, morale and motivation. Clearly it is inter-related with both of these things. It is not, however, synonymous with either. In very simple terms, job satisfaction may be described as an individual's feeling about, or attitude towards, his job. To use very subjective language, a satisfied worker would probably describe himself as 'happy' in his work.

Job satisfaction and job performance

To a considerable degree, concern for employee job satisfaction has been based on the belief that 'a happy worker is a productive worker'. With regard to absenteeism, there appears to be a fairly consistent negative correlation with job satisfaction; though even so there is some suggestion that the correlation may be weaker for skilled workers and higher level white collar staff. A similarly strong negative correlation emerges between satisfaction and turnover, i.e., the more satisfied a member of staff, the less likely he is to leave.

But it is in the relation to productivity that the 'happy worker' theory appears weakest. In a 1955 review of earlier studies, Brayfield and Crockett [18] suggested that there was little evidence of any relationship between satisfaction and job performance; a conclusion confirmed by Vroom [11] in 1964. Why should this be so?

No easy or certain answer exists. It should be noted that most studies failing to find a link have involved workers engaged in relatively structured tasks with little scope for individualism. In the one or two instances where a correlation between satisfaction and productivity has been found, workers involved have usually been management or professional staff, with considerable job opportunity for autonomy and self-fulfilment. Whether or not this is indicative of a response to a particular employer's behaviour is debatable. It is perhaps more realistic to assume that such staff are more likely to have an overriding professional commitment or that, given the opportunity to pursue their own chosen career, they would derive satisfaction whatever the circumstances.

Such a prospect highlights perhaps the principal reason for the absence of any clear-cut relationship. Job satisfaction is very largely a matter of individual attitude. A more radical explanation is proferred by Porter and Lawler based on their expectancy theory model [12]. Their argument is that instead of satisfaction being a determinant of performance, in reality performance of a task can provide satisfaction.

In view of the conclusions discussed above, it is logical to ask whether management should continue to concern itself with job satisfaction. The answer must surely be in the affirmative. Although research suggests no correlation between satisfaction and output, it appears that there is a link with both labour turnover and absenteeism. A happy worker may not necessarily be a productive worker, but he is probably less likely to engage in negative behaviour giving rise to disciplinary or industrial relations problems.

ABSENTEEISM

Although absenteeism can be a symptom of job dissatisfaction, so too can the repeated absence of colleagues lead to dissatisfaction among other staff and so contribute to reduced corporate effectiveness. It is therefore an aspect of worker attitude and behaviour deserving of management attention.

In order to monitor levels of overall, departmental and individual absenteeism a system of record keeping and statistics must be developed. Various methods of calculating absence rates may be used. The more common include:

Absenteeism rate (or lost-time %)

$$\frac{\text{No. of working days (or hours) lost in period}}{\text{Total potential working day (or hours) in period}} \times 100$$

Annual duration per person

$$\frac{\text{No. of days lost in year}}{\text{Average population at risk during year}}$$

In addition, some insight and benefit may be derived from attempting to categorize each absence according to a range of characteristics. Just as there are people who are accident prone, so too, it would appear are there staff who are absence prone. Absence should therefore be noted on an individual basis.

This is another area where Pareto's 80:20 theory [19] is often found to apply, the bulk of absence being generated by a small hard core of employees. The age or sex of employess, the day of the week or time of the year may all be correlated with a pattern of absence requiring managerial intervention. The reasons given for absence should be noted, analysed and, where appropriate, investigated. Equally it is sometimes worthwhile attempting to reach behind such excuses and determine other common factors. Monotonous work, poor pay, inept supervision, bad working conditions, etc., may all be the root cause of repeated absence.

In addition to such measures the following may be considered:

☐ a self-certification system for all absence, combined with a requirement to contact the appropriate supervisor as soon as the absence commences
☐ a periodic reminder to employees of their contractual obligation to attend regularly at their workplace
☐ reassurance that legitimate absence will not be punished or frowned upon, and that provision exists to assist staff in such circumstances.
☐ the introduction of medical examinations or disciplinary procedures for long-term, repetitive or unjustified absence
☐ training for supervisors in the handling of absence in a firm but sympathetic and fair manner.

In each case some flexibility is obviously desirable in dealing with individual circumstances. Nevertheless, some overall consistency and visible justice are essential.

MORALE

Like job satisfaction, morale is a word commonly used and commonly understood which nevertheless appears to defy consistent definition. Although tempted to rely on McCormick and Tiffin's [20] suggestion that 'anyone using the term should make its intended meaning clear' we suggest that morale is a product of individual job satisfaction and group cohesiveness. Determinants of morale will thus be determinants of these two factors. Similarly the consequences of any given level of morale will be those normally associated with the existence or absence of cohesive work groups and individual job satisfaction.

WHY DO PEOPLE WORK?

Why do people work? Why is it that even after winning a small fortune on the football pools, many individuals choose to continue working?

Today, it is generally accepted that most individuals do not simply come to work in order to collect a salary or wage. Most are also interested in other things; in particular to seek fulfilment of individual and social needs through intrinsic job satisfaction. A study by Morse and Weiss [21], for example, revealed that 31% of the workers interviewed claimed that they would continue working even if it was not financially necessary, because of their relationships with colleagues. The two researchers went on to conclude that work induced 'a feeling of being tied into the larger society, of having something to do, of having a purpose in life'.

The importance of money as a reason for working may not, however, be dismissed. A growing body of evidence suggests that an individual's attitude to work is a function of his occupation, cultural background and socio-economic status. Generally it would appear that professional workers and persons in the higher socio-economic groups are more likely to be intrinsically orientated than their blue collar or lower socio-economic counterparts.

THE AFFLUENT WORKER — J.H. GOLDTHORPE

Such differences in attitude have formed the basis for several studies, one of the most important of which is undoubtedly that conducted by Goldthorpe *et al.* [21] This examined the attitudes of 229 manual workers employed in the car, ball-bearing and chemical plants in the Luton area. All were regarded as affluent when compared with the bulk of manual workers, and moreover compared favourably with a sample of lower-grade white collar staff employed by the same organizations.

The investigation revealed that most of the workers involved stayed in their jobs principally because of the high pay they could earn. Few enjoyed or expected to enjoy their work, a minority being concerned with pay to the exclusion of all other factors. Only a very small number had serious aspirations for promotion, many suggesting that supervisory jobs were simply not worthwhile in economic terms. Interviews revealed that 60% of the more skilled men involved and 80% of the semi-skilled, claimed not to have a single 'close friend' with whom they worked. Workmates and friends were seen as separate categories. Similarly 76% of the skilled and 66% of the semi-skilled suggested that they would be 'not much bothered' or 'not bothered at all' if moved to another job away from the men with whom they currently worked. Many had moved house or come down the social scale from more interesting jobs. In each case the reason was the same — money.

Almost all (86%) stated that they 'got on' with their supervisor; their criteria being reflected in comments such as 'he leaves you alone', 'he keeps himself to himself'. Goldthorpe concludes that such workers tend to have a basically 'instrumental' approach to work.

He suggests that for them, work is a means by which money is obtained in order to achieve objectives totally external to the work-place or job. Such workers are:

particularly motivated to increase their powers as consumers and their domestic standard of living, rather than their satisfaction as producers and the degree of their self-fulfilment in work.

He argues that such a tendency results from the erosion of traditional working class life owing to urban redevelopment and greater geographical mobility. Under such circumstances, family life becomes the dominant factor for many and with it a concentration on work as an economic necessity:

It is in our view probable that, in the conditions of modern British society, the tendency will increase for industrial workers, *particularly unskilled or semi-skilled men*, to define their work in a largely instrumental manner [22].

Such attitudes are contrasted with those of white collar and other manual workers of a 'more traditional kind'. Although Goldthorpe argues that *all* workers tend to have some degree of instrumentality in their work attitude, he acknowledges that for many, work is a 'solidaristic' or group experience from which satisfaction is derived. Indeed, work may become a central life interest. For the average white collar or skilled worker, the prospect of work as a central core around which life is organized is all the more likely; for the professional worker, the integration of work and non-work may be total. Such attitudes may be clearly identified in the Trist and Bamforth coalmining studies described earlier, and in Salaman's [23] study of the work orientations of architects and railwaymen. In both instances the individuals involved were proud of their work skills and had developed a group culture: in both instances, a considerable degree of overlap existed between work and non-work activities and relationships.

From these studies and many others it is apparent that work means different things to different people. For some, a job is simply a means of obtaining money; for others an all-consuming interest. Precisely how an individual relates to his job depends on a whole variety of factors, including technology, class and occupation. The significance for management is clearly that before attempting to deal with workers individually or as a group, an understanding must be established of the employee's perception of his role at work.

REFERENCES

1. Guest, D. (1983). 'What's new in motivation', *Personnel Management*, May, pp. 20–23.
2. Maslow, A.H. (1943). 'A theory of human motivation', *Psychological Review*, Vol. 50, pp. 370–396.
3. Maslow, A.H. (1970). *Motivation and Personality*. Harper and Row.
4. Alderfer, C.P. (1969). 'An empirical test of a new theory of human needs', *Organisational Behaviour and Human Performance*, Vol. 4, No. 2, pp. 142–175.
5. For example, see: Lawler, E. and Suttle, J. (1972). 'A casual correlation test of the need-hierarchy concept', *Organisational Behaviour and Human Performance*, Vol. 7, No. 2, pp. 265–287.
6. Blackler, F. and Williams, R. (1971). 'People's motives at work' *in* Warr, P.R. (Ed.), *Psychology at Work*. Penguin.
7. Herzberg, F. *et al.* (1959). *Motivation to Work*. Wiley.
8. Locke, E.A. (1973). 'Satisfiers and dissatisfiers among white collar and blue collar employees', *Journal of Applied Psychology*, February, pp. 67–76.
9. Myers, M.S. (1964). 'Who are your motivated workers?' *Harvard Business Review*, Jan–Feb, pp. 73–88.
10. Whitehill, A.M. (1976). 'Maintenance factors: a neglected side of worker motivation', *Personnel Journal*, October, p. 516.
11. Vroom, V.H. (1964). *Work and Motivation*. John Wiley.
12. Porter, L.W. and Lawler, E.E. (1968). *Managerial Attitudes and Performance*. Richard D. Irwin.
13. Campbell, J.P. and Pritchard, R.D. (1976). 'Motivation theory in industrial and organisational psychology' *in* Dunnette, M. (Ed.), *Handbook of Industrial and Organisational Psychology*. Rand McNally.
14. Adams, J.S. and Jacobsen, P.R. (1964). 'Effects of wage inequities on work quality', *Journal of Applied Psychology*, No. 67, pp. 19–25.
15. Lawler, E.E. (1973). *Motivation in Work Organisations*. Brooks-Cole.
16. For a full discussion see: Steers, R.M. and Porter, L.W. (1983). *Motivation and Work Behaviour*. McGraw-Hill.
17. Dollard, J., Doob, W., Miller, N.E., Mower, O.H. and Sears, R.R. (1939). *Frustration and Aggression*. Yale University Press.
18. Brayfield, A. and Crockett, W. (1955). 'Employee attitudes and employee performance', *Psychological Bulletin*, No. 12, pp. 396–428.
19. Vilfredo Pareto (1848–1923) noted that 'the significant elements in a specified group usually constitute a relatively small proportion of the total items in the group'. This is commonly known as the 80:20 law.
20. McCormick, E.J. and Tiffin, J. (1975). *Industrial Psychology*. George Allen and Unwin.
21. Morse, N.C. and Weiss, R.S. (1955). 'The function and meaning of work and the job', *American Sociology Review*, Vol. 20, pp. 191–198.
22. Goldthorpe, J.H., Lockwood, D., Beechhofer, F. and Platt, J. (1968). *The Affluent Worker; Industrial Attitudes and Behaviour*. Cambridge University Press.
23. Salaman, G. (1973). 'Two occupational communities' *in* Weir, D., (Ed.), *Men and Work in Modern Britain*. Fontana.

5
Management and motivation

Earlier we suggested that if the most effective use is to be made of manpower, it is essential that management understands not only how people behave, but also why. Such knowledge is valueless, however, unless provision is also made for an environment that enables and encourages employees to achieve personal and corporate goals. A major factor contributing to the work environment is management behaviour. Even the most motivated of employees can very soon become bitter and frustrated when confronted by insensitive or uncaring management. The way in which a manager deals with subordinates will to a considerable degree be determined by the assumptions he makes about people in general and in particular, people at work.

DOUGLAS McGREGOR — THEORY *X* AND THEORY *Y*

In *The Human Side of Enterprise*, Douglas McGregor [1] describes two very different sets of assumptions, which he calls 'theory *X*' and 'theory *Y*'.

Theory *X* managers, he suggests, make the following assumptions about their subordinates:

- ☐ The average human being has an inherent dislike of work and will avoid it if he can
- ☐ because of this human characteristic of disliking work, most people must be coerced, directed or threatened with punishment to get them to put forth adequate effort toward the achievement of organizational objectives
- ☐ the average human being prefers to be directed, wishes to avoid responsibility, has relatively little ambition and wants security above all.

A theory *Y* manager assumes that:

- ☐ the expenditure of physical and mental effort in work is as natural as play or rest

☐ external control and the threat of punishment are not the only means for bringing about effort toward organizational objectives. Man will exercise self-direction and self-control in the service of objectives to which he is committed

☐ commitment to objectives is a function of the rewards associated with their achievement

☐ the average human being learns, under proper conditions, not only to accept but to seek responsibility

☐ the capacity to exercise a relatively high degree of imagination, ingenuity and creativity in the solution of organizational problems is widely, not narrowly, distributed in the population

☐ under the conditions of modern industrial life, the intellectual potentialities of the average human being are only partially utilized.

McGregor suggests that management attitudes and behaviour have too long been based on theory X and goes on to argue that theory Y is more consistent with recent psychological and sociological research. Just as the principle of theory X is the 'the carrot and the stick' so the principle underlying theory Y is the integration of personal and corporate objectives.

McGregor's theory has sparked off much management thought, discussion and criticism. Much of this, it is suggested, has arisen from a misunderstanding of the theory. McGregor does not come down firmly one one side or the other. Neither, as it is often suggested, does he intend the two theories to be seen as two extremes; rather he describes them as 'qualitatively different'. Neither theory offers a money-back guaranteed recipe for success. Neither is in fact a style or method of management. Each is a set of assumptions that may lead to various strategies. Which set of strategies is appropriate must be judged in the light of the individual situation.

E.H. SCHEIN — MANAGEMENT'S ASSUMPTIONS ABOUT PEOPLE

An alternative set of assumptions are put forward by Schein [2]. In roughly the order of their historical appearance he describes four theories.

Rational economic man

☐ Man is primarily motivated by economic incentives and will do that which gets him the greatest economic gain

☐ Since economic incentives are under the control of the organization, man is essentially a passive agent to be manipulated, motivated and controlled by the organization

☐ Man's feelings are essentially irrational, and must be prevented from interfering with his rational calculation of self-interest

☐ Organizations can and must be designed in such a way as to neutralize and control man's feelings and therefore his unpredictable traits

To these Schein adds McGregor's theory X assumptions.

Social man

☐ Man is basically motivated by social needs and obtains his basic sense of identity through relationships with others

☐ As a result of the industrial revolution and the rationalization of work, meaning has gone out of work itself and must therefore be sought in the social relationships on the job

☐ Man is more responsive to the social forces of the peer group than to the incentives and controls of management

☐ Man is responsive to management to the extent that a supervisor can meet a subordinate's social needs for acceptance

Self-actualizing man

☐ Man's motives fall into classes that are arranged in hierarchy:
  (i) simple needs for survival, safety and security
  (ii) social and affiliative needs
  (iii) ego satisfaction and self-esteem needs
  (iv) needs for autonomy and independence
  (v) self-actualization needs in the sense of maximum use of all his resources. Even the lowliest un-talented man seeks self-actualization

☐ Man seeks to be mature on the job and is capable of being so

☐ Man is primarily self-motivated and self-controlled

☐ There is no inherent conflict between self-actualization and more effective organizational performance

Complex man

In his introduction to complex man, Schein suggests that organization and management theory has tended to over-simplify and generalize conceptions of man. He considers that man is more complex than suggested by the rational economic, social or self-actualizing man theories. As society becomes more complex, so too does man, thus rendering generalizations all the more meaningless. He suggests that:

☐ man is not only complex, but also highly variable

☐ man is capable of learning new motives through his organizational experiences, his motives ultimately being determined by interacting between initial needs and organizational experiences

☐ man's motives in different organizations or different sub-parts of the same organization may be different

☐ man can become productively involved with organizations on the basis of many motives, his ultimate satisfaction and the ultimate effectiveness of the organization depends only in part on the nature of his motivation

☐ man can respond to many different kinds of managerial strategies, depending on his own motives and abilities and the nature of the tasks; in other words, there is no one correct strategy that will work for all men at all times

An examination of Schein's four sets of assumptions indicates close links with McGregor's X and Y theories. However, the principal advantage of the Schein theory is that it avoids the rather misleading apparent polarization of McGregor's assumptions. Instead it concludes that no universally applicable management strategy exists; rather that strategy must be contingent on the situation. In this conclusion, Schein is supported by a wide range of studies revealing no simple or clearly defined relationship between rewards, employee satisfaction and effective performance or productivity. Employees are individuals and will perform most effectively when comprehended and treated as such.

In a review of traditional organization structures, Fox [3] urges that management should accept this concept of individuality. He suggests that it is unrealistic to view the organization as a monolithic structure, since in fact it consists of a pluralistic combination of sometimes consistent, but often divergent, individual and group interests. Management should accept that conflict is neither unnatural nor necessarily negative in relation to the achievement of corporate goals. Time should be taken to examine the cause of conflict rather than dismissing it as irrelevant, management's job being to achieve the highest possible degree of consensus, rather than attempting to impose stereotyped attitudes or goals.

LEADERSHIP

Having discussed the assumptions underlying the manner in which a manager behaves, let us now consider the nature of such behaviour. Although 'management' and 'leadership' are often used as synonyms, we suggest that they are not in fact the same. This was clearly demonstrated, for example, by Mayo's bank wiring room study, in which it became apparent that whereas a formal supervisor existed, he was not in fact the group leader. An unofficial leader had emerged, and it was he who directed and controlled group activity. A leader may emerge anywhere or at anytime. Unlike the manager, he is not dependent for his authority on the existence of a formal organization structure. Instead, his authority rests on the willingness of people to follow him.

Management and leadership are not therefore the same. One is involuntary — the other voluntary. In practice, however, it is not always possible to distinguish between the two. Indeed, there is probably very little value in attempting to do so. What is important is that whereas a manager who is not a leader may nevertheless achieve results, such results are likely to be only a fraction of what might be achieved if he was both manager and leader. To be truly effective an individual must seek to amalgamate his managerial role with leadership.

What is leadership? Definitions vary widely, but for clarity that proposed by French [4] is probably unbeatable:

> A leader may be defined as a person who influences others in the direction of the leader's goals. Effective leadership within the context of the organization may be defined as the influencing of individual and group behaviour toward the optimal attainment of the enterprise's goals.

It is thus a vital management ingredient.

LEADERSHIP THEORIES

There have been a great many studies of leadership, most of which have taken place in the USA. For convenience, they can be grouped into three main schools or theories:

1 trait theories
2 style theories
3 situational theories

Trait theories

Trait theory is based on the idea that there is a set of personal characteristics or traits that an individual must have in order to be a leader. Examples such as integrity, charisma, ambition and courage are factors commonly cited. However, despite considerable research, no one universal set of traits has yet been identified. A further weakness is that the theory attempts to examine leadership in isolation. This is clearly unrealistic. A leader does not function alone. Leadership must therefore be seen as an interactive process involving leader, followers and their environment.

Style or behaviour traits

Rather than examining what leaders are, style or behavioural theories consider what it is that leaders do and how they do it. Most concentrate on two factors:

☐   the extent to which a leader relies on power or participation
☐   the extent to which he emphasizes people or production

One of the best known of such theories is that proposed by Rensis Likert [5]. He describes four 'systems of management':

System 1   Exploitative — authoritative
System 2   Benevolent — authoritative
System 3   Consultative
System 4   Participative group

System 4 emphasizes managerial trust and confidence in subordinates. Wide use is made of group decision making and supervision; the communication of ideas and information up and down the organization being encouraged, reward being based on group participation. On the basis of his research, Likert argues that managers adopting System 4 are consistently most effective in setting goals and achieving them.

Blake and Mouton [6] have developed a 'managerial grid' describing various combinations of managerial concern for production with concern for people. In order to integrate group and corporate goals, they suggest that the manager must develop a 9.9 style, i.e., high concern for people and production. Both the Likert System 4 and Blake and Mouton theories are, of course, very similar to McGregor's theory Y. In each case, the emphasis is on the integration of individual, group and corporate goals via need satisfaction and in particular by the creation of opportunities for self-fulfilment.

One final method of categorizing management style is taken from research by Lewin *et al.* [7]. They describe three management styles: autocratic, democratic and laissez-faire. An autocratic manager makes decisions and issues instructions that he requires to be obeyed. Such decisions are made without prior reference to subordinates and are issued without explanation. A democratic manager encourages group involvement in planning and achieving objectives; orders are issued only after consultation and explanation. The manager is in every respect a group member. The laissez-faire manager can hardly justify the title. He abandons control, leaving the group entirely to itself.

Leadership style — research

The Ohio State University studies

Literally hundreds of studies have been conducted to test the theories outlined above. One of the most comprehensive series was conducted at Ohio State University [8]. Statistical analysis of 1500 manager behaviour descriptions revealed that there were two major dimensions of leader behaviour, 'initiating structure' and 'consideration'. 'Initiating structure' refers to behaviour geared to organizing, planning, controlling and achieving corporate goals. 'Consideration' includes behaviour indicating mutual trust, respect and warmth between the leader and his group. The study showed that although the two dimensions were independent, effective leaders were above average in both dimensions, whereas ineffective leaders were below average in both.

The Prudential Life Insurance Company study — Katz et al. [9]

Sections of the company were categorized as achieving either high or low productivity. Section supervisors were interviewed about their attitude to their own jobs, their subordinates, their superiors and the company. On the basis of this information, each was described as either 'employee centred' or 'production centred'. When comparisons were made it became apparent that high productivity sections were supervised by employee-centred supervisors. Supervisors in charge of low productivity sections were production centred.

Lewin et al. [7] — handicraft classes

An early and at first sight unusual study was conducted by Lewin et al. in 1938. Groups of 10-year-old schoolboys were invited to volunteer for after-school handicraft classes. They were divided into groups, each group being put in the charge of an adult. Each adult adopted a specific leadership style: autocratic, democratic or laissez-faire. In the democratic group, the leader discussed with the group members what they could do and requested a group decision. Throughout the study he involved himself with the group in a positive fashion. The autocratic leader did not invite discussion. Rather he imposed on his group what the democratic group had decided. He gave instructions little by little, and although friendly, never participated as a member of the group. The laissez-faire leader did nothing, leaving his group to their own devices.

Autocratic leadership resulted in two types of behaviour. Some members became highly aggressive, whereas others became apathetic and withdrawn. Their aggression both directly and indirectly was directed towards the leader. However, behaviour within the group was equally aggressive at times. In the absence of the leader, all work ceased. When told they could keep their completed models, many of the boys destroyed them.

In the democratic group things were rather different. A high level of group cohesiveness existed. The leader was accepted and liked. Work continued whether the leader was present or not, and was both greater in quantity and of a higher standard than that of the other groups.

The laissez-faire group may be summarized in one word: chaos. Little or no work was done, the group behaving in a totally uncontrolled fashion whether or not the leader was present.

In order to test the results, group members were moved from group to group: the results remained constant.

The results of the studies described above have been duplicated and indeed elaborated on many occasions. However, to suggest that adoption of an employee-centred style of leadership will always result in increased effectiveness would be misleading. As we suggested earlier, leadership may never be considered in isolation. Account must also be taken of other factors contributing to the situation in which the leader finds himself.

Situational theory

From our own day-to-day experience we know that what we do and how we do it is very often dictated by factors outside our control; we find ourselves in a given situation and react accordingly. In essence this is the situational theory. Factors such as the characteristics of subordinates, organizational tradition, the nature of the task to be completed, cultural influences, etc., have all been shown to affect leader behaviour. Thus, it is argued, leadership style and behaviour can never be prescribed in anticipation of a situation. No ideal style or mode of behaviour exists. Rather, the leader must diagnose the situation, tailoring his behaviour appropriately.

In a development of the situational theory, Fiedler [10] proposes his 'contingency theory'. He argues that leader effectiveness is dependent or contingent on three variables:

☐ leader—member relations: the extent to which group members like and trust a leader
☐ task structure: the degree to which the nature of tasks is well-defined
☐ position power: the extent of the leader's formal authority

Fiedler's hypothesis is that different leadership styles are suitable when dealing with different combinations of the three factors. He concludes that:

In a very favourable or very unfavourable situation for getting a task accomplished by group effort, the autocratic, task-controlling, managing leadership works best. In situations intermediate in difficulty (for example poor leader — member relations, high task structure, and weak position power) the non-directive, permissive leader is more successful.

Vroom and Yetton model of managerial decision making

A relatively recent managerial style model is proposed by Vroom and Yetton. [11]. Focussing on the degree to which a manager should involve staff in decision making, they propose that the decision-making approach must be adapted to the attributes of the problem.

They identify five styles ranging from:

AI —   The leader makes the decision using information personally possessed

to, at the other end of the spectrum:

GII —   The leader shares the problem with the group, and acts more as a chairperson in generating and evaluating alternatives in search of group consensus.

The model is geared to achieving a high quality decision that is accepted by those who must execute it. To achieve this, seven key questions are posed, the first three concerned with decision quality and the other four with decision acceptance. When presented in the form of a decision-tree, the seven questions identify which of the five leadership styles is likely to produce optimal results.

What these theories confirm is the absence of a perfect leadership formula. For maximum effectiveness, a leader must be prepared to modify his style to meet the needs of the situation. This is easier said than done. Most of us find it difficult to change long-established attitudes and modes of behaviour. The achievement of the degree of attitudinal or emotional dexterity and flexibility required by such theories is unlikely, therefore, to be easy. Indeed, some would argue that it is impossible. In some cases this may be so; in others, however, some degree of flexibility may be achieved using various training and developmental techniques (see Management development, Chapter 15).

THEORY AND PRACTICE

We have now briefly sampled much of the more commonly accepted theory about why individuals work, what it is they seek at work, how they may be encouraged to work harder. Just what do these theories mean in practice?

Such theories must surely revolutionize our whole approach to management. Scientific management theories that dominated the pre- and immediate post-Second World War period are largely discredited. People are not machines and do not respond as such. Employees bring to the workplace individual attitudes, needs and problems. If treated in an uncaring mechanistic fashion they soon become alienated, expressing their frustration in negative behaviour, often directed against or at least detracting from the achievement of corporate objectives. Management behaviour aimed at satisfying individual needs and thus minimizing such problems can hardly be described therefore as altruistic.

Acceptance of the need to make work a more satisfying experience can be seen in all aspects of management policy and practice, ranging from the introduction of 'Flexitime' to the appointment of worker directors and the application of Management by Objectives. However, the area that has attracted most attention during the last 10 years is undoubtedly job design.

JOB DESIGN

It is principally through the design and re-design of jobs that the theories outlined above may be made truly meaningful for the average worker, whether he be blue or white-collar. Although other applications are important, their impact, when compared with what may be achieved through job design, becomes almost superficial. Methods of humanizing work through job design may conveniently be classified under three headings:

- ☐ job rotation
- ☐ job enlargement
- ☐ job enrichment

In view of the vast range of recently available material dealing with practical applications, we will restrict ourselves to an explanation of each method and a limited number of examples; further reading may be found at the end of the chapter. In particular, the reader is referred to Bailey's [12] excellent book, *Job Design and Work Organisations*, which gives very detailed consideration to proposals for matching people and technology so as to achieve both productivity and employee involvement.

Job rotation

The most basic form of re-design is job rotation. Staff are trained in various skills and moved from job to job at intervals on a determined or voluntary basis. Job interest is increased by opportunities to learn and develop new skills. However, frequent moves may disrupt social relationships, and the method is really only of value when no other alternative is possible. Rotation has been used with some success by the Polaroid Corporation. Production operative jobs are rotated with more interesting and varied jobs in research and development, quality control and engineering [13], Renault use job rotation at its Le Mans factory [14], where workers carrying out car assembly on a traditional production line basis are moved from job to job every hour.

Job enlargement

Job enlargement may be horizontal or vertical. Vertical job enlargement is generally known as job enrichment and is discussed later. Horizontal job enlargement involves the widening of duties by adding new tasks, thus making it less specialized and monotonous, and stimulating the development of new skills. Experiments with job enlargement have frequently produced excellent results. One of the best known British examples was carried out at Philip's Scottish factory in 1966 [15]. The factory manufactured electric fan heaters on traditional mass production lines, each line being manned by between 6 and 14 workers. Management was faced with acute labour relations and production control problems. The existing production method was scrapped and, after consultation with staff and unions, was replaced by a scheme in which each operative builds a complete heater. Job satisfaction increased, production defects were reduced by 50%, output rose by 10%.

Job enrichment

Job enrichment or vertical job enlargement differs from horizontal job enlargement in as much as it offers opportunities for involvement in the planning, organizing or controlling of a task. It thus offers much greater scope for satisfaction of status and self-fulfilment needs than is provided by rotation or enlargement. Examples of the successful application of job enrichment are legion. Before 1970, the South Eastern Electricity Board organized its consumer accounting department on a highly specialized basis, individual clerks carrying out repetitive and very simple tasks [16]. A decision was taken to computerize the system while at the sme time making jobs more rewarding. After consultation with staff representatives, a new scheme of work was introduced involving each clerk in responsibility for a specific group of consumers. Each clerk now deals with all correspondence, etc., relating to his group of consumers, instituting and completing accounting procedures as required. Following the introduction of the scheme, output increased, absenteeism was virtually eliminated and vacancies in the department were highly contested.

ICI were pioneers in the application of job enrichment. As one of a series of experiments the company advised a group of sales representatives that they need no longer submit individual customer sales reports, except in instances where they felt it appropriate. They were also allowed greater discretion in dealing with customer complaints, problems and pricing. Both job satisfaction and sales increased significantly.

Group application of job design

The cases described so far are all examples of individual employee job design or re-design. Some of the most outstandingly successful schemes have been those involving groups of workers. This is hardly surprising, since such schemes offer the opportunity of achieving not only employee satisfaction through work that is itself intrinsically valuable, but also satisfaction through the development of cohesive work groups.

An experiment that has received widespread attention is that conducted by Volvo in Sweden. During the early 1970s, Volvo was experiencing severe recruitment and labour relations problems despite relatively high wages. The company had plans for a new car factory at Kalmar in Southern Sweden. Initially plans were made for a traditional mass production plant layout. However, at the instigation of Pehr Gyllenhammar, the Volvo president, these plans were scrapped in favour of a revolutionary new design that would maintain production efficiency while offering considerable scope for employee job satisfaction. Trade union representatives were actively involved in all aspects of planning the new plant.

The factory began production in February 1974. Traditional mass production methods were replaced by groups of 15–20 workers. Each group was given its own hexagonal work area, which was separated from those of its neighbours by a buffer zone. Each group assembled a major component, or sub-assembly. Although management determined an output target for each group, how this was achieved was up to the group concerned, each group organizing itself and determining its own work speed.

An independent survey conducted by the Swedish Productivity Council in 1976 showed that 90% of workers involved liked the new working method, and in particular identified themselves with the quality of the product. Financial aspects of the experiment were, however, less satisfactory. Improvements in quality had not been fully achieved, though labour turnover and absenteeism were better than at other Volvo plants. Production times and indirect costs mirrored those elsewhere, but this ignored the 10% extra equipment cost of the group-based factory when compared with traditional production-line plants.

In response to criticism, Volvo executives argued that it was never intended that the new plant be seen as an experiment to be compared with other plants. Rather that it was part of a corporate commitment to a new philosophy of employment and production technology. Nevertheless, since then the economics of the plant have improved radically, albeit with some limited qualification of the original work control arrangements. In a recent joint employer/union report [17] it was noted that man-hours per car had fallen by 40% since 1977. This had been matched by an improvement in quality and quantity control. The plant was now the most labour efficient of the company's plants in Sweden.

Contributing to this improvement it was suggested, was the introduction of advanced work measurement techniques to balance workloads and reduce the number of assembly hours per unit of production. Similar modification of traditional car assembly methods has been carried out by another Swedish company, Saab-Scania, and by Volkswagen in Germany, again with claimed success. Outside the car industry, 'autonomous group' working arrangements have been used by the Philips Organization in many countries in connection with the manufacture of both components and assembled products, and in the UK by other major companies including Shell, Ferodo and ICI. Scottish and Newcastle Breweries have applied group job design to the organization of men loading and unloading delivery lorries [19]. Teams that formerly were closely supervised now organize themselves, control the issue of stock and determine delivery schedules. Instead of two supervisors, only one is employed on each shift, his role being to act as a 'consultant'. Considerable improvement in job satisfaction was reported following the introduction of the new schemes.

Does job design work?

In view of the experiments described above, one might be forgiven for considering this a ridiculous question. However, there are suggestions that job enlargement/enrichment is not the panacea some would have us believe. Many successful experiments have been reported, but rather fewer unsuccessful ones; yet common sense surely tells us that not all could be successful. Those that have produced promising results on closer examination can very often be seen to be imprecise in definition of cause and effect. In very many cases the actual job enlargement/enrichment process has been only one of several variables that might have produced the reported results. Thus, for example, in the Scottish and Newcastle Breweries study, the enrichment scheme was accompanied by supervisory training, consultative meetings, worker training, a new payment scheme and an improved work environment, any or all of which might have contributed to the experiment's success. Such points may also be made regarding experience at Volvo, and methodological aspects, e.g., the measurement of resulting job satisfaction, may similarly be criticized.

Nevertheless, examinations of 'failed' experiments fall prey, in several cases to exactly the same arguments. Needham [19] describes the failure of an initially successful scheme in a UK plant of a major multi-national electronics group. In conclusion he proposed that 'the idea still embraced by many personnel managers that job re-design leads to greater self-regulation looks increasingly dubious'. Yet in describing the reasons for failure he mentions the transfer into the work force of a displaced group of elderly and disabled workers, frequent design changes, a failure to maintain management control systems, a redundancy programme, and a hardening of management attitudes in the face of recession. To argue the cause and effect of failure with any degree of precision under such circumstances is, in our opinion, unsafe.

A more fundamental question, however, is to what extent enlargement or enrichment is desired by employees. Research demonstrated that a high proportion of schemes involve redundancy, which presumably would not be welcomed by most staff [20]. Is it possible for example that an enriched job might become so demanding that it outstrips the ability or inclination of an individual employee, thus leading to potentially greater frustration than a more repetitive task [21]? Is it possible, indeed, that some workers might prefer a repetitive task [22]? A growing body of evidence suggests that this might very well be the case, and that some workers prefer it and indeed may find highly repetitive work motivating. Charles Hulin and Milton Blood [23] suggest that enrichment techniques may only be appropriate to certain groups in the work-force, in particular, white collar and supervisory staff and 'non-alienated' blue collar workers. Similarly the studies of Goldthorpe *et al.* [24], discussed earlier, showed how certain workers simply did not seek intrinsic job satisfaction, their orientation to work being wholly instrumental. Generally it is as an individual rises through the organizational hierarchy that intrinsic work values become more important; yet most enrichment programmes have been directed at the shop-floor worker. Is it perhaps that job designers in their enthusiasm have assumed in others their own reactions to work which they perceive as boring?

There are also other non-motivational problems. A common argument is that the costs involved are potentially so high that goods produced would no longer be competitive. Certainly it does appear that the cost of equipping and stocking factories using enriched work systems is often higher than in conventional plants; e.g., Volvo at Kalmar. In addition, in return for the greater flexibility required of the worker, and for the greater responsibility he assumes, as well as for the withdrawal of restrictive practices of various kinds, a frequent element in the enrichment package is a general increase in wages and salaries. Such increased costs may of course be recovered through more efficient, better quality work, produced in an atmosphere of greater job satisfaction and improved industrial relations. However, research has produced conflicting results and many managers remain unconvinced and resistant to change. Trade Union reaction has often been antagonistic. Whether such antagonism is based on fear of redundancy, loss of membership or, as claimed, a preference for job satisfaction derived from participation in policy formulation rather than more pleasant work is not determinable. The case for enrichment appears neither fully proved or accepted. Yet it has worked well in some cases. What are the factors which tip the balance in favour of success?

Introducing work design

No foolproof recipe for success is possible. Nevertheless, by examining those experiments that have succeeded, certain guidelines may be recognized.

Our starting point must surely be to examine the jobs within our organization to see if in fact they can be enlarged or enriched. Cooper [25] suggests that wherever possible these should be in areas that are likely to have a real impact on the organization's effectiveness, since this will stimulate credibility and free managers form day-to-day responsibilities, permitting more time to be allocated to planning and development.

If it is clear that opportunities for job re-design exist, as indeed they usually do, the next question to be asked is whether or not the staff concerned would welcome such an exercise. Change of any kind is likely to be resisted, at least, initially. Care must be taken therefore to discriminate between a lack of enthusiasm based on resistance to change and that which results from staff being perfectly satisfied with current work systems. A new system imposed on an unwilling workforce clearly is unlikely to produce positive results. It is notable that in most experiments that are generally accepted as having been successful, management made a point of involving staff at a very early stage. If staff are to contribute willingly, it must be made clear what are the potential benefits as well as allaying fears or redundancy, loss of pay, etc. All staff, both directly and indirectly affected should be involved or at least kept informed of developments. Particular attention will have to be paid to trade union representatives and junior management.

Reference has already been made to the possible reaction of trade unions. However, trade unionism and job enrichment are not incompatible, if careful and early consultation is arranged, and indeed union participation is a salient feature of many successful schemes.

Just as trade unions feel threatened, so too may junior managers and supervisors. They will have a dual part to play, in as much as it will be necessary for them to adjust to a new role of adviser and counsellor while at the same time training staff to accept additional job responsibilities. Supervisors will themselves often need help in making such an adjustment, a loss of authority often causing temporary frustration.

Experience at Clark's Shoes in Somerset [12], suggests that supervisory training at an early stage on the need for change, the new working arrangements, the management of change and the supervisor's revised role is an essential element in ensuring smooth introduction and post-implementation periods. As details of the scheme become more refined, more general training of staff both in relation to technical area and group working together with other preparatory work may commence. In many cases, new systems have been introduced on a pilot basis, the pilot scheme being protected until established and evaluated.

Principles of job design

What should be the characteristics of the re-designed job? Naturally these will depend on the job involved. In general terms however, it should:

☐ be reasonably demanding, and include an optimal variety of tasks in terms of complexity
☐ provide for learning opportunities on-the-job
☐ provide for at least some minimum level of decision making by the individual
☐ provide for some degree of social support and recognition
☐ appear meaningful in as much as it is a complete job or makes an indentifiable contribution to the finished product
☐ be neither too short nor long a work cycle
☐ provide an opportunity for the employee to be involved in target setting with provision for results feedback
☐ contain some element of auxiliary or preparatory work
☐ demand some level of skill or care worthy of esteem

In addition, in relation to group based schemes, jobs should:

☐ promote or provide opportunities for interlocking social relationships particularly under circumstances of stress, interdependence or where there is little perceivable individual contribution to the end product

and where linked or grouped together should, combined:

☐ make a whole task that is meaningful
☐ contain scope for group standard setting and receipt of results
☐ provide for communication of individual and group feelings on the effectiveness of the job design [26]

QUALITY CIRCLES

Although not strictly a form of job-redesign, quality circles nevertheless encompass many of the same principles and benefits as the techniques described above. It is therefore convenient to consider them here.

Originally developed in the USA, quality circles have been adopted by the Japanese where it is now estimated that in excess of 10 million workers are involved in their operation.

A quality circle is a small group of employees, usually from the same working group, who voluntarily meet together on a regular basis, (usually in work time) to discuss quality problems, investigate causes, recommend solutions and, when given authority, take necessary remedial action. In Japan the application of circles has extended to take in areas such as costs, productivity and safety.

In the UK around 400 organizations are currently understood to be experimenting with their application. Well documented examples are Rolls-Royce and STC [27]. At Rolls-Royce, membership of groups extends across several organizational tiers and departmental boundaries, reflecting the complex technical nature of the work done. The main objectives of the exercise were to raise the level of quality consciousness and restore pride in craftsmanship. The company estimates that circles saved around $£\frac{1}{4}$ million in their first 3 years of operation with the promise of longer-term benefits through improved working relationships and capabilities. At STC, the programme was installed as part of a company exercise to reduce scrap rates. In addition to this, other recent projects tackled by circles have included the re-siting of equipment for greater efficiency and safety, modifications and redesign of equipment, and alterations in methods of moving materials around the plant. Although financial benefits are measured, STC believes that the principle gains are to be made elsewhere. Examples are more lasting improved styles of supervision, improved communications, greater employee skills and commitment to corporate rather than individual or group objectives.

Like the methods of job redesign considered above, quality circles are no easy answer to organizational problems: their introduction and operation requires care and continuing support. Lessons learned from successful schemes, including Rolls-Royce and STC suggest that to be effective:

☐ Circles must be allowed to develop before any real success is likely to be achieved. Their introduction should therefore be carried out quietly and without undue publicity until results can be demonstrated. Failure to do this may result in group and organizational disenchantment or embarrassment

☐ Circles must be supported by management at all levels. Such support must be demonstrated in time and money to allow unfettered operation

☐ Group members and group leaders will require training. Practice varies, but all members will need some training in methods for collecting data, problem solving techniques, presentation skills. Interpersonal skills training will also tend to improve group effectiveness and creativity

☐ A 'Co-ordinator' or 'Facilitator' should be appointed to monitor the formation and operation of circles. His role is to advise, train, co-ordinate and stimulate activity, but not to interfere or relieve circles of their problem solving talk

☐ Attention must be given to management styles in the organization. Despite senior management support, efforts will be abortive if the style of management does not allow for subordinate initiative or freedom of action

☐ Trade unions and other employee representatives should be involved at an early stage

In relation to this last point, trade union attitudes towards quality circles would appear to be that they are a 'belated recognition of employees' expertise and knowledge'. Although there is little evidence of union resistance to their introduction, it is clear that they are generally tolerated only where it can be demonstrated they do not challenge existing union machinery or practices. It also seems likely that unions will wish to discuss the distribution of any savings accumulating from quality circle proposals. On this point, it is noteworthy that neither the Rolls-Royce nor STC schemes reward circle members for their suggestions, despite the fact that both companies operate separate financially based suggestion schemes.

Equally important is the attitude of managers: particularly those in day-to-day contact with circle members. A number of studies [28] have suggested that management resistance is a common problem arising from alienation, a lack of consultation prior to introduction, failure to understand the potential benefits, a persistent drain on resources or a slight on previous managerial performance, etc.

From time to time it has been suggested that quality circles are just the latest management fad, or are only appropriate to Japanese culture. Experience will prove such claims true or false. What is clear is that while repeated claims of success are made, few organizations appear to have made any serious attempt to evaluate schemes in a manner which isolates them from other variables, or seeks to measure contribution in quantitative rather than qualitative terms [29]. Nevertheless, for the moment it would appear that, world-wide, a growing number of companies are sufficiently satisfied with the financial and human relations benefits accruing from such schemes to continue and, in some cases, extend their use.

REFERENCES

1. McGregor, D. (1960). *The Human Side of Enterprise*. McGraw-Hill.
2. Schein, E.H. (1970). *Organisational Psychology*. Prentice-Hall.
3. Fox, A. (1974). *Man Management*. Hutchinson.
4. French, W. (1974). *The Personnel Management Process*. Houghton Mifflin.
5. Likert, R. (1971). *New Patterns in Management*. McGraw-Hill.

6. Blake, R.R. and Monton, J.S. (1964). *The Managerial Grid*. Gulf Publishing.
7. Lewin, K., Lippitt, R. and White, R. (1939). 'Patterns of aggressive behaviour in experimentally created social climates', *Journal of Psychology*, Vol. 10.
8. Stodgill, R. and Coons, A.E. (1957). *Leader Behaviour: Its Description and Measurement*. Ohio State University.
9. Katz, D., Maccoby, N. and Morse, N.C. (1950). *Productivity, Supervision and Morale in an Office Situation*. University of Michigan.
10. Fiedler, F.E. (1967). *A Theory of Leadership Effectiveness*. McGraw-Hill.
11. Vroom, V.H. and Yetton, P.W. (1973). *Leadership and Decision Making*. University of Pittsburgh Press.
12. Bailey, J. (1983). *Job Design and Work Organisation*. Prentice Hall.
13. Foulkes, F.K. (1969), *Creating More Meaningful Work*. American Management Association.
14. Butteriss, M. (1975). *Techniques and Developments in Management*. IPM.
15. Thornely, D.H. and Valentine, G.A. (1975). 'Job enlargement: some implications of longer cycle jobs in fan heater production', *in Making Work More Satisfying*. HMSO.
16. Taylor, L.K. (1973). *Not For Bread Alone*. Business Books.
17. SAF/LO. (1984). *Volvo Kalmar — After 10 Years*. SAF/LO.
18. SPRL. (1974). *Worker Participation in Britain*. Financial Times Business Study.
19. Needham, P. (1982). 'The myth of the self-regulating work group', *Personnel Management*, August, pp. 29–31.
20. Kelly, J.E. (1982). *Scientific Management, Job Redesign and Work Performance*. Academic Press.
21. Oldham, G. et al. (1976). 'Conditions under which employees respond positively to enriched work', *Journal of Applied Psychology*, August, pp. 395–403.
22. Fein, M. (1970). *Approaches to Motivation*. Hillsdale.
23. Hulin, C.L. and Blood, M.R. (1968). 'Job enlargement, individual differences and worker responses', *Psychological Bulletin*, Vol. 69, pp. 41–55.
24. Goldthorpe, J.H. et al. (1968). *The Affluent Worker: Industrial Attitudes and Behaviour*. Cambridge University Press.
25. Cooper, R. (1974). *Job Motivation and Design*. IPM.
26. Emery, F.E. and Thorsrud, E. (1969). 'Some hypotheses about ways in which tasks may be more effectively put together to make jobs', *in Form and Content in Industrial Democracy*. Tavistock Institute.
27. Collard, R. (1981). 'Quality circles in situ', *Personnel Management*, October.
28. Hill, F.M. (1986). 'Quality Circles in the UK: a longitudinal study', *Personnel Review*, Vol. 15, No. 3.
29. Sherwood, K.F. et al. (1985). 'Quality Circles – can we evaluate them?', *Personnel Review*, Vol. 14, No. 1.

6
Communication

In this book, reference is made to the need to gain employee commitment, to involve staff in decision making, to maintain a free flow of information between management and other organizational personnel. Specific techniques and procedures are discussed that are intended to encourage consensus, motivate staff to better performance, avoid dispute or confrontation.

In each case effective communication is assumed. Yet a common complaint heard in all types of organizations is that effective communication either does not occur at all, or does so only spasmodically — or selectively. Repeatedly in our research in both public and private sectors, employees at all levels echoed such sentiments.

A BASIC MANAGERIAL SKILL

Communication is a basic skill of any manager. The adequate performance of his managerial functions depends on it and this is reflected in the considerable proportion of managerial time devoted to it. Henry Mintzberg [1] suggests that, on average, communication occupies 70–80% of the average manager's workload. What is communication?

COMMUNICATION: A DEFINITION

Definitions vary, but communication may be described as the activity whereby an individual or group conveys, consciously or unconsciously, information to another individual or group and at the same time accurately conveys meaning and understanding. As will be discussed later, such a task is no mean achievement.

In the definition above you will note that we refer to 'information' rather than 'facts'. Managers are usually concerned that facts be communicated. They often do not realize the need to communicate attitudes and feelings as well and to determine the attitudes and feelings of subordinates. To a considerable degree the efficiency of communication of facts depends on:

1   the recipient knowing the communicator's attitude as well as the facts
2   the communicator knowing what is the recipient's attitude and likely reaction before and after communication has occurred.

Unconscious communication must not be overlooked. By *not* communicating a manager may communicate. Thus the cry, 'nobody tells my anything', is typically much more than a plea for facts; rather it reflects an assumption of perceived status that may or may not be the case.

THE PERSONNEL MANAGER AND COMMUNICATION

As indicated above, we consider communication an unavoidable portion of any managers task. Why then have we included it in a textbook specifically dealing with personnel management, or is this just another aspect of the trash-can hypothesis described earlier?

It is included for two reasons. First, an examination of the function of the personnel specialist reveals that his task is unlikely to be carried out successfully unless he is a competent communicator: selection, training, counselling, negotiating and even dismissal, if they are to be carried out effectively, all rely on competent communication. Second, because of its 'people basis' in many organizations, the personnel specialist is referred to by other managers for advice on how to communicate with subordinates and how to handle problems that are essentially communication based. The ability to communicate is thus a key personnel management skill.

THE COMMUNICATION PROCESS

In developing such practical communication skills it is useful to have in mind a model of the communication process. This can be shown in diagrammatic form (see Fig. 6.1). The information to be communicated forms in the mind of the individual who wishes to communicate (the Sender). This is conveyed from his mind to his hands, vocal chords or other means of communication through a coding process. The message is then transmitted in words, gestures or some other fashion to the Receiver, who through one or more of the five senses receives and decodes the message absorbing it into his mind.

During the journey from Sender to Receiver, other influences (Noise) may interfere in the process, modifying, disrupting or blocking the

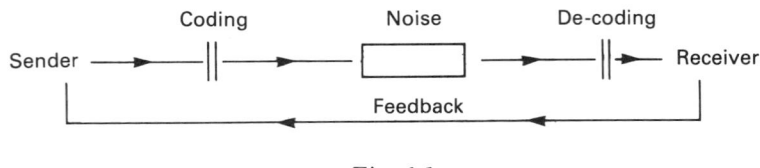

Fig. 6.1

original message. In addition to such barriers, obstacles to effective communication may occur during the coding and decoding stages.

Though it may not always occur, ideally feedback should link back from Receiver to Sender so that the effectiveness of communication may be assessed. It should be noted, however, that even where feedback does occur it may be subject to the same barriers as the original communication. What are the barriers?

BARRIERS TO COMMUNICATION

The principal barriers to communication may be grouped under three headings:

☐ organizational
☐ semantic
☐ human relations

Organizational

In some organizations it is observed that formal channels exist through which information is required to pass either up or down the organization structure. Such an arrangement, it is sometimes argued, aids communication. However, particularly in larger organizations, a message may, as a result, have to pass through many levels, repeatedly being received and re-transmitted until, hopefully, the original message reaches its intended destination.

What happens in practice, of course, is often very different. Consider the childrens' party game 'Chinese whispers' where a message is passed from child to child in a circle until the first child receives a usually unrecognizable version of his original message. Inevitably when subject to repeated transmission and re-transmission, messages are distorted or lost altogether.

In the organizational context, the problem tends particularly to affect downward communication. This can lead to apathy, frustration and eventually often tends to force reliance on the 'grapevine'.

An equally serious organizational problem is often the failure to allow for upward communication; management being content with passing information downwards with little or no concern for feedback.

Semantics

In attempting to communicate with one another, individuals at work and elsewhere do so for most of the time using words either orally on in writing. Words are little more than symbols that, regrettably, may mean different things to different people. This is further compounded by the existence of different meanings for the same word or words that sound the same but are fundamentally different in meaning.

Words quite properly used may nevertheless lack precision or be dependent upon re-inforcement by some other method of communication. Thus, for example, the expression 'quite nice' may vary in meaning from recommendatory to damning; in isolation it is impossible to tell which. Abstract words are a rich source of confusion. Consider the range of meanings that might attach to the word 'co-operation' particularly in the context of a manager – subordinate relationship.

Jargon can be a real barrier to communication. Although extremely useful to those familiar with its meaning, for others, jargon may be as incomprehensible as the most rare dialect or foreign language.

Human relations

Earlier we described the personnel manager's involvement in communication as being due, in part, to its 'people basis'. This is well illustrated in considering the range of human relations obstacles.

The content of the message, the manner in which it is communicated and received and thus the extent to which the process is successful may be determined not only by its actual construction or content but also by preconceptions that both Sender and Receiver have about each other. An unpalatable piece of information may nevertheless be accepted as valid if the Receiver has confidence in the Sender. The same piece of information conveyed by somebody mistrusted by the Receiver is likely to elicit a very different response.

Such circumstances may not necessarily rest on any particular relationship. The individuals concerned may well not know each other at all but nevertheless seek to categorize or stereotype the other's likely behaviour, reaction or motives. A common example of this is the entrenched attitudes that frequently occur in industrial disputes. Such attitudes may well be founded on a purely irrational basis. However, they may also reflect very real differences in background and experience that cause intended communication to be coded or decoded in a manner that destroys its original meaning.

Messages may, of course, be totally outside a Receiver's previous experience or understanding. The tendency under such circumstances is either to reject the message completely or to sift it, accept portions that are understood and thus acceptable and reject others. It is not hard to imagine the consequences of such a situation in the workplace, particularly in an atmosphere perhaps already strained by earlier misunderstanding.

As seen earlier, the manner in which coding or decoding occurs may, as well as reflecting an individual's personal values or experience, also reflect those of his immediate working group. Under such circumstances, the success or failure of the communication process will, to a considerable degree, be determined by the extent to which it is acceptable to group norms and the extent to which the group exercises control over its membership.

Just as experience has a part in determining the success of communication, so too has emotion. Fear, anger or insecurity may well block communication altogether or distort it beyond recognition.

Other problems have to do with the enormous, but limited capacities of the human brain. Information may simply be presented too quickly or in a form that is not easily absorbed. As a result, overload occurs and information is either rejected or a state of general confusion may occur. Inadequate time for mental adjustment may be given so that an individual is required to accept information before an earlier communication is thoroughly absorbed. Frequently failure occurs simply because an individual forgets or omits to listen.

LISTENING

On average, we tend to forget half of what has been said to us within a few hours. After two days, we can probably only recall, with any degree of accuracy, around a quarter. Much of this is due to poor listening. The underlying reasons are numerous, ranging from our comparative speeds of listening and thinking, to pre-occupation with some other problem, to fatigue. Frequently, however, problems occur as a result of premature evaluation. Since we think faster than we speak, a natural tendency is to fill the gaps in the communication process with evaluation of messages received so far, rather than listening carefully to the communication as a whole. Such a situation is particularly likely when emotions are involved; frequently, of course the time when complete and effective communication is most required.

COMMUNICATION MEDIA

Before going on to consider how such obstacles may be overcome, it is worthwhile to examine briefly the main media used in the communication process. These fall into three broad categories:

- oral
- written
- non-verbal

Oral communication

The principal advantage of oral or spoken communication is its directness. The communicator, through face to face communication, reinforced with gesture or inflection, can convey both feeling and attitude more easily. Relationships are clearer and questions more simply and rapidly dealt with. Through questioning, or observing other cues, understanding may be relatively easily checked and misunderstanding minimized. However, its nature does not permit subsequent checking or review, and as a result long-term confusion or misunderstanding may occur. Typically it also lacks the precision and accuracy of the written form.

Written communication

The relative permanence of written communication is its principal advantage. Readers can refer to it at will, check and double-check so as to ensure understanding. As a result it is probably easier to comprehend. As indicated above, the written form is typically more carefully prepared than oral forms. It presents a means of evidence and wider dissemination of the communication is possible. Its permanency can, however, be its undoing. Commitment of communication to paper or some other medium is typically more expensive and may easily get out of hand: the organization indulging in 'red-tape', becoming increasingly bureaucratic and protectionist with all the inevitable undesirable consequences. On occasions, of course, a written record may also be inconvenient for a variety of other reasons — particularly when an earlier decision is regretted!

Non-verbal communication

In addition to such methods of communication, various other non-word based media may be identified. Facial movement, touch, gestures, symbols, posture, proximity, location, etc., may all convey a message, or qualify, re-inforce or give the lie to a verbal communication. An increasing amount of attention has in recent years been given to so called 'body-language'. Its proponents argue that by observing physical movements, gestures, stance, etc., one may better understand what is in the mind of a speaker whatever the words he uses.

OVERCOMING BARRIERS TO COMMUNICATION

Having considered the potential barriers to effective communication and identified the inherent weaknesses of the principal modes, how may these be overcome?

To offer a guaranteed formula for success is impossible. Were it otherwise, poor communication would not be such a ubiquitous problem. Indeed, several barriers identified above, particularly those that are attitudinal in origin, may be impossible to breakdown or at least not in the short term. However in relation to others, some guidelines may at least be offered:

- ☐ Communicators should be made aware, through training, of the obstacles that may interfere with effective communication. At the risk of a truism, it is only when an individual begins to understand a problem that he stands a chance of proficiently overcoming it
- ☐ Without appearing condescending, a communicator must consider the person or persons with whom he wishes to communicate and tailor his message and mode of delivery accordingly
- ☐ Simple language should be used wherever possible. Clarity of expression and simplicity of construction will minimize misunderstanding or rejection
- ☐ Messages should be communicated to the right people. Unless receivers understand the message, recognize its significance or value, or know why they are receiving it, the process will be pointless
- ☐ Feedback should be encouraged in order to determine comprehension
- ☐ Several media should be used together, or in series, so as to reinforce each other. Re-inforcement may also be achieved through limited repetition
- ☐ An attitude that suggests speechmaking or lecturing should be avoided
- ☐ Problems of distortion as a result of messages passing through a multiplicity of organizational tiers should be overcome by structural arrangements which facilitate free and rapid flow of information. It may also be considered appropriate to encourage staff at all levels to consult and communicate on a less rigid basis
- ☐ As well as becoming more able in projecting ideas, staff should be encouraged and assisted to become better listeners: listening with understanding rather than judgement until the latter is appropriate
- ☐ The most appropriate medium or channel of communication must be selected. It is not intended to discuss here the merits and demerits of the various media. Several are dealt with in other sections of this book: others are well documented elsewhere. There exist however a wide range of channels, some facilitating two way communication, others permitting upwards or downwards communication only. Examples are notice boards, house magazines, suggestion schemes, joint consultation, employee annual reports, staff appraisal, committees, group meetings: each has its uses and limitations

It is important, however, not to fall into the trap of believing that adherence to the guidelines above and selection of the correct channel is all that is required. In the discussion of barriers to communication above, reference was made to the importance of attitudes and in particular the effects of trust and mistrust, confidence and lack of confidence. A manager, or indeed any other, who through his day-to-day behaviour alienates others and destroys confidence and trust may well find it extremely difficult subsequently to communicate even the most favourable of tidings in an effective fashion. Achieving good and complete communication throughout an organization takes time and effort even under the most favourable of circumstances. Although fundamental to all management functions it is with motivation that communication is most intricately woven. As in the case of motivation, it is when the needs of all concerned are best understood and provided for that the communication process is most likely to succeed.

REFERENCE

1. Mintzberg, H. (1973). *The Nature of Managerial Work*. Harper and Row.

PART 2: FURTHER RECOMMENDED READING

McCormick, E.J. and Tiffin, J. (1981). *Industrial Psychology*. George Allen and Unwin.
Brown, J.A.L. (1975). *The Social Psychology of Industry*. Pelican.
Argyle, M. (1974). *The Social Psychology of Work*. Pelican.
Taylor, L.K. (1980). *Not for Bread Alone*. Business Books.
Davis, L.E. and Taylor, J.C. (Eds) (1979). *Design of Jobs*. Goodyear.
Bailey, J. (1983). *Job Design and Work Organisation*. Prentice-Hall.
Cooper, R. (1974). *Job Motivation and Job Design*. IPM.
Butteriss, M. (1975). *Techniques and Developments in Management*. IPM.
Kelly, J. (1982). *Scientific Management, Job Redesign and Work Performance*. Academic Press.
Steers, R.M. and Porter, L.W. (1983). *Motivation and Work Behaviour*. McGraw-Hill.

PART 2: SAMPLE EXAMINATION QUESTIONS

What, in terms of management theory, is the distinction between a formal and an informal organization? What are the advantages and disadvantages of informal groups from a managerial point of view? What can managers do to overcome the disadvantages?   CIB

Discuss the possible consequences of using inter-group competition as a means of increasing performance.   IAM

What factors within an organization influence the development of cohesive work groups?   IAM

Are autonomous working groups any longer appropriate in manual work?
          IPM

'From management's viewpoint, job enrichment is a far better motivational tool (if it works) than money, because it generates improved performance at minimum cost.' How far would you accept this verdict?   ICSA

Do the present recessionary economic conditions, with record post-war levels of unemployment and pay settlements below the rate of inflation, in any way undermine the work of popular motivational theorists?

Illustrate your answer by relying on the beliefs of FOUR such theorists.   CBSI

(a) Describe fully the assumptions underlying one of the following theories of human motivation:

 (i) Maslow's need-based theory;
 (ii) Herzberg's motivation-hygiene theory.

(b) In relation to the theory you have described, what are the implications for management?   CACA

Evaluate any major theory of motivation published since 1950, with special reference to the theory's practical applications (e.g., in your own organization, or in an organization with which you are sufficiently familiar).   ICSA

It is often said that the Hawthorne studies constitute a landmark in the understanding of human behaviour at work. To what extent is such a comment justified?   ICSA

What are the motivational principles behind 'job enrichment' and what are the problems associated with its introduction? How might these difficulties be tackled?   ICSA

To what extent are pay differentials and financial inventives consistent with the findings of current motivation theories?   ICSA

Critically discuss the application of Herzberg's theory of motivation to the practice of job enrichment. What problems may be encountered by those wishing to implement such a scheme?   IPM

Evaluate the contribution of theories of motivation towards our understanding of pay as a motivator.   IPM

Evaluate the effectiveness of both formal and informal work groups in the modification of individual behaviour at work.   IPM

How useful is the concept of 'morale' for the personnel manager?   CBSI

Summarize the current state of knowledge on the concept of 'leadership style', and assess the significance of this concept for personnel policies.   ICSA

How can a knowledge of motivation help managers? Illustrate and explain your answer with examples.   IOB

What is the relationship between motivation and performance? What factors influence motivation?   IOB

Douglas McGregor advanced two sets of propositions about human beings in an organization, which he labelled theory X and theory Y. What do you understand by theory X and theory Y? What application potential do these respective theories have for management?   CACA

'Best performance is obtained in those undertakings where supervision is employee centred'. Explain in detail Likert's concept of 'employee centred supervision'.   CBSI

Many managerial problems in an organization are the result of poor or non-existent communication. Identify and comment on what you consider to be the principal barriers to efficient communication. Suggest some steps for overcoming these barriers to communication.   CACA

Define and comment on the term 'communication' and discuss why it is important to the efficiency of an organization. What do you understand by the principal systems of upward, downward and horizontal communication flow within an organization?   CACA

It has occasionally been argued that all interpersonal problems within organizations could be resolved by effective communications. How far would you agree with this contention?   ICSA

Bill Brown, your friend and fellow section leader, possesses many admirable qualities and skills. He is clear-headed and logical, a good organizer and planner, and has a good understanding of the technical aspects of his work. Despite all this, his staff often seem to be puzzled because he does not always make himself clear to them, and, as a result, mistakes are made and the staff become annoyed and frustrated.

How would you help Bill Brown to communicate more effectively?   CIB

What are the advantages and disadvantages of a participative style of management? How can the potential benefits be maximized?   CIB

There are many barriers to communication. What can the sender of a message do to make sure it is clearly conveyed? What can the receiver do to grasp the meaning of the message as accurately as possible?   CIB

Jill Knight has been in charge of her group for 3 months. It appears to be completely demoralized. Productivity is low, absenteeism is high, no one co-operates. As Jill's boss, what advice would you give her on how to improve the group's performance? What would be the signs of success?   CIB

Your manager believes that successful leaders are born not made. He says that certain personality traits like integrity, courage and vision are the vital ones.
  (i) Give your views on the importance of personality traits in leadership.
 (ii) Explain the current views on personality theories of leadership and what you understand by styles of leadership.
(iii) Explain the importance of situational leadership.   CIB

The advantages of strong and cohesive work groups include greater interaction between members, mutual help and social satisfaction, lower turnover and absenteeism and often higher production. State and discuss FIVE factors likely to promote cohesiveness in a working group.   IAM

(a) Is there any relationship between motivation and frustration?
(b) Describe, if possible with examples, the defence mechanisms that may be adopted by employees who frequently experience frustrations at work.
(c) How can management seek to minimize job frustration   IAM

'Work and leisure are complementary in the sense that individuals typically compensate for lack of satisfaction in the one by seeking higher levels of satisfaction in the other.' How far do you agree?   IPM

'When considering staff motivation Building Societies should be more concerned with groups than individuals.'

Discuss possible reasons for this statement and to what extent you agree with it.   CBSI

Management often gives great emphasis to the importance of effective internal communications. Why is this and what can be done to improve them?   CBSI

From the evidence of behavioural research, what are the factors to take into account when designing effective working teams?   CBSI

Part 3
Staffing

7
Manpower planning

In the present economic and commercial environment, there is an increasing need for manpower resources to be managed in a professional way. It might be suggested that the future is so uncertain that planning in the manpower area is a waste of time! We would suggest that the converse is true. Provided flexibility is built into the process, there is no reason to feel that a systematic approach is not worthwhile. The alternative of reacting to events through a sort of 'crisis management' cannot be acceptable to any organization that aims to succeed in the present environment.

Although statistical techniques and technology are available to assist the manpower planner, these alone are no substitute for commercial awareness, practicality, and not least a strong feel for the human aspects of manpower management. Planning without due regard to the views of staff, as expressed through trade unions and other representatives, is courting failure [1].

Manpower planning covers a range of activities, and definitions vary according to one's viewpoint. It can take place at national level, and a range of government bodies, such as the Department of Employment, are involved with various employment issues. We are mainly concerned here with company or organizational manpower planning, which should be of major concern to the personnel manager. At this level manpower planning has been defined as:

> a strategy for the acquisition, utilization, improvement and retention of an enterprise's human resources [2].

This definition indicates clearly the wide range of activities involved in forecasting, planning and managing an organization's labour force. It might also suggest that the activity of manpower planning is synonymous with personnel management itself. Indeed it is probably true to say that a great deal of the work of *implementing* the manpower plan forms the bulk of the day-to-day work of the personnel function.

If we draw upon the above definition, it is clear that the policies and strategies developed through the manpower planning process will eventually be converted into the following familiar activities:

☐   recruitment of staff
☐   training and development of existing staff
☐   transfers and promotions
☐   wages and salaries (the cost of staff will be a vital part of the
     planning process)
☐   allocation and use of accommodation
☐   redeployment and staff redundancy
☐   collective bargaining and productivity issues

In fact, virtually all staffing matters will be affected by, or affect, the
manpower planning and management function.

THE MANPOWER PLANNING PROCESS

From the outset it is essential to stress that manpower planning does
not form a discrete function and must of necessity be linked to the
organization's broader objectives. It is a dynamic process that must be
subject to constant review, and the methodology presented below is
unlikely to fit neatly into every organizational plan. It is usual to
consider the macro and micro levels separately and also the supply and
demand aspects. However, any separation is purely for facility of
analysis and all aspects are, of course, closely inter-related.

The approach

In manpower planning, as with most planning operations, we need to
answer the following questions:

☐   what is the present position?
☐   how was it arrived at?
☐   what do we wish to achieve?
☐   How can we achieve it?

A manpower planning group that will include specialists and line
managers from various sections of the organization will have to cover
the following seven inter-related areas of activity or 'steps' towards
creating the 'manpower plan'.

1   manpower objectives as part of corporate plan
2   manpower audit (external) — an assessment of the external
    environment with regard to labour markets, etc.
3   manpower audit (internal) — the numbers and categories of
    present employees, productivity, mobility, wastage, etc.
4   supply forecasting
5   demand forecasting

6 implementation
7 control

Objectives

It should be stressed from the outset that manpower planning is only an integral part of the overall corporate planning process and is in no way independent. Any objectives regarding manpower will therefore be inter-related with those concerning such things as capital expenditure, marketing, re-organization, diversification and of course, financial forecasts. This position can be illustrated most simply with a diagram (see Fig. 7.1).

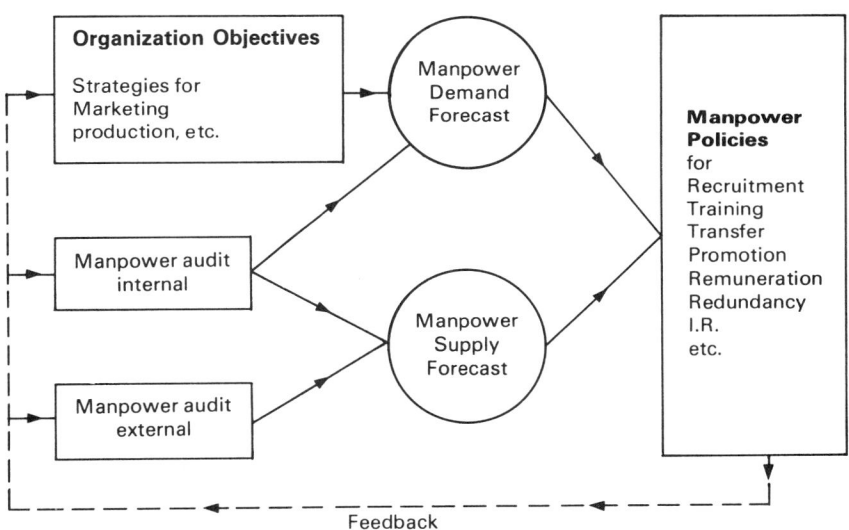

Fig. 7.1

Although considerably simplified, Fig. 7.1 clearly illustrates the integration of manpower considerations with the corporate plan and the interaction of supply and demand upon personnel policies that must in turn be converted into specific programmes. The feedback 'loop' is intended to highlight the dynamic nature of manpower planning. Difficulties in producing the right numbers and quality of staff at the right time will obviously affect the operation of the organization. Corporate objectives may have to be altered in the light of this feedback in order to redress any imbalance in human resource requirements. The days when manpower resources were expected to adjust to business demands through recruitment or redundancy are gone. Manpower considerations will often take the lead nowadays instead of reacting to events. For example, difficulties with staff retraining may affect the timing of the introduction of new technology or a particular work system. Industrial relations problems may equally cause management to adjust plans for reducing production capacity in a particular plant.

Manpower audit — external

The national labour market is extremely dynamic and much statistical information is available concerning many factors of employment [3]. However, the reliability and relevance of this data must be assessed by the individual organization. Generally, we have an ageing labour force that contains an increasing number of female workers and enjoys a reducing number of working hours and longer holidays. We are also experiencing the paradox of simultaneous unemployment and labour shortages, the latter being predominantly in skilled occupations. Demographic forecasts also suggest that the number of school leavers will reduce significantly in the early 1990s, adding to the problems of employers. These national factors will have an obvious bearing upon the potential supply of labour, and must be fully considered. However, in order to assess the more immediate impact it will also be appropriate to consider factors that are local to the organization. Local studies will assume extra importance when considering expansion or removal to another area. Items such as population density, competition for labour and current employment levels should be carefully assessed at the planning stage. Despite high levels of unemployment in recent years, employers have been forced to recruit in remote parts of the country owing to shortages of skilled labour in the vicinity of their establishments particularly in the South East.

Manpower audit — internal

Although the external audit is conducted mainly with a view to the supply situation, the internal audit will be used in determining both supply and demand. Within the framework of the corporate plan, it should be possible to use management information in order to carry out a much more thorough audit than that of the external situation. What, then, are the aspects of the human resources that need to be analysed?

Age

The age distribution of the workforce is critical for such matters as recruitment, training, promotion, sickness, absenteeism, wastage, etc. An ageing workforce may provide benefits of maturity and experience, but these can be offset by reductions in physical effectiveness and innovation, not to mention a lack of succession. A mainly young workforce may not possess the depth of experience necessary for a stable organization. The 'ideal' distribution will depend on circumstances. In times of contraction, an older workforce will allow natural wastage through retirement, whereas a sales-led organization may require a young active workforce. A simple age distribution graph is given in Fig. 7.2

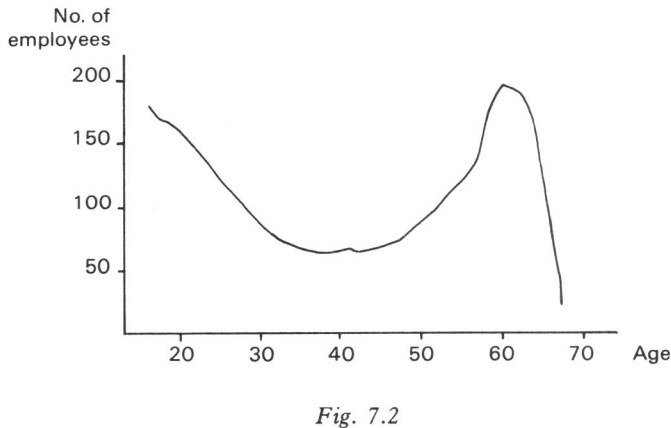

Fig. 7.2

In the example in Fig. 7.2, it is apparent that the organization has predominently young or old employees with considerably fewer in the middle age ranges. This could suggest a 'succession gap' that may require remedial measures in the areas of recruitment, retraining, etc. In order to utilize this data for a full analysis of the internal supply situation it will have to be supplemented with further management information.

Skills analysis

If age distribution data is to be meaningful, it will be necessary to use more discreet graphs than that described above. These should indicate the age distribution within specific occupations or departments. The data will then be presented in a form that management can more easily appreciate and act upon. Of itself, a basic skills inventory will be invaluable to management, and any personnel records system worth its salt should readily provide details of the skills and attributes of each employee. However, this information will require regular updating and staff appraisal would provide one opportunity for this.

Promotion and transfer

Although promotion and transfer are used by management as part of an employee development programme and for motivational purposes, they will also have a major bearing upon the succession needs of the organization. Despite the fact that employee expectations are often tempered by existing practice, it is for management to study past promotion patterns and to try to predict whether or not any changes will affect the internal supply situation. Here again, qualitative information is essential in order to assess potential for promotion at various levels.

Productivity

An essential part of any internal manpower audit is an assessment of the productivity of the labour-force. This can be achieved through basic work-study techniques and comparisons with other organizations. The information obtained can then be used as part of the overall planning process and will obviously affect management policies regarding retraining, mechanization, etc., apart from the human relations aspects and the industrial relations implications.

Costs

Manpower planning cannot take place in a vacuum with little or no regard for the economic facts of life. In order to satisfy financial criteria, a detailed analysis of manpower costs would appear essential. These could be broken down under various headings, e.g.:

- [ ]   recruitment costs
- [ ]   training costs
- [ ]   costs of remuneration, sub-divided into basic pay, overtime, etc.
- [ ]   fringe benefits
- [ ]   accommodation and other 'on' costs, such as pensions, sports facilities, canteens, car parks, etc.
- [ ]   personnel administration costs
- [ ]   relocation and severance costs

Turnover

Turnover, or more correctly, wastage analysis, has received a great deal of attention from manpower planners. The statistical possibilities are enormous, but these apart, analysis is important for practical reasons. Wastage of manpower has obvious indirect effects upon the organization and has direct bearing upon many management strategies, such as recruitment, training and promotion.

It is probably as well at the outset to deal with the semantic problems. 'Wastage' is often confused with 'turnover', whereas in fact the former is an element of the latter. Wastage only deals with severences; turnover embraces the whole recruitment – promotion – severance process.

An early and important series of empirical studies were carried out by the Tavistock Institute at the Glacier Metal Company [4]. This work suggested that wastage could be represented by a curve that could then be divided into three identifiable phases, as illustrated in Fig. 7.3.

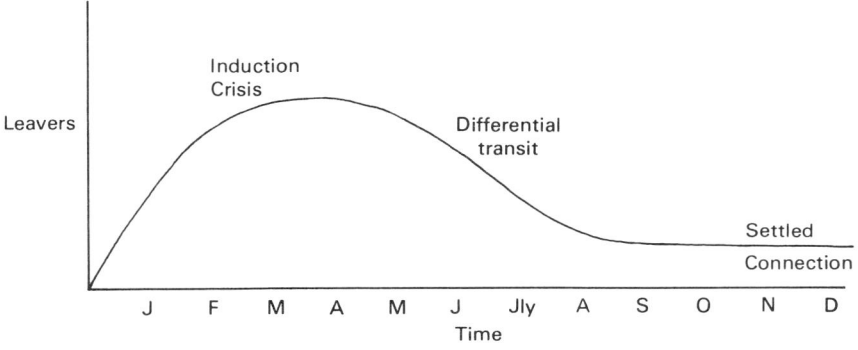

Fig. 7.3

1   *Induction crisis* — the period shortly after entry during which 'marginal' employees leave
2   *Differential transit* — the 'secondary' phase during which employees are orientating themselves within the organization
3   *Settled connection* — the phase of becoming a settled long-term employee.

The three phases are not always neatly distinguishable, and the scales used for plotting the graph could vary the emphasis upon each one. However, they do generally illustrate the situation that occurs in most organizations. Despite the fact that many mathematical models have been based upon the well established unitary induction crisis model, more recent studies have identified 'multiple induction crisis' situations within some organizations.

The lesson would appear to be that the relationship between length of service and leaving is of obvious importance to management. However, it is for each organization to analyse its own data in order to highlight any idiosyncrasies.

Turnover statistics

There are various ways of measuring and expressing wastage:

1   *Labour turnover index.* This is a simple method that produces an index of 'crude' turnover expressed as a percentage. It is sometimes referred to as the BIM Index as it was introduced in a

British Institute Management booklet in 1949. (It will be noticed that the term 'turnover' is used whereas in fact it is dealing with wastage):

$$\text{Labour turnover} = \frac{\text{Number of leavers in period (usually 1 year)}}{\text{Average number employed during period}} \times 100$$

The average number of employees is arrived at by merely adding the number employed at the beginning of the period to that at the end, and dividing by two, e.g.:

$$\frac{\text{Number of leavers (say, 50)}}{\text{Average employed (say } \dfrac{240 + 260}{2}\text{)}} = \frac{50}{250} = 20\%$$

But what does 20% indicate? Is this good or bad? This can only be assessed by comparisons with previous figures and with those of other similar organizations. Even then, it does not provide qualitative information, and this aspect will be discussed below. It is also apparent that this index is not discrete. In general, length of service affects wastage, but the above index does not identify how long the leavers have been with the organization. Neither does it indicate in which occupations the wastge is occurring.

2 *Labour stability index.* This measure is intended to provide an idea of whether or not turnover is taking place at the 'fringe' or whether it is affecting longer serving employees. It is usually defined as:

$$\frac{\text{Number with more than 1 years service}}{\text{Total employed 1 year ago}} \times 100$$

The example in Table 7.1 may explain how this index refines the information provided by the crude labour turnover index. It is clear that the labour turnover index does not highlight the different wastage patterns or 'stability' rates, as does the stability index. However, this index still does not reveal the different situations that exist within some departments. One department may traditionally employ 'short service' workers whereas another may attract 'long service' employees.

3 *Skill wastage index.* The labour turnover index could also be

Table 7.1

	Labour turnover index	Stability index
Dept. A 50 employees 25 leave and are replaced	$\dfrac{25}{50} \times 100 = 50\%$	$\dfrac{25}{50} = 50\%$
Dept. B 50 employees 5 leave and are replaced 5 times	$\dfrac{25}{50} \times 100 = 50\%$	$\dfrac{45}{50} = 90\%$

supplemented further in order to identify in which occupations various levels of wastage are taking place. This can be expressed as:

$$\frac{\text{Number of jobs in category vacated during period}}{\text{Average number employed in category}} \times 100$$

It will by now be apparent that the measurement of wastage can involve a great deal of statistical refinement. It is essential however, as part of the audit, to produce the data that is most useful to the organization so that it can be used in the implementation stage of the manpower plan.

Benefits and costs of turnover

Having considered ways of analysing the levels and types of turnover, we will now turn to some of the reasons why it is of concern to management. A certain amount of staff turnover can be beneficial to an organization, but there are costs involved that may be unacceptable if 'avoidable' turnover reaches high levels.

1 *Benefits.* The following would be included amongst the possible benefits of staff turnover:

   ☐ leavers can be replaced with 'new blood' from outside the organization, thus avoiding stagnation of ideas, etc.
   ☐ provision is made for promotion of existing staff, which will facilitate career paths and aid motivation
   ☐ 'natural wastage' may be used as a method of avoiding compulsory redundancy
   ☐ it might also be said that in some cases those leaving are not

suited to the organization and by leaving they save the organization problems of discontentment or lack of co-operation

2   *Costs.* High levels of turnover can present serious problems. Financial costs, both direct and indirect, can be added to other practical difficulties. These would include:

- ☐ recruitment costs
- ☐ investment in training of staff who leave
- ☐ loss of productivity while new staff are undergoing training. Also 'work gaps' while replacement being found
- ☐ errors and wastage by new staff
- ☐ payment of overtime to existing workforce
- ☐ negative effects upon staff morale
- ☐ public relations aspects; customers, etc., may find it disconcerting to have to deal with a constantly changing staff

High turnover can be symptomatic of various problems, and we must endeavour to uncover the reasons behind it. Various consultations and investigations can be carried out, including a thorough, but confidential, exit interview with those who have resigned.

Managing turnover

A recent IMS report [5] has highlighted the need to manage turnover and suggests that organizations should:

- ☐ Anticipate it: by being aware of 'at risk' groups and ensure that terms and conditions are competitive.
- ☐ Adjust its causes: by improving supervision, career progression and job satisfaction.
- ☐ Account for non-work factors: by catering for the dual career family and reviewing relocation policies.
- ☐ Don't recruit it! by ensuring that applicants are given realistic and honest information about jobs on offer.

Supply forecasting

Having set objectives and carried out the necessary 'audits', we reach the stage where the products of these activities must be used to project future needs for manpower and the sources available to meet these needs. On the supply side, most of the preparatory work has been dealt with above. Using the analysis of internal supply, combined with the research of national and local supply situations, it will be necessary to forecast the potential supply position for the life of the plan. Obviously the short-term forecasts should be more detailed and accurate than attempts to forecast the position several years ahead. As a general comment, few organizations will compile corporate manpower plans for more than 5–7 years ahead, as after this any projections become rather speculative. A 'rolling' annual plan is quite common.

Demand forecasting

Manpower demand forecasting will be based upon activity levels indicated by the corporate plan, as well as shortages indicated by audit. From this, a forecast of the numbers and types of staff required by various departments should be possible. For instance, the sales budget should indicate the productive manpower required in a manufacturing business. Also, in these and other non-manufacturing organizations, the amount of paper work generated by the sales forecast should be a guide to the extra clerical support required. It should not be overlooked that these assessments must also take account of productivity and capital investment data.

Various techniques are used in forecasting manpower demand, ranging from sophisticated statistical models to basic managerial judgement. The methods used will depend on the back-up data available, the size and nature of the organization and the degree of expertise available. It is intended to describe the most common techniques in basic terms, but it should be remembered that in practice two or more methods will probably be combined, and managerial judgement will almost certainly form part of any forecasting method.

Managerial judgement

Using information provided by the corporate plan together with personal experience, each manager should be able to make a fairly informed estimate of his manpower requirements for the future. Often, top management prepares guidelines for departmental managers who will then set out their own forecasts on a standardized form. Then with the aid of the personnel manager and other specialist departments such as OR, O & M or Work Study, the forecasts will be compared and amalgamated into an overall manpower plan.

Work study

Where it is possible to express work in terms of units and standard times, it is not difficult to project the 'work loads' thrown up by the production budget. If the average productivity of an operator is known, it is possible to calculate the manpower required to produce the number of units budgeted for.

A simplified example may be useful:

Budgeted output for year	50 000 units	
Standard hours per unit	10	
Total hours	500 000	
Average productive hours per operator/year	1 500	
No. of operators required	333	$\left(\dfrac{500\ 000}{1\ 500} \right)$

A similar exercise could be carried out for clerical workers provided clerical work measurement techniques are used within the organization. It should be stressed that the above example is extremely simplified, and that many jobs are not capable of expression in standardized terms. Owing to the problems of changing standards and work methods, it is unwise to use this system for forecasts much beyond 1 year.

Statistical techniques

Forecasts of varying complexity can be produced utilizing statistical techniques. One method of projecting past data into the future is the use of time series. Based upon budgeted activity levels, policies concerning capital utilization, and other knowledge of the internal and external environments, a graph can be produced. This should indicate any trends, cycles or fluctuations dependent upon the situation and the data used. Although this method will graphically indicate future manpower requirements, in common with most other methods of forecasting, it relies upon the degree to which past data can be projected into the future, and the accuracy of the assumptions made.

In order to deal with the difficult problem of assessing the number of indirect workers required in the future, a system of ratios is sometimes used. If, for instance, the number of clerks per direct worker is known, this ratio can be projected into the future using the data produced regarding direct workers. These ratios could, of course, be affected by changes in productivity or work methods.

Many personnel departments will have spreadsheet software available for computers which will facilitate the manipulation of variables affecting human resource demand levels. It should be remembered, however, that, despite the degree of sophistication, demand forecasting is a notoriously difficult problem, and any projections will have to be constantly reviewed and amended where necessary.

Implementation

The objectives, information and forecasts that have contributed to the manpower plan must now be converted into policies that should produce in turn concrete programmes of action. The planning activity should provide an ideal opportunity to review the various personnel functions, and where these are not capable of meeting the criteria laid down they may need to be revised. The manpower plan will normally be sub-divided on a basis similar to that outlined below:

- ☐ Recruitment — the numbers and types of employees required over the period of the plan together with details of any potential supply problems
- ☐ Training — the amount and types of training required for both new recruits and existing employees
- ☐ Employee development — closely linked to training, this programme must provide for projected promotions and transfers
- ☐ Productivity — methods for maintaining or improving productivity including work methods, incentives, productivity bargaining and other methods of improving motivation
- ☐ Redundancy — specific plans regarding the number of potential redundancies and how these will be dealt with
- ☐ Accommodation — plans for expansion, contraction or re-location including buildings, equipment and for improving working conditions

It is apparent from the above brief summary of functional plans that manpower planning plays an important part in co-ordinating the various activities and giving them a sense of direction. On a day-to-day basis, it is essential for managers to co-operate in order that flexibility can be retained and problems dealt with as they arise.

Control

Part of the implementation process will be a system of manpower control. But what is meant by control? As with all budgets or plans, it is essential to measure the projected position against the actual and to take remedial action where necessary. But what criteria are appropriate against which to measure the levels of manpower? Various methods can be employed including:

establishment control
cost control
productivity control

The *establishment control* system merely compares the staff a particular department has been allocated by the manpower plan with its actual establishment. Any variation should then be accounted for. The problem with this system is that it tends to be rather rigid and does not provide for changes in work patterns. It also tends to become a 'head-count', and does not differentiate sufficiently between occupations. It can also fail to take account of overtime working and the sub-contracting of work to agencies.

Control against costs attempts to meet the financial criteria of the organization by converting employees into cost centres. Although this idea is extremely attractive to cost-conscious management, the whole business of manpower costing is fraught with difficulties. There is a temptation to deal with direct costs and those indirect ones that can be most easily assessed while those that are less easily allocated are ignored, with the result that effective control is not achieved.

Productivity indices, or manning ratios, attempt to compare actual manpower utilization with targets. Monitoring of productivity would appear to be an essential tool of manpower control, and it is also useful for comparing different departments or areas. It will of course be necessary to draw up some measure of performance that may be based upon output, cost, revenue and so on. However, these indicators are not always simple to derive, and the whole exercise can detract from more urgent personnel problems.

Having taken the trouble to prepare a manpower plan, it seems only reasonable to incorporate some system of control. However, a passive monitoring procedure is probably of no more use than a rigid control system. Ideally, a control procedure should be flexible enough to adapt to new situations while adhering in principle to the criteria esablished. In this way the exigencies of supply and demand can be ameliorated through a balanced programme of personnel policies.

Summary

The following is a list of points concerning the activity of manpower planning. They are all considered important. There is no order of priority, and they are in no way intended to be independant. In fact, most are inter-related:

☐ Manpower planning relies upon a sound information base. Use of computers should not deplete the amount of useful information available

☐ Of the essence, manpower planning is a multi-disciplinary activity. Good communications and co-operation between line managers, specialists and the personnel manager are essential

☐ Sophisticated mathematical models should not be a substitute for good management and human relations. People should not become statistics in a manpower plan

☐ Personnel managers should develop the expertise to understand statistical techniques and to apply them as necessary

☐ Any manpower plan should not endeavour to project too far into

the future, and should be subject to continuous review and feedback
☐ Manpower planning is notoriously difficult. It should, however, provide a framework within which decisions about an organization's human resources can be made. Thus, organizations which have planning procedures should be better placed to adapt to the many changes which occur.

REFERENCES

1. Fyfe, F. (1986). 'Putting the people back into manpower planning equations', *Personal Management*, October.
2. Anon. (1974). *Company Manpower Planning*. HMSO.
3. See, for example, *Department of Employment Gazette*, published monthly. HMSO.
4. Rice, A.K., Hull, J.M. and Trist, E.L. (1950). 'The representation of labour turnover as a social process', *Journal of Human Relations*, No. 3.
5. Bevan, S. (1987). *The Management of Labour Turnover*, IMS Report 137.

8
Preparation for recruitment and selection

Recruitment and selection is one of the most routine yet one of the most vital functions of any organization. Most employers would also agree that it is a costly and time-consuming process, and for this reason it must be planned and carried out in an efficient manner. It is, however, only part of a much larger process and relies heavily upon feedback generated by other integral parts of the manpower planning system. Without details of wastage, promotions, training and so on, it will be impossible to ascertain the quantity and quality of staff required. More importantly, without feedback it will be virtually impossible to know whether or not our recruitment methods are effective.

Efficiency, although of prime importance, is only part of the story. There is a danger that organizations will treat recruitment as a mechanistic process based upon their own needs for staff. It should be remembered that there are two parties involved and the needs of the individual must also be considered. Will the jobs that we offer provide the challenge and satisfaction required by the applicant, and will he or she be motivated to remain and progress with the organization? These questions are discussed more fully elsewhere, but nobody dealing with recruitment should fail to ask them if the process is not to become a one-sided impersonal routine.

The employment of an individual has always been a responsibility. Cynics might say that it has now become a liability. Recruitment has undoubtedly been affected by the plethora of recent employment legislation. This has added to the more 'normal' problems of take-overs, mergers, reconstructions and so on. Some of the problems of legislation and its effects upon recruitment will be returned to later. In the meantime we shall consider what is usually termed 'the recruitment process'. Basically, this consists of:

☐ Analysis (of job and potential employee) — the criterion problem job analysis, job description, person specification
☐ Attracting candidates — sources of recruitment, advertising, application forms

☐ Selection — interviews, group selection, tests, references, placement

The word 'process' is used to denote a systematic and thorough approach, rather than a cold-blooded and relentless routine. Each part of the process is equally important, and all are inter-dependent. If any operation is skimped the others will suffer and become less effective.

The criterion problem

The 'criterion problem' is an implicit part of recruitment, as of many other personnel activities. It is possibly for this reason that the consideration of criteria becomes lost amongst the more explicit and 'practical' considerations of recruitment. However, it is of little use preparing elaborate procedures and selection techniques if insufficient thought is given to the end product. A great deal of academic work has been carried out on criterion development in the United States, mainly by industrial psychologists [1]. Although a great deal of the theory becomes extremely complex, the principle is vitally important. It is therefore proposed to provide a simplified review of this area.

In the personnel context, the criterion has been variously described as 'a measure of the "goodness" of a worker' and 'that which is to be predicted'. In other words, it is a measure of the desired level of performance or of success in a job. It will be apparent that the criteria in respect of a job at the time of recruitment will relate to some time in the future. This throws up immediate problems regarding the time scale applicable to the criteria. Should we be developing measures for the early part of an employee's career, or should we be concerned with ultimate performance? It seems reasonable that we should endeavour to take an overall view of any career programme, although this is easier said than done.

In practice, a compromise also has to be reached between what is termed the *actual* criterion and the *ultimate* criterion. For example, a pilot's simulated test results may have to be used as a measure of performance in an actual flying mission. It is only where the actual criterion overlaps with the ultimate that we have what is termed 'criterion relevance'. There will, of course, be a considerable part of the actual criterion that will be unrelated to the ultimate, and the former will also be deficient in some aspects (see Fig. 8.1).

Predictors

In order to assess whether or not a particular applicant meets the appropriate criteria we use various 'predictors' or selection devices, such as interviews and tests. Unfortunately, we are now introducing a further source of inaccuracy, dependent upon the efficiency of the predictor in assessing whether or not the criteria will be met. We,

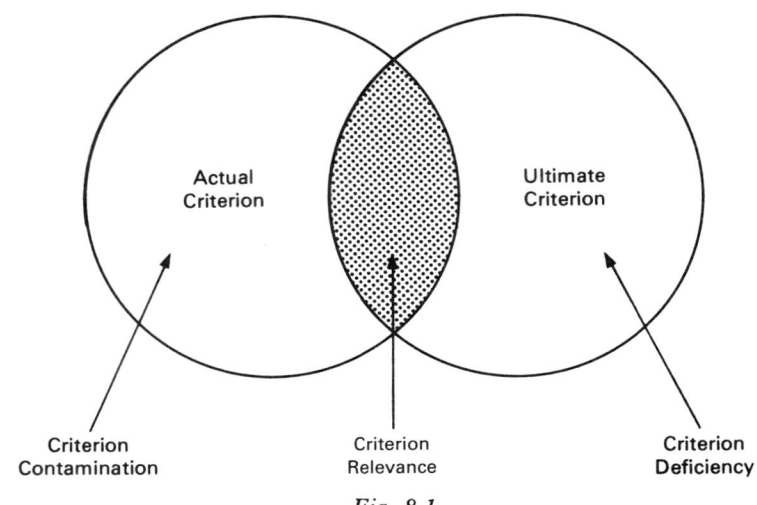

Fig. 8.1

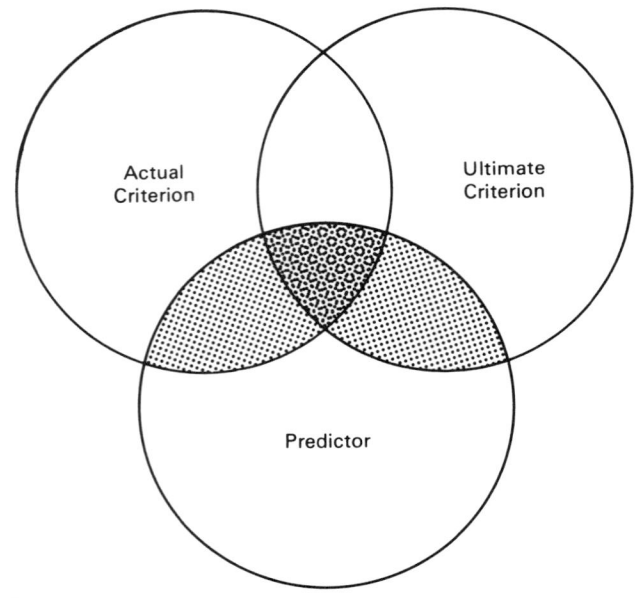

Fig. 8.2

therefore, tend to arrive at a situation as illustrated in Fig. 8.2.

It is, of course, difficult to generalize about the validity of any selection technique when each situation presents its own variables. However, newer techniques, such as 'meta-analysis', which uses large numbers of individual studies and combines the results taking account of sample size and variations in results, have produced data which is more authoritative.

From the personnel manager's point of view, the more effective the selection device, then the greater the benefit to the organization in terms of cost savings. Some opinion suggests that greater use could be made of research into selection techniques in order to improve practice in this area [1a].

Criterion development

How, then, are we to develop valid measures of performance and job success? Nagle [2] suggested the following approach:

1 Define the activity.
2 Analyse the activity.
3 Define 'success'.
4 Develop measures for each element of 'success'.

This appears to be a reasonably logical approach even though it makes the task sound rather too simple. Weitz [3] posed three questions for the personnel manager to ask himself about criteria:

1 Type — which are the best measures of performance?
2 Level — what level of performance is acceptable?
3 Time — when should the criteria be evaluated?

All these are sound questions but the answers may be somewhat more elusive. In practice, the evaluation of a 'successful' employee can be extremely difficult. Apart from the obvious measures of output or productivity others include supervisor-ratings, peer-ratings, and promotion records. However, even when considering jobs which appear simple to evaluate, it soon becomes apparent that performance can be affected by many external factors and that 'success' is not so simple to define. A classic example is the salesman. The obvious measure would be the level of his sales. However, on further investigation it might be discovered that he has taken over a particularly good geographical area from his predecessor or that he generates a great deal of bad debts. Maybe we should look for a better measure?

Dunnette *et al.* [4] suggested that the best way to discover which qualities lead to success in a job is to ask those who are already doing it successfully. In essence, their research consisted of asking a large sample of people employed in the same occupation what they considered to be the key qualities for success. This method could be effective provided a reasonable sample of respondents is available.

If we have managed to discover the attributes required for success we must then relate these criteria to definable measures and to methods of predicting these. The most sound way of testing both the criteria and the prediction methods would be to plot the progress of those selected against a 'control group' who have been hired without regard to their scores in various prediction devices. The candidates' ratings on actual job performance should then be compared with their ratings on the predictors and also with ratings for the 'unselected' group. If the scores or observations on the predictors correlate satisfactorily with actual performance ratings, further candidates should then be selected according to their scores on the predictor.

Although proper evaluation is essential, the detailed method outlined above may not be possible for practical reasons, neither may it be necessary in many situations. The cost of evaluation must be weighed against the benefits obtained and the degree of effort will depend upon the circumstances at the time of recruitment. There will be little point in developing sophisticated prediction techniques where the difference between the best and worst worker employed is negligible or unimportant. Similarly, where almost all of the applicants are capable of doing the job and there are fewer applicants than jobs available. It would appear that a compromise must be struck between sound principles and practical constraints. However, these constraints should never completely abrogate the practice of criteria and prediction development. There is no point in continuing with a recruitment method if it is unable to differentiate between those who will succeed and those who won't.

Job requisition

Apart from the overall demands of the manpower plan, which should indicate the levels of recruitment required, there may be specific demands for replacements or additional staff from various departments. These may be formal or informal, but in any case it is important to check the validity of the requisition. In larger organizations, a standard form will be used giving details of the job to be filled, the duties involved, and the calibre of person required. There may also be provisions for authorization by a senior manager where additional staff are required. If the position to be filled is not of a standard nature, or has not already been analysed, it will be necessary to proceed with job analysis.

Job analysis

Job analysis has been described as 'the process of examining a "job" to identify its component parts and the circumstances in which it is performed'. The approach and the amount of detail will depend upon the purpose for which the job is being analysed. We are concerned here with recruitment, but analysis is, of course, used for other purposes, such as training and job evaluation. It should not, however, be confused with 'task analysis', which may form part of the process, but is more commonly used in ergonomics.

There is an obvious need for investigation and collection of information. This can be obtained by various means:

Observation

This requires skill on the part of the observer. Skilled workers may make their work look unduly easy, and it may be necessary to observe several individuals. The speed of some operations may also make analysis difficult, and it may be necessary to use film. This method does not, of course, take into account the degree of mental process.

Interview employee

If this method is to be of any use it is important to inform the employee concerned of the reason for the analysis, otherwise he may be guarded and suspicious. Even then he may tend to exaggerate difficulties or overlook certain important details.

Questionnaires

These avoid the difficulties of unstructured observations, but are only as good as their initial design. There are obvious benefits of standardization from the point of view of records, but they may be inapplicable for more complex jobs.

Interview supervisor

This may produce a less biased analysis of the work of the subordinate. On the other hand, a false impression may be given owing to relationships with the present incumbents of the job or as a means of bolstering the supervisor's status. It is also possible that the supervisor has not actually done the job concerned or has forgotten some of the details.

'Critical incidents'

It has been suggested by Flanagan [5] that each job should be analysed into behaviours that are critical for its successful completion. In this way, irrelevant detail is discarded and a better idea of the type of person required for the job is obtained.

The method used for job analysis will probably depend on the circumstances, but it should be remembered that the information obtained will form the basis of the job description and the specification of the individual to be recruited by the organization.

Job description

A job description has been described by Flippo [6] as 'an organized, factual statement of the duties and responsibilities of a specific job'. It will include an identification section together with details of responsibilities, relationships, and the basic content of the job which has been identified through job analysis. An example of a recruitment job description form is given in Fig. 8.3, although the format could vary depending on the type of job and organization requirements.

It will be noticed that the form in Fig. 8.3 contains two columns in which parts of the job that are either difficult or unpleasant can be highlighted with an appropriate note. In similar vein to Flanagan (see above), Professor Alec Rodger [7] maintains that it is important to assess:

☐ whether the job applicant will cope well with certain aspects of the job
☐ whether he will enjoy certain aspects

Unless these 'difficulties and distates' are sufficiently highlighted in the job description, based upon the incumbent's experience and/or the interviewer's knowledge, these crucial areas may be missed at interview. The result might well be a disillusioned employee followed by resignation.

Many job descriptions deserve the criticism of being 'meaningless pieces of paper' that tell little of the real day-to-day problems of the job concerned. Unless some life is breathed into them, as suggested by Rodger, they are hardly likely to assist the interviewer in matching the person to the job.

Management level

Although the normal job description form can be adapted for most types of job, management and supervisory posts create particular problems. J. Munro Fraser [8] has suggested that a statement of duties is inappropriate since an estimated 80% of managerial time is spent in 'talk'. He proposes a list of responsibilities linked to quantifiable standards. An alternative form of managerial job description would be to break down responsibility into constituent parts under such headings as Act, Recommend, Advise, Delegate, and so on. Despite the fact that an executive job is non-repetitive, Flippo [6] considers that all executive jobs contain common functions, and suggests a description under the following headings:

1 Job objectives — what is the scope and nature of the job?
2 Organizing — what authority and influence has the manager over the organization and its personnel?

JOB DESCRIPTION FORM
FOR RECRUITMENT

		D	U
JOB TITLE			
NAME AND JOB TITLE OF MANAGER			
DEPARTMENT SITE			
SUMMARY OF OBJECTIVES			
MAIN AND KEY DUTIES			
RESPONSIBILITIES FOR RESOURCES/STAFF			
NUMBER AND NATURE OF RELATIONSHIPS			
WORKING CONDITIONS, AMOUNT OF TRAVELLING			
HOURS OF WORK, OVERTIME, HOLIDAY			
PAYMENT			
UNUSUAL FEATURES			
POSSIBLE TRANSFER AND PROMOTION ROUTES			

D = DIFFICULT
U = UNPLEASANT

Fig. 8.3

3 Planning — what type of projects are undertaken?
4 Policy making — on what committees does incumbent sit, and
   what part is played in decision making?
5 Direction — what contacts does manager have with personnel,
   and how does he motivate subordinates?
6 Control — what types of control authority does manager have?
7 Operation — what is the manager's personal operational involvement within his specialist area?

Despite the fact that certain jobs are difficult to commit to written
form, the effort is normally salutory and often assists with other areas
of personnel management. However, it is never a once-and-for-all job,
and if the job description is to be worth the paper it is written on, it
must be reviewed, and up-dated where necessary, at regular intervals.

Person specification

The terms 'job specification' and 'person specification' are often used
synonomously. We have chosen the latter purely to avoid confusion
with 'job *description*' in usage.
    A person specification is a development of the job description, and
deals with the qualities required by somebody ideally suited to the job.
It is much more qualitative than the job description, and should paint a
picture of the type of person required. From this it will be seen that we
are again involved in the criterion problem. We are trying to marshall
qualities that are considered necessary for success in a job under various
headings.
    Many person specifications are based upon the seven-point plan of
Alec Rodger [7] or J. Munro Fraser's five-fold grading system [8].
    The basic headings for a seven point plan are as follows [7]:

1 *Physical make-up* — appearance, speech, health, etc.
2 *Attainments* — education, training, experience, qualifications
3 *General intelligence* — intellectual capacity
4 *Special aptitudes* — manual dexterity, verbal ability, literacy,
   numeracy
5 *Interests* — intellectual, practical, social, artistic, sporting
6 *Disposition* — steadiness, self-reliance, influence, acceptability
7 *Circumstances* — domestic circumstances, age, mobility

The five-fold grading system (Munro Fraser) [8] are:

1 *Impact on others* — appearance, speech and manner
2 *Acquired qualifications* — education, training, experience
3 *Innate abilities* — 'brains', comprehension, aptitude for learning
4 *Motivation* — level of objectives, determination and achievements
5 *Adjustment* — emotional stability, ability to get on with others and
   to withstand stress

Both of the above methods provide a well-established and useful framework for a person specification, and an example of the way each might be used for the same job is given in Fig. 8.4.

There are also many other 'frameworks' available that are advocated by their inventors. These include Schein's 'general classes of variable' [9]:

1 Biographical information and work history
2 Intellectual level and aptitudes
3 Specific areas of knowledge or specific skills
4 Attitudes and interests
5 Motivation, personality and temperament

as well as Sidney and Brown's 'nine-point plan' [10]:

1 Personal data
2 Physique
3 Education and technical qualifications and experience
4 Work and other experience
5 Mental abilities
6 Social roles
7 Initiative
8 Emotional stability
9 Motivation

It is not suggested that any of the above systems are followed slavishly. Each organization will need to adapt and develop its own form of specification in accordance with its particular needs and circumstances.

It is also important to note that both Rodger's and Munro Fraser's systems are primarily linked to methods of interviewing that grade candidates under the various headings (although Rodger's plan was originally devised for occupational guidance rather than recruitment). We shall return to these methods in the section on interviewing.

Application forms

Despite the fact that some employers consider that letters of application can tell them quite a lot about a candidate, they are often unstructured and may omit important details. For this and other reasons most employers tend to design application forms for use by job applicants. A well-designed application form can fulfil the following functions:

☐ provide information on candidates in a standardized and easily comparable format
☐ supply details appropriate to person specification and exclude irrelevant material
☐ provide a basis for selection administration, interview and subsequent records

Seven-point plan

Essential	**Desirable**
Physical make-up	
Good health record. Acceptable bearing and speech. No serious uncorrected impairment of sight	Pleasant appearance, bearing and speech
Attainments	
'O' level English language or equivalent. Ability to type, and to operate office machines. Experience of general office work	'O' level maths or equivalent, RSA II typing. Experience of using simple statistical information. Experience of staff supervision
General intelligence	
Above average	
Special aptitudes	
Reasonable manual dexterity. Facility with figures	
Interests	
	Social activities
Disposition	
Persuasive and influential. Self-reliant	Good degree of acceptability, dependability and self-reliance. Steady under pressure
Circumstances	
No special circumstances	

Five-fold grading system

Essential	**Desirable**
Impact on other people	
Acceptable bearing and speech	Pleasant manner, bearing and speech
Qualification and experience	
'O' level English language or equivalent. Ability to type, and to operate office machines. Experience of general office work	'O' level maths or equivalent. RSA II typing. Experience of using simple statistical information. Experience of staff supervision
Innate abilities	
Quick to grasp a point	Able to assess priorities and make decisions
Motivation	
Personal identification with service given by section. Interest in efficiency of administration	
Adjustment	
Steady, self-reliant, good at making friendly relationships with colleagues at all levels	Able to cope with stress and pressure from different user departments

Fig. 8.4 A person specification for Office Services Supervisor

When designing an application form, regard must be given to both content and layout. As far as possible, the details requested should reflect the person specification framework used for listing the criteria for the job. Layout should assist applicants, so avoid ambiguity, poor spacing and questions that cause embarrassment or indignation. The IPM Code of Practice on Recruitment advises against asking a whole range of detailed personal questions on religion, medical problems, next of kin and family circumstances. Many of these could well be left until interview, or even postponed until after selection.

It is often advisable to design different forms for different levels of job. Unskilled manual applicants will probably be intimidated or frustrated by a long, detailed form. A much simpler version would be more satisfactory from everybody's point of view. This is not to suggest that *any* application form should be complex and difficult to complete. Remember that you are trying to encourage applicants, not put them off! An example of an application form for what might be termed 'middle-range' jobs is given in Fig. 8.5. It should be stressed that this is *not* to scale, and the spacing provided is not, therefore, ideal. It should also be said that no form can be put forward as a 'model' for all organizations. Each will have to consider its own requirements and priorities for the type of jobs in question. We would anticipate the form being of A4 format and having a plain front page (apart from name and job) clearly marked CONFIDENTIAL. We have seen many forms marked 'Private and Confidential' which contain a great deal of personal information on the front page, which seems to defeat the object to some extent.

REFERENCES

1. For a review, see, Cascio, W.F. (1982). *Applied Psychology in Personnel Management*. Reston Publ. Co. Chapter 6.
1a. Makin, P. and Robertson, I.T. (1986). 'Selecting the best selection techniques', *Personnel Management*, November.
2. Nagle, B.F. (1953). 'Criterion development', *Personnel Psychology*, Vol. 6, pp. 271–289.
3. Weitz, J. (1961). 'Criteria for Criteria', *American Psychologist*, Vol. 16, 228–231.
4. Dunnette, M. (1969). *Personnel Selection and Replacement*. Tavistock.
5. Flanagan, J.C. (1954). 'The Critical Incident Technique', *Psychological Bulletin*, Vol. 51.
6. Flippo, E.B. (1984). *Principles of Personnel Management*, 6th Edn. McGraw-Hill.
7. Rodger, A. (1952). *The Seven-Point Plan*. NIIP.
8. Munro Fraser, J. (1978). *A Handbook of Employment Interviewing*, 5th Edn, Macdonald & Evans.
9. Schein, E.H. (1980). *Organisational Psychology*, 3rd Edn. Prentice-Hall.
10. Sidney, E. and Brown, M. (1961). *The Skills of Interviewing*. Tavistock.

Position or type of work sought	Job ref.	

Surname (block letters)	Other names (in full)	Title

Address		Postcode

Home telephone number	Work telephone number	

Date of birth	Place of birth	Marital status	Sex

Nationality	(Give work permit details where applicable)

Please tick (√) the box (or boxes) below which you consider best describes your ethnic origins

Afro-Caribbean		Asian		Other (please specify below)	
African		European (incl. UK & Irish)			

This information is requested in order to comply with the requirements of the Code of Practice on Race Relations issued by the Commission for Racial Equality.

Educational Qualifications

Secondary Education

School	Subjects Studied	GCE/CSE	Grades Obtained	Date

Further Education

College/University	Qualification Obtained Subject and level	Subjects Covered	Date

Professional Qualifications obtained or being pursued

College/University	Qualification Obtained	Subjects Covered	Date

mployment History

Please start with your present or most recent employment and work backwards				
Date started	Date left	Name, location and nature of business of employer	Position held and main duties	Final salary and reason for leaving

urther Details

Please use this space to supply more information regarding your skills, experience, achievements and responsibilities and relate these to your reasons for applying for this job. (Please be as concise as possible, but use an extra sheet of paper if necessary.)

Additional Information

Do you suffer from any disability?   If registered disabled, please state registration number
Please give details of any serious illnesses or operations over the last 10 years

Do you have a criminal record or criminal charges pending?   Yes/No
If yes please give details on separate sheet

Do you hold a clean driving licence?   Yes/No

Where did you hear of this vacancy?

When are you *not* available for interview?

---

ease give the names and addresses of two referees, one of which should be your present employer

Present employer ——————————————   2 Other ——————————————

_____   _____

_____   _____

_____   _____

ay we contact before interview   1 Yes/No   2 Yes/No

ie information which I have given in this form is to the best of my knowledge true.

Signature of Applicant   Date

ig. 8.5 Employment application form (not to scale)

9
Recruitment

SOURCES OF RECRUITMENT

Assuming that the need to fill a post has been clearly established and justified, it will be necessary to review the supply side of the recruitment process. Although there is no neat solution, a popular practice is to divide the sources on an internal/external basis. The general principle of whether to recruit internally or externally is often the subject of heated discussion, and strong views may be held on this topic [1].

Internal sources

Promotion

In many cases it may be possible to promote a subordinate to fill the vacant post. This should not present difficulties where a system of appraisal and staff development is in operation and has obvious motivational advantages.

'Sideways' appointment

It may be possible to transfer somebody of similar seniority from another department or area. Although this is sometimes frowned on, it can help to develop and broaden the individual's experience and is often used as part of a management development programme.

The advantages of internal recruitment include the following:

☐ it increases the morale and motivation of the workforce
☐ it reduces costs of advertising, recruitment, induction and training
☐ the internal appointee and the organization are 'known' to each other.

Some of the disadvantages claimed are:

☐ the organization may stagnate without 'new blood'

☐ a sideways move may only transfer the recruitment problem elsewhere

☐ internal promotions may cause friction amongst existing staff

External sources

The sources of external supply are in theory boundless, but in practice there are well established methods of obtaining staff. The costs involved will vary, and not all sources will be suitable for every job category. It is basically a question of 'horses for courses', and experience will indicate the most suitable source for filling a particular type of post. Some of the more common sources of supply are as follows.

Direct advertising

This can have the advantage of reaching very large numbers of potential candidates, but can also be costly (see section on Advertising below).

Government employment agencies

These include Jobcentres, which serve those seeking work as well as employers looking for staff. The service provided is free but the degree to which applicants are assessed and matched to vacancies may also be limited.

Private employment bureaux

These are particularly useful for clerical staff and 'temps', but there are several specialist and execuitve agencies in the larger cities. A commission is usually charged for a successful introduction.

Schools, colleges and universities

Direct contact can be made with careers officers and careers conventions are arranged at many universities. Many larger organizations recruit direct to fill their demand for young trainees and graduates.

Introductions by existing staff

Where vacancies are internally circulated, existing staff often recommend a friend or relative. This can be a fruitful source, as they are unlikely to recommend somebody who will not live up to their recommendation. However, heavy reliance on this method might lead to difficulties over equal opportunities due to the 'closed' nature of the system.

'Head-hunting'

Where a person of particular talent or rare expertise is required, it may be necessary to search out somebody already in employment and induce him to change jobs. Consultants are sometimes employed to seek out a suitable candidate. Although this practice is considered unethical in some quarters, it is generally accepted that it may be the only option open where a particular type of expertise is required.

There are all kinds of variations on the above themes and two or more methods can, of course, be used simultaneously. There are occasions where it will be imperative to recruit externally. Where there is a choice, however, the advantages and disadvantages of external recruitment are basically the converse of those given above in respect of internal recruitment.

ADVERTISING

Recruitment advertising, like any other form of advertising, is ideally dealt with by a specialist. The preparation and placement of an advertisement for maximum effect is something that many are prepared to attempt but in which few succeed. Larger personnel departments either employ their own experts or can afford to retain an advertising agency. However, there is no reason why the high cost of advertising should not be put to good effect, provided experience is used to supplement some basic ground rules:

☐ recruitment advertising should be aimed at an 'appropriate' audience
☐ the advertisement should produce an adequate number of replies (too many may be as bad as too few)
☐ the contents should arouse interest and provide sufficient detail to prompt a response from the correct level of applicant

All of the above points are really saying the same thing — an advertisement should contact and communicte with a representative group of people who are both qualified to do the job and interested enough to apply for it. Applying these basic criteria, we must use media and techniques to meet various recruitment requirements.

Media

The main types of printed media for recruitment advertising are:

☐ national newspapers
☐ specialist journals
☐ local or regional newspapers

The costs for both display advertising and per column centimetre in each medium will usually correspond to the order in which they are listed. Although it is difficult and dangerous to generalize, a rule of thumb guide would be to use local newspapers for junior or manual jobs. If the job requires a specialist or skilled employee, professional journals or specialist magazines will probably produce a suitable response. For senior management posts the nationals are probably the most appropriate medium, although specialist journals may also be ideal for particular types of post. Technical information on circulation and readership can be obtained from various sources, but there is no substitute for the organization's own research of response to its advertisements. This can be achieved relatively simply either by using codes to be quoted on applications or through a direct question in the application form. (See 'Evaluation' below.)

Design and content

The actual design and layout of an advertisement can either be left to a specialist or, in most cases, proofs will be supplied by the media and the layout can then be agreed. Visual presentation is important and many organizations follow a house style and use a 'logo' with which members of the public can identify. Some years ago Esso carried out some research into recruitment advertising. Surprisingly, they found that the actual size of the advertisement did not seriously affect the response. However, display advertising was more productive in respect of clerical vacancies.

Apart from the technical considerations, and not overlooking the complexity of the whole subject, it is possible to specify some minimum requirements for the contents of a recruitment advertisement. Every advertisement should at least contain:

- [ ] the job title or reasonable description of the job
- [ ] the name and/or a brief description of the organization
- [ ] the location
- [ ] the rewards – either specific or a range
- [ ] an outline of responsibilities and any special or unusual aspects of the job
- [ ] the minimum experience and qualifications required, with age range where appropriate
- [ ] reply instructions appropriate to the type of job being advertised
- [ ] An 'equal opportunities' statement.

Follow-up

Assuming that the advertising has been successful, enquiries should be received shortly after its appearance. The type of communication will depend upon the reply instructions contained in the advertisement. Respondents may have been asked to call personally, telephone, write a letter of application or send for a standard application form and further details. The method used will usually depend on the organization's preference and the type of job being advertised. The key is to make it as simple as possible for applicants to respond.

Although some consider that a letter of application provides an indication of the writer, it is generally accepted that for most situations a standardized application form is more useful. It is felt that the form can be designed to supply the information required by the organization and that it eliminates irrelevance. It also simplifies the process of comparing candidates and forms the basis for interview should this be considered desirable. (For a more detailed discussion of application forms, see Chapter 8, page 125.)

If a fair number of applications are received, a systematic method of processing them should be used. It may be advisable to use a control sheet or appropriate computer software to record what action has been taken in respect of each applicant. If it is likely to take more than a few days to assess the applicants, letters of acknowledgment should be sent. When assessment has been completed, the 'possibles' will usually be invited for interview and those who are considered unsuitable will be sent a letter that should leave them with a good impression despite any disappointment. The period between the initial contact and a possible interview is crucial, and delays or unclear communications could cause the loss of good candidates. An advertisement is only as good as the back up it receives.

Evaluation

If a fair amount of recruitment advertising is handled it is as well to evaluate the success or otherwise of various ads. Many organizations maintain a control book in which all advertisements are recorded with copies of the actual ads placed. Key references can be used, such as codes or room numbers, in order to identify the source of the application. Don't forget to retain envelopes when using references!

Various checks can be made on each advertisement, such as the cost per short-listed applicant or the cost per recruit. The number of appointments/interviews per initial application is a good way of assessing the 'selectivity' of the advertisement. The lower the ratio the more accurately targeted the advertisement.

Don't forget to evaluate the failures as well as the successes. If few suitable applications are received or no appointment made, questions need to be asked:

☐   was the medium appropriate?
☐   was the design attractive and the advertisement well placed?

☐ were the terms and conditions offered competitive?
☐ was the timing wrong (bank holidays, newspaper strike, etc.)?
☐ were the reply instructions appropriate?

With a little methodical research it is not difficult to evaluate advertisements effectively, and use this information for the future.

REFERENCE

1. For a treatise on the advantages of 'internal recruitment', see Courtis, J. (1985). *Cost Effective Recruitment*, 2nd Edn. IPM.

10
Selection

A whole range of selection techniques or 'predictors' is available to the personnel specialist. Apart from the application form itself, there are various types of interview and a whole battery of testing devices that attempt to measure various attributes, such as aptitude, intelligence and personality. However, many organizations continue to rely on an application form followed by a face-to-face interview for all but exceptional situations. Bearing in mind what has already been said regarding the importance of reliable and valid criteria and prediction devices, there follows a review of the main selection techniques.

INTERVIEWING

The interview is undoubtedly the most commonly used selection device. It is also subjected to more abuse and incompetence than any other. The main problem lies in the fallacy that anybody can successfully conduct an interview. In fact, excellent interviewers are the exception rather than the rule, and anyone who interviews candidates for recruitment on a regular basis will require thorough training in the basic 'rules' of good procedure. Hopefully this will be complemented by experience and the personality of the interviewer.

Objectives

The objectives of the selection interview may be stated as:
1. To assess whether the candidate is willing and able to do the job successfully and is suitable to the organization.
2. To enable the candidate to assess whether the job and organization are suitable to him/her.
3. To give a good impression of the organization by providing a fair and well constructed interview.

It must always be remembered that interviewing is a two-way process. No interviewer should be arrogant enough to assume that the candidate will automatically accept the job on the basis of one advertisement. The public relations aspects are also important as not everybody will get the job but they may well be future customers or business associates of the organization.

It should be remembered that the initial interview is often followed by a further interview with the applicant's prospective manager before the final decision to appoint is made. The interviewing skills of line managers will vary enormously, and although they may be guided by the personnel manager the final decision will invariably rest with them.

Some organizations use a panel interview in order that all interested parties can take part. In our view, the stated advantages of panel interviews are outweighed by the failure to create a natural situation for the candidates. It is extremely difficult to obtain a valid impression of someone who has been placed in a stressful and unnatural environment. If the candidates have sufficient time available it might be preferable to hold shorter and less formal interviews with each of the members of the panel on a one-to-one basis.

Hints and tips are no substitute for thorough training in interview technique, but the following rudimentary guidelines may help to illustrate some of the basic considerations for those responsible for interviewing:

☐ Base the interview upon a thorough job description and person specification that set out clear criteria. (e.g., seven-point plan, 'difficulties and distates', 'critical incidents', etc.)

☐ Ensure that the interviewer is thoroughly conversant with all data concerning the job and the applicant *before* the interview commences

☐ Interviews should be held in comfortable surroundings, free from interruption. Allow enough time for adequate discussion

☐ Prepare a criterion-related check-list against which to rate the applicant (Rodger or Fraser models may be useful as guides)

☐ Begin the interview in a conversational manner in order to help candidate to relax

☐ Ask open-ended questions rather than those only requiring yes/no answers

☐ Follow interviewee's lead where possible, and endeavour to probe relevant areas in depth

☐ Be attentive, but do not react in a way that will reveal disapproval or prejudice

☐ Allow the interviewee to talk freely, but endeavour to ensure that all information that you require is obtained

☐ Avoid being influenced by 'halo effects' and 'stereotypes'

☐ Leave difficult questions until a rapport has been established, but end on an agreeable note

☐ Note taking is useful, but should preferably be left until immediately after the interview, as it can be distracting

Subjectivity and bias

One of the greatest criticisms concerning interviewing is that it is 'too subjective'. It is claimed that interviewers allow their judgement to be influenced by 'halo effects' and 'stereotyping'. The former refers to the situation in which a particular characteristic displayed by a candidate, such as verbal fluency or an interest in sport will influence judgement in other areas. Stereotyping usually refers to bias that arises from attributing cultural generalizations to individuals such as 'all long-haired men are irresponsible' or 'all foreigners are untrustworthy'. Although these situations do arise and are to be avoided, it is unlikely that total objectivity can ever be achieved when dealing with human situations. Subjectivity is natural, but bias and prejudice are unfortunate and possibly unlawful.

Validity and reliability

The selection interview has been widely criticized concerning both its consistency when used on different occasions and/or by different interviewers as well as its ability to predict successful job performance.

Although research findings vary with regard to reliability, the influence of factors referred to above on the part of the *interviewer* inevitably affects the consistency of results.

Despite a great deal of pessimism concerning the validity of the interview, some more recent studies such as the review by Arvey and Campion [1] have been somewhat more sanguine, particularly in respect of the panel interview. However, this optimism should not be overstated, and relatively the prediction rating of interviews remains low.

The whole matter should be kept in proportion, and clearly the interview remains as popular as ever. In certain areas, the interview has proved particularly effective. Ulrich and Trumbo [2] noted from a wide range of studies that areas described as 'personal relations and motivation to work' were well assessed by the selection interview. What must be remembered is that human beings are involved on both sides of the selection procedure. Consequently, acceptability may be as important as scientific validity.

HOW CAN THE INTERVIEW BE IMPROVED?

If the criticism concerning the interview, much of which is fully justified, is to be countered, how can we improve it as a selection device? The need for adequate preparation and training has already been stated, and basic guidelines for conducting the interview have been suggested. The systems of person specification suggested by Rodger and Munro Fraser have been outlined in Chapter 8, and whether or not these are used or adapted, the importance of thorough groundwork cannot be stressed enough. This approach should assist reliability by standardizing the areas to be covered by the interviewer in accordance with the person specification. Unless we endeavour systematically to assess the candidates against pre-determined criteria, the interview will revert to the haphazard subjective technique referred to by its critics. Panel interviews are sometimes used in the hope that individual subjectivity will be neutralized and that the joint prediction concerning the candidate's suitability will be more valid than that of a single interviewer. These may merely result in a number of subjective judgements that may be compromised or subverted by a strong member of the panel, however, unless the same principals are applied. We have already referred to the problems of stress created by this practice.

The chief proponents of the interview have recommended the use of the person specification as an interview plan. By using one of the frameworks suggested, the interviewer can ask questions to assess the extent to which the candidate matches up to the appropriate criteria. An example of an interview plan based on Rodger's seven-point plan is given in Fig. 10.1.

Carlson *et al.* [3] carried out a review of research findings and concluded, *inter alia*, that:

1   Structured interviews (of the type recommended by Rodger and Fraser) are more consistent and valid than unstructured ones
2   Interviews should form part of an overall selection procedure according to relevance
3   Interviewers require intensive training
4   Feedback is necessary if prediction is to be improved

Despite the many criticisms of the interview, Bernard Ungerson [4], who admits to favouring 'objective' selection, sums up the situation rather well:

However successful, in the future, objective methods come to assess personality characteristics, interviews will always be necessary. They will be needed because they meet the expectation of candidates for human contact with potential employers, because there are some characteristics which can be assessed only by visual and conversational contact, and because information and impression must flow from the potential employer to the candidate. Other techniques cannot meet these needs.

Follow up

If the validity of interviewing within an organization is to be assessed, a follow-up procedure must be incorporated. Thomason [5] refers to the fact that an organization can never check on the suitability of the candidates who 'got away'. However, assuming that those employed are the best part of the original sample, data concerning them must be invaluable in checking the validity of recruitment techniques.

Some organizations use special forms to check predictions made at the time of selection against actual performance in aspects of the job. To what extent it is possible to take a 'scientific' approach to validation of this type we are not sure. Despite the obvious difficulties involved, it would seem futile to continue recruiting staff without checking the effectiveness of the methods used.

Candidate's name _____ Date _____

Category	Questions	Preferred 1 2 3 4 5 6 7 8 9 10	Actual 1 2 3 4 5 6 7 8 9 10
Physique	a. Has he any physical defects or disabilities of occupational importance? b. Does his appearance, his bearing and speech make a suitable first impression? c. Has he had, or does he suffer from any adverse medical condition?		
Attainments	a. What general educational opportunities has he enjoyed? b. How well has he done in relation to them? c. What occupational training has he had? d. What occupational experience has he had? e. To what extent has he benefited from it?		

General intelligence	a. How would you assess his intelligence in relation to the general population?
	b. How would you assess his intelligence in relation to people of similar education?
	  (1) Is his general knowledge good?
	  (2) Is he well-read, well informed?
	  (3) What are his powers of reasoning?
	c. Has he used his inherited intelligence effectively?
	d. Has he ever taken an intelligence test?		

Special aptitudes	Does the applicant appear to have an aptitude for the special type of activity shown in the job specification? (A copy of the job specification is attached)		
Interests	a. Does the applicant appear to derive particular satisfaction from (1) social		

(2) practical
(3) constructive
(4) physically active
(5) intellectual, activities?

b. What levels of achievement has he set himself and to what extent has he succeeded in attaining them?

Disposition

a. Does the applicant appear to have the temperament and character to play the role that the job involves?

b. Is he temperamentally suitable to meet the demands of the job with regard to:
(1) Reliability
(2) Acceptability
(3) Leadership or influence over others.
(4) Self-dependence or prepared to accept responsibility
(5) Initiative
(6) Sense of humour

Circumstances

a. Are his domestic circumstances likely to conflict with the demands of the job?

b. What kind of job has his background and previous work led him to expect?

c. What frustrations does he meet in his present job?

d. Are the prospects of the job under consideration likely to satisfy him in respect of prestige and remuneration?

Additional

a. Has he any queries about the job specification and the conditions of employment?

b. Is there any question he thinks the panel should have asked him? Is there anything about himself he would like to tell the panel?

Fig. 10.1 Interview assessment form

GROUP SELECTION/ASSESSMENT CENTRES

The Civil Service and some other large organizations sometimes use group selection techniques as part of the recruitment process. It is normally only appropriate to relatively senior appointments and where there are several 'likely' candidates. Typically, a group of about 6 to 8 applicants will attend a session during which they will be requested to discuss topics or carry out tasks that are set by a panel of assessors. The main point of the technique is to provide an opportunity to observe the applicants in a problem-solving situation within a group setting. As a great deal of a manager's time is spent in solving problems and communicating with other people, it is considered that this form of assessment is particularly appropriate.

Increasingly, group selection is becoming just one aspect of a wider 'assessment centre' which might last for 1–2 days and encompass a range of other selection devices including interviews and psychometric tests. In this way, both inter-personal and individual skills can be assessed in a structured and comprehensive manner.

The arrangements and processes are not dissimilar to those of an assessment centre set up for development and potential assessment of existing staff. Again, these are being used increasingly by larger organizations and further reference is made to these in Chapters 12 and 15. Whatever the emphasis, it is clear that the assessors need to be well trained and mindful of the criteria for the task in hand.

This leads us to some of the problems of such selection techniques. Apart from the need for experienced and unbiased assessors, there is the problem of acceptability. Some applicants are unwilling to 'compete' in a group situation: others tend to overreact in either an extrovert or introvert manner. It is also an expensive and time-consuming activity. For these reasons, it may be advisable to carry out pre-selection tests in order to arrive at an optimum group for assessment.

Group assessment is a useful technique for selecting personnel for jobs where social skills are particularly important. However, it can only be used in conjunction with other methods of assessment, modern assessment centres attempt to provide a broader range of these.

TESTS

Many larger companies, particularly in the USA, use 'objective' selection tests as part of their recruitment programme. However, their use is not as widespread as some of the literature would lead one to believe, and smaller organizations tend to rely on other techniques. There has also been a great deal of rationalization of testing in the USA since a Supreme Court decision in the early 1970s in which strict guidelines were laid down concerning the validity of testing devices.

Despite this caveat and in view of the enormity of the task of selecting staff successfully, any aid to prediction is welcome. As with most techniques, there are some basic principles that bear remembering.

Relevance

Any test must be based upon sound job analysis and man specification. When the criteria for success in the job have been established, it must be decided which of these, if any, are measurable by tests. If no test is relevant, use some other technique.

Reliability

Reliability refers to the consistency of the results obtained. In other words, a person who takes the test on different occasions should obtain the same, or a very similar, result. If the results vary significantly, the test is valueless.

Validity

If the test is reliable we can assume that *something* is being measured. The problem is then to ensure that it is measuring the attributes that it is being used to measure. This is normally referred to as '*content*' or '*construct validity*', and although test designers will produce correlation coefficients, it should be remembered that the attributes themselves are only abstractions. Although construct validity is of obvious importance, a test must also possess '*operational validity*'. In other words, it must be applicable to the type of job and situation in which it is being used. This will require a great deal of evaluation work within the organization.

Types of test

A full discussion of all aspects of the many types of test available is not possible here, but for a practical and concise guide Holdsworth's [6] short publication is recommended.

Skill/attainment tests

Often of a practical nature, these tests enable an employer to assess in a direct manner whether or not the applicant has the necessary abilities for the job. Work samples, such as typing a document or operating a computer, are often used.

Intelligence tests

These are used fairly widely in the armed forces and the Civil Service for selection purposes, but less so in industry. However, commercial use has increased in recent years, even though the number of users remains fairly small. Intelligence tests are usually in written form and consist of several problems that attempt to measure verbal, numerical or perceptual ability. Most are given with a time limit and can be marked in order to produce percentile scores. These can then be ranked against contemporaries or larger comparative groups. Intelligence tests can only cover certain aspects of 'intelligence', and some researchers consider that intellect has many facets that cannot be adequately tested.

Aptitude tests

The six main aptitudes that are relevant to selection are verbal, numerical, spatial, mechanical, manual dexterity and clerical. Of necessity, aptitudes have to be fairly specific, and it is not possible to measure groups of tasks that do not require a common capacity. For instance, it would not be possible to measure 'managerial aptitude', as management tends to involve a whole range of tasks. Some aptitudes cannot, of course, be separated completely from general intelligence, but tests are well developed under all of the above headings. In most categories there are well established 'package deals' of tests available from various sources. Toplis et al.'s book [6] reviews some of the better known ones and more detailed information can be obtained from the designers. Here again, relevance is as important as the general reputation of the test in respect of validity and reliability.

Personality tests

Personality testing is a mine-field for the unwary or inexperienced. 'Personality' is generally accepted to be important for many jobs, but it is also extremely difficult to get to grips with. We often refer to people as being 'reliable', 'energetic', 'sociable', or 'self-starters'; but what do these expressions mean, and how do we discover whether a job applicant possesses such attributes? In truth, many researchers are unable to agree on definitions of such things as extroversion, introversion, neurosis and so on. However, tests have been developed that can be adapted for selection purposes and these fall into two main categories.

Personality questionnaires attempt to probe the candidates' interests, ideas and beliefs. They may be answered verbally or in writing. Although many tests have built in 'lie detectors', faking is an obvious problem in a recruitment context where applicants are trying to create a good impression. The other area of difficulty is in the interpretation of the answers.

A more indirect method of assessing personality is used in a group of 'projective tests'. These are based on a belief that a person will project his/her personality through the performance of a task or the interpretation of objects or situations. The use of this type of test is rare in the selection situation, and they are confined largely to clinical or more general psychological use.

It is apparent that the interpretation and scoring of this type of test is even more difficult, and it is definitely a job for a psychologist who has received specialist training in this field.

Although personality tests are highly developed in the clinical field, it is probably true to say that until research produces better correlations between personality attributes and job success, even where these attributes can be defined, these types of tests should only be used after careful consideration.

REFERENCES

Although references are not a selection technique as such, they can act as confirmation or otherwise of the selection decision, and most offers of jobs are made 'subject to satisfactory references'. The only worthwhile reference will be obtained from the applicant's previous employer or educational establishment, and even with these it is sometimes necessary to 'read between the lines'. Referees tend to be extremely cautious and are loath to give a bad reference. This could be based upon ill-founded fears of a libel action, sympathy, or purely because they want to get rid of the employee in question. If in any doubt, a telephone call may help to clarify the position.

What a reference will at least provide is confirmation of the candidate's previous employment. Standard reference forms are useful for illicitng such information as job title, length of service, rate of pay, etc., and these are widely used. The type of information that typically might be requested on a standard form is outlined below:

Employment details
    Job title
    Period for which employed
    Main duties
    Salary

Personal history
    Absenteeism
    Lateness
    Health
    Honesty

Opinion of referee
    Job performance
    Personality/relations with others
    Suitability for proposed employment

It will be noticed that the details are divided into 'facts' and 'opinions'. In view of what has been said above, the latter should be treated with some scepticism and only acted upon where there is good reason to do so.

OTHER TECHNIQUES

Situational interview

A technique known as the 'situational interview' has been developed over recent years which claims to improve the predictive validity of the selection interview. It is based on the premise that an individual's stated intentions will indeed relate to behaviour in the job. Based upon the 'critical incidents' of the job, a series of questions is developed around the types of behaviour required to carry out the job successfully. In other words, how would the candidate behave in particular situations? Clearly, this technique would require considerable development if it is to be used rigorously but its proponents claim that the effort is worthwhile.

Biodata

There has been some debate recently about the effectiveness of using biographical data as an indicator of success in the job, despite the fact that its use in practice appears to be minimal. Basically, the technique relies upon matching such things as age, experience, qualifications and family background against those of existing employees considered to be 'successful'. An extended application form/questionnaire may be used to obtain the information from applicants.

Despite the claimed validity of this approach, the development of the criteria requires a great deal of time and they will need to be reviewed and updated from time to time.

PLACEMENT

Once the offer has been confirmed, the 'recruitment process' is virtually concluded. However, it is vitally important to ensure that full details of the agreed starting date are passed to the department concerned in order that the necessary arrangements can be made.

It bears repeating that the whole selection process relies on the feedback obtained concerning the new employee after placement. Even before the regular appraisal system has commenced, a report should be obtained from the new employee's supervisor or head of department. If he does not appear to be settling in well the reason should be ascertained. If the feedback obtained is at variance with the assessment at the time of selection, all details should be carefully checked and where necessary either the criteria and/or the method of selection should be reviewed and modified. Selection performance can only be judged by results, and unless these results are fed back into the system, it will never reach optimum effectiveness.

INDUCTION OF NEW STAFF

As we mentioned when referring to staff turnover, many organizations experience an 'induction crisis' — staff who fail to settle and leave within a few weeks of joining. Poor induction may be partly to blame. Even where new employees do not actually leave, they may well be less efficient if they feel anxious and unfamiliar with the job and the organization.

How should induction be approached?

Much will depend upon the size and resources of the organization. However, the main objectives remain the same:

☐ to welcome new employees and help them to settle
☐ to familiarize them with the organization and the job
☐ to communicate information on company policy, duties, health and safety, etc.

Induction really starts at recruitment when new employees may be introduced to other staff and shown around. Larger organizations may have a formal programme on the first day of work with talks, films, etc. All organizations should extend this initial activity with less formal induction at the place of work. A conscious effort must be made to assist the new member of staff to settle in as smoothly as possible. Special attention should be paid to school leavers, women returning to work, disabled employees and racial minorities. A checklist may be useful to ensure that new staff have received all the necessary information and support and Personnel may be charged with the responsibility of recording the induction activities.

REFERENCES

1. Arvey, R.D. and Campion, J.E. (1982). 'The employment interview: a summary and review of recent literature', *Personnel Psychology*, No. 35, pp. 281–322.
2. Ulrich, L. and Trumbo, D. (1965). 'The selection interview since 1949', *Psychological Bulletin*, No. 53, pp. 100–116.
3. Carlson, R.D. *et al.* (1974). 'Improvements in the selection interview', *Personnel Journal*, Vol. 50, No. 4. April.
4. Ungerson, B. (Ed) (1983). *Recruitment Handbook*, 3rd Edn Gower Publishing Group Ltd.
5. Thomason, G. (1981). *A Textbook of Personnel Management*. IPM.
6. Toplis, J., Dulewicz, V., Fletcher, C. (1987) *Psychological Testing: A practical guide*. IPM.

11
Legal aspects of recruitment and employment

When advising on the recruitment of new employees the personnel manager must be mindful of the many legal consequences of employing, or indeed not employing, a particular individual. Although much of the employment legislation is referred to in the appropriate chapters, it is intended to confine this section to matters immediately impinging upon recruitment and selection and areas which do not fit easily elsewhere. It is, of course, impossible to cover the legislation in any detail in a book of this nature and for those requiring chapter and verse there are many publications available apart from the statutes themselves [1]. However, it is worth highlighting some of the key areas for consideration.

THE CONTRACT

A contract of employment may be oral or written. Generally speaking it will follow the normal rules of contract, subject to certain common law and statutory restrictions. Although the law does not require the contract itself to be in writing, each employee (but see below for exceptions) must be given a *written statement of particulars* of certain terms and conditions of his contract within 13 weeks of commencement of his employment (Employment Protection (Consolidation) Act 1978, S.1).

Certain employees such as registered dock workers, seamen, and those working mainly outside of the UK are excepted from these provisions. Also, employees working less than 16 hours per week are not legally entitled to the statement, unless they have been continuously employed for 5 years or more, when the minimum requirement is 8 hours per week.

The written statement should provide the following particulars:

1. Identity of employer and employee.
2. Date employment began.
3. Rate of remuneration and payment intervals

4 Hours of work
5 Entitlement to holidays and holiday pay
6 Sickness provisions and sick pay
7 Pension rights, including whether or not a contracting out certificate is in force
8 Periods of notice required to terminate contract (see Chapter 30, p. 323 for statutory minimum)
9 Disciplinary rules applicable to employee
10. Details of person to whom employee can apply if dissatisfied with any disciplinary decision relating to him or for purposes of expressing a grievance

Where there are no provisions in respect of any of the above matters, e.g., there is no sick pay, the statement should state this. Also, the statement may refer to other documents that contain the necessary details, such as an employee handbook or an agreement with a trade union. However, these documents must be 'readily accessible' to the employee.

Although there is no prescribed layout for this written statement, most organizations either design a standard format or use a commercially printed form. It should be noted that any changes in the terms covered by the written statement must be notified to the employee *in writing* within one month of the change.

Failure to provide the necessary statement or amendment entitles the employee to complain to an industrial tribunal. The tribunal is empowered to imply a term of the statement and prescribe the necessary particulars to be included.

SEX DISCRIMINATION

Discrimination in employment on grounds of sex or marital status is unlawful under the Sex Discrimination Act 1975. Although we tend mostly to consider discrimination against women, the act applies equally to the treatment of men, except in connection with pregnancy and childbirth!

Discrimination may be 'direct' or 'indirect'. *Direct discrimination* occurs where a woman or a married person is treated less favourably than their counterparts. This will apply to both refusing or failing to offer employment as well as to the terms of employment offered. *Indirect discrimination* may occur where an employer applies a requirement or condition of employment which is such that:

1 the proportion of women or married persons able to comply is considerably smaller than the proportion of men or unmarried persons; and
2 the employer cannot show it to be justifiable; and

3   it is to the detriment of the person concerned because she or he cannot comply with it.

Examples of indirect discrimination might include a demand for certain physical requirements, such as strength, height or even age, that are not applicable to the type of job and cannot be justified.

It will be apparent that the sex discrimination legislation is particularly pertinent to recruitment and selection and the personnel manager should be aware of the pitfalls. Advertisements containing such words as 'salesgirl', 'stewardess', or 'postman' should be avoided, unless qualified by a note to the effect that men and women are free to apply. Application forms should be vetted to ensure that no questions are included that could imply discrimination and interviewers should also be trained to avoid questions of a discriminatory nature. Selection tests should not discriminate unjustifiably.

There are of course situations where an employer is allowed to discriminate on grounds of sex in cases where this is a 'genuine occupational qualification'. This could apply to such things as models, actors or even lavatory attendants.

Unlawful discrimination is often difficult to prove, and there is a great deal of case law in this area. The personnel manager will need to advise on current issues and also give a lead in formulating the organization's policy in respect of sex discrimination on all aspects of employment, including recruitment.

Where an individual considers that he/she has been refused employment owing to unlawful sex discrimination, the complaint can be referred to an industrial tribunal within 3 months. The tribunal may order compensation where it considers the complaint well founded.

On a broader front, the Equal Opportunities Commission may investigate organizations and has wide powers to deal with cases of discriminatory practices, including a court injunction if this is considered necessary to halt the situation. The Commission has issued a Code of Practice that includes the recommendation that employers should monitor and keep records of the recruitment and progress of women. The Sex Discrimination Act 1986 extends the provisions of the 1975 Act to firms of 5 or fewer employees and some private households. The Act also requires employers to treat all employees similarly with regard to compulsory retirement age and any age-related promotions or training. Other provisions remove restrictions under the Factories Act and other legislation concerning women's working hours, e.g., night work in factories.

EQUAL PAY

When recruiting, it is essential that the terms and conditions offered to a woman are equal to those for a man applying for the same job. This will include such things as holiday entitlement, sickness benefits, etc., as well as basic salary or wage. The Equal Pay Act 1970 stipulated that she should be employed on:

☐ 'like work' or
☐ 'work rated as equivalent' under a valid job evaluation scheme.

However, the Equal Pay (Amendment) Regulations 1983 provide that applicants may claim equal pay for work of 'equal value'. As before, claims will be made to an industrial tribunal but in these cases a member of a panel of experts (designated by ACAS) will be instructed by the tribunal to consider the case and report back. Since the regulations came into effect many claims have been lodged. Others have been settled informally. Some cases have become *causes célèbres*. The *Financial Times* reported one case of a female VDU operator in the printing industry who received an increase of £100 per week as a result of claiming equal value with a male typesetter. Quite clearly, personnel managers will need to anticipate claims of this type and review, in particular, job evaluation schemes [2] and reward policies in the light of the legislation.

RACIAL DISCRIMINATION

Another area of recruitment charged with emotion is that of discrimination on grounds of race. As in the case of the statute referred to above, the Race Relations Act 1976 refers to many topics other than recruitment. However, the Act has obvious implications for employers and the personnel department should carefully review recruitment policies and criteria for selection. Indirect discrimination would cover such things as insisting upon a good command of English when this is not essential in order to carry out a job properly. Employers should also be wary of complaints concerning application forms and tests that can only be understood by English speakers, despite the practical difficulties involved. Those who choose to ignore foreign qualifications do so at their peril.

Unlike its predecessors, the 1976 Act provides direct access to the industrial tribunals for those who claim discrimination against them. The Commission for Racial Equality also has wide-ranging powers to issue codes of practice and carry out investigations. The latest Code issued in 1984 recommends 'Ethnic Monitoring'. The level of records and monitoring expected will depend on the size and resources of the organization. The main aim is to encourage employers to analyse the selection, training, promotion and other employment policies towards racial minorities.

Some organizations, such as Mars Ltd, have carried out ethnic monitoring for some years as part of a wider policy towards the 40 or so nationalities that they employ. The issue of monitoring obviously raises several issues, but problems of confidentiality, etc., should not overshadow the positive aspects [3].

PAST CRIMINAL CONVICTIONS

The Rehabilitation of Offenders Act 1974 provides that, after a period of time, persons who have been convicted of criminal offences and who have served their sentence, with exceptions, need not disclose those convictions to a potential employer.

The Act introduces the concept of a 'spent' conviction. The time required for convictions to become 'spent' will depend on the nature of the sentence, and will run from the date the sentence was imposed. Generally speaking, sentences carrying penalties in excess of 30 months' imprisonment can never become 'spent'.

A person whose conviction has become spent is known as a 'rehabilitated person'. They are not obliged to disclose:

1   details of spent convictions,
2   the offence for which convicted, or
3   any circumstances surrounding the conviction.

The implications for recruiters, particularly in respect of questions at interview are important. If an applicant is asked whether he has any criminal convictions, he is entitled to answer 'no' if these are spent. Failing to employ a person purely on grounds of a spent conviction or subsequent dismissal for the same reason may well lead to a successful application to an industrial tribunal by the individual concerned. There are exceptions to the above provisions in respect of various professional applicants, such as police officers, doctors and teachers.

UNION MEMBERSHIP

Even where union membership or 'closed shop' agreements are recognized by employers, new members of staff cannot be forced to join the union. Any remaining provisions to enforce a 'closed shop' have now been repealed by the Employment Act 1988.

On the other hand, it is also unlawful to dismiss or take action short of dismissal against staff who wish to join or take part in the activities of an independent trade union under previous legislation.

From a practical point of view, it would appear that employers still have the right to *engage* union or non-union members, but after that employees have the legal right to belong, or not to belong, to a union without undue interference from their employer.

The industrial relations aspects of closed shops are discussed in Chapter 26, page 295.

MATERNITY RIGHTS

Employers of female staff will need to be aware of various rights in respect of pregnancy and maternity. These rights are largely contained in the Employment Protection (Consolidation) Act 1978 (EPCA 1978) as amended by the Employment Act 1980 (EA 1980).

Ante-natal care

Under the Employment Act 1980 a pregnant employee has a right to paid time off for appointments in respect of ante-natal care. Time off, during working hours, must not be 'unreasonably refused' but the law recognizes the need for evidence of pregnancy and an appointment card to be produced to the employer if requested.

Dismissal

An employee may claim unfair dismissal if the principal reason for the dismissal is her pregnancy unless the employer can show that her condition causes her to be incapable of carrying out her work. If, however, there is a 'suitable' available vacancy to which she is able to transfer, this must be offered by the employer.

Maternity Pay

Previous statutory rights to maternity pay have been superseded by Statutory Maternity Pay (SMP), introduced by the Social Security Act 1986 supplemented by Regulations. These provisions are somewhat complex and mainly concern those personnel managers administering the system. However, outline particulars are given in Chapter 21, page 236.

Return to work

An employee (with similar length of service to that referred to above) who has been absent due to pregnancy is entitled to return to work with her original employer within 29 weeks of the date of confinement. The EPCA (1978) provided a right to return to the employee's original job and notification of intention to return was not particularly rigorous. This caused obvious problems for employers with regard to maintaining vacancies for staff who may or may not decide to return to their jobs.

The EA 1980 redressed the balance somewhat in favour of employers and in order to claim the right to return to work an employee must:

1. Inform her employer in writing at least 21 days before her absence:

     (a) that she will be absent due to pregnancy;
     (b) the expected week of confinement;
     (c) that she intends to return to work with her employer.

2.   Respond in writing within 14 days of receiving a request from her employer, confirming her intention to return. (This request may be made not earlier than 49 days after the date of confinement.)

3.   Give at least 21 days written notice of the date on which she intends to return.

The EA 1980 also allows employers to offer 'suitable alternative employment' to a returning employee where, for various reasons, it is not practicable to reinstate her in her old job.

Despite a slightly improved situation from the employer's point of view, there are still many practical implications of these statutory rights. Procedures and paperwork will have to be prepared in order that staff are notified of their rights and arrangements made for monitoring staff absent due to pregnancy. Replacement staff will also need to be informed clearly of the conditions under which they are being employed.

REFERENCES

1.   See, for example, Department of Employment booklets, issued free at local offices of the Department.

2.   Fouracre, S. and Wright, A. (1986). 'New factors in job evaluation', *Personnel Management*, May.

3.   Crofts, P. (1984). 'Counting on monitoring for racial equality', *Personnel Management*, March.

PART 3: FURTHER RECOMMENDED READING

Bramham, J. (1988). *Practical Manpower Planning*, 4th Edn, IPM.
Bowey, A.M. (1974). *A Guide to Manpower Planning*. Macmillan.
Hackett, P. (1982). *The Recruitment Handbook*. NOP.
Sidney, E. and Brown, M. (1961). *The Skills of Interviewing*. Tavistock Institute.
Dunnette, M.D. (1966). *Personnel Selection and Placement*. Tavistock Institute.

PART 3: SAMPLE EXAMINATION QUESTIONS

Define the term 'manpower planning'. What are the advantages for an organization that decides to follow a policy of providing future manpower needs from within its own resources.   CACA

John Hoskins is the manager of a branch of a business in which your bank has acquired an interest. As the local bank personnel officer you discover that John Hoskins's branch has a very large turnover of staff — significantly higher than colleagues who recruit in the same vicinity.

Closer examination reveals that the bulk of the turnover is among young trainees recruited locally by Mr Hoskins himself. 60% tend to leave in the first month of employment.

Mr Hoskins recruits on the basis of a 10-minute interview because he believes 'you can sum anyone up in that time'. He blames the turnover on local schools who 'fill kids' heads with ideas above their station'.

What selection methods would you introduce to John Hoskins to help him to improve his selection?

What would you suggest in terms of his attitude to local schools?   CIB

If you were asked to advise on the methods an organization should use for the effective recruitment and selection of 'management trainees', what guidelines could you offer? Indicate, in addition, the training which you would expect such individuals to receive in order to equip them to fill managerial positions.
ICSA

Outline the process of manpower planning and examine its practical application in ONE of the following types of organization:
(a) an aircraft manufacturer;
(b) a multinational oil company;
(c) a national railway network;
(d) a university, college, or polytechnic;
(e) a firm manufacturing 'white goods' (washing machines, freezers and refrigerators).   ICSA

What are the main methods of supply and demand forecasting used in manpower planning?   IPM

How can personnel specialists improve the quality of selection decisions made in an organization?   IPM

What methods would you use for short-listing when you have a very large number of candidates for a single vacancy?   IPM

'Manpower planning is often regarded as a luxury that only large companies can afford'. What are your views on this statement?   IAM

What contribution can a recruitment specialist make to the selection of staff in a highly technical function of which he has a limited amount of knowledge?   IAM

What are the key points to bear in mind in preparing and placing a job advertisement?   CBSI

How can the personnel manager set about developing sound practices in his organization in the field of race and sex discrimination?   CBSI

You have been asked to draft a standard contract of employment for cashiers. What terms and conditions would you include and why?   CBSI

A vacancy has occurred in your section. Your manager has asked you to set up a system of selecting a replacement. How would you go about it?   CIB

What are the main factors that affect the rate of staff turnover? Why is staff stability important?   CIB

Interviewing is a critical part of the selection process.
What do you consider are the crucial elements in a successful selection interview?
What are the limitations of the interview as a tool of selection?   CIB

Your manager is alarmed at the increase in labour turnover among junior employees in your branch/department within the last year. You are asked to analyse the possible causes and put forward recommendations that might help to solve the problem.   CIB

Imagine you are preparing to recruit a personnel manager, with responsibilities encompassing the broad spectrum of personnel issues, including policy-making, industrial relations, and manpower planning. Produce the following, with a reasoned justification for your views where appropriate:

(a) the recruitment methods to be adopted in order to generate an acceptable number of competent short-listed candidates; and
(b) the selection techniques to be used if the right person is to be chosen.   ICSA

How is labour turnover measured? What are the advantages and disadvantages of labour turnover? At what point does turnover cease to be 'good' and become 'bad'?   ICSA

(a) For what purposes is job analysis carried out?
(b) Describe the advantages and disadvantages of three different techniques commonly used in job analysis.
(c) Describe the principal stages in preparing a manpower plan.
(d) Explain the various methods of bringing manpower supply and demand into equilibrium.   CBSI

Part 4
Appraisal and development

12
Staff appraisal

The term 'appraisal' in this sense means the evaluation of the performance and/or potential of employees. It is also sometimes referred to as merit rating. Although several of the techniques used are similar, it is important to discriminate between staff appraisal and job evaluation. Staff appraisal attempts to evaluate the individual employee and the extent to which he succeeds in his present job and shows promise for the future. Job evaluation considers the job alone and its comparative worth or importance for the organization.

Staff appraisal is an integral part of any manager's function. Indeed, whether intended or not, it occurs on a day-to-day basis in determining how to get work done and which members of staff to allocate to which duties. The choice is between an unplanned, casual approach and a formal, conscious, planned process. If formal, a traditional method may be used measuring employee characteristics or performance. Alternatively, a behavioural approach may be taken, involving both employee and manager in the determination of mutually acceptable goals.

A survey carried out by the IPM in 1985 revealed that of the 306 organizations concerned, 82% formally operated performance review schemes. Of these, most considered the performance of management personnel; 78% included first line supervisors; 66% clerical and secretarial workers; 55% professional/scientific staff and only 24% skilled and semi-skilled workers.

OBJECTIVES

These may conveniently be grouped under two headings — management information and motivation.

Management information

☐ The provision of information about existing and potential manpower strengths and weaknesses as a basis for manpower and corporate planning

- [ ] To provide a basis for determining salary reviews, promotions, transfers, redundancies, dismissals, etc.
- [ ] The determination of training needs on an individual and group basis
- [ ] To provide a means of auditing the adequacy of other personnel procedures, and to identify criteria against which to measure predictors

Motivation

- [ ] The identification and communication of individual strengths and weaknesses — 'letting the employee know where he stands'
- [ ] The stimulation of higher performance, development of potential, and increased job satisfaction

A useful contribution made by the 'systems' approach to management is that it describes the personnel function as an integrated whole made up of various subsystems each of which contains an area of personnel management activity. Staff appraisal is identified as a crucial component of such a system, linking and providing a focal point for all other activities. Indeed Cummings and Schwab [2] describe it as the 'glue or cement' binding together the personnel management function.

This central role, however, creates a major difficulty. A single staff appraisal scheme is often intended to meet a multiplicity of varying objectives, each requiring different timescales, criteria and appraisal attitudes. In attempting to reduce these to a single process, a compromise may be achieved satisfying none and fraught with difficulty. Randell et al. [3] argue that the answer lies in a division of the appraisal process. They recommend that reward, performance and potential reviews be carried out 'not only separate in time, but also in paperwork, procedure and responsibility'. The principal force behind such an argument is that division separates those aspects of staff appraisal that relate to salary administration and negotiation from those intended to contribute to individual and organizational development and control. Many other writers support this view. However, although studies show that most employers divorce appraisal from any negotiation, at least on a time basis, there is little evidence to indicate that many are adopting Randell's three-stage approach. Anstey et al. [4] indeed suggest such fragmentation is unnecessary, since in any appraisal interview, no matter what its objective, the appraiser is constantly required to adjust his role and approach.

OUTLINE PROCEDURE

In essence, most appraisal schemes have the following pattern:

1   A report on each employee to be appraised is prepared. Usually
    this is done once or twice a year.
2   Each employee is interviewed.
3   Follow-up action is taken as determined by the report and
    interview.

APPRAISAL TECHNIQUES

A wide range of techniques are available, some encountered more
frequently than others. We will deal here only with the more commonly
used:

☐   Linear scales
☐   Behaviourally anchored rating scales (BARS)
☐   Results orientated schemes

Linear scales

The linear scale or graphic scale is without doubt the most commonly
used of appraisal methods. The appraiser is given a form in respect of
each employee to be appraised. The form lists several factors or
characteristics against each of which is a scale. The appraiser is
required to indicate on each scale his assessment of the employee in
respect of that factor or characteristic. This may mean placing a tick
somewhere on a numerical scale or in one of a series of boxes each
representing a distinct degree of the factor under consideration.
Examples of the more usual types of scale are shown in Fig. 12.1.

Careful selection of factors to be assessed is essential. Not only must
they be relevant to the type of employee being appraised, but also,
wherever possible, capable of objective measurement. Two types of
factor tend to be used: traits, e.g., reliability and co-operation; and
results, e.g., quantity and quality of work. Although most forms of this
kind use a mixture of the two, there is an obvious advantage in
emphasizing results since this tends to lend greater objectivity. The 1985
IPM survey indicated that 63% of appraisal forms were results
orientated. The same report revealed a decrease but still significant
number of schemes using traits (29% as compared with 34% in 1977).

Typically, appraisers are required to rate each employee in respect of
a dozen or more factors. However, as the number of factors increases so
overlapping tends to occur, making it more difficult to identify
accurately the factor to be appraised. Indeed, it has been suggested
that, for practical purposes, only two factors need be considered —
ability to do the present job and quality of performance.

The linear scale method is relatively simple to design, understand
and use. No reliance is placed on the ability of the appraiser to express

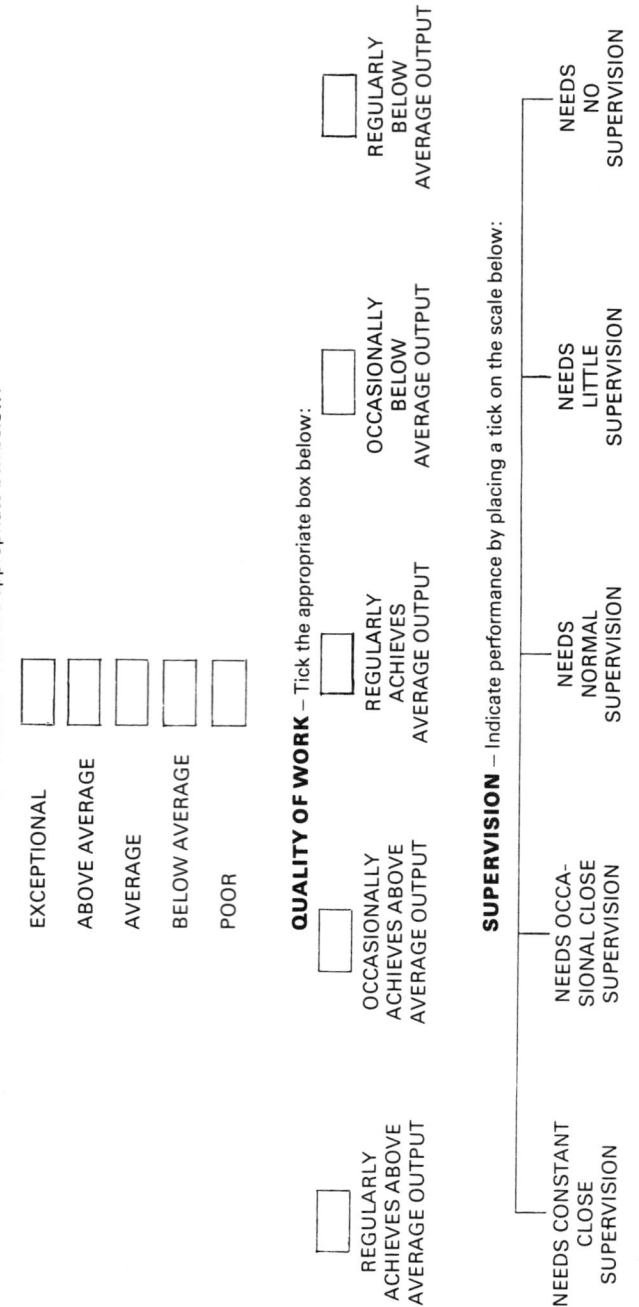

Fig. 12.1 Some linear scales used for appraisals

himself in wriitng, and information is provided in standard form. However, the major limitation remains subjectivity. The fact that a tick appears somewhere along a scale or in a box in no way guarantees that a careful, objective weighing of all the facts has occurred. To a limited degree, however, safeguards may be built in by careful form design, and concentration on questions that may be objectively answered, i.e., results rather than trait based.

Behaviourally anchored rating scale (BARS)

A relatively recently developed group of methods of appraisal is the behaviourally anchored rating scale. In developing a BARS scheme, it is usual for a group of staff with a good working knowledge of the job in question to identify and define several important dimensions or aspects of the job. These might be, for example, communication, planning, meeting deadlines, etc. In relation to such dimensions, the group then describes examples of behaviour along a scale between effective and ineffective behaviour. When appraising, the appraiser is required to identify which mode of behaviour most appropriately describes the employee under consideration and to score him accordingly on the scale. Proponents of BARS claim many advantages. Theoretically it should reduce error due to subjectivity (see below). Since it is typically developed by those who will use it, it should encourage appraiser confidence. The job-related basis should provide employee acceptability and a useful starting point for counselling. However, against such arguments it must be said that its development is highly time consuming and results in a multiplicity of appraisal systems since each job will normally require a unique rating scale [5]. Although it is claimed as more objective, several studies have suggested that in comparison with traditional methods its advantage is small.

Results orientated schemes

In previous editions of this book reference was made to the use of MBO (management by objectives) as a basis for appraisal. While formal MBO schemes are only used by a relatively small number of organizations (30% in the 1985 survey [1]), its influence is evident in many of the results orientated schemes currently in use.

Typically, objectives are set and at a following subsequent appraisal interview performance is measured on the extent to which these have been achieved. Such an arrangement is wholly consistent with Douglas McGregor's 'uneasy look at performance appraisal' in 1967 [6].

In some cases, it is apparent that individual objectives are firmly linked to pre-determined corporate objectives. However, a consensus view is that employee participation in both goal setting and performance is to be encouraged with each employee being encouraged to prepare his own list of proposed objectives as a basis for discussion and agreement with his superior. Similarly, it is argued that the employee, not his superior, should be invited to evaluate his own performance, his superior acting always as a counsellor and aide in problem solving rather than a critic.

Such schemes provide, of course, a very real opportunity for the integration of individual and corporate targets and, at the same time, have much to offer as a means of motivation and personal development. As a method of appraisal, however, they have a number of major limitations. Since targets are set on an individual basis they do not provide a ready means of comparison between employees for purposes of promotion or salary award. Although they may increase the objectivity with which such decisions are made, some other method of appraisal will still be necessary for such purposes. Secondly, goal achievement is often dependent on others and may to a considerable degree be outside the employees' control. Finally, goals are often difficult to define and are rarely consistent over an useful period of time.

WHO SHOULD APPRAISE?

In most cases, appraisal is carried out by an employee's immediate superior. Since generally he will have day-to-day contact with the employee concerned, he should be well equipped to evaluate and counsel. Indeed, as already noted, even in the absence of a formal appraisal scheme, it will be necessary for him to appraise staff as part of the day-to-day process of getting work done.

Several studies have shown that appraisal by several superiors may help to eliminate many of the problems of individual subjectivity inherent in the appraisal process. Further, it is suggested that a group of appraisers may collectively possess greater knowledge of an employee and his behaviour. [7].

It is important however that all appraisers are competent to appraise, in as much as they have real knowledge of the employee. Otherwise, the process may degenerate into collective guesswork or the corruption of accurate assessments by those made without real knowledge.

In many organizations a compromise is achieved by having appraisals reviewed by the supervisor's immediate superiors. This is the case, for example, in the British Civil Service.

Some use is also made of:

☐ appraisal by colleagues
☐ appraisal by subordinates
☐ self-appraisal

Of these, appraisal by colleagues and self-appraisal are increasingly encountered in the UK.

Appraisal by colleagues and subordinates (multi-appraisal)

Several studies, principally in the USA, have been made of assessment by colleagues and subordinates. 'Buddy rating' (rating by colleagues) has for example been used to assist in determining promotions in the US Armed Forces and by several major American companies. Assessment by subordinates has been used as a means of improving supervisor performance by the Esso Company; the Gulf Oil Corporation have used a combination of subordinate, colleague and superior appraisals [8].

Neither method has received widespread support. It is suggested that the criteria adopted by subordinates and colleagues will differ from those used by superiors, and that the consequent appraisals will be of limited value in fulfilling organizational objectives. Further, that the possibility of such appraisals determining promotions or salary increases will limit the degree of objectivity brought to bear.

On the other hand, organizations using this approach argue that colleague or subordinate assessments are often more accurate and specific. Also that when made by staff whose opinion is respected by the appraiser, appraisals may be particularly effective in modifying behaviour. To encourage this, at least one major UK manufacturing company invites appraisees to select up to six appraisers from any corporate level. To be selected is considered both an honour and a heavy responsibility.

Studies are not consistent in their findings. A survey carried out at IBM in 1964 [9] showed clear agreement between colleague ratings and promotions determined by management. Other studies, however, have demonstrated no consensus at all.

Self-appraisal

So far we have discussed appraisal by superior, subordinates and colleagues. Logically, we must also consider self-appraisal. It is, of course, wholly consistent with much behavioural theory and in particular with McGregor's theory Y. Its application has received increasing attention, both in the USA and more recently the UK.

However, it is important to discriminate between true self-appraisal and self-assessment as part of a participative supervisor/subordinate appraisal. So far as true self-appraisal is concerned, it appers until recently to have been little used. This is probably because of the obvious problem of bias. Although several studies have shown that generally subordinates' ratings tend to be more favourable than those made by their superiors, often the same studies have suggested that a root cause may be that superiors and subordinates disagree regarding the responsibilities of a job, their relative importance, etc. As a result of perceptual differences, they are in fact virtually assessing performance in different jobs.

Recent studies [10] suggest that most people are able to assess their own performance and even predict their future performance. The real problem is their willingness to do so. The use of self-assessment as part of a joint appraisal exercise, however, is widespread. The 1985 IPM survey referred to above indicated that 55% of organizations involved were using employee-prepared interview forms, compared with only 28.3% in 1977. Our research suggests that this trend has accelerated. It is argued that by involving employees in this way, the appraisal is transformed into a joint problem solving exercise in which the superior is no longer trying to tell the employee about his strengths and weaknesses, but is rather responding to the employee's own assessment of himself. In this way appraisal becomes more constructive, less defensive and more meaningful as a method of improving job satisfaction and performance.

Two examples of UK organizations successfully using this form of joint appraisal are Pilkingtons and British Leyland, though there are many others. Work by Meyer [11] suggests several benefits likely to accrue from such a scheme; particularly in respect of staff who are 'marginal performers'. Following self-appraisal-based interviews, he suggests that staff are more likely to cope subsequently with their jobs and to accept criticism as being fair while making a contribution to the resolution of disagreement during the interview.

However, in respect of two groups of employees, he suggests that the approach may not be successful. These are staff who have never previously been formally appraised, and those who depend heavily on their supervisor for direction; either because of personal make-up or their supervisor's authoritarian management style.

APPRAISAL OF POTENTIAL

So far, we have concentrated on the appraisal of what an employee has done or is doing. Earlier you may recall we included 'the provision of information about existing and potential manpower as a basis for manpower and corporate planning' in our list of staff appraisal objectives.

Peter Drucker [12] suggests that 'to try to appraise a man's long-range potential is a worse gamble than to try to break the bank at Monte Carlo'. Similarly, Randell and his colleagues [3] describe it as 'probably the most technically difficult aspect of staff appraisal' and 'also probably the most dangerous'. Although we acknowledge such warnings, it must be stated that one of management's prime responsibilities is to plan. Even with advanced mathematical techniques any forecast is liable to be inaccurate whether it relates to the national birth rate, corporate sales or the management potential of an employee. Forecasting in all of these areas has to be carried out using as a basis the best available information.

Evidence suggests that most organizations with appraisal schemes consider potential assessment a worthwhile exercise. Two questions spring to mind:

☐ how may potential be assessed?
☐ who is best qualified to assess it?

Assessment

Although accepting that any assessment of this kind can only be subjective, it would appear that the only starting point is to attempt to relate current job performance to the demands of possible future posts. Obviously however, past performance can never be a totally reliable predictor. The fact that an employee has behaved in a certain way in certain circumstances is no guarantee that he would again behave in a similar way in different or indeed the same circumstances.

Further, as an employee moves up the management ladder, so the nature of his work will inevitably change. The emphasis will increasingly move from pre-occupation with organizing and motivating to planning and controlling. A less departmentally introvert attitude will be required. Time scales will usually extend and progress be most subject to influences outside the manager's direct control. In one sense, this reveals the inadequacy of relying on current performance as a basis for projection. In another it provides the solution. Rather than rely on consistency of overall behaviour, we must instead try to identify behaviour that reveals that an employee has learned skills and attitudes of the kind called for in a more senior post.

Who should assess potential?

We have already suggested that in most organizations it is an employee's immediate supervisor who is generally considered to be best equipped to assess his performance.

When day-to-day performance is concerned, this may be a wholly realistic attitude. With regard to the assessment of potential it is perhaps more limited. It is surely unreasonable and unrealistic to expect a superior to be able accurately to assess a subordinate's ability to cope with the demands and exigencies of posts at management levels of which the superior has no first-hand knowledge. Indeed supervisors frequently show a marked reluctance to engage in such activity. In order to overcome this problem, it is often the practice to involve the supervisor's supervisor in this part of the appraisal procedure, as well as for overall review purposes as discussed above.

Assessment centres

As an alternative, the use of an assessment centre might be considered.

Though widely used in the USA, surveys suggest that they have until recently attracted little attention in the UK, perhaps because of their relatively high cost. Nevertheless, a growing number of employers [21] clearly feel that their use is a worthwhile investment. Techniques used usually duplicate those used for management trainee selection and management development puposes [13]. Over the course of 2–4 days assessments are made on the basis of a series of tests, interviews, individual and group projects and business games; together with the observations of assessors supervising the assessment sessions. Normally at least one of the assessors is an industrial psychologist.

Assessments are not principally concerned with what an employee has done or can do — rather how he is likely to act in the future given a specific role.

The 1986 IPM report revealed that the use of assessment centres in the UK was very limited, in fact only 18% (4% in 1977). It suggested that employers were still to be convinced of their advantages when compared with more traditional methods. However, Ungerson [14] argues that there was a good case for using professionally staffed centres, since these can, and do, produce better forecasts of performance than those made by line managers. Nevertheless, in general terms it seems that the value of reports of this type is largely a function of the knowledge that assessors have of the employing organization, its methods and its values. In the absence of such knowledge, assessments may be little more than a measure of the employee concerned against the assessor's individual conceptions of what makes for success.

RELIABILITY AND VALIDITY

Whatever appraisal method is used, whoever appraises whom, appraisal must be both reliable and valid if it is to be of value. The problems involved in establishing accurate predictors when recruiting staff have already been discussed. Similar problems exist in relation to appraisal (see Chapters 9 and 10).

LIMITATIONS AND PROBLEMS

To a very large extent the multiplicity of appraisal methods reflects both changes in management fashion and an awareness of the fact that no ideal method has yet been devised. Nevertheless, an appreciation of the problems and limitations that exist at least provides an opportunity for steps to be taken to minimize their effect.

The principal problem associated with appraisal is of course appraiser attitude and subjectivity. Others arise from a whole range of sources. Some of the most important are discussed below.

The Halo effect and stereotyping

These have already been discussed in connection with recruitment and selection (see Chapters 9 and 10).

Constant error

Different people have different standards — some higher, some lower. Thus some appraisers will give consistently high or favourable ratings, although others give ratings that are consistently low or unfavourable, even though the staff concerned may be of equal merit. A similar situation may occur as a result of varying departmental policies. This creates obvious difficulties in making comparisons between staff rated by different appraisers.

Central tendency

As has already been mentioned, a common appraiser tendency is for all employees to be rated within a very narrow band, usually 'average', or sometimes 'above average'. This *may* accurately reflect the true state of affairs, i.e., most employees being considered *are* average performers. However, in many cases, this 'middle-of-the-road' appraisal may indicate that the appraiser is either fearful or resentful of his judicial role. In other cases, it may demonstrate a complete lack of thought, the appraiser having perhaps merely 'gone through the motions' of staff appraisal while in fact only wishing to rid himself of the task as quickly as possible. Equally, of course, it may be that he knows so little about the staff concerned that 'average' ratings provide a convenient escape route.

Recency

Appraisal procedures in most organizations are carried out once a year. This means that the appraiser will be reviewing performance over an extended period. Unless adequate records have been maintained, the most accurately remembered behaviour will be that of the month or so preceding the appraisal. Owing to the very fact that the period immediately precedes the appraisal or owing to factors totally unconnected, this behaviour may be wholly unrepresentative.

Weighting

Frequently in the application of rating to salary administration, factors are allocated various values or weights. The appraisal complete, scores awarded for the various factors are totalled. This overall total determines rank order and often additional renumeration. How weights are allocated is a potential source of distortion. Although statistical methods exist that assist in eliminating the problem, they tend to be complex and time consuming. Generally therefore comparative weights are determined by subjective and often compromise judgements.

Not only may an inappropriate weight give rise to distortion; so too can the spread or cluster of ratings. The more widely spread are ratings in respect of one factor when compared with others, the greater will be its real rather than intended weight.

Other problems

In addition, a range of other subjectivity problems may occur from time to time. The 'similar-to-me' error is a tendency to favour appraisees who are similar to the appraiser in attitudes or background. Attributional bias may present problems: appraisers tending to see the causes of poor performance as wholly attributable to appraisees rather than, at least in part, determined by factors outside the appraisees' control. There is a recognized tendency to rate higher status personnel more favourably than junior staff. Regrettably appraisals may also on occasion be affected by simple bias whether it be on sex, racial or religious grounds.

ELIMINATION AND REDUCTION OF PROBLEMS

How may we seek to overcome these problems? The initial answer is training. Care spent in training both before and during the operation of an appraisal scheme has been shown on many occasions to be a vital pre-requisite for success [19].

If an appraisal scheme is to succeed it is essential that appraising staff understand and are committed to its purpose, and appreciate the potential pitfalls. The problems of commitment will, of course, be reduced if managers and supervisors have been involved in the initial development of the scheme. However, this will not always be possible. The first step is therefore to explain how appraisal fits into organizational policy, its relationship with other aspects of personnel activity, its objectives, its problems, and in particular its consequences and benefits for line managers. Wherever possible senior management should be actively involved in the training process in order that they may be seen to be taking appraisal seriously.

The next step is to give potential appraisers experience of appraisal and where appropriate, appraisal interviews. This should not only allow practice of interviewing skills, but should also attempt to reveal to appraisers actual examples of their own bias and error. Various methods are available: case studies, role playing with video tape feedback, group discussions and analysis have all been found useful.

A detailed description of the application of such a training scheme may be found in Randell et al. [3], though, from our experience it is often this aspect of a scheme's introduction that receives least time and attention.

How else may we improve appraisals? Reference has already been made to the need to select factors or characteristics that may be accurately recognized and objectively evaluated rather than amorphous traits incapable of precise definition or illustration. The careful design of forms has been shown to affect significantly the accuracy of appraisals (though many schemes now minimize their role [20]).

Various statistical methods are available to aid adjustment for appraiser subjectivity or to eliminate problems of unintended factor weights.

Just as preparatory work before introduction is important, so too is the regular monitoring of the appraisal scheme. Without this, a well planned, well introduced scheme may rapidly deteriorate and so become valueless. Checks on reliability and validity should be maintained and attempts made to identify lenient or hard raters and those prone to other sources of error. In this as in many areas, 'refresher' training may help to remind appraisers of the dangers inherent in the appraisal process.

THE APPRAISAL INTERVIEW

One of the most contentious aspects of appraisal is whether or not an appraisal report should be openly discussed with the employee concerned.

Arguments against discussion are generally based on two points:

☐ that reports which it is known are to be discussed are likely to be less reliable
☐ that managers dislike conducting appraisal interviews, are 'uncomfortable when they are out in the position of playing God' and consequently are ineffective when forced to do so, even to the point of re-arranging schemes beyond recognition and without approval [15]

Both points tend to be at least partially supported by research. Nevertheless, without feedback of results, appraisal can have little developmental value, since an employee can hardly be expected to improve if he is not aware in what way his performance is deficient. Further, the consequences of an honest and open exchange of information and ideas must be compared with the possible negative consequences of an appraisal procedure shrouded in secrecy and suspicion.

Statistics suggest that most organizations with formal appraisal schemes favour an open approach. In the 1985 IPM survey, for example,

64% of organizations concerned revealed appraisal reports in full; 28% in part. In only the remaining 8% were reports entirely closed.

The survey also showed that where reports were not fully open, it was assessments of potential that were most often not revealed. Our experience suggests a continuing trend towards openness, several schemes, e.g., British Leyland, providing for each appraisee to receive a copy of his fully completed appraisal form.

Effects of appraisal interview on subordinates

At the beginning of this chapter we described appraisal as being a motivator. This is based on the assumption that people like to know 'where they stand' and that by providing such information, employees may be stimulated to achieve higher standards of performance.

In practice, it appears that the reaction of staff is very mixed. Indeed many theorists argue that rather than acting as a motivator, the 'sandwich' of good and bad comments, which commonly constitute appraisal interviews, promotes in most employees a stereotyped, negative and defensive attitude. If appraisal is to succeed, it is obviously important to discover why such a response occurs and how it may best be avoided.

One of the most informative series of studies of appraisal and its effects is that conducted by Meyer et al. [16] at the General Electric Company. These studies concluded that:

- [ ] criticism has a negative effect on performance
- [ ] praise has little effect one way or the other
- [ ] performance improves most as a result of participative goal setting
- [ ] coaching should be a day-to-day, not once-a-year activity
- [ ] separate appraisals should be held for different purposes

In the light of these studies, many traditional forms of appraisal appear to be fraught with difficulty; and it is on this basis that arguments in favour of a more participative or results orientated approach are generally developed.

The manager – subordinate relationship

Since it is usually a subordinate's immediate superior who initially appraises him, the effects of the interview may also be examined in the context of their day-to-day manager – subordinate relationship.

The formality of an appraisal interview may be unacceptable to staff used to a consultative style of management with a high degree of informal communication. Reaction may thus be more favourable when dealing with staff unused to participation. Alternatively, it may be that staff who are satisfied with their supervisor and his style are more likely to be satisfied with his conduct of an appraisal interview [19].

Effects of interview style

Just as it is important to consider an appraiser's day-to-day management style, so it is important to examine the more immediate impact of his interview style.

Maier [17] identifies three general styles:

☐ tell and sell
☐ tell and listen
☐ problem solving

Tell and sell

In the tell and sell interview, the appraiser starts by telling the subordinate where he stands and then attempts to sell the employee a pre-determined course of action. Unless the appraiser is gifted with salesmanship and patience, the interview may become acrimonious, the appraiser resorting to coercion, the employee becoming increasingly alienated, and both seeking to save face.

Tell and listen

The tell and listen type is reflected in most appraisal schemes. The appraiser tells the subordinate how he has been assessed and then invites him to respond. Since he is invited to participate, the subordinate is less likely to feel frustrated by his inability to question or alter the appraiser's assessment. Communication becomes a two-way process, providing a opportunity for each participant to learn from the other. It is assumed that under such circumstances, an employee will adopt a less defensive attitude and so be more amenable to change.

The realism of such assumptions, however, must surely be open to doubt, since, even given the opportunity to state his case, an employee may feel inhibited by a desire not to appear a trouble maker, or may simply feel that it is futile to attempt to change the mind of the appraiser. The success of such a method therefore depends very heavily on the attitude of the appraiser and in particular on his ability to listen, summarize and reflect the subordinate's feelings.

Problem solving

The problem-solving interview differs significantly from the other two styles. The interview takes the form of a problem-solving discussion. The employee is encouraged to identify his problems and suggests ways of solving them. Appraiser and subordinate are partners in the process; the appraiser listening and using exploratory questions to stimulate fresh ideas in the subordinate's mind. Motivation is provided by subordinate's increased freedom and responsibility together with the resulting intrinsic job interest. Though focusing on the employee's contribution, such an interview demands high standards of appraiser skill and ability.

Which style should be adopted?

Generally the consensus appears to be that a problem-solving approach or perhaps a tell-and-listen style should be used. Several studies suggest that the problem-solving approach in particular aids in breaking down the negative role stereotypes often adopted by appraiser and appraisee, and further that it can be identified as leading to post-appraisal job satisfaction and productivity.

Others qualify this suggestion. Meyer [18] argues that a highly participative approach is most appropriate when used with appraisees who have a high need for independence, whereas it may prove unsatisfactory when used with others with a high dependence need. Similarly, tell and sell is likely to be most appropriate when dealing with new or inexperienced staff: indeed, such staff may be frustrated by a participative, problem-solving style.

Discussion of potential assessment

Reference has already been made to the difficulties involved in identifying satisfactory measures or indicators of potential. Problems of this kind are generally given as reasons for not discussing this portion of the appraisal. In reality, however, the anxiety expressed by so many managers about how to handle the question of potential and promotion is often more due to fear of adverse employee reaction, or embarrassment in having to counsel an employee who obviously overestimates his own ability and prospects.

In assessing potential, account must of course be taken of an employee's wishes, and this implies that the future must be discussed. However, whether the assessment be good or bad, the appraiser may be presented with something of a 'Catch 22' situation. How does he approach the task of counselling an employee who has no prospect of further promotion? In fairness, the employee ought probably to be given the facts; but how can this be done without crushing his morale or perhaps losing the services of a limited, but otherwise satisfactory, employee?

In many respects the counselling of a very able employee may prove no easier. For example, the appraiser may be faced with a situation in which an employee, though extremely well qualified for promotion, in fact has few immediate prospects owing to a lack of organizational growth or his path being blocked by staff unlikely to move in the near future. A 'low key' interview may depress an able employee and leave him with the impression that he is not appreciated. An over-favourable interview may raise his expectations that when not satisfied may lead to frustration. In either case the result may again be the loss of a valuable member of staff.

Follow-up

Regrettably, the all too common fate of appraisal forms is to be filled, filed and forgotten. If appraisal is not to fall into disrepute as elaborate 'window-dressing' it is important that any action agreed during the interview is implemented; whether by the appraiser or the appraisee. Practice varies — some organizations providing for 'action to be taken' to be recorded on the appraisal form; other organizations using a separate form, a copy of which is given to the employee. Whatever procedure is adopted, management must ensure that promises are kept, or, if some action has been agreed but cannot for some reason be taken, that the employee concerned is given an explanation. Where the subordinate has agreed to undertake certain action, this too should be followed-up, the immediate supervisor ensuring that the subordinate receives appropriate counselling and assistance.

FACTORS FOR SUCCESS — A SUMMARY

Despite warnings about the imminent collapse of traditional staff appraisal schemes, it is apparent that their use continues and indeed shows signs of flourishing. This does not, of course, mean that all are equally successful. However, whether introducing a new scheme or attempting to improve an existing one, it is obviously helpful to identify factors which significantly influence prospects of success. Most have already been mentioned; the more important are summarized below:

☐ Top management must be seen to be actively committed to appraisal and ready to set an example by appraising and being appraised.

☐ For its success, an appraisal scheme has to be operated and supported at all management levels. As wide a range of staff as possible should therefore be involved in the formulation of the appraisal scheme: it should not be seen as an exclusively personnel function.

☐ Methods and procedures should be selected that closely fit the objectives and policies of the organization, while at the same time remaining as simple in operation as possible. It should again be remembered that the scheme will largely depend on the contributions of line managers in various disciplines. An over-elaborate scheme may not be generally understood or accepted and may invite meaningless platitudes.

☐ To reach a position where employees anticipate appraisal with pleasure is probably too much to ask. However, much can be done to avoid outright hostility. Hostility often arises from fear, ignorance, lack of involvement or suspicion of unfairness. It is important therefore that the scheme is seen to be as 'fair' as possible, many organizations providing an appeals procedure for employees who consider themselves unfairly treated. All staff should be given a full explanation of the scheme, preceded where appropriate by discussions with trade union or staff representatives.

□ Adequate training must be provided for all appraisers before they become involved in appraisal and, in particular, appraisal interviews.

□ Provision should exist to ensure that staff receive feedback of results and that agreed action is taken or an explanation given.

□ The introduction of the scheme should not be seen as a once-and-for-all task, but should allow for constant monitoring and improvement to ensure continuing reliability, validity and overall acceptability. Particular attention should be given to problems or suggestions fed back from line managers.

REFERENCES

1. Long, P. (1986). *Performance Appraisal Revisited*. IPM.
2. Cummings, L.L. and Schwab, D.P. (1973). *Performance in Organisations*. Scott, Foresman.
3. Randell, G.A., Packard, P.M.A., Shaw, R.L. and Slater, A.J. (1974). *Staff Appraisal*. IPM.
4. Anstey, E., Fletcher, C. and Walker, J. (1976). *Staff Appraisal and Development*. George Allen & Unwin.
5. Borman, W.C. and Dunnette, M.D. (1975). 'Behaviour based versus trait orientated performance ratings', *Journal of Applied Psychology*, Vol. 60, No. 5, October, p. 561.
6. McGregor, D. (1957). 'An uneasy look at performance appraisal', *Harvard Business Review*, September/October.
7. Klimoski, R.J. and London, M. (1974). 'Role of the rater in performance appraisal', *Personnel Psychology*, No. 59, Winter, pp. 445–451.
8. Stimson, J. and Stokes, J. (1980). 'How to multi-appraise', *Management Today*, pp. 43–53.
9. Roadman, H.E. (1964). 'An industrial use of peer ratings', *Journal of Applied Psychology*, August.
10. Mabe, P.A. and West, S.G. (1982). 'Validity of self evaluation: a review and meta-analysis', *Journal of Applied Psychology*, No. 67.
11. Meyer, H.H. (1980). 'Self appraisal of job performance', *Personnel Psychology*, No. 33, pp. 291–295.
12. Drucker, P. (1968). *The Practice of Management*. Pan.
13. Dulewicz, V. (1982). 'The application of assessment centres', *Personnel Management*, September, pp. 32–35.
14. Ungerson, B. (1974). 'Assessment centres – a review of research findings', *Personnel Review*, Vol. 3, No. 3, pp. 5–13.
15. Rowe, K.H. (1964). 'An appraisal of appraisals', *Journal of Management Studies*, Vol. 1, No. 1, pp. 1–24.

16. Meyer, H.H., Kay, E. and French, J. (1965). 'Split roles in performance appraisal', *Harvard Business Review*, January/February, pp. 123–129.
17. Maier, N.R.F. (1959). *The Appraisal Interview*. Wiley.
18. Meyer, H.H. (1980). *Ibid*.
19. George, J. (1986). 'Appraisal in the public sector: dispensing with the big stick', *Personnel Management*, May, pp. 32–35.
20. Anderson, G. *et al.* (1987). 'Appraisal without form filling', *Personnel Management*, February.
21. Stevens, C. (1985). 'Assessment centres – the British experience', *Personnel Management*, July, pp. 28–31.

13
Promotions and transfers

As a follow-up to staff appraisal and for many other reasons, it is often necessary to move staff from one job to another within an organization. Such moves generally fall into one of two categories:

☐ promotions
☐ transfers

PROMOTIONS

Promotion occurs when an employee is transferred from one job to another, the new job involving greater responsibility, status, improved remuneration and often better working conditions. It demonstrates a management intention to fill a vacancy using talent already within the organization, rather than recruiting from outside. The benefits and problems associated with such a decision have already been discussed when considering recruitment policies (see Chapters 9 and 10).

For most staff, promotion prospects are important. Promotion offers opportunities for satisfaction of status and social needs, and may make more real the prospect of self actualization at work. However, it must not be assumed that all employees wish to be promoted. For some, the rewards may not be considered adequate recompense for additional responsibility. Others may feel that the effects on their social and domestic life will be too great; some may doubt their ability to cope with the additional load.

Nevertheless, whether individual staff wish to be promoted or not, it is important that an organization formulates a clear promotion policy and procedure.

Seniority versus ability

The major problem in formulating policy is determining an acceptable basis for promotion decisions. Normally policies are based on either ability or seniority, seniority in this sense meaning length of service. Each has its advantages and its advocates.

Although seniority rewards loyalty and long service it in no way guarantees able management. Indeed many able and willing staff may feel forced to seek employment elsewhere rather than wait for 'deadmen's shoes'. Though its effects on morale may be favourable, in as much as staff are not passed over, its effects on motivation may be less acceptable — staff knowing that their turn will come if they wait long enough. For these and other reasons management will normally wish to base its policy on ability, often in the face of employee or trade union pressure to adopt seniority.

Such pressure may prove irresistible unless management is able to demonstrate the fairness of its policy. Perhaps with some cause, it will often be assumed that persons are promoted not on grounds of merit but as a result of favouritism or for 'political' reasons. If these assumptions are to be disproved, it will be necessary to show that decisions have in fact been based on objective criteria such as regular staff appraisal reports, independent assessments or perhaps test or examination results.

In practice, a compromise may be the answer, many organizations giving preference to senior staff 'where all other things are equal'.

Selection for promotion

Having agreed the criteria for promotion, a further consideration must be how staff are to be selected. Again practice varies widely. In many organizations, promotions are determined by management and announced as a *fait accompli*: in others, vacancies are advertized internally, and employees wishing to be considered are invited to apply. Although the former has the advantage of speed and thus economy, such benefits may prove false economy if staff consider management's action in any way unfair or underhand. A policy of internally advertizing all vacancies is probably then to be recommended, except in cases where there is a natural successor or other special circumstances exist.

If such a policy is not to be devalued, staff must be free to apply for any vacancy for which they consider themselves suited, whether in their own department or not. However unwelcome the potential loss of an able member of staff may be, supervisors must resist the temptation to block applications or dissuade employees from applying. In order to guard against instability, however, it may be wise to insist that staff serve a specified period in a job before being free to apply for other posts.

Training for promotion

A policy of promotion from within is unlikely to benefit employer or employee unless a supply of properly trained staff exists from which to choose. Although many examples exist of staff learning by 'being thrown in at the deep end', such a policy suggests an abrogation of management's planning resonsibility and is unlikely to produce satisfactory results particularly in the short-term. Both in training and in any subsequent promotion, it is, of course, essential to ensure equal opportunity, unaffected by sex, creed, colour, race or marital status.

TRANSFERS

The need to transfer staff may occur for several reasons instigated by management or staff. Often the circumstances leading to a transfer are of a highly sensitive nature and so it is valuable if management has a considered and well known transfer policy to which to adhere.

Such a policy will normally make clear the circumstances in which a transfer will be permitted, arrangements for training and re-settlement, and the effects, if any, on pay and other benefits. In developing policy, account must of course, be taken of situations likely to make transfer necessary. The most common are briefly discussed below.

Fluctuations in demand for staff

In even the best ordered of organizations, demand for staff is likely to fluctuate. As a result, it is quite possible that an organization might have a surplus of staff in one area, and a shortage in another. Under such circumstances it may be mutually advantageous that staff be transferred.

As an alternative to redundancy the transfer may be welcomed. Even so, a worker moving to a new job will in most cases require a period of adjustment, during which time to unscramble a mixture of emotions and again seek to satisfy social, status and in particular, security needs. The problem will be particularly acute where an employee sees the transfer as a demotion, whether or not this is in fact the case.

Where demotion has occurred, it may be possible to soften the blow by continuing to pay the worker at his earlier, higher rate. Generally, however, this will only be viable where the transfer is seen as a short-term measure, or seems likely to be reconciled fairly quickly in some other way. In the long-term, such an arrangement is likely to cause dissent among other workers being paid at the normal, lower rate.

Staff development

Transfers may also be used as a means of planned staff development or training. By being transferred in accordance with a pre-determined plan, staff may be given the opportunity to experience or learn several different jobs. Such an arrangement not only potentially provides a multi-skilled and therefore more flexible labour force, but also enables staff to appreciate more fully their role and makes possible the introduction of job enlargement and enrichment programmes. In particular, job rotation is often used as part of a management development scheme (see Chapters 14 and 15).

Requests for transfer may also be made by individual members of staff anxious to broaden their experience. In such cases, every effort should be made to ensure that this is indeed a worker's true motive and that he is not using it as a convenient means of overcoming some other problem; also that he has the ability or aptitude to benefit from a transfer. Subject to these conditions, arrangements should be made wherever possible to comply with his wishes, since alternatively he may seek to satisfy his ambition elsewhere.

Staff ability or attitude

Occasionally it may become apparent that an employee is not suited for his current post. The problem may be one of faulty selection. It may be that an employee though once capable is no longer, owing to ill health or old age. Alternatively he may simply have been in a job too long and become disenchanted or bored. The problem may be one of attitude, an individual employee continually indulging in disruptive behaviour or failing to get on with his supervisor or colleagues.

Such cases will naturally have to be diagnosed and treated on their individual merits: older and disabled workers being treated with particular sympathy. Whatever the reason, transfers should never be seen as any easy solution or device by means of which supervisors may pass on their more troublesome or incompetent subordinates to an unsuspecting colleague.

14
Training

INTRODUCTION

Training in the UK has increasingly become part of a wider area of political debate and activity. Although many statements have been made about the need for employers to take responsibility for their own training, unemployment and a mismatch of skills has required a range of initiatives from the government over the last 20 years or so.

The Industrial Training Act 1964 set up the Industrial Training Boards (ITBs). These were charged with the task of stimulating training in their respective industrial sectors, setting standards and acting as a collection and redistribution agency for funds. The latter function created sufficient bureaucracy to detract from the others, and the Employment and Training Act 1973 greatly reduced the impact of the notorious 'levy/grant' system. Subsequently, it was decided that the ITBs were still too bureaucratic, and in 1981 the Secretary of State abolished 17 of the existing 23 boards.

The Manpower Services Commission and its successor, 'The Training Agency', have been charged with stimulating a range of training at national level and a plethora of initiatives have been forthcoming, the latest known as the Employment Training Programme (inevitably this has been shortened to 'ET' as with all the previous acronyms!).

Clearly, training has wide social and economic ramifications which many consider can only be dealt with at national level. Despite this, it is also apparent that a great deal of responsibility for the training and development of staff rests with employers.

The IPM Code of Practice on Continuous Development [1] states, *inter alia*, that if learning activity in an organization is to be fully beneficial both to the organization and its employees, the following conditions must be met:

☐ The organization must have some form of strategic business plan. It is desirable that the implications of the strategic plan, in terms of the skills and knowledge of the employees who will achieve it, should be spelled out.
☐ Managers must be ready and willing (and able) to define and meet needs as they appear, all learning needs cannot be anticipated; organizations must foster a philosophy of continuous development.

☐ As far as practicable, learning and work must be integrated; this means that encouragement must be given to all employees to learn from the problems, challenges and successes inherent in their day-to-day activities.

☐ The impetus for continuous development must come from the chief executive and other members of the top management team (the board of directors, for example); the top management team must regularly and formally review the way the competence of its management and workforce is being developed.

☐ Investment in continuous development must be regarded by the top management team as being as important as investment in research, new product development or capital equipment; it is not a luxury which can be afforded only in the 'good times', indeed the more severe the problems an organization faces, the greater the need for learning on the part of its employees and the more pressing the need for investment in learning.

LEARNING THEORY

Any person involved in the design of training courses or in the application of training techniques will not be fully prepared without a basic understanding of the learning process. A great deal of research has been carried out in this area, and it is only possible here to refer to some of the basic principles in the hope that those interested will read further on the subject [2].

Drive, stimulus, response, reinforcement

There are four generally accepted basic concepts which make up the learning situation.

Drive, or motivation, is obviously necessary if any activity is to take place. Human drives may be instinctive or learned, and in training programmes we are more likely to be concerned with meeting learned drives, such as the need for recognition or the satisfaction in mastering a job.

Stimulus is also necessary in order to elicit a response. In a commercial setting, these 'cues' may take various forms from a signal on a screen to the colour of a particular form or the appearance of a steel component. The tone of voice or expression of a colleague is also a typical stimulus.

Response to a stimulus is sometimes predictable, but in complex human situations it is often difficult to connect responses to specific stimuli. Howevver, it is necessary to learn to diagnose behaviour in terms of stimulus and response if training is to be effective.

A **reinforcer** is something that serves to increase or maintain the strength of a response. In human situations, examples are not difficult to find. Such things as money, promotion or praise are commonly used in the business environment.

Conditioning

Reinforcers, or rewards, feature strongly in a great deal of training that is based upon 'instrumental' conditioning. The work of B.F. Skinner involving animals is well known in this respect and forms the basis of a great deal of training methodology, particularly in physical skills. It has been found, for instance, that learning is more permanent when we reward correct behaviour only part of the time and not after every correct response. The timing of the reinforcement is also crucial: the closer it follows a correct action the more effective it is likely to be.

Knowledge of results

One of the most important stimulants to learning is feedback or knowledge of results. Whether the feedback is positive or negative, it is essential if behaviour is to be influenced sufficiently. If one is learning to shoot a rifle it would be impossible to adjust aim without knowing where the previous shot hit. Similarly, in a management context it would be extremely difficult if no feedback was received concerning the effects of the policies adopted.

Presentation

When presenting material or a task to a trainee, the question of partial or whole presentation may arise. The whole method of presentation is generally to be preferred where the intelligence of the learners is high and the material being studied is meaningful and unified. The part-presentation system has proved superior where a task involves a complex sequence of operations that are interdependent.

The length and frequency of training sessions could also be important. Generally, the spacing out of sessions is desirable, particularly with regard to physical skills, and the rest periods usually assist in respect of such things as fatigue, boredom and consolidation of learning. More intelligent or experienced trainees learning material that is meaningful may respond better to longer training sessions.

Guidance

Although trial-and-error learning is not often advocated, too much guidance may be an equally bad thing. Although a moderate amount of guidance is desirable in order to avoid the formation of bad habits, the trainee should be allowed to develop a certain amount of 'insight', particularly in the more complex situations. 'Discovery learning' can be extremely effective in encouraging participation and enthusiasm.

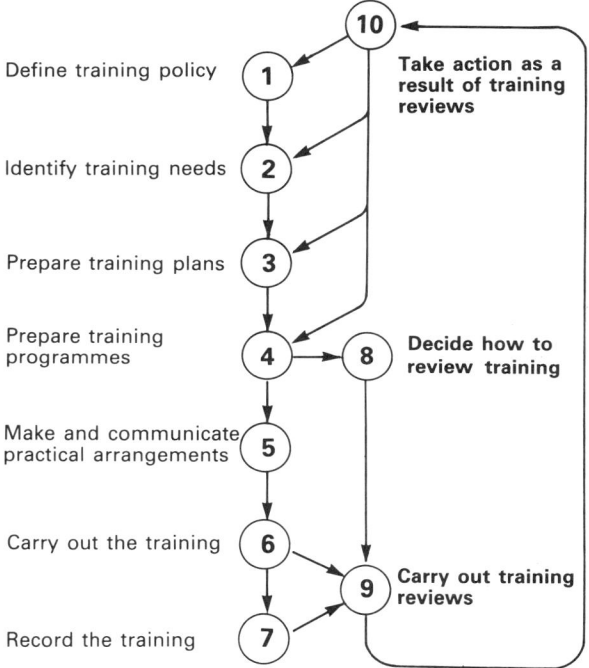

Fig. 14.1 A systematic approach to training (courtesy of HCITB)

Transfer of training

It is obviously important to know whether the knowledge or skill gained during training can be applied in the work situation, particularly when assessing off-the-job training. There are various theories concerning the transferability or otherwise of various types of training to different situations, but it is important to ensure that, as far as possible, the transfer is positive. It should be remembered that apart from having no effect at all, the learning in one situation could have a *negative* effect when transferred to another.

A SYSTEMATIC APPROACH TO TRAINING

If training within an organization is to be effective regarding both costs and results, a systematic approach is necessary. Although practical difficulties are recognized in following any methodical system, a framework similar to that illustrated in Fig. 14.1 is suggested if we are to avoid 'training for training's sake'.

Training policy

A training policy should be formulated to meet the organization's overall requirements in conjunction with policy in other areas. It will of necessity be in fairly broad terms, but this should not be an excuse for woolly, meaningless exhortations and ideals. The policy should include statements regarding:

- ☐ the links between the organization's overall objectives and training
- ☐ the purpose and priorities of training and resources to be committed
- ☐ the person(s) responsible for training
- ☐ the types of training to be developed, opportunities available to staff and general administration

A clear policy is vitally important both as a guide for those responsible for training and as a method of informing staff of management's intentions concerning the provision of training.

The letter and spirit of the Sex Discrimination Act 1975 and the Race Relations Act 1976 will also need to be incorporated in respect of training opportunities. (An example of a Training Policy statement is given in Chapter 1, page 8).

Training needs

'Training needs' can be considered at different levels:

Organizational

- ☐ What knowledge and skills are required now and in the future?
- ☐ What is the shortfall between the capabilities of our staff at present and what we require of them?
- ☐ How much training is required to get to the position we wish to reach?

Individual

- ☐ What is your job?
- ☐ How effectively can you do it at present?
- ☐ What will your job be in the future?
- ☐ What training if any do you require to:
  - (a) do the job as effectively as possible?
  - (b) cope with changes in the job?
  - (c) provide you with confidence and satisfaction?

The actual method of obtaining answers to these questions will be quite diverse. Corporate and manpower planning activities should give the answers to questions concerning general demands for knowledge and skills. The actual levels of performance of the workforce can be measured by various productivity indices available to the organization. These broad indications must be followed through at the individual level, however. Staff appraisal presents one opportunity to discuss any inadequacies in performance and to relate these to possible training initiatives. Other, less formal, discussions and meetings between staff and supervisors should also indicate individual or group training needs.

Training plan

Training plans may be prepared for a certain period of time or cover a particular training initiative. Training programmes will be incorporated into the plan together with details of the staff to be trained, the budget available and the person(s) responsible.

Training programmes

The term 'training programme' tends to suggest a library of prepared courses to which people are subjected at suitable intervals. Unfortunately that may be rather close to the truth in some organizations, but hopefully these are in a small minority. It is hoped that, by following the approach suggested in this chapter or something similar, training 'programmes' will be geared to the needs of the various categories of persons employed by the organization. It is obvious that these needs will vary a great deal, depending on the individuals or groups concerned and the particular problems that they face at any particular time. The training may involve updating and assimilation of knowledge or the learning of new skills. Whatever the training, each programme should at least specify its objectives, the timetable, methods and personnel involved, as well as methods of review.

Some of the more perennial training programmes are discussed below.

Induction training

This often consists of a short course or programme of items aimed at assisting new recruits to adjust to the organization and to provide them with background information. Typical courses include talks and films about the organization's structure and facilities and the provision of literature containing regulations and useful information. The degree of formality will depend upon the organization concerned but an induction course is normally considered valuable from a staff relations viewpoint (see also Chapter 10, page 146).

Apprenticeship

Apprenticeship schemes can cover a range of trainees from graduates to craft apprentices. Apart from initial training in respect of the organization and its systems, the prime objective is to develop a range of skills. This is usually achieved through a combination of on-the-job training and day-release or short courses at colleges or training centres. It is to be hoped that the period of apprenticeship will also provide ample opportunity for the acquired skills to be applied to various tasks and situations. One of the major criticisms of apprenticeships in the past has been the menial work and time wasting sometimes experienced by the participants, and many schemes have been improved accordingly.

Clerical/administrative training

This is often neglected area, owing sometimes to the lack of definition concerning the objectives of the jobs involved and the knowledge and skills required to do them efficiently. Much training takes place on an informal basis through the trainee's immediate superior or an experienced colleague. On-the-job training may be supplemented with in-company courses or the opportunity to obtain qualifications through day-release.

Much activity in recent years has centred upon the introduction of computerized office systems and information processing, where training is often shared by the manufacturers or designers of the systems.

Supervisory training

The supervisor has been referred to as 'the man in the middle'. In the modern industrial situation he can feel extremely isolated. He may feel that the shop steward is usurping his authority from below and that management does not give him the support he deserves. However, it is dangerous to generalize both in assessing the attitudes of supervisors and the provision of training. Although some problems will be common to many supervisors, others may be unique. It seems, therefore, logical to analyse the skills and knowledge required by the *individual* supervisor before providing training.

The problems that arise as a result of inter-personal relationships or organizational procedures are probably best dealt with internally. The best internal courses are participative and based upon real problems experienced by the supervisors concerned. They will also encourage co-operation with colleagues and help them to identify with other parts of the organization. Group discussions, case studies and projects are all appropriate training methods for this situation.

External courses may be useful for exposure to new ideas or management techniques. However, care must be taken in checking the relevance and utility of any proposed courses to the individual attending.

Management training

Management training and development has received much attention in recent years and requires a great deal of consideration. It is discussed more fully in Chapter 15.

Training methods

There are many training methods available, ranging from the tried and tested to more modern techniques. However, methodology should not be used for reasons of conformity or for the indulgence of trendy fads. It should be closely linked to the needs of the particular situation and based upon sound principles. Bass and Vaughan [3] suggest that a technique will be judged adequate to the extent that it appears likely to:

☐ provide for the learner's active participation
☐ provide the trainee with knowledge of results
☐ promote the transfer of training experience to the job
☐ provide reinforcement for appropriate behaviour
☐ provide for practice when needed
☐ motivate the trainee to improve his performance
☐ encourage the trainee to accept and adapt to change

Training may take place on-the-job or off-the-job, either internally or externally. Each of these environments will have advantages for particular applications, and the venue will be one of the considerations when deciding upon methods. It is not possible to discuss the many training techniques used in any detail in a book of this nature and further reading is recommended. However, a brief summary of some of the more common methods is given below.

'Sitting next to Nelly'

This probably is still the most common method of training. Learning by demonstrations and example, as well as 'learning by doing', are at the centre of this approach. Main problems are that the training is rarely planned and 'Nelly' may not set a good example.

Job rotation

Traditionally employed for management trainees or 'high flyers' in order to provide experience of a wide range of operations within an organization. If the programme is not carefully planned and administered a great deal of time may be wasted.

Job instruction

Job instruction training was developed during World War II as a systematic approach for use by supervisors when training subordinates. It is based upon four steps that consist of preparing the trainee, presenting the knowledge, allowing the trainee to perform the job and following up by checking performance. It is a logical approach, and forms the basis of a great deal of traditional training.

Lectures, talks and discussions

These are probably among the most common methods of transmitting information and can be formal or informal. Although lectures are an economic method of communication, they should be supplemented with other methods of learning. Informal discussions and talks may provide more opportunities for participation by trainees.

Case studies

These may be used on an individual or group basis. Their main advantage is in presenting trainees with 'real life' problems with which they may be able to identify. They should be stimulating and relevant to the learning objectives.

Role playing

Normally used in supervisory and management training. A background situation is provided and the participants assume the roles of persons involved. It is usually hoped to strengthen inter-personal skills and to provide an insight into the different viewpoints and interests represented. Commitment on the part of trainees and positive criticism are required if the method is to be successful.

Simulation

Apart from the pure forms of simulation, such as vestibule training, 'in basket' exercises and business games have been developed. These are a development of the case study and role play, and attempt to simulate real-life situations as far as possible. They can constitute an extremely stimulating experience and will also encourage learning provided they are properly designed and administered.

Films, video

Many organizations use visual aids, such as training films and videos, as part of their training programmes. The visual impact and humour of many of the modern productions provide a valuable contribution to many types of training. There is a danger of using this form of communication at the expense of a properly planned training module, but provided clear objectives are set there is no reason for this to occur [4].

Computer based training (CBT)

Computers were introduced to training many years ago as part of 'programmed learning' schemes. The computer is good at imparting standard information and enabling the trainee to check the degree to which he has assimilated the particular knowledge or skill. New technology can, however, be used in a range of applications of training. It is particularly suited to training that has a high procedural content, but it can also be linked to other equipment in order to assess performance. British Gas is currently assessing the use of CBT across a range of training activities [5]. It is, of course, appropriate for those working in remote locations such as gas rigs.

Training records

In order to control training activity and costs, proper records are required. Training received by each employee should be recorded to provide data for manpower audit purposes.

Evaluation of training

Sir David Orr, chairman of Unilever, summed up the problem of evaluating training. Referring to the £100 million his company would be spending on training in the current year he stated: 'we are less able to calculate the return on that expenditure than we are for any other investment'. Nevertheless, the amount of expenditure indicates the degree of Unilever's commitment to training, and Sir David advocated the improvement of methodology.

Despite this note of pessimism concerning the difficult subject of evaluation, those responsible for training should not adopt a defeatist attitude. If training is to be as effective as possible, some attempt at evaluation must be made. In view of the huge amounts of money spent on various training techniques, the amount of time and money spent assessing their effectiveness is relatively small. Often it does not stretch beyond asking the trainees or their supervisor whether or not they think they have learned anything.

How, therefore, should the problem of evaluation be tackled? Several approaches have been suggested by different writers and a great deal of academic research has also been carried out.

Bass and Vaughan [6] regard the problem as twofold:

1 To determine whether the training procedures actually result in the desired modification of employees' behaviour.
2 To determine whether the training outcome has any demonstrable relationship to the achievement of the organization's goals.

It is also recognized, however, that it is desirable to know firstly, whether the techniques employed are the most effective and secondly, how the effectiveness of training compares to other approaches to developing the capability of the workforce, such as improving selection procedures or re-designing jobs.

Hamblin [7] suggests that the problem of improving the evaluation of training can be described in three questions:

☐ How can we improve the criteria by which training is evaluated (i.e., how do we pick on the *right* training objectives?)
☐ How can we improve our methods for gathering the information on the basis of which we evaluate the training?
☐ How can we use the evaluation to improve the training?
(It will be noted from Fig. 14.1 that methods of review are decided *before* the training is carried out.)

All three questions are inter-connected, and they all require an answer if the evaluation is to contribute towards improving overall performance. What evaluation procedures can be employed therefore?

Hamblin refers to five levels at which evaluation can take place:

1 **Reactions**. This refers to the trainees' response to the training. It can only serve as a useful measure if the trainer knows what type of reaction he is seeking. The sole objective may be to obtain the reaction 'I enjoyed that!', and if this is the case the reaction level of evaluation will be quite adequate.

2 **Learning**. Most training will have certain 'learning objectives' and they will be evaluated by an assessment of skills or knowledge gained at the termination of the training course.

3 **Job behaviour**. Apart from an assessment of terminal behaviour it will be necessary to evaluate whether there has been a transfer of learning to the actual job and whether or not this is sustained.

4 **Organization**. This level goes beyond job behaviour and tries to evaluate the effects of training upon the organization in respect of such things as quality of work, productivity and morale.

5 **Ultimate value**. This refers to the affects upon the ultimate goals of the organization whether it uses financial criteria to measure the cost effectiveness of training or, in the case of a less profit motivated organization, as an indication of the growth of individuals, which may in turn benefit the organization as a whole.

The five levels are, it is suggested, links in a chain. Training leads to reaction which leads to learning which leads to changes in job behaviour which lead to changes in the organization which lead to changes in the achievement of ultimate goals. Although most managers would prefer to evaluate training at levels 4 and 5 only, it will be apparent that this is extremely difficult, and in some cases impossible. There are so many other variables affecting organizational goals that it is difficult to isolate the training input. However, sensible evaluation at the lower levels may give some indication of these effects, and it is in any case a valuable exercise to ensure that none of the links in the chain has snapped.

A broad discussion of American research and opinion concerning the problems of training evaluation, particularly in respect of management training, is contained in a book by Campbell et al. [8]. It reviews the whole spectrum of viewpoints from the 'pragmatic' to the 'scientific'. The latter group includes Soloman and MacKinney who take the view that unless proper control groups are set up in order to check results, there is little point in bothering to evaluate training at all. On the other hand, researchers such as Andrews consider that the opinions of the trainees themselves and their associates are the most practical and useful method of assessment. Whatever methodology we use, the basic problems will remain. It would appear that we must continue to ask the three questions posed by Hamblin in the hope that the answers are forthcoming.

REFERENCES

1. Institute of Personnel Management (1987). *National Committee for Training and Development*. IPM.
2. For a succinct review see Bass, B.M. and Vaughan, J.A. (1973). *Training in Industry: The Management of Learning*. Tavistock Institute.
3. Bass, B.M. and Vaughan, J.A. (1973). *Training in Industry: The Management of Learning*, Chapter 7. Tavistock Institute.
4. Roberts, K. (1984). 'The slide to video', *Personnel Management*, April.
5. Rinn, B. (1984). 'Taking stock of computer based learning', *Personnel Management*, June.
6. Bass, B.M. and Vaughan, J.A. (1973). *Training in Industry: The Management of Learning*, p. 140. Tavistock Institute.
7. Hamblin, A.C. (1974). *Evaluation and Control of Training*. McGraw-Hill.
8. Campbell, J.P., Dunnette, M.D., Lawler, E.E. and Weick, K.E. (1970). *Managerial Behaviour Performance and Effectiveness*, Chapter 12. McGraw-Hill.

15
Management development

One of the best definitions of management development we have encountered comes from a management statement of a large brewing company. Management development is regarded as:

> a series of processes, activities and events in the company which are designed to improve performance now and in the future and to provide for future management needs

Although a rather lengthy definition, it does pick up several important points concerning the objectives and activities of management development. Firstly, it makes clear that development is a continuing activity. Secondly, it indicates that it is much more than training. Also, there is a clear impression of development for both the needs of the organization and the individual manager.

THE DEVELOPMENT PROGRAMME

Most management development programmes will use various techniques to achieve certain objectives in line with the organization's overall plans and policies. These objectives would normally include:

- ☐ the improvement of current job performance
- ☐ the development of potential in order to meet contingencies and to succeed to higher posts
- ☐ the motivation of managers through the setting of performance criteria and suitable rewards
- ☐ the creation of a climate which is conducive to individual growth and self development

The last of these objectives stresses the need to take into account individual views and requirements. The word 'programme' should be interpreted as a planned strategy rather than a rigid regime to which all are subjected.

Organizational needs

The organization's needs for managers in the right number and with appropriate skills should be part of the manpower planning process (see Chapter 7). Information concerning forthcoming retirements or transfers can be used to predict vacancies and to prepare candidates accordingly. However, even in the short-term, managers can resign or suffer ill health and those chosen as 'first line' successors may be amongst this number. In view of this, any planning must contain a degree of flexibility and should not concentrate solely on immediate successors.

In the longer term, the matching of posts with 'likely successors' will become even more difficult. Those responsible for management development will need to concern themselves with developing a sufficient number of managers at various levels to meet the anticipated general need. It is more prudent to approach development on a broad front than endeavour to groom one or two 'high flyers' for specific jobs.

Individual needs

Having considered the organization's needs for a supply of trained and capable managers we must now turn to the individual and his ability to fulfil these needs. In order to assess the manager's abilities and inadequacies, a combination of counselling and appraisal will be required. Some developmental techniques, such as management by objectives (MBO), incorporate a regular appraisal as part of the methodology. Apart from appraising the manager's present performance, it will also be necessary to consider his potential.

Potential appraisal is best kept separate from performance appraisal in the view of some commentators. It is a key operation for succession planning, and is often carried out by a manager at least twice senior to the person being appraised. This is considered advisable in order to reduce any subjectivity that may be shown by an immediate boss and also to introduce a person with knowledge of more senior posts. The job is sometimes carried out by a small panel that will include a senior personnel manager.

The assessment of potential will be based upon track record, various reports and sometimes upon a 'potential' appraisal interview. This is fraught with similar pitfalls to those of the performance appraisal interview (see Chapter 12, page 171), but it is necessary if an exchange of views concerning aspirations and training needs is to take place. The appraisal should, *inter alia*, produce the following information:

- [ ] the level of the manager's motivation for advancement
- [ ] his willingness to take responsibility
- [ ] his ability to communicate
- [ ] the areas of skill and knowledge which need to be developed

☐   details of any remedial training required

Assessment centres

A more objective method of potential assessment would be through the use of 'assessment centres'. These are basically sessions that managers attend and participate in various tests and projects. The activities will have been planned to reflect the qualities required for management posts at a higher level and will normally be assessed by senior managers from the organization concerned or occasionally by external consultants. It is considered that assessment centres predict potential more accurately than other methods of assessment. They are not widely used in the UK, due partly to the cost of organizing appropriate sessions that will possibly last for two or three days. However, usage is increasing particularly by larger organizations. Apart from the assessment of potential, they are also considered to be beneficial to the managers participating in the activities. The development aspects of assessment centres should not, therefore, be overlooked.

An individual programme

After both performance and potential appraisal, the areas of training and development must be identified together with a suitable method for achieving them. There are four main areas of skills that can be acquired:

☐   technical (knowledge)
☐   administrative
☐   social
☐   decision making

The first two are specific, the last two general, and because of this a great deal of attention has been given to the latter in many management training programmes. It is important, however, not to over-generalize at the expense of specialist training, which may be crucial for certain situations.

As a minimum, most managers will require the following from a management development programme:

1   To know what is expected of him.
2   To be given an opportunity to perform — 'self-development' cannot take place if too many restrictions are placed on managers or no challenge provided.
3   To know how he is doing — through both formal and informal review and feedback.
4   To receive guidance when required.
5   To be rewarded according to his contributions — managers

cannot be expected to develop without incentive. This might include 'non-reward' of poor performance.

TECHNIQUES

There are a great many methods of training and developing managers each with their own followers. There has been a significant growth of 'packages' in recent years that endeavour to train 'en masse' in the hope that the individual manager will gain something. Although these often appear attractive to the personnel manager of an organization wishing to develop its managers, care should be taken in the seletion of courses.

External courses

As stated, there is a whole range of courses available run by various organizations and covering the spectrum of specific and general skills. Apart from checking out the reputation of organizers, the personnel manager must satisfy himself that the courses selected meet both the organization's criteria and the needs of those participating in the course.

The Coverdale Organization is one of several offering 'self-development' programmes. The methodology is based largely on group discussions and exercises that are designed to bring out the strengths and weaknesses of the individuals concerned and to encourage new approaches to problem solving and working with others. The sessions usually last for one week, and two or more sessions are recommended, separated by a longer period performing normal work duties.

External courses have an obvious appeal to both the training manager and the participants, but they should not become a 'soft option' that does not stand up to proper evaluation.

Internal courses

Many larger organizations have established their own management training facilities in which a range of advanced techniques is used. The main advantage of internal courses is that they can be directed more specifically towards the needs of the organization and indeed the individuals concerned. The courses may combine on-the-job training with more formal short courses and packages. Many consider that there is no substitute for actually 'doing the job', and many organizations arrange for managers to be exposed to as much 'experience' as possible. This might include project work, secondments, conferences, group work and job rotation.

'Action learning'

One advocate of 'learning by doing' is Reg Revans. He has devised 'action learning projects' for many managers from different organizations. This may involve a spell of several months in a different division or even with an entirely different organization. During this period they will endeavour to tackle problems without the normal constraints of hierarchy or pre-conceived ideas. Revans takes a radical view of management education, and the following are amongst the propositions he puts forward [1]:

☐ men and women learn only when they want to learn . . . not at the will of bosses who send them off on courses . . .
☐ learning is a social process, that in solving together some problem of common interest the learners help each other . . .
☐ it is barren to argue without testing one's conclusions in specific action (a criticism of case studies, etc.)
☐ even deliberate action is a waste of time unless its specific consequences are assessed against a set of declared expectations

Revans' arguments have powerful appeal to the 'common sense' of the practical manager. However, advocacy of one particular approach usually tends to over-simplify the situation.

T-group training

Also referred to as 'laboratory training' or 'sensitivity training', T-group training aims to develop increased awareness of self and others within the participating group. Programmes were developed in the USA during the 1940s at the National Training Laboratories and these have now been adapted and used over a wide range of countries and organizations. Although the types of programme and their objectives and methodology vary greatly, there follows a brief description of the subject in the hope that those interested will read further from the wide range of literature available [2].

T-group sessions usually involve a small discussion group that meets under the direction of a 'trainer'. He will take no part in the discussions, except for a short introduction or where he feels that intervention is required. The main objectives of the exercise are to increase the participants' awareness of their own feelings and reactions towards others and to help them to deal with inter-personal relations. This may involve a change in attitudes owing to the often intimate nature of the discussions.

The sessions may last for anything from a couple of hours to two weeks or more, but the average duration would probably be two days. Although in the early days laboratory training dealt mainly with 'stranger' groups, i.e., people drawn from different organizations, increasing attention is being given to 'cousin' or 'family' groups where the participants are drawn from the same organization, or even the same department. Apart from the objectives for the individual, it is also hoped to concentrate more on team building and organizational problems in the latter cases.

Although T-group training has been practised for many years now and is regarded by many as extremely beneficial, it still has its critics. Because the discussions can become extremely intense and personal, those who are sensitive or emotionally unstable may become distressed and could suffer from the experience. It is therefore essential that the participants should be screened before commencement and that the 'trainer' is himself trained to conduct the session.

Finally, the validity of T-group training is brought into question. Proponents argue that, properly conducted, the experience is beneficial to the participants and assists in dealing with human relations problems. However, apart from the problems of proper control and the negative effects that are experienced in some cases, the most contentious point is the transfer of training. One of the main problems appears to be the fact that the laboratory is culturally far removed from the workplace, and if the effects are to be felt at organizational level the training will need to be adapted in order to reach a wider audience.

Management by objectives

Management by objectives (MBO) is a widely used method of management development. Its strongest advocates are Drucker and Odiorne in the USA and Humble in the UK. A great deal of literature and films are available extolling its virtues and describing the basic process:

1 The manager discusses and agrees the objectives of his job for a future period with his boss. Certain specific goals or targets will be agreed in line with overall organizational objectives and special consideration will be given to the manager's contribution to improving performance.

2 At the expiry of the period they will jointly review performance as compared with the objectives.

3 Problem areas are discussed and areas for improvement are agreed. New targets are set for the subsequent period.

This process requires a great deal of co-operation and understanding on the part of participants and some systems introduce an 'advisor' who sits in on the objective setting discussions in order to ensure that targets are realistic.

The main proponents of MBO consider that its basic philosophy is fundamental to good management. It can incorporate many elements including motivation, appraisal, reward, participation and planning. However, there is a danger of following the system too rigidly without the true commitment of top management or of attempting to install a 'partial system'. In its most bureaucratic form the system can become extremely complex and laden with paperwork. Humble [3] has stated:

> . . . at its best, MBO is a system that integrates the company's goals of profit and growth with the manager's needs to contribute and develop himself personally . . . it is not a new wonder tool that can replace intelligent or sensitive leadership and its misuse can cause more harm than good.

Job rotation

Although rapid job rotation of management trainees has fallen into disfavour in recent years, properly planned job experience with different departments can provide useful contributions to the development of some managers.

Coaching

Many managers and supervisors gain a great deal from working for a boss who is prepared to give them guidance and responsibility. Coaching, however, involves more than merely understudying a boss who may or may not be interested in the development of his subordinate. It requires commitment by both parties to a planned programme of practical development that will include regular interviews at which progress and problems can be discussed. Much will depend on the personalities of the parties involved and the ability of the manager responsible for coaching. For a detailed discussion of this technique, see Singer's book on the subject [4].

CONCLUSION

Many of the techniques outlined above are potentially useful. They should not however be adopted as panaceas for organizational ill-health. The development of managers involves the creation of a climate in which they can grow and gain from the challenge and experience of their day-to-day work. This task cannot be delegated to the personnel manager or the training officer. It requires a firm commitment from top management to provide the opportunities and rewards which will encourage managers to reach their full potential (see also Organization Development, page 363).

REFERENCES

1. Revans, R. (1980). *Action Learning.* Blood & Briggs.
2. Simpson, B. (1984). 'T-Groups, T.A., N.L.P. . . .', *Personnel Management,* November.
3. Humble, J. (1972). *Manangement by Objectives.* BIM.
4. Singer, E.J. (1979). *Effective Management Coaching,* 2nd Edn. IPM.

PART 4: FURTHER RECOMMENDED READING

Pratt, K.J. (1985). *Effective Staff Appraisal — a Practical Guide.* Van Nostrand Reinhold.
Randell, G.A. *et al.* (1985). *Staff Appraisal* 2nd Edn. IPM.
Anstey, E. *et al.* (1976). *Staff Appraisal and Development.* George Allen & Unwin.
Fowler, A. (1983). *Getting Off to a Good Start.* IPM.
Pepper, A.D. (1984). *Managing the Training and Development Function.* Gower. *A Guide to Systematic Training.* (1982). HCITB.
Revans, R.W. (1971). *Developing Effective Managers: A New Approach to Business Education.* Longman.
Roberts, T.J. (1974). *Developing Effective Managers.* IPM.
Hague, H. (1973). *Management Training for Real.* IPM.

PART 4: SAMPLE EXAMINATION QUESTIONS

If you were designing a performance appraisal procedure, how would you go about it? What sort of appraisal procedure would you advocate, and why? (Answer this question by reference to a specific organization or organizations.)
ICSA

Examine the advantages and disadvantages of a policy of promoting from within the organization as opposed to the alternative of recruiting from outside. How might the disadvantages be overcome?
ICSA

As senior manager of an established company, you feel that there is a case for a more formalized executive promotion policy. Justify your case and describe what you consider are the main objectives of such a policy and the techniques required to put it into effect.
IAM

(a) 'A sound performance appraisal scheme is an essential requirement for management development to be effective.' Disuss.
(b) What other functions does an appraisal scheme fulfil in an organization?
CBSI

'Good managers make good managers.' Discuss the validity of this proposition, with particular reference to the benefits to be derived from formal management training/development programmes.
ICSA

'Performance appraisal is a waste of time if it consists principally of an assessment of performance over the past twelve months; it should concentrate more or less exclusively on planning for the future.' Discuss.
ICSA

Outline what you would consider to be appropriate objectives and suitable content for an induction training programme to be administered to all new employees in the head office of a large multi-national enterprise. How might the effectiveness of such a training programme be evaluated and validated?
ICSA

Comment on the likely differences in perception when determining the training needs of individual employees as compared with those of the employing organization. IPM

Six months ago a regional manager of your bank decided to introduce a rating system for employees based on the following qualities:

loyalty, dependability, initiative, interest in work and sense of responsibility.

These ratings were to be used for appraisal and counselling purposes, to identify training needs and promotion possibilities, and as a factor in salary adjustments. The decision was conveyed by letter to all the managers who might be involved in the rating system and the letter also stated that the system would function from the first day of the next month.

When employees heard the news there were immediate protests. The Staff Association made urgent representations to head office, who were taken by surprise, not having been party to the introduction of the scheme. (Regional managers in the bank are encouraged to develop their own ways of appraising staff in their territory.) The regional manager said that he thought the scheme, which he had come across while attending a management course, was a distinct improvement on the existing bank-wide appraisal system. He also said that it was the duty of management to manage and not to be thrown off course because of protests from the Staff Associations on matters of no concern to them.

You have been asked to advise on this problem.

What is your analysis and what would you propose? CIB

Why are periodic individual appraisals important? What would you expect to be included in such an appraisal for an accountant? CACA

In your bank you are a supervisor who is responsible for the induction training of new recruits.

What arrangements would you make for the effective induction of a trainee who has just left school:

(a) when he visits the bank immediately before starting work
(b) during his first year of employment

Your answer should indicate the various people you would expect to be involved in the induction process, and bring out clearly the reasons for their involvement. CIB

(a) What methods exist for identifying the training requirements of an organization?
(b) Why is it important to identify training needs? CBSI

What are the benefits of evaluating training? How would you ensure evaluation is carried out effectively? CBSI

What elements are there in a systematic approach to training policy? Illustrate your answer with examples. CBSI

What are the arguments for and against linking performance appraisal with BOTH
(a) Promotion decisions, and
(b) Pay decisions?   IPM

How can systems of performance appraisal be effectively linked with management development?   IPM

'Performance appraisal is unassailable in theory, but unworkable in practice'. Discuss this verdict, preferably using the example of your own organization or another with which you are familiar.   ICSA

(a) What do you understand by the systematic approach to training?

   (Illustrate your answer with references to the training of a specific type of employee, such as copy-typists, engineering apprentices, or sales represent-atives. Note that these categories are only examples quoted for illustrative purposes, and the candidate is free to use other instances if desired.)

(b) Why is the systematic approach occasionally ignored, either as a whole or in part?   ICSA

(a) For what purposes may an organization institute a policy of systematically appraising staff performance?
(b) describe TWO of the following methods of appraising staff performance:
      (i) Ranking or rating
      (ii) Critical incidents
      (iii) Management by objectives   IAM

Prepare a statement of policy for use by the training function of an organization.
                                                                                IAM

(a) In relation to administrators, review the respective merits and de-merits of training
      (i) On the job
      (ii) Off the job.
(b) Describe in each case, two techniques of 'off' and 'on the job' training applicable to management development.   IAM

What does the phrase 'management development' mean? How is it best accomplished?   ICSA

By what means should an organization determine (a) when operational problems justify formal training solutions, and (b) how to make use of normal work activities as training opportunities?   IPM

Part 5
Rewards and incentives

16
Money and motivation

INCENTIVE THEORY

Dictionary definitions of the word incentive include 'motivator' and 'incitement to action'. The motivational force of an incentive is therefore crucial, and ideally no organization should administer 'incentives' in ignorance of their true effectiveness. But this is easier said than done. Motivation in general is discussed elsewhere, and we shall confine ourselves to incentives in the context of wages, salaries and fringe benefits in this section.

The great debate

Does money motivate? Is it irrelevant? Where does it rank compared with other incentives? These questions have been the basis of a great deal of controversy and research over many years. Despite the work of Mayo, Maslow and Herzberg, many industrialists still lean towards Taylor's view of 'rational-economic' man. However, productivity, if this is the objective, is made up of many ingredients apart from monetary reward. Even Taylor's famous Dutchman was also subjected to changes in work method and tool design.

Theory and practice

At the theoretical level, Vroom's expectancy theory of motivation provides a logical view of money as an incentive. He considers that the motivational effect of money will depend on how badly an individual needs to attain certain goals and the extent to which he considers that money will be instrumental in helping him to achieve them. Drawing upon expectancy theory, Porter and Lawler [1] have contributed an important viewpoint to this subject. They consider that pay *is* an important incentive and one that can satisfy needs at all of Maslow's famous levels. The following are some of the principles they consider crucial if pay is to act as a true incentive:

1 Pay must be geared to performance.
2 Pay must be seen to be geared to performance.

3 Employees must be informed of how their pay and any increases are evaluated.
4 Sufficient information should be made available to enable individuals to compare their pay with that of their colleagues.

The last point was found to cause a great deal of anxiety in those questioned during research, and secrecy is considered by Porter and Lawler to be no substitute for a properly evaluated system. It should be said, however, that a totally 'open' system could also create obvious problems in some circumstances.

Why incentive schemes go wrong

A great deal of empirical work has been carried out in order to investigate the incentive effects of money and to try to discover why some incentive schemes appear to succeed whereas others fail. It appears that many schemes in the past have been ineffective largely owing to poor communications and mistrust. Apart from the well-known bank wiring room observations, both Roy [2] and Whyte [3] have spent long periods working alongside employees on various bonus and piecework schemes. The often unfounded mistrust appears to lead to social norms, and group pressures are brought to bear upon the individual, leading to restricted production and 'gold-bricking'. Lawler [4] describes this situation diagramatically as in Fig. 16.1.

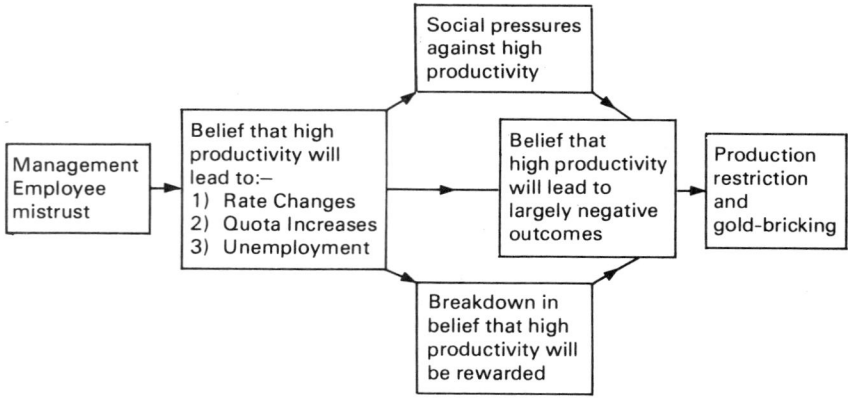

Fig. 16.1

ATTITUDES

In Britain the work of Goldthorpe *et al.* [5] at Vauxhall Motors highlighted an interesting view of the workers' attitude to work and money. Many production workers did not appear concerned with the intrinsic quality of their work, provided that they could maximize their earnings in order to pursue their particular interests outside work. Although this may appear a natural attitude for those engaged in monotonous work, McDougall [6] found in a study involving over 2500 executives, that money also came high up the list of incentives for most of them. The latter study also confirmed Lawler's view that financial reward should be seen to be linked to individual performance if it is to act as an incentive.

To state that money is an incentive is not enough. We have seen that in the wrong climate the statement does not in any case hold good. The problem remains complex. It is about objectives, individual attitudes, social and political pressures, and of course, physical and mental capabilities. Pay systems must endeavour to meet the objectives of the organization by using the knowledge gained to date concerning the ability of money to motivate while recognizing the practical limitations.

STAFF STATUS/HARMONIZATION

In many organizations, a clear distinction is still made between 'weekly paid' and 'salaried' staff. The obvious distinctions between wage earners and salaried staff relating to the frequency and method of payment are by no means the most significant. The whole basis of calculating the reward is often different and it has been said that an employee receives wages for 'what he does' whereas a salary contains a considerable element for 'what he is'. This whole question is fundamental to the calculation of job worth to the organization, and its roots lie largely in tradition rather than with any objective rationale. Traditionally, salaried staff have received better terms of employment regarding such things as hours, holiday, pensions, etc., although the increasing scope of collective bargaining is narrowing these differentials in many cases. Even so, new fringe benefits are constantly introduced, particularly in the case of senior salaried staff, and these are discussed below. Despite the fact that some large organizations, including ICI and the Central Electricity Generating Board, are providing salaried status for all employees and that the salaried proportion of the workforce is growing, the continued differentiation that remains in many organizations is considered by many to be devisive. It is seen as a perpetuation of the 'them and us' situation that exists between salaried staff and manual workers, which is described by writers, such as Lockwood in his 'The Blackcoated Worker' [7].

There are, of course, many social pressures for the maintenance of segregated pay systems, some based upon traditions of 'cash in hand'. Despite the fact that the remaining *statutory* rights to this form of pay have been removed by the Wages Act 1986, questions of overtime, etc. will remain areas of contention.

Despite these difficulties, increasing numbers of employers are moving towards 'harmonization' of terms and conditions of employment. Apart from attempting to eliminate some of the problems referred to above, the aim is to increase the flexibility of the workforce by breaking down barriers between groups. It is, of course, also administratively desirable to reduce the variations in terms and conditions and to pay all staff by cashless methods. Provided that these changes are properly introduced through consultation and negotiation, there is no reason why both staff and the employer should not benefit. In the context of what has been discussed in this chapter we shall now consider various aspects of pay administration.

REFERENCES

1. Porter, L.W. and Lawler, E.E. (1968). *Managerial Attitudes and Performance*. Irwin-Dorsey.
2. Roy, D. (1955). 'Efficiency and the Fix.' *American Journal of Sociology* Vol. 60.
3. White, W.F. (1955). *Money and Motivation*. Harper & Row.
4. Lawler, E.E. (1971). *Pay and Organisational Effectiveness: A Psychological View*. McGraw-Hill.
5. Goldthorpe, J.H. *et al.* (1968). *The Affluent Worker: Industrial Attitudes and Behaviour*. Cambridge University Press.
6. McDougall, M. in White, M. (1975). *Motivating Managers Financially*. IPM.
7. Lockwood, D. (1966). *The Blackcoated Worker*. Unwin.

17
Job evaluation

We would define job evaluation as:

a *systematic* method of assessing the *relative* worth of a range of *jobs* as the basis for a pay structure.

Some words in this definition have been stressed to make the following points:

- [ ] Job evaluation is systematic to a greater or lesser extent but it cannot claim to be scientific. Subjectivity and judgement are involved.
- [ ] Job evaluation is concerned with relationships, not absolute values. The worth of a job to an employer is affected by markets, negotiations and other factors.
- [ ] Job evaluation is only concerned with the job. Individual effort or performance must be rewarded separately if this is appropriate.

Uses

Job evaluation can be used in any situation where for one reason or another pay relativities between various jobs have become anomalous or 'unfair'. This could be due to technological change, which has caused concomitant changes in the content of different jobs. It could also be the result of an outdated pay system that has been allowed to drift into a state of confusion and decay. Management may have negotiated piecemeal settlements with different groups of workers owing to particular pressures. Whatever the motive for carrying out the job evaluation exercise, if done properly it should provide a framework that staff are able to understand and that is capable of absorbing new jobs and changes in job content as they arise.

Limitations

Despite its advantages, job evaluation is not free from criticism. It is accused of disguising what is inevitably a subjective operation with a plethora of 'pseudo-scientific mumbo jumbo'. Although this is hardly fair criticism of well administered schemes, any job evaluation exercise has its limitations.

Job evaluation can only effectively provide a structure to which basic rates of pay can be attached. It therefore becomes less appropriate where pay is to be based largely upon performance. Neither is it concerned with absolute wage levels or the actual difference in pay between one job and another. These can only be determined by other factors, such as supply and demand of labour, custom and practise, the relative bargaining strength of the job holders and the ability of the employer to pay.

Advantages

According to ACAS [1], a properly introduced and maintained job evaluation scheme can lay the foundation for fair and orderly pay structures and thus improve the climate of industrial relations. More specifically, it is suggested that job evaluation can help management, unions and workers:

☐   establish acceptable differences in the wage rates between jobs, thus removing any existing anomalies and inequities in pay
☐   create simpler, more easily understandable, pay structures
☐   reduce the number of grievances over relative wages
☐   provide a yardstick by which grievances or claims about jobs can be judged, and so help avoid arbitrary decisions
☐   lessen time spent on dealing with such grievances and claims
☐   fit new jobs into existing pay structures, thus easing technological and organizational change

The analytical process that forms an integral part of most job evaluation schemes is usually a salutory experience in itself. It often highlights problems in areas such as selection, training and working methods.

THE JOB EVALUATION PROCESS

The introduction of a job-evaluated pay system from drawing board to implementation can take many months. A programme will have to be carefully drawn up to cover the various stages of the operation.

Preparatory

Consultation and communication are probably the key words for the successful introduction of a job evaluation scheme. The job is often given to a group or committee, and where the employees are represented by trade unions it would appear sensible to form the committee on a joint basis. This committee can then investigate the feasibility of a scheme and, if appropriate, decide upon a strategy for its introduction.

Among the tasks of the committee will be the selection of a method most appropriate to the circumstances prevailing within the organization. It will then have to prepare a strategy to deal with such things as policy, communications and consultation. Procedures will have to be established to deal with the mass of detailed investigation and negotiation that will almost certainly be necessary. A certain amount of initial training may also be required for some of the members of the committee in the technical problems of introducing a scheme. It is as well to be forewarned of difficulties by someone with experience of similar programmes.

Analysis and assessment

Following communication with the workforce concerning the objectives and mechanics of the exercise it will be necessary to commence the spadework. A great deal of detailed job analysis may be necessary, and although existing records could provide a good foundation for this work, the analysis for job evaluation purposes may require a particular format. It is also important to agree any job description with the employees and their union representatives if appeals at a later date are to be kept to a minimum.

Once every job in the system has been analysed, the evaluation process can commence. The degree of difficulty will depend upon a combination of factors including the size of the organization and the number of jobs involved, the method being used and the degree of unity amongst members of the committee. As already stated, several subjective elements will be brought to bear upon this part of the operation, and it can become an extremely lengthy process.

Building and pricing the structure

Following the evaluation of individual jobs and the establishment of their relationships to each other, it is usual to divide the spectrum of jobs into some kind of graded structure. 'Natural' grading points sometimes present themselves, and grades may be formed around 'benchmark' jobs where these have been identified. The grading system may throw up further anomolies within the original evaluation and these will have to be reconciled. It must be remembered that traditional relationships represent a strong influence upon decisions at this stage. Too much downgrading is, of course, also considered undesirable.

Now comes the crucial operation of placing the new grades against the monetary scale. From the union side, there will obviously be considerable pressure for the new grades to be placed as high up the scale as possible, and a certain amount of 'overlapping' of scales is normal. It must be remembered that until this stage of the operation, monetary values have not been consciously considered under some schemes. The exercise has merely involved the comparative value of one job with another, based upon job content criteria.

Negotiation, implementation and control

Although the stated objectives of most job evaluation schemes do not include the improvement of actual pay levels, in practice the employees and their representatives will usually be looking for some improvement in pay. The actual pay levels for the new grades will be the subject of negotiation, but owing to the number of upgradings that tend to take place, the overall wage bill will usually be higher at the end of the operation.

The agreed new pay structure will have to be announced and introduced on an agreed basis, and this may be phased where the ramifications are significant. Even after the scheme has been implemented it will be necessary to monitor the early stages and provide procedures for dealing with subsequent appeals, re-gradings and the grading of new jobs. The original committee or a sub-committee thereof may meet from time to time to deliberate upon these matters.

METHODS OF JOB EVALUATION

There are many job evaluation techniques available, from basic rule of thumb systems to those that are extremely complex in their most advanced forms. The methods are usually divided into two main groups:

1 'Non-analytical' or 'non-quantitative' methods
2. 'Analytical' or 'quantitative' methods

A recent Court of Appeal decision held that a non-analytical scheme is no defence under S1(5) of the Equal Pay Act 1970 to a claim for equal pay for work of equal value. Employers should, therefore, be advised to consider carefully the use of non-analytical methods.

Some of the more common systems are outlined below starting with non-quantitative methods.

Ranking

This method is concerned with ranking whole jobs by comparison of job descriptions. The descriptions are not usually analysed and those responsible, whether a representative committee or a group of top executives, simply compare each job with the others in order to decide whther it is more or less demanding or equally so. In practice, the job descriptions may actually be stacked in descending order of value, or a set of cards may be prepared for similar use. Alternatively, a form may be prepared containing a column for each department and the jobs will be ranked within these columns.

The 'vertical' comparison may present less difficulty than the 'horizontal', which will involve comparing jobs across departmental boundaries in order to decide in which grade they should be placed. For this purpose, it may be preferable to introduce certain factors of the jobs, such as knowledge, skill, responsibility, etc. Although this may help in coming to terms with the comparison of an accountant with an engineer, it may also introduce the kind of complication that the method is intended to avoid. Most problems arise in ranking jobs of a similar level, and in order to overcome this a system of 'paired comparisons' is sometimes used. Basically, this involves comparing each job on a 'win, lose or draw' basis, and awarding points accordingly. Benchmark jobs may also be identified in order to form anchor points within the overall system.

Provided the above modifications are not carried to extremes, the ranking system retains its main assets of speed and simplicity. The main criticisms of the system include the detailed knowledge required by those administering the scheme and the tendency towards rule of thumb judgements which will inevitably be seen as unfair.

Job classification or grading

This is in effect a reversal of the ranking system as the organizational structure is divided into several hierarchical grades into which jobs are placed. Each grade will be assigned an identifying number or letter accompanied by a description of the type of work and level of ability required for jobs within that grade (see Fig. 17.1). Several benchmark or key jobs are also identified as an indication of the level of the grade to which each is assigned. The Institute of Administrative Management publishes a similar scale of grades for use in evaluating clerical jobs [2].

The classification method is relatively cheap to administer and simple to operate and understand. It does, however, lack flexibility and the

---

Grade 1 — Tasks requiring little or no previous experience and which are closely supervised

Grade 2 — Routine tasks carried out in accordance with clearly defined rules and procedures

Grade 3 — Routine tasks that require some experience, aptitude and initiative

Grade 4 — Tasks that require some qualifications or supervisory ability

Grade 5 — Tasks requiring professional or specialized knowledge, non-routine decision making and supervision of a minimum number of staff

---

Fig. 17.1 An example of grade definitions

ability to deal with complex job situations. It is ideally suited to fairly rigid hierarchical organizations, such as the Civil Service.

Points rating (or assessment)

This is an anlaytical or quantitative system and is probably the most common method in use at the present time. Instead of comparing whole jobs, the method involves breaking down each job in accordance with a number of 'factors'. Typical factors would be such things as skill, responsibility, working conditions, etc. A maximum number of points is then allocated to each factor, jobs are analysed under each of the factors and points are awarded. The total points score for each job places it in its appropriate rank order. The factors are usually weighted so that suitable emphasis may be given to factors that are considered more important. Some factors may also be broken down into 'degrees' that will indicate various levels within the factor and the number of points to be awarded. A typical list of factors with weighting would be as follows:

Factor	Weighting	Points
Education and training	20%	120
Experience	10%	60
Supervision	15%	90
Decisions	20%	120
Complexity of work	25%	150
Responsibility for assets and materials	10%	60
	100%	600

The factor 'Experience' may be divided into degrees as follows:

Degree 1	0 – 3 months	10 points
2	3 months – 1 year	20 points
3	1 – 2 years	40 points
4	2 – 5 years	60 points

The job of selecting factors is made simpler if separate schemes are prepared for different categories of work, e.g., clerical, manual, managerial, although trends in 'harmonization' and 'equal value' may mitigate against this in future.

Once the factors and points have been agreed, it is usual to 'test run' some benchmark jobs in order to ensure that the system does not produce absurd results. The panel or committee will then award points to every job using a detailed job description that should have been

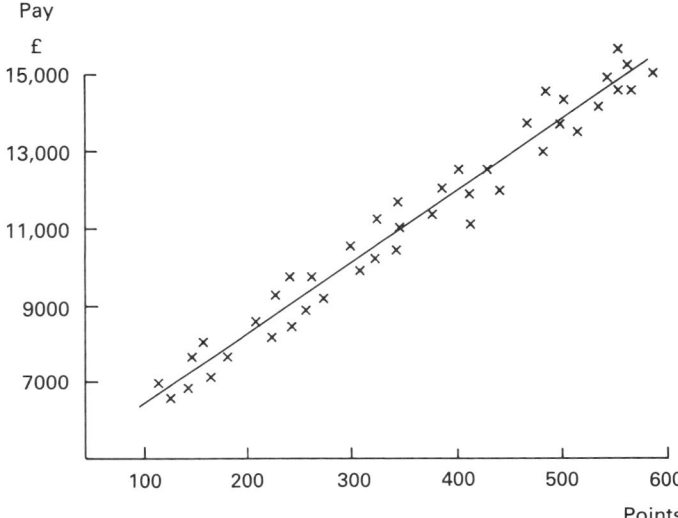

Fig. 17.2 A scattergram showing trend line

prepared after job analysis. Once the jobs have been evaluated, it is normal to produce a scattergram that will indicate the points rating of each job against rates of pay as shown in Fig. 17.2. It may also highlight certain 'anomalies', i.e., jobs which are at present underpaid or overpaid. The former can probably be upgraded with few problems, but the latter may have to be frozen or 'red-circled' until such time as the pay of other similarly graded jobs catches up with them.

This graph will produce a trend line and will often indicate natural break points that might be used for superimposing grades onto the chart. Particular attention should be paid to the spread and range of each of the grades created. A fair degree of 'overlap' is usually considered desirable for purposes of internal flexibility (an illustration of grades is given in Chapter 18, page 223).

Points rating has been criticized for undue complexity and a false impression of scientific objectivity. However, provided it is well administered, it is a method that is not difficult to understand and that contains a fair degree of logic. Above all, it rates highly with employees, in that it is 'seen to be fair' — one of the most important considerations for any job evaluation method.

Factor comparison

This method is also analytical, but although it embodies the principle of factors used in points rating these are usually confined to a maximum of about five factors. Typical factors for hourly paid jobs would be:

1   mental requirements
2   skill requirements
3   physical requirements
4   responsibilities
5   working conditions

Job descriptions are prepared and 'key jobs' are selected on both a vertical and horizontal basis. These are then ranked under each of the factors and placed upon a key scale graded in monetary units. The assessors must decide how much of the current pay received by the holders of the key jobs relates to each factor. All other jobs are evaluated on a similar basis and placed on the ranking scale. 'Adjustments' are then made where considered necessary.

This method, although using the principles of both points rating and ranking, appears to be unduly complex. Although monetary values are often disguised by the use of a points conversion system, the fact remains that existing pay levels are being used as major criteria in the evaluation of jobs, and this would appear to defeat the object of the exercise to some extent.

Other systems

Other methods of job evaluation are available, many having been developed by management consultants. The Hay/MSL Guide Chart Profile system has been adopted by many organizations. This has similarities to the standard points rating approach but concentrates on three groups of factors under the headings 'know-how', 'problem solving' and 'accountability'. Paterson's system of 'decision banding' allocates jobs to particular 'bands' based upon their fit with the decision levels described by each band. This system has similarities to job classification referred to earlier in that it creates 'boxes' and then allocates jobs to them if they appear to fit the description on the box. Decision banding appears to be most appropriate to managerial areas as it fails to consider criteria other than decision making, such as skill or responsibility.

Conclusion

It is worth repeating for those considering a system of job evaluation that it is not a panacea for the ills of a bad pay structure. However, it does enable the organization to build a new framework or hierarchy based upon a systematic approach. There will always be a fair degree of subjectivity, but the benefits will be real if it is approached in a constructive and open manner. Not only must the system be fair, it must be *seen* to be fair. Currently, this must take account of the equal pay for work of equal value ammendments to the Equal Pay Act (1970), as well as trends towards flexible working and harmonization of terms and conditions [3].

REFERENCES

1. ACAS (1976). *Guide No. 1: Job Evaluation.* ACAS
2. IAM (1983). *Office Job Evaluation.* IAM
3. Fouracre. S. and Wright. A. (1986). 'New factors in job evaluation', *Personnel Management*, May.

18
Salary administration

Salary administration, according to McBeath and Rands [1]

> is about equitable salary relationships, which, in an age of participation with progressively greater disclosure of salaries, means getting these relationships — internally and externally — right for all to see.

This definition contains wide implications for those responsible for planning and regulating a salary system.

There follows a consideration of the main elements of salary administration under the following headings:

☐ policy and objectives
☐ planning and design of a structure
☐ salary reviews and control
☐ increments, merit awards and bonuses
☐ fringe benefits

POLICY AND OBJECTIVES

An organization's policy with regard to salary administration will be to a large extent reflected in the aims and objectives that it sets. Apart from the attitudes of the management, any salary policy must take account of:

☐ market rates, both local and national
☐ legislation on equal pay, taxation, etc.
☐ the needs and aspirations of employees, both as individuals and groups
☐ the practices of competitors with regard to absolute pay levels, structures, and reward 'mix'

- [ ] the needs of the organization to recruit, retain and motivate personnel
- [ ] the need for any structure to be based upon evaluation that is 'seen to be fair'
- [ ] the organization's ability to finance and control salaries

The degree to which each of the above factors are taken into consideration will probably depend on the organization's overall philosophy.

It is considered important that line managers, trade unions and staff are consulted on the formulation of policy and any major changes to it. Policy may be produced in the form of a written statement and details may be contained in a manual.

The aims and objectives might include:

- [ ] the evaluation of the relative worth of every job by means of a proper system of job evaluation
- [ ] the reward of the relative performance and contribution of every employee shall be taken into account
- [ ] the overall level of salaries paid shall be competitive with those of similar organizations
- [ ] the system will provide for the regular review of individual salaries to provide for progression
- [ ] flexibility will be provided to accommodate changes in market rates, inflation, etc.
- [ ] the system will be applied as openly and fairly as possible

This overall policy and any specific aims should act as a guide in the detailed planning and operation of the scheme decided on.

DESIGNING A STRUCTURE

A sound basis for a salary structure is a methodical job evaluation scheme as described in Chapter 17. In the case of salaried staff most methods of job evaluation will result in a range of job grades or scales that span the financial spectrum and usually identify 'families' of jobs that have received similar valuations. Although most organizations have salary 'scales' of one sort or another, the actual design and operation varies considerably.

Rate for age scales

Although not used generally, a straightforward age scale may be used for junior staff and trainees, particularly within the public sector. The problem with this type of scale is its rigidity, which does not take account of individual merit. It must also be kept under constant review in order to allow for changes in market rates. In order to overcome the former problem, a certain range for merit is often included at each age, as shown in Fig. 18.1.

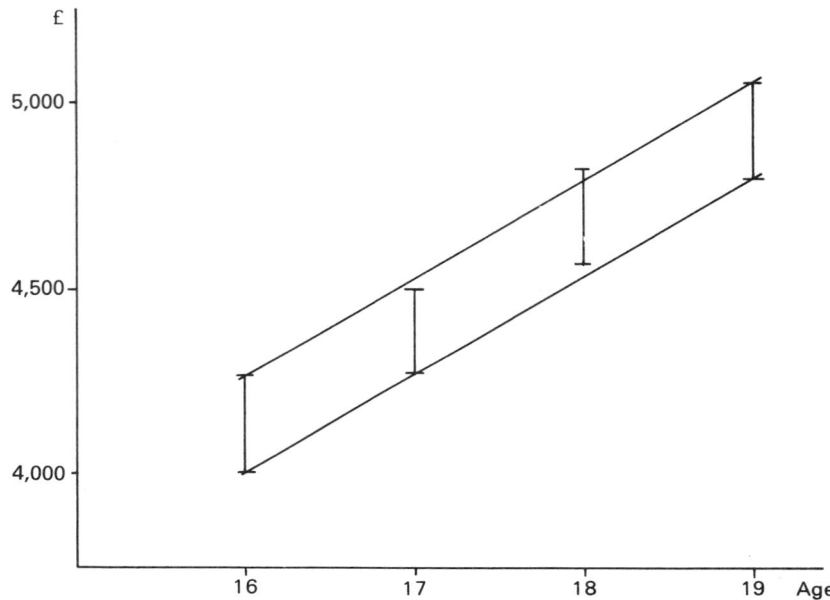

Fig. 18.1 A simple rate for age scale with merit ranges

Fixed incremental scales

Under this system, each job is graded and a range of grades, usually overlapping, is agreed. Although the grades may appear similar to those shown in Fig. 18.2, the main distinction will be the inclusion of several incremental 'points' on each grade. Staff will tend to progress from one point to the next on an annual basis, as of 'right'. They may also be upgraded, within limits, on criteria that will often stress seniority and service. This approach to salaries is commonly found in the public sector.

The main advantages of this system are that it is simple to administer and budgets can be prepared with some certainty. Employees are rewarded for loyalty and have the advantage of regular increments. Incremental systems of this type do not, however, inspire high levels of performance and may fail to motivate younger members of staff.

A degree of flexibility has been introduced into incremental scales in some organizations. Quite simply, this involves dispensing with 'automatic' increments and awarding them according to performance.

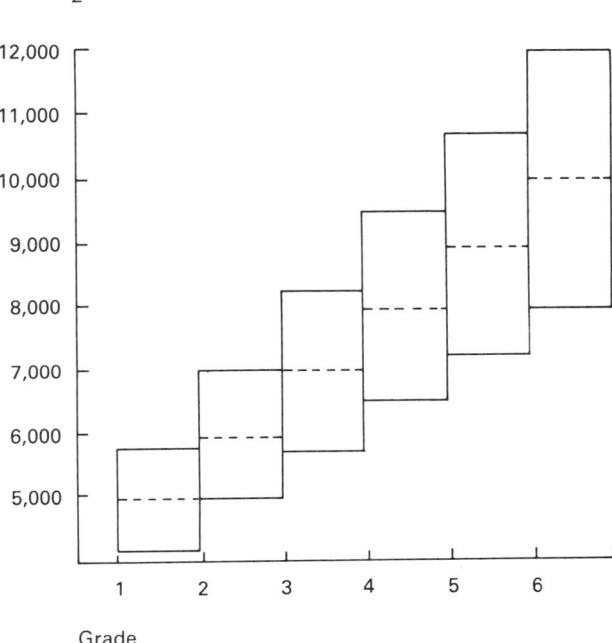

£

Fig. 18.2 Merit structures using a range of 40% of the median for each grade

Under this scheme a double increment could be awarded or an increment could be withheld. In this way, high performers can be 'accelerated' up through a particular grade.

Merit scales

Most organizations in the private sector use a system of merit scales. Although based upon similar principles, the detailed design and its application will vary considerably. Most structures will comprise a series of overlapping scales or grades. The range of the grades and the degree of overlap will depend upon individual circumstances and the objectives of the organization. An example of these types of 'grade box' is given above in Fig. 18.2.

It will be observed that the degree of overlap in Fig. 18.2 increases progressively, and this is usually considered beneficial in providing flexibility where jobs are re-graded under a job evaluation scheme, and for giving scope to reward both long service and merit.

The actual degree of flexibility in awarding merit increases will also depend upon the policy of the organization concerned. In some cases this is at the discretion of the manager making the award and is completely flexible. Other schemes set 'norms' for increases that tend to make the system similar to the more rigid incremental method. Guidelines are usually set out in writing giving the accepted 'high', 'low' and 'average' merit increase, and the manager will usually apply these norms quite rigidly.

The advantages and disadvantages of merit salary schemes are basically the converse of the fixed incremental approach. For management there may be less financial control, depending on the type of system used, but motivation of staff may be increased. Some employees may feel that reward of performance is fairer than reward of service and be duly motivated; others may feel that the system smacks of favouritism and is too uncertain.

The above is merely a brief outline of the most common salary structures. There are many variations on these themes and it is up to the designer to decide upon the features which his organization finds most acceptable and to incorporate them into a suitable structure.

SALARY REVIEWS

Salaries need to be reviewed regularly both overall and on an individual basis. General reviews usually take place in response to inflationary pressures or changes in market rates. Any changes in the structure or overall levels may be made unilaterally or through negotiation where staff are represented by a trade union. Where fixed increments are not paid, the question of merit rises may have to be included in any general review in order to ensure that the organization is not creating financial difficulties for itself.

Individual salary reviews normally take place annually. Even where 'automatic' increments are paid some organizations supplement these with an additional merit award or reserve the right to withold an increment. This review is a major operation and often forms part of the appraisal process. There tends to be two schools of thought concerning the integration of performance appraisal and salary review and some managers feel strongly that the salary or 'reward review' should be kept entirely separate. The reader is referred to Chapter 12 for a more detailed consideration of this topic.

Whatever the method of review used, it will be necessary to maintain detailed individual records in order to assess the employee's progress with regard to pay. It is obviously desirable to maintain each employee on an 'ideal' salary path according to his progress and aspirations. Although line managers are invariably responsible for the actual award if any, most organizations have a review policy as part of the overall scheme and guidelines are usually laid down in order to assist the manager in his decision. These may cover:

☐ overall budget
☐ maximum and minimum increases
☐ criteria for regrading and promotion
☐ relationship between performance and size of reward

The degree of rigidity with which these guidelines are applied will vary from one organization to another. Provided the manager has received sufficient information and training concerning the organizations salary policy any flexibility is unlikely to be abused.

PERFORMANCE- AND PROFIT-RELATED PAY

The motivational aspects of pay have already been discussed in Chapter 16. However, in the present climate it is worth discussing certain aspects of salary policy in more detail. Apart from the regular reviews referred to above, many organizations are attempting to build greater flexibility into their systems in order to encourage higher levels of performance and commitment.

'Employers are becoming less concerned with structures, norms and averages and more concerned with attracting and retaining the right individuals in the face of serious skill shortages', states Barry Curnow [2] in an article which also suggests that 'job size' is now less important than the individual's results and achievement. Clearly, it might be considered that this only applies to a few 'high flyers' and those with scarce skills and, to some extent, this is true. The financial services sector is a prime example [3]. However, there are signs that greater margins for performance are being built into the salaries of a wider range of staff.

Apart from pay increases based on individual performance, many employers have set up various profit-sharing schemes usually based on share ownership under various government-approved plans. More recently, the government has introduced, in the 1987 Finance Act, a tax-relief incentive for 'Profit-related Pay' (PRP). Briefly, this is part of the employee's pay which is formally linked to the profits of his employer. This proportion is at present limited to 20% of pay or £3000, whichever is lower, but half of this amount may be received free of income tax. Obviously, the employer's scheme has to be approved by the Inland Revenue and there are number of complications [4].

Linking rewards to performance and profit in this way appears attractive to certain employees and in good times. However, many staff require stability and security, and although these views may appear old-fashioned, those responsible for reward policy will no doubt consider them alongside those referred to above.

CONTROL

In view of the high proportion of overall costs that salaries represent, particularly in service industries, a systematic method of control is essential. In smaller organizations this may consist of regular checks against overall budgets, but in a large organization it may be advisable to maintain control on a departmental basis.

Any control system must be based on sound information and much data concerning present and future manning levels on a departmental basis should be produced as part of the manpower planning process (see Chapter 7). Summaries should be prepared by each department showing actual numbers employed broken down into grades, estimated staff movements, overtime and an allowance for annual awards and inflation. Once agreed, this will form the departmental or divisional budget for the forthcoming period. Various statistical techniques are used in order to assess variations from the 'mid point' of pay grades and the degree of 'attrition' within each grade. In simple terms, the latter refers to the gradual reduction of pay levels within a grade owing to the replacement of higher paid employees with new, lower paid ones.

REFERENCES

1. McBeath, G. and Rands, D.N. (1976). *Salary Administration*, 3rd Edn. Business Books.
2. Curnow, B (1986). 'The creative approach to pay', *Personnel Management*, October.
3. Goodswen, M (1988). 'Retention and reward of the high achiever', *Personnel Management*, October.
4. IDS Study 397, November 1987.

19
Wage administration

In Chapter 18 we referred briefly to the difference between salaries and wages that traditionally has been as much about status as the actual differences in payment method. Elsewhere we refer to the 'wage/work bargain' because wages have become a central item on the agenda of collective bargaining in most industries, not only in respect of absolute amounts but also the system of calculating and awarding pay. Wage earners sometimes referred to as 'hourly paid' employees usually work at the 'sharp end' of an organization and success depends on the amount of effort and loyalty that they are prepared to contribute. These facts must be borne in mind by those designing and operating wage payment systems.

Organizations cannot isolate themselves from external factors when considering wages. Every student of economics will be familiar with theories of marginal productivity and the market concepts of labour. There is not the opportunity here to discuss wages theory, but both the economic and social influences on wage structures are excellent background for the practitioner as well as the student.

OBJECTIVES

From a management point of view, the payment of wages will perform the function of securing and retaining suitable workers and motivating them to achieve the goals of the organization as effectively as possible. However, these objectives could be sub-divided and considered in more detail, depending on the particular work situation. They may include:

- ☐ effort or performance
- ☐ learning or skill
- ☐ responsibility
- ☐ acceptance of change
- ☐ cooperation

It will be virtually impossible to achieve all of these objectives, and management must decide upon its priorities. The method of payment should then be selected accordingly.

Workers will also have objectives that may be satisfied to a greater or lesser extent by pay. These will vary according to the attitudes of the individual or work group but most workers would probably require a good proportion of their income to be stable and almost certainly require that their wage be 'fair' when compared with others doing similar work. A balance will need to be struck between the objectives of management and those of the workforce when considering the method or payment to be employed.

WAGE PAYMENT METHODS

Before considering the various methods of wage payment it should be stressed that every organization should have a sound job structure that has been properly evaluated, preferably with the participation of relevant trade unions (see Chapter 17). This structure should take account of differentials between grades and any variations in actual payment methods between one section of the workforce and another. Within this overall structure, which may be extremely complex in a large organization, the following methods of payment may be used.

Time rates

Time rate, also known as day work, hourly rate or flat rate, is the most common method of payment used in British industry overall. This type of payment is most common in situations that do not lend themselves to payment of results; i.e., where output cannot be related to effort and cannot be specifically measured. The main criticism of time rate is the lack of any performance incentive element. Organizations have tried to overcome this in various ways, which are discussed below.

Payment by results (PBR)

A National Board for Prices and Incomes report [1] offered the following definition:

> Payment by Results may be broadly interpreted to mean any system of wages or salaries under which payment is related to factors in a worker's performance other than time spent at his employer's disposal. However the term is most commonly applied in a more restricted sense to payment systems which attempt to establish a formal relationship between pay and output or effort.

The simplest form of PBR is 'straight piecework' where the employee receives an agreed price for each unit of output. In theory the system is easily understood and has a high incentive effect. However, various adaptations, such as progressive and regressive rates, have been attempted to meet variations in technology and working methods, and have tended to introduce undesirable complications. Also, in the wrong climate the system of rate fixing, which is at the heart of most piecework systems, can cause various output restrictions which nullify the original objective of increased output (see Chapter 16, page 208). Other 'indirect workers' such as maintenance staff may also demand a 'lieu bonus' as reward for their contribution to any increase in output. Many industrial relations problems are, in fact, caused by disputes over PBR systems. However, a good scheme operated in the right climate can increase production and reward operators prepared to work hard whilst reducing the amount of supervision required.

Apart from piecework, other schemes have been developed, most of which are based upon time standards. Bonuses may be paid upon the operator's efficiency over and above a set standard. In other 'time saving' plans, such as the Halsey–Weir and the Bedaux Point, any time saved through working faster than the standard time is subsequently shared on an agreed basis between the employer and the employee. This approach has been used on a plant-wide basis by large car manufacturers, such as BL, in recent years, combined with other methods of improving productivity.

Whichever method is chosen, payment on an output basis is only really appropriate where:

1   Output standards can be set and are measurable.
2   Output is controlled by the efforts of the individual/group.
3   Quantity of output is more important than quality.

Measured daywork

Measured daywork has been introduced by some of the large manufacturers, such as Ford, Vauxhall and Philips Electrical, largely to overcome many of the industrial relations problems inherent in PBR. In 1973, the Office of Manpower Economics [2] reported that Measured Daywork (MDW) covered nearly 10% of the national workforce, and that this proportion was growing. Basically, pay is fixed on the understanding that the employees maintain a specified performance level. It does offer more stability in earnings at the inevitable expense of less flexibility in output. The 'acceptable' output level is obviously of crucial importance, and more supervision is required in order to ensure compliance with standards. However, when introduced with care it has proved to be successful in providing a premium level of pay for a sustained level of performance.

Plant-wide incentive schemes

These systems normally provide for a bonus based on overall *labour* performance. They should not be confused with profit-sharing schemes which usually reflect the performance of all the factors of production. The best known examples of plant-wide systems are the 'Rucker Plan' and the 'Scanlon Plan'. Many American companies have found these plans most successful, but they are not widely used in Britain. The Rucker Plan is based on 'added value' attributable to the manufacturing process. The Scanlon Plan is more flexible, and is usually based on the current wage bill's ratio to sales value of production. Despite certain differences in philosophy, the general idea is to encourage worker participation in the improvement of efficiency and productivity. The schemes rely as much on cost savings as increased output, and a system of committees is employed to consider staff suggestions.

As with any all-embracing system, problems have been experienced in intergroup relationships and differentials have had to be introduced to appease disgruntled skilled workers. Other problems have arisen in companies engaged in cyclical industries where wide fluctuations in bonus have occurred. Some employers hold back a proportion of bonus to boost the months in which little or nothing would normally be received. Despite claimed success in some organizations, it is generally considered that these systems are only suitable for firms that operate in very stable conditions. Even here they have the inherent disadvantage of all plant-wide schemes — remoteness of the incentive from the individual.

Profit-sharing schemes

Some organizations, such as ICI and John Lewis, extend a share of profits to most of their employees. The philosophy behind most schemes is that profit sharing encourages effort, loyalty and cooperation. However, for a scheme to achieve these objectives, the basis of calculating 'profits' will have to be clearly spelt out and must be seen to be fair. The proportion of normal pay represented by the profit element will also need to be worthwhile, probably a minimum of 5–10%. The main disadvantages of these schemes are that the reward, usually annual, is too remote to affect behaviour, and that profits can be affected by factors outside the control of the workers.

CHOOSING AN APPROPRIATE SYSTEM

As can be seen from the brief review above, there are many different kinds of payment systems that may be directed towards the individual, a group, or an entire plant. We have already referred to objectives and these will obviously feature strongly when selecting a suitable system.

Lupton and Bowey [3] suggest four questions that the manager needs to ask:

1 What should the objectives of the firm be when installing or modifying a payment scheme?
2 What payment systems are available to choose from?
3 How should the firm go about deciding which of the available schemes is best suited to its circumstances?
4 Which of the available schemes satisfies its objectives?

They add that management is obviously attempting to influence worker behaviour which in itself is a difficult thing to do. Given this problem, Lupton and Bowey consider that there are four main groups of influences that affect the operation of a payment scheme:

1 Technology — the machinery and production methods employed by an organization will influence the attitudes and amount of discretion of the employee.
2 Labour markets — the supply and demand for labour could have effects upon both absolute levels of pay and the method of calculating payments.
3 Disputes and disputes procedures — the effectiveness or otherwise of these procedures could decide whether or not pay systems can be kept under control.
4 Structural characteristics — things, such as multi-unionism and plant-level bargaining, as well as the age and sex distribution of the workforce can affect the type of payment system and its successful administration.

The above factors are broken down into 23 'dimensions' that may be used to produce a 'profile' of an organization, which it is suggested can be used in the selection of a payment scheme. These appear to be somewhat complex for practical purposes, although the principles outlined are obviously sound.

CONCLUSION

Many pay and incentive schemes have been developed over the years, each claiming to be better than its competitors. Fashions change and schemes rise and fall in popularity. It is suggested, therefore, that no scheme is good or bad in itself, but only in relation to the circumstances in which it is operated. Those responsible must attempt to answer the questions posed above after an objective analysis of the schemes available, in the context of the organization's own environment.

REFERENCES

1. NBPI. (1968). *Payment by Results Systems*, and *Supplement*, Report No. 65, HMSO.
2. Office of Manpower Economics. (1973). *Measured Daywork*. HMSO.
3. Lupton, T. and Bowey, A. (1983). *Wages and Salaries*, Chapter 3. Gower.

20
Fringe benefits

Fringe benefits are forming an increasing proportion of the total rewards received by the employees of many organizations. Some of the benefits provided by employers over and above the basic salary, such as paid holiday, subsidized meals, sick pay and pensions, have become accepted as 'normal'. Other benefits that are more accurately termed 'fringe' have developed rapidly in recent years, partly in response to competition for senior personnel, partly for reasons of cost effectiveness, and also to alleviate the effects of government pay restraint and taxation. Remuneration specialists are devising new 'perks' all the time, and some of the benefits received by staff of the more generous employers are described below.

Insurance

Life assurance, medical insurance and permanent disability insurance are among the most common types of cover offered to employees. Benefits may be entirely free to senior executives, whereas other staff may be offered advantageous discounts on premiums. Private medical schemes, such as BUPA, are commonly offered on a group discount basis.

House purchase

Many organizations will make bridging loans available to assist with house purchase at little or no interest. Larger organizations offer mortgages at low rates of interest. Although these mortgages used to be considered a tie to the employer some newer schemes have considerably reduced the number of 'strings' attached to the mortgage.

Company cars

For many jobs a company car is considered a 'normal' part of the remuneration package whether or not it is a necessity. It is estimated that more than 65% of cars sold in this country are purchased by organizations for staff use, and when the costs of running a car out of net income are calculated, it is not difficult to appreciate the growing popularity of this particular 'perk'.

Loans

Several organizations arrange loans, usually interest free, to assist with various personal expenditures, such as car purchase or home improvements. It is also common practice nowadays to provide a loan to cover the cost of an annual season ticket to enable employees to take advantage of the discount involved.

Share option schemes

One of the fastest growing benefits in recent years has been employee share schemes. Schemes vary, but normally allow qualifying staff to purchase shares in their company on advantageous terms. There are tax restrictions on these benefits concerning disposal, etc., but there are also considerable tax advantages. Apart from the possible financial benefit, many of the companies that have introduced these schemes undoubtedly see them as a means of increasing employee involvement in the organization and its objectives but, in practice, benefits to the organization may be limited [1].

Miscellaneous

Apart from the specific benefits mentioned, a whole variety of other items may be provided dependent upon the policy of the organization and, of course, the grade of the employee. These may include such items as fees to professional bodies, supply of clothing, assistance with school fees, free or subsidized holidays, subsidized travel, sports and social facilities (often taken for granted) and discounts on purchases from company shops.

TOTAL REMUNERATION

It is estimated that employee benefits now constitute more than 30% of the payroll costs to the employer and the trend is upwards. Particularly at the higher levels where the impact of personal taxation is greater, organizations talk in terms of the 'total remuneration package' for their employees. Unlike salary, benefits may or may not fulfil the needs of an individual, and the employer's generosity may be wasted if the benefits are not those that are attractive to the employee. Remuneration specialists are now employed by many organizations to review the package offered and to reconcile the wishes of the employee to considerations of tax saving and cost effectiveness. There is a trend towards the American 'cafeteria' system of benefits for senior staff, whereby the employee chooses from a range on offer in accordance with his personal needs. Although some commentators consider fringe benefits to be unethical, particularly at the executive level, they would appear to represent a realistic and popular approach to remuneration, given the prevailing circumstances.

PROS AND CONS OF FRINGE BENEFITS

Employers will need to take account of various factors when developing a remuneration package. As we have already stated, there has been a marked tendency to increase the fringe benefit element of the rewards to employees. Before adopting or increasing benefits, employers should be aware of the main issues, which would include the following.

Advantages

- [ ] can be tax effective for employee and cost effective for employer
- [ ] fulfil expectations of staff in line with social trends and competition
- [ ] can increase loyalty and staff satisfaction. (By providing for welfare needs of staff and financial perks tied to the job, e.g., reduced mortgage, staff are likely to remain with employer. Tangible benefits, such as company cars, will also increase satisfaction with employment rewards.)

Disadvantages

- [ ] benefits may not be appropriate to or appreciated by all staff
- [ ] costs to employer of providing benefits can increase without any real added benefit to employee owing to inflation
- [ ] staff may take fringe benefits for granted and still demand higher cash rewards

It is for each organization to work out its own policy on the degree to which fringe benefits form part of the reward package, taking account of the above points.

PUBLICITY

As we stated above, one of the main problems with fringe benefits is staff taking them for granted. In order to avoid this, some organizations supply staff with an annual statement of remuneration and benefits. This will show the employee's rate of pay together with accrued pension rights, life assurance, holiday entitlement and other benefits. Although employers should endeavour to avoid a patronizing tone, this approach certainly acts as a reminder to staff of the full value of benefits provided over and above their salary.

REFERENCE

1. Poole, M. and Jenkins, G. (1988). How employees respond to profit sharing', *Personnel Management*, July.

21
Legal aspects of pay

EQUAL PAY

The Equal Pay Act 1970 and the Equal Pay (Amendment) Regulations will need to be complied with concerning pay and other terms and conditions of work. This subject is discussed more fully in Chapter 11, page 150.

METHOD OF PAYMENT AND DEDUCTIONS FROM PAY

The Wages Act 1986 removed any *statutory* right to have payment of wages made in cash. This will now be a matter of contract but deductions from pay are controlled by the Act. No deduction from pay is lawful unless:

(a) it is required or permitted by a statutory or contractual provision, or
(b) the employee has given prior written consent to the deduction.

Deductions from workers in retail employment for such things as cash shortages are limited to 10% of gross pay on any payday.

ITEMIZED PAY STATEMENT

Under the Employment Protection (Consolidation) Act 1978 (EPCA) employers must provide a written statement of gross pay, deductions and net pay at or before the time of payment of all employees.

GUARANTEE PAYMENTS

Where an employer is unable to provide work for employees on days when they would normally work, he must pay a sum not exceeding a specified daily rate (as fixed from time to time by the Secretary of State). The maximum entitlement is 5 days in any quarter, and it will not be payable to employees laid off in connection with a trade dispute or if the employee refuses 'suitable alternative employment'. Under the EPCA 1978, as amended, the employee may complain to an industrial tribunal who will order payment if this complaint is well founded.

PAID TIME OFF

The EPCA 1978 provides for several circumstances under which an employee is entitled to time off with pay. Trade Union officials are entitled to 'reasonable' time off to carry out *union duties* or undergo relevant training (see ACAS Code of Practice No. 3). Employees under notice of dismissal owing to *redundancy* are also entitled to 'reasonable' time off with pay in order to seek work.

There are also provisions allowing time off for employees carrying out *public duties*, e.g., a member of a local authority, and for *Safety Representatives* to carry out their duties in accordance with the Safety Representatives and Safety Committees Regulations 1977.

The Employment Act 1980 created a statutory right for pregnant women not to be unreasonably refused time off with pay for *ante-natal care* appointments.

MATERNITY PAY

From April 1987, the Social Sercurity Act 1986 replaces existing maternity pay with 'Statutory Maternity Pay' (SMP). Employers will be responsible for paying SMP but will be able to recover these payments from government funds in a similar manner to SSP. The provisions are extremely complex and involve a two-tier system of benefit for women. 'Lower rates' are available to those who have been employed for more than 6 months, and complying with other conditions, whereas 'higher rates' are due to those with at least 2 years' qualifying service [1].

Employees must also give their employer notice and medical evidence of absence due to pregnancy in order to qualify. SMP will normally be paid for a maximum of 18 weeks in accordance with entitlement and at rates set by the Secretary of State. Personnel managers and those responsible for payroll administration will need to take advice from the DHSS and familiarize themselves with the complex provisions.

MINIMUM RATES OF PAY

There are no general regulations concerning minimum rates of pay as such, but for many years certain categories of workers have had their pay regulated by Wages Councils. These were originally conceived in the early part of this century to protect workers in the 'sweated trades', who tended to be geographically scattered and unrepresented by trade unions.

Wages Councils normally comprise a small number of independent members, one of whom is usually the chairman, together with the representatives of employers and workers. They are appointed by the

Secretary of State for Employment and their powers have been varied by a range of legislation and regulations, most recently in the Wages Act 1986. They continue with their central function of fixing minimum rates of pay for the workers under their jurisdiction and Wages Council Orders are enforced by the Wages Inspectorate.

The 1986 legislation took all people under 21 years of age out from the control of the Wages Councils on the grounds that they were being 'priced out of the market' and that employers were not prepared to pay statutory minimum wages. Wages Councils are also charged with taking into account local market rates and employment conditions when making orders, and the Secretary of State has wide powers to regulate their proceedings.

Many employees in industries, such as catering, retailing and laundries, still have their rates of pay set by Wage Councils, but the debate continues as to whether they are 'protected' by the councils or forced into unemployment due to the employers' inability to pay these rates.

HOLIDAY PAY

It may come as a surprise to many that there is generally no statutory entitlement to holiday pay. Any payment made for holidays will be subject to agreement between employer and employee.

SICK PAY

Payment for periods of illness will normally be covered by the contract of employment and is one of the particulars that should be included in the 'written statement' of terms and conditions for each employee.

Under the Social Security and Housing Benefits Act 1982 most employees are now entitled to 'statutory sick pay' (For further details see Chapter 23, page 259.)

REFERENCE

1. Gill, D. (1987). 'SMP: a not so immaculate conception', *Personnel Management*, April.

PART 5: FURTHER RECOMMENDED READING

Thomason, G. (1980). *Job Evaluation*. IPM.
Scott, K. (1983). *Office Job Evaluation*. IAM.
Bowey, A. (ed.). (1982). *Handbook of Salary and Wages Systems*. Gower.
Armstrong, M. and Murlis, H. (1980). *A Handbook of Salary Administration*. Kogan Page.
Smith, A. (1983). *The Management of Remuneration*. IPM.

PART 5: SAMPLE EXAMINATION QUESTIONS

Define job evaluation.

What are the strengths and weaknesses commonly associated with job evaluation systems?   CIB

Write short notes on money as a motivator.   CACA

Outline a system of payment that you would regard as appropriate for lecturers on the course you have just completed, or on a similar course of which you have had recent experience. Include either or both job evaluation and incentive elements, explaining why you would use the methods you advocate.   IPM

To what extent are pay differentials and financial incentives consistent with the findings of current motivation theories?   ICSA

What are (or should be) the objectives of an organization's pay policy? A recently published textbook on personnel management has argued that 'Traditionally, compensation policies have been biased in favour of organization goals to the detriment of employee needs.' How far would you accept this generalization? Illustrate with examples.   ICSA

What are the essential considerations which building society personnel managers must take into account when determining a salary administration policy.   CBSI

'People only come to work for money'. Discuss.   CIB

(a) Describe the main objectives of job evaluation and briefly describe a method of achieving these.
(b) Discuss the place of job evaluation in a modern reward policy employed by a building society.   CBSI

'The financial services market is characterised by growth, increasing segmentation and greater competition.'

What are the implications of this statement for the pay and benefit schemes of building societies?   CBSI

What are the strengths and weaknesses of job evaluation? How might the weaknesses be overcome or minimized?   ICSA

Discuss the advantages and disadvantages of profit-sharing as a means of attracting, retaining and motivating employees.   ICSA

Define a 'fringe benefit'. What are the arguments for and against using them as part of a remuneration package?   CBSI

You work for an organization in which there is considerable dissatisfaction about the fairness of the salary system. There seems to be no sound basis for individual pay awards. There are allegations of favouritism. Relatively unskilled people seem to be paid as much as those who are highly skilled. Newcomers can earn as much as long-standing employees. What action would you take to remove the dissatisfaction?   CIB

Some employers who have moved wage-earning employees to salaried status have been surprised that the employees do not then seem to assume the same attitudes to their work as those who are already salaried. Why do you think this is?   IPM

There is an increasing variety of benefits in remuneration packages. What are the reasons for this, why is the greatest variety available only to management and professional employees, and what are the effects on IPM employment costs?
                                                                      IPM

In which types of situation would you use which types of financial incentives, and why?   IPM

Part 6
Health, safety and welfare

22
Health and safety

For reasons closely connected with the development of personnel management, health and safety in many organizations has been and still is considered a part of the 'welfare function'. However, as a result of several forces including, public concern, technological and medical advance and increasing statutory pressure, the nature of health and safety work is both changing and increasing in importance. Increasingly it forms a separate specialism under the general personnel umbrella. Whether in future it continues to be a personnel responsibility, or is attached to the production function, or perhaps exists as a separate functional entity, remains to be seen though. A survey by Torrington and Hall [1] suggested an almost even division between personnel and technical functions.

A MANAGERIAL RESPONSIBILITY — WHY?

Why should management give health and safety increasing attention? Indeed, should it be considered a managerial responsibility at all, since accidents and disease are in no way exclusive to the workplace?

The facts are that management is required, whether it wishes or not, to give more attention to such matters. Government, trade unions, insurance companies, the public, increasingly demand that employers provide a safe and healthy work environment. Management has to accept that it has social responsibilities and that it exists in a world that is increasingly socially aware. Examined nationally, the costs are high. During the last decade the number of working days lost to the nation due to incapacity resulting from accidents and prescribed diseases has regularly exceeded working days lost as a result of industrial disputes.

Setting aside moral or statutory duties, it makes sense for management to be concerned. To a very considerable degree, the success of an organization is determined by the ability and effectiveness of its staff. Injured or sick staff are unlikely to achieve optimum performance. The cost of sickness and accidents cannot therefore be ignored.

THE COST OF ACCIDENTS

Even a series of relatively minor accidents may soon begin to adversely affect profitability. Costs incurred might include:

- [ ] damage to plant or materials
- [ ] cost of wages to the injured employee
- [ ] cost of supervisor's time spent in dealing with the incident and consequences thereof
- [ ] cost of safety officer's and safety representative's time
- [ ] cost of wages paid to workers uninjured but involved in or stopping work during or after the incident
- [ ] cost of administrative procedures
- [ ] recruitment and training costs of replacement workers
- [ ] cost of decreased production from the employee immediately after his return to work
- [ ] cost of overtime made necessary by the incident
- [ ] insurance premium costs
- [ ] legal costs
- [ ] loss of profit resulting from sales cancelled owing to production delay
- [ ] medical costs both directly incurred as a result of the incident and the indirect cost of providing medical services
- [ ] loss of staff, customer or community goodwill

Examined in this way, it is difficult to see how management can fail to be concerned. Nevertheless, it is apparent that both in the UK and elsewhere, successive governments have considered it necessary to establish statutory rules and procedures forcing employers to accept their responsibilities.

STATUTORY CONTROL

In 1833, the first Factories Act was passed by Parliament. During the next 140 years, literally hundreds of additional pieces of legislation were introduced, each with the objective of ensuring a healthier and safer work environment. Despite good intentions, the result was chaotic. In 1970, the Robens Committee was formed to consider occupational health and safety law and practice. Its report was published in July 1972.

Briefly, its findings were that:

- [ ] there was too much law
- [ ] much of the law was unsatisfactory and difficult to understand
- [ ] a variety of agencies were involved in law enforcement, as a result

of which overlapping and confusion occurred while at the same time diffusing available expertise
- [ ] the emphasis should move from negative enforcement by external agencies, to a self-regulatory system
- [ ] employers should increasingly give attention to accident prevention rather than dealing with individual incidents as they occurred
- [ ] responsibility for health and safety should be considered an employer/employee partnership based on clearly stated policy and effective organization
- [ ] such policy should take account not only of employer/employee interests, but also of possible consequences for the public generally

These findings and recommendations provided a basis for the Health and Safety at Work, etc., Act 1974 (HSWA).

THE HEALTH AND SAFETY AT WORK, ETC., ACT 1974

Objectives

The objectives of the HSWA are:

- [ ] to secure the health and welfare of persons at work
- [ ] to protect persons other than persons at work against risks to health or safety, arising out of, or in connection with the activities of persons at work
- [ ] to control the keeping and use of explosive or highly inflammable or dangerous substances. Preventing people acquiring, possessing or illegally using such substances
- [ ] to control the emission of noxious or offensive substances from any area

Persons protected by the HSWA

With the exception of those employed as domestic servants in a private household, the Act applies to all persons at work whether they be employers, employees or self-employed. Approximately 7 million workers not previously protected by health and safety legislation are now included. Statutory provisions also extend to people who are not employees, but may be affected by work activities.

Employers' duties to employees

General duties

Section 2 of the Act provides that 'It shall be the duty of every employer to ensure, so far as is reasonably practicable, the health, safety and welfare at work of all his employees. In particular, an employer must:

☐ provide and maintain plant and systems of work that are safe and without risks to health
☐ make arrangements for safety and absence of risks to health in connection with the use, handling, storage and transport of articles and substances
☐ provide such information, instruction, training and supervision as is necessary to ensure the health, safety and welfare at work of his employees
☐ ensure the maintenance of any place of work in a condition that is safe and without risks to health, and the maintenance of means of access and egress from it that are safe and without such risks
☐ provide and maintain a working environment for his employees that is safe, without risks to health and adequate as regards facilities and arrangements for their welfare at work

At first sight, such provisions seem merely to re-iterate the pre-statute common law position. However, the consequences for employers are in fact far reaching. Whereas previously an inspector would have to show that a specific rule had been broken before being able to take action, it now appears that all he must do is to show that an employer has failed to carry out a general duty.

Safety policy

Except for those with less than five employees, all employers are required to formulate and publish a written statement of general policy with respect to the health and safety of employees, and the organization and arrangements for carrying out that policy. Provision is also to be made for policies to be regularly revised and for such revisions to be communicated to staff.

The Act does not recommend any specific policy statement content, the intention being presumably that employers will wish to tailor policies to their individual circumstances. However, the Health and Safety Executive has published guidelines. In summary form, these recommend that:

☐ the statement should declare the employer's intention to provide the safest and healthiest working conditions possible
☐ top management should lay down broad policy principles which should then be elaborated and interpreted as appropriate for the needs of various organizational levels and locations
☐ the statement should identify the officer responsible for fulfilling the policy together with others who have responsibility for implementing the policy

☐ a description of joint consultative committees, etc., for health and safety should be included together with a list of members of such consultative committees, etc.

☐ the statement should make clear the importance of health and safety precautions and the role of all employees in maintaining a safe and healthy work environment

☐ management's intention to achieve a healthy and safe environment through training and effective supervision should be emphasized, together with management proposals to achieve such ends

☐ rules and regulations dealing with specific hazards should be stated. Details of ways of dealing with other common hazards, e.g., machine safety guards, protective clothing, etc., should also be included

☐ procedures for the reporting and recording of accidents should be described together with arrangements for analysing and communicating accident data to management and the safety committee

Safety representatives and safety committees

The Act provides for the appointment of employee safety representatives by recognized trade unions. This provision was implemented by the Safety Representatives and Safety Committee Regulations 1977 and came into force in October 1978. A Code of Practice relating to the requirements placed on safety representatives and on employers has been published by the Health and Safety Commission.

Employers have a duty to consult with representatives for the purpose of making arrangements for promoting and developing health and safety measures. If required to do so by employee representatives, an employer must also set up a safety committee. The function of such a committee shall be to keep under review the measures taken to ensure health and safety at the workplace.

To enable safety representatives to carry out their duties, the Code of Practice recommends that employers should give them information on:

☐ the plans and performance of the undertaking in so far as they affect the health and safety of employees

☐ hazards and the precautions necessary to eliminate or minimize them, including any information provided by consultants, designers, the manufacturer, importers or suppliers of any article or substance used or proposed to be used at work

☐ records and statistics of accidents, dangerous occurences or notifiable industrial diseases

☐ any other relevant matter, including measurements taken by the employer in the course of checking the effectiveness of health and safety precautions.

The Act also provides that representatives shall be entitled to time off with pay for performing their duties and in order to undergo reasonable training. Where a representative is refused time off, or is refused pay, he has a right of complaint to an industrial tribunal, which may award compensation.

In addition to the general duty to consult with employers mentioned above, safety representatives have other specific duties. These are:

- [ ] to investigate potential hazards and examine the causes of accidents
- [ ] to investigate employee complaints relating to health or safety
- [ ] to make specific or general representations to the employer on matters affecting the health and safety of employees
- [ ] to represent employees in consultations with and receive information from inspectors of the Health and Safety Executive
- [ ] to attend meetings of safety committees
- [ ] to carry out inspections of the workplace at least every three months (or more frequently with the approval of the employer). Inspections may also be carried out if there has been some significant change in the conditions of work, or if an accident or notifiable disease has occurred

Duties of employees

It may be recalled that one of the recommendations of the Robens Committee was that responsibility for health and safety should be considered an employer/employee partnership. It is reasonable therefore that statutory duties should be imposed on employees. These are contained in Sections 7 and 8 of the Act.

It is the duty of every employee while at work:

- [ ] to take reasonable care for the health and safety of himself and of other personnel who may be affected by his acts or omissions
- [ ] to co-operate with his employer or any other person in the performance of statutory requirements

In addition, no person shall intentionally or recklessly interfere with or misuse anything provided in the interests of health, safety or welfare in accordance with statutory provisions.

THE HEALTH AND SAFETY COMMISSION

The Health and Safety Commission was set up by the HSWA to provide a single body with overall responsibility for health and safety at work. Consisting of 9 members drawn from both sides of industry, it took over the responsibility for health and safety matters from several government departments.

The functions of the Commission are:

☐ to make whatever arrangements are considered necessary to ensure health and safety at work

☐ to provide a focal point for initiatives on health and safety at work

☐ to encourage and make arrangements for training, information and research

☐ to submit proposals for regulations to the appropriate Minister

☐ to appoint a Health and Safety Executive

THE HEALTH AND SAFETY EXECUTIVE

The executive, as its title suggests, is responsible for enforcing statutory provisions and regulations, and for carrying out other work in accordance with directions and guidance given by the Commission.

It controls a single inspectorate, which was originally formed by all existing factories, mines and quarries, nuclear installations, alkali and clean air, and explosives inspectors being transferred to the Executive in 1975. In this way it achieves yet another of the Robens Committee recommendations.

The Executive is also responsible for administering the Employment Medical Advisory Service.

HEALTH AND SAFETY REGULATIONS AND CODES OF PRACTICE

The HSWA is an enabling act, i.e., it provides regulation-making powers. As mentioned earlier, one of the problems the Act is intended to solve is the vast range of pre-1974 health and safety statute and regulations.

Although much of this continues to be enforceable, it is intended that some 31 Acts and over 500 subsidary regulations shall eventually be revised and replaced by a system of regulations and codes of practice designed to maintain or improve the standards of health and safety established by existing legislation.

Regulations may be made by the appropriate Minister, usually as a result of proposals made by the Health and Safety Commission. Ministerial powers under the Act are in fact extremely wide, allowing for example, the repeal, modification or replacement of existing statute without need for Parliamentary approval.

Codes of practice are intended to provide practical guidance in respect of any duty imposed by a regulation, the HSWA or any other existing statutory provision. They may be issued by the Commission subject to the approval of the Secretary of State and after consultation with appropriate bodies.

It is important to appreciate the significance of a code of practice. A code is merely a guide to good practice. Breach of a code is not therefore an offence. However, if criminal proceedings are instigated in respect of a matter dealt with by a code, then failure to adhere to the code may be given in evidence. Normally this will be considered proof of guilt, unless it can be shown that the law was complied with equally effectively in some other way.

Enforcement

Enforcement is generally the responsibility of Inspectors appointed by the Health and Safety Executive.

However regulations may also be made requiring local authorities to be responsible for aspects of enforcement under the guidance of the Commission. In order to carry out his duties, an inspector has wide powers of entry, inspection and testing.

Improvement and prohibition notices, and prosecution

Where an inspector considers that a person is contravening one or more statutory provisions, he may issue an improvement notice. This includes details of why the notice is served, and requires the contravention to be remedied within a specified period.

Where he considers that an activity involves a risk of serious personal injury, he may issue a prohibition notice, directing that the activity must stop until remedial action is taken.

In both cases there exists a right of appeal to an industrial tribunal. If, however, a person on whom an improvement or prohibition notice is served fails to comply, then he is liable to prosecution.

As an alternative, or in addition to serving a notice, an inspector may prosecute any person contravening a statutory provision. A person found guilty of an offence is potentially liable to a fine, an unlimited fine and/or imprisonment. Certain continuing offences also carry a fine for every day on which the offence occurs. In all cases, the onus of proof lies with the accused.

Improvement and prohibition notices and the comparative ease with which a prosecution may be brought under the HSWA represent a considerable strengthening of the inspectorate's powers. It is apparent that these powers are being used with around 5000 notices being served each year.

IS THE ACT WORKING?

To what extent is the HSWA succeeding in achieving its objectives and in particular, those objectives directly associated with the health and safety of employees?

When first introduced, the Act was widely welcomed. However, Prentice [2] voiced a commonly supported caveat:

Hopefully, the new legislation will at least dent the macabre accident statistics, but legislation by itself will make only a faint impression. A new philosophy aimed at changing attitudes must go in train with legal penalties.

To what extent is this new philosophy apparent?

Generally it would appear that attitudes are changing, and that both management and employees at all levels are more health and safety conscious. Health and safety education and training has become a growth industry, ranging from already well-established lifting and handling type courses to graduate and post-graduate courses in occupational health and safety. The Royal Society for the Prevention of Accidents (ROSPA) and the British Safety Council (BSC) between them currently train around 30 000 people a year. Training boards and professional bodies, e.g., the Institute of Building, together with the MSC are actively committed to training for safety.

Organizations and companies such as the Central Electricity Generating Board, the Singer Company (UK) Ltd, Massey Ferguson and BP, with already well-established health and safety provisions, have tended to consider statutory provisions as minimum acceptable standards; on occasions anticipating statutory regulations. Thus for example, the CEGB has had trade union appointed safety representatives since January 1978 and Singer since July 1976. Even small firms, it would appear [3], have generally made some effort to exceed minimum statutory requirements. It would appear therefore that there is no lack of activity geared to the objectives of the HSWA.

Whether or not all of this activity is as effective as it might be is open to doubt. Nevertheless, such efforts would appear *slowly* to be having some effect in at least stabilizing the numbers of serious accidents and fatalities occurring in the workplace.

In 1976, the Health and Safety Executive published a survey [4] of the roles and functions of 23 safety officers. Only 7 were considered adequate by the Executive. In November 1978, Professor Richard Booth of Aston University was described [5] as being 'sharply critical of the competence of a number of safety advisers'.

A study by Beaumont *et al.* [1], although acknowledging the existence of a growing number of safety personnel, revealed that in only a half of the companies studied was there employed a full-time safety specialist. Of these, a high proportion had received training of some kind ranging from one-day to one-week courses. However 13% had received only in-plant training, and 16% had received no training whatsoever. Staff occupying safety roles generally, it appeared, were long-serving employees with no safety background, mainly 45 years of age and older. Where carried out on a part-time basis, the allocation of safety duties appeared to occur in an almost haphazard fashion, often moving from production personnel to stores staff or purchasing.

Although such findings may well reflect the reality of managing in a recession, one might be forgiven for suggesting that also implied is a low level of priority; companies in many cases merely going through the motions of compliance with statute.

The problem however is not solely one of management attitude or adequacy. In a study [6] of safety practice in a British chemical plant, it became apparent that there existed within the plant two safety environments. First the formal, consisting of managerial policy as contained in written rules, regulations and procedures, rules which among other things satisfied statutory requirements. Second, an informal system enforced by group pressures. All operatives involved felt that the formal system was impossible to follow and so developed informal practices to 'take care of the unsuitability of rules made by those who were believed to have no practical day-to-day involvement in chemical plant operation'.

In several instances, supervisors and managers 'turned a blind eye' to breaches of safety regulations, under pressure from top management to achieve higher productivity.

None of this is, of course, very new. As we have already seen, many organizations have a similar formal/informal organization structure. The reaction of these workers and first-line supervisors to rules imposed from above is a perfect example of what Gouldner [7] suggested occurs in what he called a 'mock bureaucracy'. Nevertheless, the study demonstrates a major problem for management. In formulating safety policy, account must be taken not only of management statutory and moral responsibilities, but also of the manner in which such a policy may be made meaningful and acceptable to those affected by it. Potentially, safety representatives and committees would appear to be at least a part of the answer.

Too much law?

A final consideration of the 1974 Act's implementation has to do with the extent to which it has met the Robens Report complaint of too much legislation. Despite early promises, it is clear that the volume of legislation has not diminished. Much of the pre-1974 safety statute still continues to exist, and rather than being replaced appears to be added to by new codes and regulations, British Standards and guidance notes. Added to these are existing and promised regulations arising out of EEC membership. This new material generally appears much more detailed than earlier provisions. Although this undoubtedly meets criticism that no standards are generally available against which to measure compliance with statute, implicit is a firm adherence to increasing statutory control rather than the self-regulation recommended by Robens.

IMPLICATIONS FOR MANAGEMENT

The implications of the HSWA for management are very clear. The Act emphasizes that management's responsibility includes all aspects of health and safety at work. In particular, management is required to formulate policies and provide organization structures to ensure that its responsibility is fulfilled. Policies and guidelines for policy formulation have already been discussed. Organization for health and safety is dealt with below.

There is however, a further important point of emphasis. If the objectives of the Act are examined, it becomes clear that a management policy based on post-incident action will not do. The emphasis is very clearly on prevention rather than cure. As early as 1921, Heinrich [8] in a review of over 5000 cases of potential accidental injury referred to a 300:29:1 ratio, i.e., for every 330 accidents of the same kind, involving the same persons, 1 will result in serious injury, 29 in minor injuries and 300 in no injury.

When an employee, either because of his repeated unsafe action or repeated exposure to an unsafe mechanical condition, suffers 300 no-injury accidents before he sustains even a minor injury, surely there can be no lack of opportunity in preventitive effort.

Although Heinrich deals with industrial safety, preventitive medicine, of course, attempts to tackle the problem of health hazards in exactly the same way, i.e., identify and analyse the potential hazard before it occurs, and develop and implement measures to prevent, or at least minimize, its effects.

ORGANIZATION FOR HEALTH AND SAFETY

Section 2 of the HSWA, it may be recalled, requires that employers must, in addition to preparing a health and safety policy, indicate the organization for carrying out that policy. Guidelines to policy drafting issued by the Health and Safety Executive suggest that individuals and their responsibilities should be defined.

Where functional expertise exists to advise line management, then the relationship of these functions should be made clear and the extent of their functions defined in relation to safety and health. However, research carried out by Beaumont *et al.* [1] suggests that this is frequently not the case.

Responsibility exists, of course, at all levels from managing director to the most junior worker on the shop floor.

At senior management level there exists a responsibility to ensure policy formulation, its adequate resourcing and enforcement. Line managers have the prime responsibility for ensuring that organizational objectives are achieved in a healthy and safe fashion. Theirs, too, is responsibility for training and hazard identification, supported as appropriate by functional specialists. At minimum, assistance should be available from a designated safety officer.

Safety officer

The specific duties of a safety officer will naturally vary from organization to organization. In a very large organization, safety officers may be appointed to cover specialist health or safety areas; in a rather smaller concern, the health and safety function may be attached to some other member of staff, for example the welfare officer or works manager. His authority may similarly vary from purely advisory to functional. Generally it is better that he be seen as an adviser, since this in no way conflicts with or diminishes the responsibility of line management. His main duties will include:

- ☐ to advise management at all levels and in all specialisms on matters of safety
- ☐ to advise during the design, development, modification or installation of buildings, plant, processes, etc.
- ☐ to advise on the installation of safety measures and procedures
- ☐ to advise on safety clothing
- ☐ to investigate and report on accidents
- ☐ to maintain and analyse safety records
- ☐ to advise on and carry out safety training as requested
- ☐ to advise on health and safety publicity
- ☐ to liaise with management, safety representatives, the safety committee and Health and Safety Executive inspectors

ACCIDENT PREVENTION

The Concise Oxford Dictionary defines an accident as an event without apparent cause, or an unforeseen course of events. In the industrial context, however, it is very clear that this definition lacks precision. Reference has already been made to the work of Heinrich who suggested that for every one serious injury and 29 minor injuries suffered by a worker, 300 other accidents would occur in which the workers would suffer no injury, 300 accidents providing an early warning of the existence of a particular hazard. Even a brief examination of the Health and Safety Executive's Annual Reports will show with monotonous and alarming regularity how most accidents are caused by the same predictable, and thus avoidable, causes year after year. Generally, it is accepted that whereas an accident may be unplanned, it is usually not unforeseeable. Accidents are in fact, the final phase of a chain of unsafe acts, or unsafe acts and conditions. If these activities can be identified, then accidents may be avoided.

Accident prevention therefore will involve:

☐ analysing accidents in order to learn by mistakes made
☐ engineering for safety
☐ carrying out regular safety inspections
☐ training and encouraging staff to be safety conscious

Accident analysis

As a basis for analysis, it is essential that *all* accidents, however minor, are investigated, recorded and reported. Normally the supervisor responsible for the employee concerned will be required to ensure that this is done, though in very serious cases, the safety officer or more senior line management may be involved. If reports are to be of value, it is vital that all accidents are reported and that reports contain useful information rather than a series of platitudes. Whether complete information is received will to a very large extent be determined by management attitude. Quite understandably, staff may feel recluctant to report incidents that could easily be 'hushed-up' if they anticipate criticism or disciplinary action. Although disciplinary proceedings may on occasions be necessary, staff will undoubtedly feel encouraged if they feel that reports will be positively received and that they are playing an important role in further accident prevention. Reports on accidents will of course only tell a part of the story. To take account of this it may be worthwhile arranging that 'near-accidents' are also recorded. Indeed, according to Heinrich, this may prove the most fruitful source of data.

If reports are to be of real value, they should also attempt to identify the cause, or more likely causes, of the incident. Initially these may be broken down into two categories: unsafe acts and unsafe conditions. These will be further divided, the intention being to establish specific problems which may be tackled and remedied, or which, though meaningless in themselves may, when collated with other data, indicate a trend.

The context in which the incident occurred should not be overlooked. Research has shown that situational factors, including job type, style of management, day or night shift, period of shift elapsed, age and sex of worker, and many others may all be significant.

An overall assessment of performance may also be of value either as a means of inter-firm comparison, or more usefully as a means of comparing departmental or plant performance and so highlighting problem areas. A commonly calculated index is:

The injury incidence rate, which is expressed as the number of reportable injuries (i.e., involving three days or more absence) per 1000 workers:

$$\frac{\text{Number of reportable injuries in period}}{\text{Average number of employees in period}} \times 1000$$

Engineering for safety

A considerable amount of attention has been given to safety engineering in recent years, its advocates at times apparently considering it a panacea for industrial accidents. Indeed, the HSWA imposes statutory duties on designers and installers of plant and equipment. In practice, it does not render all other precautions redundant. There are many cases recorded of workers over-riding, circumventing or removing safety devices. Nevertheless, despite such apparent foolishness, safety guards, fail-safe systems and other safety devices should be built in or added to equipment wherever possible. Protective clothing should be supplied where appropriate. Consideration should also be given to general environmental conditions. Good standards of heating, lighting, ventilation and housekeeping are all important in helping to eliminate accidents.

Safety inspections

Before the HSWA, statute provided for the regular inspection of pressure vessels, boilers, lifts and certain other plant. General inspections could, and still can, be made by Health and Safety Executive inspectors. The HSWA provides that Safety Representatives may carry out inspections at 3-monthly intervals, and in many organizations these are already carried out by members of safety committees. Normally, however, inspections will be the responsibility of supervisors and will be conducted on a fixed daily or weekly basis in accordance with pre-determined checklists. Spot checks may also be carried out by the supervisor, his superior, the safety officer, safety representatives or members of the safety committee. More often than not, the success of such checks is in identifying unsafe conditions rather than acts. Whatever the inspection method adopted, it must be ensured:

☐ that remedial action is promptly taken where a hazard is identified
☐ that inspections do take place and are not sacrificed for the sake of more immediately supervisory problems.

Safety training and publicity

Safety training is an esential part of any accident prevention scheme, and should commence immediately a member of staff is employed. As part of normal induction training, employees should be made aware of their responsibility for health and safety, general and special hazards, the use of safety clothing and equipment, the availability of medical services, safety rules and procedures for reporting accidents. After induction, further safety training may be necessary in connection with an individual's particular job.

The need for training does not, however, end at this point. Training is a continuous process. Changes in technology may give rise to new hazards. Refresher training may prove necessary where standards within a particular work group appear unsatisfactory. Further general training, e.g., lifting and handling, may also be considered worthwhile.

In addition to formal training, several other methods are available to publicize and re-inforce the safety message. These include posters, literature, films, exhibitions, safety award schemes and safety competitions, sometimes with cash prizes. Not surprisingly, the more successful of such schemes appear generally to be group based and require some degree of active employee participation.

OCCUPATIONAL HEALTH

In larger organizations, some form of occupational health service may be available. Medical services provided will generally fall into two categories: curative and preventitive. Until fairly recently, occupational medicine has concentrated largely on curative aspects, i.e., dealing with accidents and minor illness occurring in the workplace. Although such work continues to be important, the emphasis in occupational medicine as in occupational safety is increasingly on prevention. The main functions of an occupational health service are therefore:

☐ to provide treatment for injuries and illness occuring at the workplace
☐ to carry out medical examination of staff joining the organization or returning to work after sickness or accident
☐ to identify hazards
☐ to provide continuing medical examinations and screening services
☐ to provide medical advice both to individuals and the organization in relation, for example, to the installation of new technology, work processes, etc.

The potential contribution of such a service not only at a general caring level, but also in relation to the effectiveness and profitability of an organization is reflected in the sophisticated occupational health departments established by a growing number of major employers. British Telecom, for example, with around $\frac{1}{4}$ million employees, has established an occupational health service with more than 50 full-time occupational physicians, nurses and technicians, supplemented locally by part-time doctors. The medical staff carry out a wide range of occupational health services. While safeguards exist to protect normal medical ethics and codes of conduct, the service is closely integrated into both personnel and line management structures, linking it to the primary purpose of the business while clearly establishing the roles of each specialist function. In explaining BT's attitude its chief medical officer suggests:

> You might then ask why we took on such a massive programme. The answer might sound trite, but it is one thing to say 'our employees are our most valuable resource', another to behave as if you believe it. Thus it is important that we explore every route towards reduction of preventable disease in BT and reduce erosion of this resource to a minimum [9].

REFERENCES

1. Torrington, D.I. and Hall, L. (1987). *Personnel Management: A New Approach*. Prentice-Hall International.
2. Prentice, G. (1974). 'The safety rep: his roots and role', *Personnel Management*, November, pp. 36–39.
3. Donnelly, E. and Barrett, B. (1981). 'Safety training since the Act (1981)', *Personnel Management*, June, pp. 44–47.
4. Health and Safety Executive. (1976). *Safety Officers: Sample Survey of Roles and Functions*. HSE.
5. Anon. (1978). *Personnel Management*, October, pp. 26–27.
6. Gill, J. and Martin, K. (1976). 'Safety management: reconciling rules with reality', *Personnel Management*, June, pp. 36–39.
7. Gouldner, A.W. (1955). *Patterns of Industrial Bureaucracy*. Routledge and Kegan Paul.
8. Heinrich, H.W. (1959). *Industrial Accident Prevention*. McGraw-Hill.
9. Hughes, G. and Fingret, A. (1987). 'BT's direct line to occupational health, *Personnel Management*, October, pp. 68–71.

23
Statutory sick pay (SSP)

While occupational sickness arrangements have existed in many organizations for some time, with effect from April 1983, under the provisions of the Social Security and Housing Benefits Act 1982 (amended by the Health and Social Security Act 1984 and Social Security Act 1985) employers are responsible for paying to their employees statutory sick pay (SSP) in respect of the first 28 weeks of absence through sickness. Any such sum is recoverable from the State by holding back payment from National Insurance contributions paid monthly to the Inland Revenue. The principal effect of the new scheme is thus to transfer the administration load from State to employers. An outline of the basis of SSP is provided below. A number of excellent handbooks are available dealing with its administrative intricacies [1].

EMPLOYEES INCLUDED AND EXCLUDED

Generally SSP is payable to all employees if they are sick for 4 or more days in a row. However, several groups of employees are excepted. These are:

☐ employees who are past State pension age on the first day of sickness
☐ employees who are taken on for a specified period of no more than 3 months
☐ employees whose average weekly earnings are less than the lower weekly earnings limit for National Insurance contribution
☐ employees who go sick within 57 days of a claim in respect of one of a number of State benefits, including sickness benefit, invalidity pension, maternity allowance, unemployment benefit
☐ employees who have not yet started work
☐ employees who go sick during a stoppage of work as a result of trade dispute, unless they can prove that they did not take part in the dispute
☐ pregnant employees who are off sick during the time starting 11 weeks before their expected date of confinement and ending 6 weeks after
☐ employees who have already received 28 weeks' SSP in an earlier employment and there is less than 56 days elapsed since the last SSP payment

☐ employees who are sick while abroad outside the EEC
☐ employees in legal custody

PROCEDURE FOR CLAIMING SSP

In order to claim SSP an employee must demonstrate:

☐ that his day of incapacity for work is part of a *period of incapacity for work*, i.e., 4 or more consecutive days
☐ that the day is within a *period of entitlement*
☐ that the day is a *qualifying day*

These terms are explained below.

A period of entitlement

This period starts with the first day of capacity for work and ends when:

☐ the period of incapacity has ended
☐ an employee has received his full 8 weeks entitlement to SSP in the tax year or period of incapacity
☐ a pregnant employee reaches the 11 week before her anticipated date of confinement
☐ an employee's contract of employment ends
☐ an employee goes abroad outside the EEC
☐ an employee goes into legal custody

A qualifying day

A day when the employee is required by his contract of service to be available for work, i.e., a normal working day.

Any employee satisfying the above conditions is entitled to SSP at a flat rate for a maximum of 28 weeks from the same employer in any one period of entitlement or tax year. After such entitlement is exhausted, the employee may qualify for State Sickness Benefit, which is administered by the Department of Health and Social Security. Entitlement to SSP also extends to part-time staff, provided they earn the requisite amounts.

NON-PAYMENT OF SSP

For various reasons, circumstances may arise wherein an employer feels it inappropriate to pay SSP. Any private arrangement that sets out to limit, modify or exclude entitlement is void. However, if the withholding of SSP is due to a disagreement regarding entitlement, the Act provides that an employee may request a written statement explaining the employer's decision. This may then be referred for a decision to the Insurance Officer based at the local DHSS office. From here there exists a right of appeal.

SELF-CERTIFICATION

With effect from June 1982, doctors are no longer required to issue sick notes until 7 days' absence from work. Instead, employees are required, in respect of less than 7 days' absence, to obtain and complete forms that self-certify absence through illness.

IMPLICATIONS FOR MANAGEMENT

As indicated earlier, the net effect of the provisions described above is to shift a large proportion of administrative procedures formerly carried out by the DHSS and general practitioners onto employers and, to some degree, employees. In consequence, it is necessary for sickness and absence records systems to be refined and extended to take account of statutory requirements and to provide management with data to control self-certification. Such a need is illustrated in the experience of one company that, while acknowledging an increase in absence since self-certification was introduced, admitted that this was 'likely due to the fact that absence recording had been previously non-existent or unrealiable'.

In addition to recording self-certified absence and providing for its investigation and control, provision is also required for giving details of SSP decisions to employees, providing employees with exclusion or transfer forms so that they may claim state benefit, and the maintenance of statutory records both during and after the period to which they refer. Depending on company needs, such systems might be manual or computer based. To deal with these, several software packages are readily available compatible with a range of sizes and types of computer.

Other practical consequences have to do with self-certification. Although *prima facie* a licence for employees to take time off work whether sick, or malingering, the evidence suggests that generally this has not occurred. A study published by Incomes Data Services [2] showed that although most organizations had seen absence levels remaining static, where employers had tightened-up control systems, sickness absence had declined. Such findings are supported by earlier studies at Metal Box [3], where self-certification was introduced in 1981. Although the number of 2- and 3-day absences increased following the scheme's introduction, this was compensated for by a reduction in longer-period absences, suggesting that employees were monitoring their own sickness and returning to work when they felt well, rather than relying on the expiry of a doctor's certificate.

It will be noted that reference is made above to the tightening of control systems. The absence of a system of absence recording and analysis or one which is administered in a sloppy way invites abuse. Arrangements should exist, so that:

- [ ] employees know what is expected of them when they are sick in terms of reporting their absence, certification, etc. They should also be made aware of the risks of disciplinary action arising from abuse of the system.
- [ ] managers are aware of their responsibilities in terms of recording and reporting absences as well as interviewing staff on their return to work.
- [ ] absences are analysed so as to indicate not only individuals absent from work, but also other trends, e.g., departments, skill groups, nature of illness, etc., associated with higher than normal absence rates.
- [ ] procedures are available for the investigation of any apparent trends or the seeking of medical advice on individual cases.

REFERENCES

1. Gill, D. (1983). *How to Implement Statutory Sick Pay*. IPM.
2. IDS (1974). *Sick Pay and SSP*. IDS.
3. Howard, G. (1982). 'Self-certification at Metal Box', *Personnel Executive*, December, pp. 31–33.

24
Welfare

As discussed earlier, the birth of Personnel Management resulted largely from middle-class reaction to the treatment of workers during the nineteenth century. Often based on religious beliefs, the concern of campaigners was for the physical, mental and moral welfare of workers and was manifested in the paternalistic management style of employers, such as Boulton and Watt, and Robert Owen. This pre-occupation with welfare dominated the personnel management function for many years. Indeed, it was not until 1931 that the now Institute of Personnel Management abandoned its 'Institute of Industrial Welfare Workers' title.

A CHANGING ROLE

Increasingly as a nation we have accepted responsibility for the general welfare of people both at and away from work. Today, persons in need can seek the assistance and protection of the many welfare services offered by central and local government and a multiplicity of other agencies. Many areas traditionally considered welfare matters, e.g., holidays, pensions, insurance and low-interest mortgages, are now matters for negotiation as part of a total remuneration package. Other areas, e.g., health and safety are very largely controlled by statute, and with their increasing technical complexity are tending to be transferred out of the personnel function altogether. In many ways, therefore, the original role of the welfare officer has been usurped. This does not however mean that welfare is an anachronism. Modern methods of production, management and life condition us to new demands and attitudes; subject us to new pressures. The role of the welfare officer has simply changed.

WELFARE SERVICES

In view of the various modifications of the welfare role, what remains? Welfare services may best be categorized as:

- [ ] personal services
- [ ] group services

Personal services

The nature of personal welfare services will logically be determined by the needs of individual employees. Generally, services will take the form of counselling employees in difficulty or at potentially difficult stages of life. Employees may, for example, have domestic, legal or financial problems.

Although many would argue that such matters have nothing to do with an employer, the reaction of the worker to such problems is likely to significantly affect his performance at work. An example is the behaviour patterns of individuals approaching or in the process of divorce. With one in three marriages in the UK ending in divorce and the consequent psychological consequences lasting for perhaps two or three years, employers are unwise if they simply adopt the attitude 'it's nothing to do with us'. The Marital Information and Divorce Advisory Service (MIDAS) [1] has proposed that during the worst year of the experience, individual performance may be reduced by two-thirds. Absenteeism on grounds of ill-health, to resolve legal and family problems and as a result of accidents (to which the divorcing or recently divorced appear particularly prone) may further reduce an employee's contribution. For an employer to arrange counselling so as to minimize such effects, or to reduce stress by providing expert advice on legal or financial matters may well be a sound investment.

If divorce is, at least in part, a reflection of a more stressed society, so too are increasing rates of alcoholism. The effects of alcoholism are well documented. It is typically associated with physical disability and impaired emotional, occupational and social skills. Given American estimates that between 5–10% of a workforce is likely to be affected by a drink problem and that absenteeism may be four times higher than average among such employees [3], the matter is clearly something that management should consider with concern, and provide for in supervisor training, disciplinary procedures and counselling facilities.

Stress and personal problems may, of course, arise from a whole range of sources, and staff simply need a hand to get through difficult or trying circumstances. In each case, the role of the welfare officer is to help the employee to solve his own problems, and not to solve problems for him. Although he may become involved in liaison with management colleagues and agencies outside his own organization, the welfare officer must resist the temptation to get personally involved or begin to direct rather than advise an employee. Often problems may be very simply resolved merely by the provision of accurate information, or by putting an employee in touch with a specialist adviser within or outside the organization. On other occasions, employees will come to a welfare officer not for advice, but merely to talk about a problem as an aid to determining or confirming their own solutions [4].

Group services

Of group services commonly offered, some are well established, e.g., sports and social clubs (though this in no way confirms their value); others, e.g., child-care facilities are indicators of relatively recent trends. Which services are offered will, of course, depend on the philosophy and finances of a particular organization. Further determinants may be the type of industry involved, or an organization's location. Among the more common are:

- [ ] subsidized canteen or restaurant facilities
- [ ] subsidized living accommodation
- [ ] child-care facilities
- [ ] subsidized or free transport facilities
- [ ] purchase discount schemes
- [ ] sports and social clubs, 'industrial concert' tickets, subsidized holiday travel arrangements
- [ ] company scholarships
- [ ] benevolent funds

WHY SHOULD WELFARE ACTIVITIES BE PROVIDED?

There is little evidence to prove that welfare facilities will increase productivity. Pioneers in the field, such as Cadburys at Bournville and Lever Brothers at Port Sunlight, proceeded on the basis that if staff were placed in congenial surroundings they would work harder. However, Herzberg et al. [2] (you will recall) suggested that such facilities were hygiene factors, not motivators. They do not stimulate people to work harder; rather they prevent dissatisfaction.

Why then should facilities be provided? As mentioned above, at one time welfare facilities were provided in an atmosphere of all encompassing paternalism. Outside Japan, such an attitude is largely unacceptable today. Instead, it is increasingly accepted that management has a more conservative but nevertheless important social responsibility for the general wellbeing of staff. The provision of welfare services thus fulfills a social responsibility to which staff are entitled.

Although for some organizations, such a role would be adequate justification for welfare expenditure, it is probably fair to say that the number of such organizations is declining. Even in the area of staff welfare, management is tending to be more cost effectiveness aware. What then is welfare's economic role? Among the organizational benefits claimed are:

- ☐ improved job satisfaction
- ☐ improved morale
- ☐ easier recruitment
- ☐ an enhanced public image
- ☐ reduced labour turnover

However, in many cases these claimed benefits are probably rationalizations for the existence of facilities.

Improved job satisfaction or morale will not necessarily contribute to productivity, and indeed the influence of welfare seems likely to be incidental when compared with other factors. Prospective employees do not generally place welfare facilities at the top of their shopping list when jobhunting. What tend to be more important are salary, the nature of work involved, security and prospects for promotion. Although welfare may be of importance in marginal cases, it is often the case that organizations paying the best salaries and wages also offer the best welfare facilities. Similarly, an employee considering leaving rarely seems likely to be dissuaded by thoughts of comparative welfare provisions (though Flowers and Hughes [3] suggest that these may be important in retaining unskilled manufacturing employees). For many employers, therefore, the returns that accrue as a result of welfare expenditure are doubtful, largely unquantifiable and must in most cases be considered an act of faith.

PRINCIPLES FOR PROVIDING WELFARE FACILITIES

If company welfare provisions are to benefit employees or employer, it is important that they are regularly reviewed. In carrying out such a review, what are the principles to be borne in mind?:

- ☐ *The return to the organization should a least equal the cost of the facilities provided*
  The difficulty of achieving this has already been discussed. Nevertheless, as an objective it can be recommended.

- ☐ *Facilities should satisfy a need*
  Facilities should only be supplied if they satisfy a need. This is an obvious maxim, but often overlooked. Provision of a service that nobody wants can frequently turn into a demand to stop wasting money and start paying more wages. To ask employees what they want is often equally hazardous. Usually facilities in demand will be highlighted by staff without prompting by management.

- ☐ *Paternalism should be avoided*
  One of the main dangers in the provision of welfare services is that an impression of old-fashioned paternalism may be created. In

some countries a paternalistic attitude is perfectly acceptable. In Japan it is normal practice, many organizations looking after staff and their families literally from birth to death. In return, the average Japanese worker spends his whole working life with one company, identifying himself totally with it, and sometimes beginning his working day with communal prayers of thanksgiving to the spirit of the company. Such a management attitude is unlikely to find favour with the average British worker, and a welfare policy based on such a basis is thus likely to do more harm than good.

☐ *As many employees should potentially benefit as possible*
Although staff should never be coerced into taking advantage of welfare facilities, the facilities offered should potentially benefit as many employees as possible. A minority service is unlikely to produce an acceptable return, and indeed may stimulate division or elitism.

A technique to meet this criterion found in the USA, though not to any degree in the UK, is the so-called 'cafeteria' approach. As its name suggests, the principle of the system is that each employee is credited with a welfare benefits expenditure limit within which he is free to choose benefits so as to most closely meet his own needs. Such a system, it is argued, overcomes complaints from employees who consider company money wasted or derive no benefit from company schemes owing to their personal circumstances. It is argued that it also encourages the use of welfare facilities, employees becoming more knowledgeable in the process and hopefully more satisfied in consequence. The potential administrative nightmare associated with such a scheme is all too obvious; nevertheless, it does represent an attempt to translate welfare provision from its traditional role to something more meaningful, valued by staff and thus potentially of value to the employing organization.

REFERENCES

1. Marital Information and Divorce Advisory Service. (1984). *Surviving Divorce: Men Beyond Marriage*. MIDAS.
2. Herzberg, F., Mausner, B. and Snyderman, B. (1959). *Motivation to Work*. Wiley.
3. Flowers, V.S. and Hughes, C.L. (1973). 'Why employees stay', *Harvard Business Review*, July/August, pp. 54–55.
4. Orlans, V. (1986). 'Counselling services in organisations', *Personnel Review*, Vol. 15, No. 5, pp. 19–23.

PART 6: FURTHER RECOMMENDED READING

Selwyn, N.M. (1982). *Law of Employment*. Butterworths.
Whincup, M. (1983). *Modern Employment Law*. Heinemann.
Slade, E.A. (1983). *Tolley's Employment Handbook*. Tolley.
Arscott, P. and Armstrong, M. (1976). *An Employer's Guide to Health and Safety Management*. Kogan Page.
Martin, A.O. (1967). *Welfare At Work*. Batsford.

PART 6: SAMPLE EXAMINATION QUESTIONS

It has often been said that the responsibilities of the personnel function include the 'welfare' of employees in the organization. How far would you agree with this proposition? What would you consider to be the future of the 'welfare' role in personnel management?   ICSA

Identify the components of an effective health and safety policy for an organization. What steps should be taken to ensure that the policy is implemented and does not become a mere collection of platitudes?   ICSA

What are the strengths and shortcomings of the Health and Safety at Work Act?   IPM

In the general field of health, safety and welfare how do the roles of the following differ:

(a) Personnel Officers   (b) Safety Officers
(c) Occupational Health Nurses   (d) Line Supervisors?   IPM

The emphasis in health and safety within any building society should be on accident prevention. What specific training schemes would you implement in order to encourage this philosophy?   CBSI

(a) What are welfare services. You should illustrate your answer with practical examples.

(b) What benefits does the employer gain from the provision of welfare services?   CBSI

Discuss the arguments for and against the inclusion of safety within the personnel function.   CBSI

In 1972, the Royal Commission on Safety and Health at Work reported that unnecessarily large numbers of days are lost each year through industrial accidents, injuries and diseases, because of the 'attitudes, capabilities and performance of people and the efficiency of the organisational systems within which they work'. To what extent has the situation changed?   ICSA

'Expenditure on health and safety cannot be justified on cost-effective grounds – that is why it is invariably treated as a low-priority item.' Discuss.   ICSA

Part 7
Industrial relations

25
Trade unions and employers' associations

In view of the wide-ranging ramifications of industrial relations and the ways in which the term is used colloquially, it might be as well to start with a definition. Bain and Clegg [1] have defined it as:

> The study of the rules, institutions and processes both formal and informal, structured and unstructured, of job regulation.

McCarthy [2] offers the following for those preferring a shorter but less precise definition:

> The factors affecting the wage/work equation.

Through a combination of the above definitions, it is apparent that we shall need to look at the parties to the 'wage/work bargain', the framework and rules within which they operate and the methods used to regulate this complex system.

The British system of industrial relations, like most others, is composed of three parties:

1 Workers and their organizations
2 Employers or management and their organizations
3 Government and government agencies

These three parties create a complex network of rules to govern workplace relationships, and in particular to define the status and conduct of the parties. Basically, these rules are of two kinds:

1 *Procedural* — dealing with relationships and methods of approaching problems or contingencies (e.g., disciplinary procedures) — the 'rules of the game'.
2 *Substantive* — dealing with subject matter, such as wage rates or working conditions.

It should be remembered that the parties to these rules operate in the wider social and political environment that forms part of the overall study of industrial relations. The concept of an industrial relations system can be viewed at:

- [ ] national level
- [ ] industry level
- [ ] firm or plant level

These levels are a useful theoretical device for analysing and discussing systems, but in practice, of course, the boundaries are far more blurred, and the events at each 'level' must affect consideration of the others.

The structure of industrial relations in the UK has been established largely on a 'voluntary' basis. Despite legislation that has increased substantially in recent years agreements are not normally enforceable at law as, for example, in the USA. It is based chiefly upon the organization of employees into trade unions and employers' into associations (although to a lesser extent), and on freely conducted negotiations between them — 'collective bargaining' — at all levels.

TRADE UNIONS

Structure

In the study of most organizations the term 'structure' usually refers to its internal parts and their relationship to each other. In respect of trade unions, the term usually refers to consideration of the size and type of unions and their coverage in respect of different industries and types of worker. The internal workings of a trade union are usually termed 'organization' or 'government'.

Traditionally, trade unions have been categorized into three main types:

1 *Craft* — membership based upon specific skills or occupations across industrial boundaries. One of the earliest forms of association, e.g., Amalgamated Union of Engineering Workers (AUEW)
2 *Industrial* — these cover most or all workers in a particular industry, regardless of specific occupation, e.g., National Union of Mineworkers (NUM).
3 *General* — commencing with the spread of unionism to unskilled and semi-skilled workers at the end of the nineteenth century — the 'New Unionism' — these recruit from many industries and occupations, e.g., Transport and General Workers Union (TGWU).

Although not strictly a separate category of union, the 'white collar' unions have gained prominence in recent years and are sometimes treated separately. They recruit from managerial, administrative, supervisory and technical staff and may take any one of the above three forms: examples include the National and Local Government Officers Association (NALGO) and the Association of Scientific, Technical and Managerial Staff (ASTMS).

It must be remembered that the above distinctions are by no means clear cut, and that there are other methods of categorization available. Turner [3] prefers a different 3-fold classification system — 'closed', 'open' and 'intermediate', based upon the recruitment policy of the union concerned.

Membership

Trade union membership in the UK reached a peak of 13.3 million in 1979. Since that time there has been a downward trend to around 10.5 million in 1986 (see Fig. 25.1). This reduction is mainly due to a combination of high unemployment in the 1980s and the growth of the service sector, alongside the contraction of traditional areas of unionism such as engineering and energy supply. Changes towards part-time work could also be an influence upon declining numbers as union membership is not prevalent amongst this group. The number of trade unions had also declined from a peak of 519 in 1973 to a figure of 335 in 1986. Much of this decline is due to a continuing process of mergers. Figure 25.1 also provides an historical view of the large number of unions at the end of the last century compared to the low membership.

The size of unions varies widely with over 50% being relatively small with less than 1000 members. At the other extreme are some 8 unions representing over 50% of the membership (see Table 25.1). Trends in union membership are always difficult to predict, and despite the fact that many unions have contracted in recent years, some white-collar areas, such as banking and finance, have increased their membership.

History

The trade union movement has a long and chequered history in this country, and unions have had to adapt to changes both internally initiated and imposed from outside. No enlightened study of industrial relations can be made without some knowledge of this history and further reading is recommended [5].

Internal organization

Although the internal organizational structure of unions varies, many follow the following pattern:

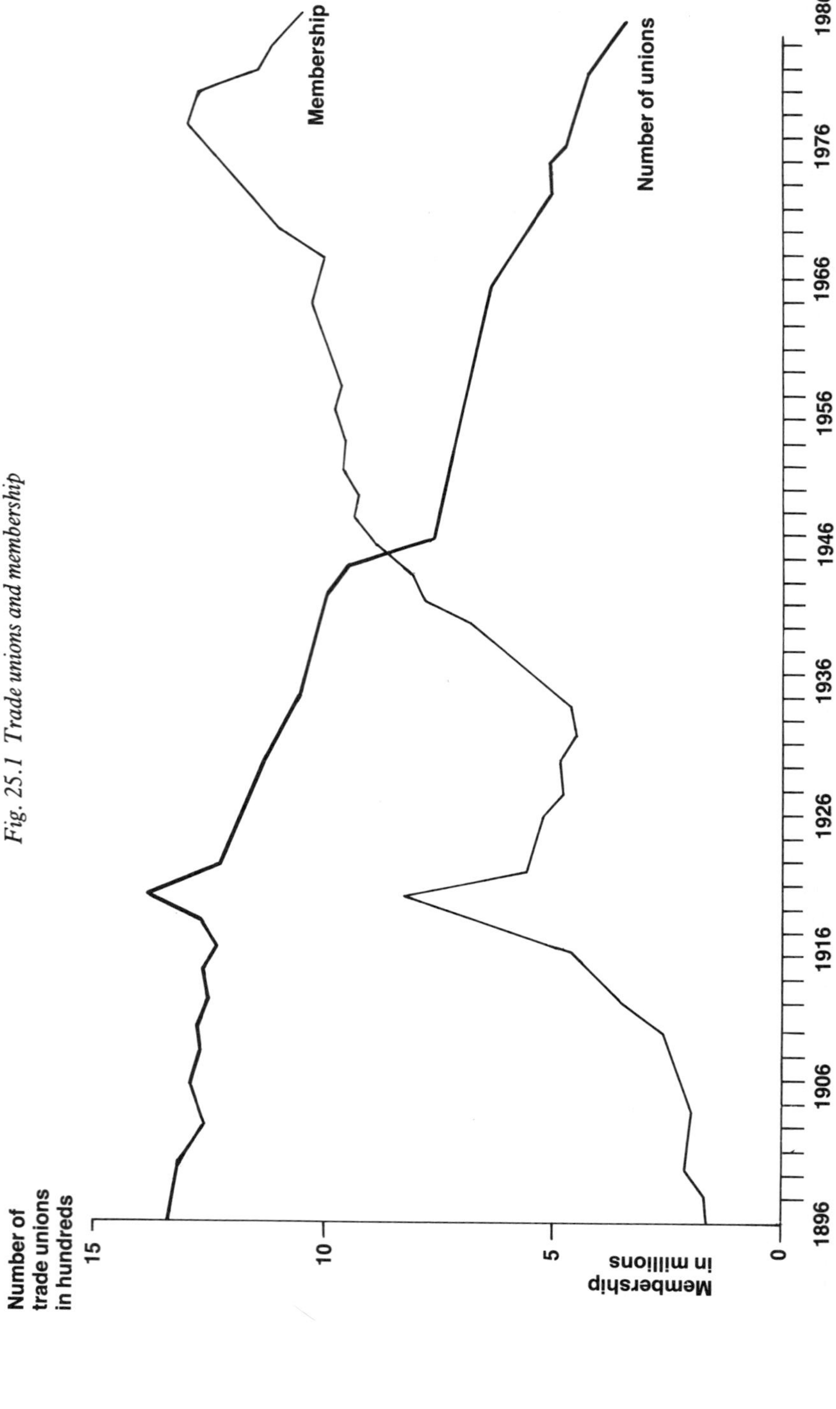

Fig. 25.1 Trade unions and membership

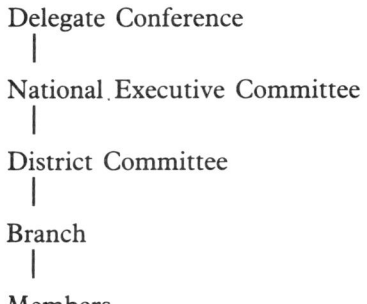

Delegate Conference
|
National Executive Committee
|
District Committee
|
Branch
|
Members

The *Delegate Conference* normally meets annually and is the main policy-making body. Delegates who attend the conference usually represent branches, and they receive a report from the executive committee on the past year. Various motions are debated, covering a wide range of subjects.

The *National Executive Committee* controls the union on a day-to-day basis. It may also form the nucleus of a larger 'council', which may

Table 25.1 Trade unions — numbers and membership, end 1986

Size	Number of unions	All membership (thousand)	Percentage of	
			Number of unions	Membership of all unions
Under 100 members	63	3	18.8	0.0
100–499	81	21	24.2	0.2
500–999	30	23	8.9	0.2
1000–2499	50	83	14.9	0.8
2500–4999	22	76	6.6	0.7
5000–9999	16	105	4.8	1.0
10 000–14 999	5	62	1.5	0.6
15 000–24 999	10	192	3.0	1.8
25 000–49 999	25	911	7.5	8.6
50 000–99 999	7	544	2.1	5.2
100 000–249 999	15	2657	4.5	25.2
250 000 and over	9	5862	2.7	55.6
*Membership unknown	3	–	0.9	0.0
All members	335	10,539	100.0	100.0

*There were three unions in 1986 whose membership was not reported, two of which were newly formed in 1986.
Source: Department of Employment *Gazette*.

meet at monthly intervals. Some of the members may be full-time salaried officials, but others may be part-time lay-members. The committee carries out similar duties to those of a board of directors, and it must be remembered that in the larger unions the responsibilities for both members and funds is considerable. The 'Chief Officer' who usually chairs the executive, can greatly influence decisions and many become national figures.

The *District Committee*, sometimes referred to as a Regional or Divisional Committee, is usually made up largely of lay-officials elected by local branches, although a full-time paid Secretary will often be employed. This committee is responsible for co-ordinating the work of the branches and bringing regional problems to the attention of the executive. In larger unions industrial problems, as opposed to administrative ones, are sometimes dealt with by regional trade groups that co-ordinate the interests of various trades or occupations within the union.

Every member of a union is assigned to a *Branch* that may be based upon a geographical area or a place of work. Branches may be administered by full-time officials, but it is more likely that lay-officials will be appointed. The Branch forms the mouthpiece for members' views, and these are passed up through the union machinery. It is also the point of transmission of union policy to the membership. Branch meetings are held at regular intervals, although often poorly attended.

The *Members* of the union require representation at the shop-floor level, and this is usually provided by an elected shop steward. The growth and importance of shop stewards in recent years demands closer study.

The shop steward/staff representative

The Report of the Royal Commission on Trade Unions and Employer's Associations [7], known as the Donovan Report, states:

> In most factories in which trade unions are strong, their members in each workshop choose one of their number to speak for them . . . he or she may go under a number of titles, but the most common is 'shop steward'.

Unlike full-time union officials, most shop stewards spend a relatively small proportion of their time on trade union duties. Elections are often informal and frequently appointments are uncontested. The job of a shop steward is not particularly popular, and incumbents are rarely opposed in office.

Much of the authority vested in the shop steward appears to be tacit rather than formally devolved. Many union rule books do not set out his duties clearly, although most shop stewards are issued with a handbook that provides guidance as to what is expected of him. The collection of membership subscriptions offers regular contact with members, but many employers now deduct union dues from pay and transfer them to the union in bulk. It is important to remember that many branches are poorly supported, and therefore the shop steward becomes the main method of communication between the union and its members, being the focal point of union activity at the workplace. Indeed, for the vast majority of members, the shop steward *is* the union.

The importance of work-place representatives is due largely to the development of plant-level bargaining in many industries (see section on Collective Bargaining, page 285). Consequently, it is probably fair to say that trade union duties have become subordinate to those in respect of industrial relations. Many are involved in a great deal of direct negotiation concerning pay and working conditions, and can wield considerable influence particularly where payment-by-results systems and overtime are operated. In larger organizations there may be senior shop stewards, or conveners, who act as spokesmen on major issues. Where more than one union has members within a firm, a joint shop steward committee may co-ordinate the interests of the various work groups. Some senior shop stewards may spend most of their time on union business, rather than the typical few hours per week. Despite the poor press that shop stewards usually receive, the Donovan Committee concluded that they were generally a moderating influence — 'more of a lubricant than an irritant'.

As has been stated above, the functions and the relationship of the shop steward vis-à-vis the union, and indeed the employer, can be somewhat nebulous. The position does, of course, vary from union to union and from one employer to another. The position was dealt with in a report by the Commission on Industrial Relations [8] and many of its recommendations were consolidated into the Industrial Relations Code of Practice [9], which was not abolished with the Industrial Relations Act 1971. The 'facilities' recommended for shop stewards include the following.

Appointment and qualifications

Trade unions and management should agree upon the number of shop stewards and eligibility for appointment. Facilities should be provided for publicity and the holding of elections.

Status

Trade unions should recognize their shop stewards through the provision of comprehensive written credentials, covering powers and duties together with his period of office and scope of representation. These credentials should also be acknowledged by management.

Co-ordination

In establishments where there are several shop stewards, whether or not of the same union, arrangements should be made for the election of a senior steward to co-ordinate their activities with the agreement of management.

Facilities

Dependent upon the shop steward's functions, union and management should endeavour to provide as a minimum:

□ time off work with pay to deal with his industrial relations duties, subject to management permission
□ details of new employees
□ accommodation for meetings
□ access to a telephone and notice-boards
□ provision of office facilities where appropriate

Training

Trade unions and management should jointly endeavour to see that the shop steward receives any training considered appropriate to his needs, and that he is kept adequately informed on the policies and objectives of both parties.

The recommendations concerning time off for industrial relations duties and training have become an entitlement under the Employment Protection (Consolidation) Act 1978, and ACAS has issued a separate Code of Practice on the subject. The remainder depend upon the degree of co-operation and enlightenment of the union and employer involved. The importance of the shop steward at the centre of British industrial relations cannot be denied. It would therefore appear beneficial to both union and management to provide the recognition and facilities recommended in the Code of Practice [10].

External organization

Unions combine in various ways in order to further their own interests. Trades Councils are formed on a geographical basis, consisting of local union branches. They provide a forum for discussing issues raised by local trade unionists and co-ordinating the movement regarding representation in civic matters. Certain unions also form Federations that represent them on a joint basis, particularly for collective bargaining purposes. There are some 40 federations, of which the largest is the Confederation of Shipbuilding and Engineering Unions.

The Trades Union Congress (TUC)

The Trades Union Congress (TUC) is perhaps the best known body outside of the individual unions. Not all unions are affiliated to the TUC, but those that are represent well over 90% of trade union members. The TUC's history goes back for well over 100 years, during which time it has become one of the most influential bodies in Britain. The highlight of the year is the annual conference (Congress), to which affiliated unions are entitled to send one delegate for every 5000 members. Resolutions submitted by various unions are passed on a whole variety of topics, and the General Council is elected for the forthcoming year.

The General Council is the executive body of the TUC. It meets each month to examine the detailed work carried out by the special committees that are part of the organization's structure. There are committees consisting wholly of General Council members, in addition to many others that may include TUC staff members or representatives of government departments and employers' organizations. The 44 seats on the General Council are allocated to 'trade groups' and there is a group to ensure representation of women (2 seats). Seats are allocated according to the size of the unions in each group, although some flexibility is provided to cater for sectional interests. Each group nominates its representative(s).

The daily work of the TUC is supervised by the General Secretary and his Assistant. He is supported by more than 100 staff at Congress House, many of whom are graduates. They are organized into five main departments — Economic, Education, Organization, International and Social Insurance. Apart from many other duties, these departments provide the back-up for the many committees referred to above. The officers within these departments without doubt form the largest group of specialists in the trade union movement.

Apart from its considerable powers to intervene in industrial disputes, either with employers or between affiliated unions, the TUC has traditionally attempted to influence events on a wider front. The historical links with the Labour Party as well known and, in the past, the TUC has had a powerful influence in the political field when governments of both complexions have been in power. Apart from direct representation, the TUC has been well represented on a number of 'tripartite' bodies such as ACAS, HSC and NEDC. However, the strained relations between the TUC and the present government illustrated by the former's recent removal from the Training Commission may suggest a changing view of the TUC's participation in national bodies.

Trade union objectives and methods

Objectives

In their classic work, the Webbs [11] described a trade union as 'a continuous association of wage earners for the purpose of improving the condition of their working lives'. Although written many years ago, this remains valid as the central aim of trade unions. It is of course, difficult to discuss generally the objectives of 'trade unionism' as these will vary dependent upon the type of union, the views of the individual officers and members and between the long and short-term.

In its written evidence to the Donovan Commission, the TUC listed the following as its main objectives:

1 Improved terms of employment
2 Improved physical environment at work
3 Full employment and national prosperity
4 Security of employment and income
5 Improved social security
6 Fair shares in national income and wealth
7 Industrial democracy
8 Advice in government
9 Improved public and social services
10 Public control and planning in industry

Although it was stated that the objectives were in no order of priority, it is significant that terms of employment are at the top of the list. It is also apparent that some of these objectives are of a wider political nature, and this is no accident. Anyone making a serious study of trade unions cannot ignore their political aims, as these are an inseparable part of their objectives.

Methods

The main methods employed by trade unions to achieve their objectives are:

1 Collective bargaining — a traditional and central feature of British industrial relations, discussed more fully below (Chapter 26)
2 Joint consultation — although shunned by some trade unionists, it offers a forum for the exchange of views (see Chapter 27)
3 Autonomous job regulation — work groups or trade unions may unilaterally change work methods or production levels; this could include strike action
4 Services to members — many unions provide various welfare facilities for members, such as sickness and unemployment benefits

5   Influence of government — the trade union movement's influence upon the Labour Party and at government level has been referred to above
6   Political action — this can include representations, demonstrations and strikes for political rather than industrial purposes
7   International activities — the TUC and other unions are affiliated to various international bodies whose aims are broadly similar to those referred to above

Of these methods, collective bargaining is by far the most important, in line with the major objective of improving the pay and working conditions of union members.

STAFF ASSOCIATIONS

Many white collar workers are represented by staff associations rather than trade unions. There has been a tradition of staff associations in areas such as the financial sector, covering insurance, banking and building societies. However, white collar unions carried out vigorous recruiting campaigns in the early 1970s and unions such as BIFU and ASTMS now represent many workers in banking and insurance. Some staff associations have thrived despite the trade unions, and the building society industry is a prime example. Here, in fact, many of the larger associations have obtained 'certificates of independence' from the Certification Officer under the Trade Union and Labour Relations Act 1974.

The objectives of staff associations in industrial relations terms could be compared to those of trade unions, although the wider ambitions of trade unionism are not evident. Terms and conditions of employment will often be negotiated through a Joint Committee, and the interests of the association's members are its prime concern. Much criticism has been levelled at staff associations in the past owing to the fact that they have been 'supported' by the employers. However, many of the larger associations are now becoming more professional and have been financially independent of employers for some years. If they are not effective in representing the interests of their members in the future no doubt the white collar unions will be ready to step in should they be required to do so.

EMPLOYERS' ASSOCIATIONS

It should first be established what is meant by 'employers' associations', although there is no precise definition. Many associations are mainly concerned with commercial matters, such as the problem of standards for certain products or methods of trading, and these are normally called 'trade associations'. From an industrial relations viewpoint, those associations that are concerned with the regulation of wages and other conditions of employment are of interest. Historically, they were formed in response to trade unionism and in order to strengthen the employer's influence over terms of employment. There are at present some 1000 employers' associations concerned with employment matters, but this figure includes local associations, such as Chambers of Commerce. They range from fairly small organizations to the huge Engineering Employers' Federation, which covers firms employing some 2 million people.

Associations also range from those with no apparent constitution to those with complex structures including local, regional and national organizational levels. Staff may vary from one part-time officer to many full-time employees. Funds are usually derived from members' subscriptions, which are usually in proportion to their payroll. An executive body is invariably elected by the members, and its power will depend upon the particular constitution.

Ironically, most associations are trade unions from a legal point of view, but in many cases they were developed as a defence for individual employers against trade unions. The main functions of these associations are:

- [ ] *Negotiation* of national agreements on wages and conditions as well as various procedural agreements
- [ ] An *advisory role* to members, providing advice on such matters as industrial relations strategy, training, pay systems, manpower planning, redundancy, etc.
- [ ] *Representation* of members' views to government and other bodies, such as EEC in respect of legislation and economic planning

These functions do, of course, vary, and there is a tendency for some of the larger companies to take over some of them for themselves (particularly negotiations). Others have resigned from associations to avoid restriction of their actions. In fact, the very large and the very small companies tend to avoid employers' associations — probably because they do not feel a need for them. It is probably fair to say that although remaining very influential, the move towards plant-level bargaining has greatly diminished the associations' role in the field of negotiations.

The Confederation of British Industry (CBI)

The CBI was formed in 1965 as the result of a merger of the British Employers' Confederation, the Federation of British Industries and the National Associaiton of British Manufacturers. This represented a centralization of the major national organizations into one body. Organization of employers' associations on a national basis was a much later development than that of trade unions. It was not until the first World War and government intervention into private industry that the organizations that formed the CBI were themselves created.

The CBI admits employers' associations, trade associations and individual companies to membership besides the nationalized industries. Its objectives include:

To provide for British industry the means of formulating, making known and influencing general policy in regard to industrial, economic, fiscal, commercial, labour, social, legal and technical questions, and to act as a national point of reference for those seeking industry's views.

It must be remembered that the CBI can only attempt to influence, but has no direct negotiating rights or control over its members. Unlike the General Council of the TUC, it cannot intervene directly in industrial disputes. It is fair to say that it has not achieved the influence and status of the TUC in the eyes of the public. However, its background and objectives are not strictly comparable, and it is its influence upon economic planning and government policy by which it must be judged.

The CBI is governed by the Council of about 400 elected members, but it operates largely through a series of standing committees. It is also represented on many national bodies and joint committees with the TUC. Labour matters are dealt with by the Labour and Social Affairs Committee, but although it formulates policy for transmission to members, the government and other bodies, its main role remains advisory. The CBI maintains international contacts through membership of the International Organization of Employers.

INDUSTRIAL RELATIONS POLICY

Each employer should consider a policy on industrial relations especially where staff are, or are about to be, represented by a trade union or staff association.

The *objectives might include*:

☐ A climate of trust and cooperation.
☐ The avoidance of conflict and disputes.
☐ The resolution of any problems by the use of agreed procedures with a view to keeping disruption to a minimum.
☐ Machinery and dialogue which provides for employees' views and rights to be recognized whilst acknowledging the need for the organization to be managed.

A *policy statement would include*:

- ☐ Above objectives.
- ☐ Statement of union recognition.
- ☐ Collective bargaining and negotiating machinery.
- ☐ Joint consultation arrangements.
- ☐ Agreed procedures.
- ☐ Workplace representation.
- ☐ Employee participation.
- ☐ Management guidelines on specific IR matters and IR aspects of other activities.

Even where staff are not represented by a formal body, many of the above principles might apply to a policy on 'employee relations'.

REFERENCES

1. Bain, G.S. and Clegg, H.A. (1974). 'A strategy for industrial relations research in Great Britain', *British Journal of Industrial Relations*, March.
2. McCarthy, W.E.J. (1969). *Industrial Relations in Britain*. Lyon, Grant & Green.
3. Turner, H.A. (1962). *Trade Union Growth, Struucture and Policy*. George Allen & Unwin.
4. Price, R. and Bain, G.S. *in* Bain, G.S. (Ed.) (1983). *Industrial Relations in Britain*, Chapter 1. Basil Blackwell.
5. Pelling, H. (1976). *A History of British Trade Unionism*. Pelican.
6. Armstrong, E. *in* Kessler, S. and Weekes, B. (Eds.). (1971). *Conflict at Work*, Chapter 2. BBC Publications.
7. Lord Donovan. (1968). *Report of the Royal Commission on Trade Unions and Employers' Assocations*. HMSO.
8. Commission on Industrial Relations. (1971). *Facilities Afforded to Shop Stewards*, Report No. 17. HMSO.
9. *Industrial Relations Code of Practice*. (1971). HMSO.
10. For a review of facilities for worker representatives, *see* Daniel, W.W. and Millward, N. (1983). *Workplace Industrial Relations in Britain*, (DE/PSI/SSRC Survey), Chapter 2. Heinemann.
11. Webb, S. and Webb, B. (1894). *History of Trade Unionism*. Longman.

26
Collective bargaining

One of the central objectives of trade unionism has been the replacement of individual negotiation of pay and other terms of employment with a collective agreement made between employers or their associations and workers' organizations. This method of negotiation and settling conditions of employment is known as collective bargaining. Flanders [1], however, disagreed with the Webbs' interpretation that collective bargaining was the collective equivalent of individual market bargaining. He contends that unions do not sell their members' labour but rather enter into a joint rule-making process. He also prefers the terms 'joint determination' or 'joint regulation' to collective bargaining.

Collective bargaining is not only concerned with agreements about terms of employment, but also with the regulation of relationships between the two parties. Procedural agreements will be entered into for settling disputes that may arise between the parties. These disputes may arise as a result of some matter not covered by existing agreements or out of the interpretation of those already entered into. The scope of collective bargaining has widened considerably over the years. Apart from basic wages and hours of work, negotiations may include such things as holidays, sick pay, training, work methods, discipline, promotion, etc. Although management tries to preserve its prerogatives in certain areas, there are no theoretical limits to the matters that could be the subject of collective bargaining. There is obviously a constant attempt by both parties to establish rights and resolve conflicts of interest, which has been termed 'power bargaining'. However, if 'voluntary' collective bargaining is to remain a viable institution, the ideologies of the parties must remain sufficiently compatible for mutual recognition to continue.

BARGAINING MACHINERY

Collective bargaining machinery refers to the bodies and channels of negotiations that have been established over the years. A typical piece of machinery at national level would comprise several unions on one side and one or more employers' associations on the other.

Apart from *ad hoc* bodies that have developed to deal with the negotiations of various industries, the more formal bodies were largely formed as a result of the recommendations of the Whitley Committee in 1916 which were:

1 That Joint Industrial Councils should be set up in well organized industries
2 That works committees, consisting of representatives from workers and management should be appointed in individual establishments
3 That the Trade Boards system of statutory wages regulation in badly organized trade should be extended. This resulted in the extension of Trade Councils and subsequently Wages Councils (see page 236)
4 That a permanent Court of Arbitration be set up
5 That the Minister of Labour should be authorized to hold enquiries into disputes

Great emphasis was given to the desirability of voluntary machinery to encourage collective bargaining although a structure for the joint bodies was recommended. A three-tier structure of committees was proposed — national, district and works — that would meet regularly and have written constitutions. Terms of reference were to include not only the traditional areas of negotiation, i.e., pay and conditions of employment, but also matters of efficiency, education, training and research. There are at present some 200 Joint Industrial Council in various industries, including flour milling and chemicals. In central and local government and the nationalized industries, there is a statutory obligation to form such bodies, and in the Civil Service they are usually known as Whitley Councils (see also Chapter 27, page 297).

Most manual workers are covered by one of many pieces of negotiating machinery at national level and in the public sector many non-manual employees also come within their scope. It is important to remember that the number of employees whose terms of employment are considered by these bodies is much greater than the number of trade unionists. Generally, the collective agreements are applied by employers in respect of all their employees, whether or not they are trade union members.

LEVELS OF COLLECTIVE BARGAINING

Collective bargaining may take place at any of the following levels:

1   Industry (national)
2   District (not common nowadays)
3   Company
4   Plant
5   Sub-plant

All of these levels could affect the pay and working conditions of an individual and they may all be taking place simultaneously.

National or *Industry-wide* bargaining is a traditional aspect of the British industrial relations system particularly in the public sector and typical negotiating machinery is referred to above. During the First World War and the inter-war years unemployment levels were generally high, and trade unions tended to see their role as one of unifying and improving the standards of workers generally. They also realized that they were strongest when negotiating at national level. Employers and government supported this national approach, as it tended to stabilize the industrial situation.

With relatively full employment during the late 1950s and 1960s, national agreements became less able to embrace the demands of trade unionists at plant and shop floor level, and two parallel systems began to emerge. These were described by the Donovan Commission [2] in 1968 as a conflicting system of 'formal' national and 'informal' local bargaining systems. This has led to a tendency for national agreements to become more limited in scope, and wages are often negotiated as minimum rates that are supplemented at local level. Other terms of employment, such as hours and holidays are, however, often treated as standard throughout an industry. The national agreement has, therefore, become a guide for minimum standards within an industry, which ensures some consistency of conditions of employment.

In the case of some large organizations that are not members of employers' associations, such as Ford, bargaining may take place at *company level*. Agreements may resemble national agreements, and are often negotiated with national representatives of the trade unions concerned.

Plant-level bargaining and shop floor bargaining has grown significantly, and is one of the most outstanding features of post-war British industrial relations. It is essentially carried out by shop stewards, although full-time officials may be involved, and agreements may cover entire plants or individual departments or sections. This has arisen partly to supplement national agreements according to local needs and conditions. It is also in response to a preference by workers, and in many cases management, to negotiate at what they consider to be a more relevant level. This development is certainly apparent when considering the composition of the average pay packet. Whereas before the Second World War the earnings of most workers were within a few per cent of the nationally negotiated rate, Donovan reported that by

1967 the 'workplace margin' had increased to about 50%. Although this has reduced slightly since that time, the margin is still considerable.

The joint DE/PSI/SSRC Survey of Industrial Relations [3] reported that levels of bargaining varied between sectors and types of worker. Plant-level bargaining was considerably more common for manual than non-manual employees. In the public sector, however, it was rare for collective bargaining over pay to take place at all at plant or establishment level. Size of establishment was also an important variable, particularly in the private sector, with plant-level bargaining being much more important in larger establishments.

PRODUCTIVITY BARGAINING

The term 'productivity bargaining', although used often, can mean different things to different people. It may, therefore, be useful to give one or two authoritative descriptions of this subject. Research Paper No. 4 of the Donovan Commission [2] states:

> The term 'productivity bargain' lacks precision, but broadly it may be described as an agreement in which advantages of one kind or another, such as higher wages or increased leisure, are given to workers in return for agreement on their part to accept changes in working practice or in organization of work which will lead to more efficient working.

The National Board for Prices and Incomes [4] commented:

> By a productivity agreement we mean one in which workers agree to make a change, or a number of changes, in working practice that will lead in itself — leaving out any compensating pay increase — to more economical working; and in return the employer agrees to a higher level of pay or other benefits.

It is worth stressing that both of the above documents distinguish between agreements that contain vague statements concerning 'the need for efficiency' and a productivity agreement of substance. One of the essential parts of any productivity agreement is a fundamental or at least meaningful change in current work methods or practice.

During the 1950s, many British companies became aware of generally low levels of productivity compared with other countries. Even where similar plant was used, it was evident that many more man-hours were used for similar levels of output. One of the main factors was the widespread incidence of overtime working in manufacturing industries. The situation was the result of many years of managerial ineffectiveness, informal bargaining pressures, custom and practice, that few people questioned or even understood. In this situation, management, which conceded collective bargaining on such things as wages and other terms of employment, was reluctant to forego its prerogative in respect of working methods. Had they been prepared to bargain in this area, the familiar pattern of formal national bargaining and fragmented workshop bargaining was hardly conducive to the introduction of change on a plant-wide basis. Any negotiation and consultation would need to include representation from all levels of the union, but take place predominantly at plant level.

One of the first and most comprehensive examples of productivity bargaining within this country took place at Esso's Fawley refinery, near Southampton, during the late 1950s and early 1960s. In a climate of rapid technical innovation and increasing international competition within the oil refining industry, Esso hired American consultants to examine operations at Fawley. The consultants challenged several traditional practices and the sustained high levels of overtime working. Management accepted most of the criticism and opened extensive discussions with union officers, shop stewards and the men, on changing some of these practices.

The refinery was divided into two main departments, employing craftsmen, semi-skilled and labourers. The craftsmen were represented by seven different unions and the non-craftsmen were mainly members of the Transport and General Workers Union. After many months of talks the management drew up a series of proposals collectively known as the 'Blue Book'. The major proposal was that overtime should be drastically reduced over a period of 2 years, basic wages being increased over a similar period by approximately 40%. Other important items included the elimination of craftsmen's mates, a relaxation of craft demarcations and flexibility in the scope of supervisors. Elimination of long-standing conventions such as washing time, set tea-breaks, etc., was proposed in exchange for a reduction in the working week from $42\frac{1}{2}$ to 40 hours. The overall pay structure was also substantially simplified by incorporating many 'special payments' into the overall rate of pay. A fundamental proviso was that there were to be no redundancies as a result of the Blue Book's proposals.

The bulk of the proposals were accepted by the unions, and as a result the company was able substantially to reduce work previously undertaken by outside contractors and man the expanding factory. The management at Esso did not rest on its laurels, but viewed productivity bargaining as a continuous process. Flanders' book on the agreements [5] is recommended for those requiring more detail than it is possible to provide here.

Despite the fact that many similar agreements followed those at Fawley, productivity bargaining has always been the subject of widespread doubts and criticism. These include claims that management is 'buying off' restrictive practices that would be replaced by others. It has also been claimed that agreements force other employers to increase pay with no concomitant increase in productivity, and that it is a short-term solution that unfairly rewards the inefficient at the expense of the efficient.

Some of these criticisms are undoubtedly based upon the evidence of many 'bad' productivity agreements. There are undoubtedly cases where ill-informed managements have entered into agreements for reasons of expediency, particularly when under pressure from various pay-restraint policies imposed by government. Much depends on the motivation of the negotiating parties and the existing industrial relations climate. There is no doubt that many managers and supervisors will take what Fox [6] describes as a 'unitary' view of the organization, believing that the workers should subscribe to 'teamwork' without extra reward. However a 'pluralistic' view might recognize that the objectives of management and workers do not necessarily coincide and that the 'teamwork' standpoint may be somewhat naive.

Despite the criticism, Flanders considers that the salutory experience of productivity bargaining holds certain object lessons, particularly for management. Firstly, he sees it as a means of eliminating the 'evil' of under-employment and systematic overtime. He considers this practice to be grudgingly accepted by many managements, who must take the initiative if change is to be accepted. In an interesting analogy, Flanders refers to management as the government and the trade unions as 'no more than a permanent opposition'. He also suggests that productivity bargaining brings consultation and collective bargaining closer together rather than being supplanted by each other, thus increasing the scope of agreements. Finally, he uses the Fawley agreements as an example of positive and innovative management, in contrast to the passive acceptance of the status quo and piecemeal reactions to problems that are so often the norm.

Productivity bargaining in the classic Fawley style has gone out of fashion. The problems it attempts to solve have not. It has been discredited by many shallow and meaningless agreements. The approach may have to change, possibly to a more continuous process, but the need for 'creative' collective bargaining remains as strong as ever.

PROCEDURES

It has already been stated that employers and employees or their representatives tend to enter into two main types of agreement — substantive and procedural. The former covers rights of the parties and terms of employment, the latter deals with the actual processes of negotiation and with methods of dealing with disputes or problems that may arise. These 'procedures', therefore, represent a set of rules that may be written or unwritten and aim to govern the conduct of the parties in the settlement of the various terms and conditions of employment.

Procedures may be established at various levels from national to plant, depending on the negotiating machinery available. The Donovan Commission Research Paper No. 2 agreed that the main functions of procedures were concerned with:

1 Trade union recognition
2 The establishment of machinery for reconciling differences

Recognition of a trade union may be partial, i.e., for representation of individual members only, or for full negotiation. A certain amount of recogition must be a pre-requisite for the initiation of any procedure and subsequent procedural agreements will reflect the degree of recognition employers are prepared to acknowledge.

Procedures may be agreed to cover a wide range of issues.

Negotiating procedures

Negotiating procedures will be quite formal and defined in writing at national level, but domestic (plant level) procedures may be relatively informal. However, various reports have recommended greater formality at domestic level, and Richard O'Brien [7] endorsed this view with the agreements made at Delta Metal. He considered that clearly written procedural agreements:

1 Imply that each side has a legitimate role to play in a proper fashion, i.e., they provide the agreed rules of the game
2 Can define acceptable standards of behaviour
3 Produce greater certainty as against custom and practice.

Grievance and dispute procedures

Grievance and dispute procedures are often part of the same process. A grievance that is recognized by the union and on which there has been failure to agree with the employer will usually be designated a 'dispute'. These procedures will cover various problems such as disagreements concerning overtime or bonus rates. Indeed virtually any term of employment may be brought into question. Most procedures follow a similar pattern, starting with a complaint to an immediate supervisor, passing through intermediate levels up to a national joint body. An outline of a typical procedure is given in Fig. 26.1.

Many procedures have been criticized for the length of time provided between the various stages. When this occurs, the employees and their representatives will become impatient and bypass or ignore the agreed procedure. The time limits included in the example are there to ensure

Outline grievance/dispute procedure

Stage 1 — Individual takes grievance to supervisor — if issue affects union members, staff representative may accompany individual. If no satisfaction within 3 working days;

Stage 2 — Staff representative to refer issue to departmental manager. If no satisfaction within 5 working days;

Stage 3 — Senior staff representative to take up with senior manager. If no satisfaction within 7 working days;

Stage 4 — Matter discussed at joint management/union committee (director level representation and possibly full-time union official). If no satisfaction;

Stage 5 — Conciliation/arbitration

Fig. 26.1

that this does not happen. Simplicity, speed and representation are probably the key words of principle for the design of a workable grievance procedure.

Other common procedures cover redundancy and discipline and dismissal, and reference should be made to the relevant chapters for further details of these.

Once procedures are agreed between union and employer they are often difficult to modify as any change to the status quo may be seen as a change in the balance of power. However, if a procedure is not to fall into disuse it must adapt to changes in circumstances. Where alterations are necessary, a third party may be useful in introducing acceptable changes.

It is apparent that procedures are a vital part of the industrial relations process. A good procedure will encourage mutual recognition and a willingness to 'abide by the rules'. In order to achieve this a procedure must be acceptable to all levels of employee representation and appropriate to the industrial setting in which it operates. As Flanders [1] puts it:

The acid test of a procedural agreement is the extent to which the rights and obligations of the parties are known and accepted by all concerned.

NEGOTIATIONS

A great deal of the subject matter of industrial relations is dealt with through the negotiation process. Negotiations may concern recognition issues, procedural matters or substantive items, such as pay or hours. As with most things, a successful negotiator requires skill, preparation and a great deal of experience. There are certain conventions, strategies and tactics that need to be learnt. There is all manner of jargon, innuendo, slight of hand and thrust and parry that form part of the process.

It is not posisble to go into the detail of the negotiation process here, but we shall endeavour to outline some of the issues in the hope that those who wish to pursue the subject will read further [8].

It should be remembered at the outset that negotiations are held with a view to reaching a settlement. Whatever the tactics, this must always be paramount in the minds of the parties involved. Let us use a pay negotiation as an example and consider the various stages of the process.

Preparation

Each party will need to assess its own strengths and weaknesses as well as those of the 'opposition', and define:

1 The target or ideal settlement it would like to achieve
2 The maximum (management) is prepared to concede/minimum (union) is prepared to accept (fall-back position)
3 The realistic offer/claim that you consider to be acceptable

If the fall-back position of the parties overlap (Fig. 26.2) there is considered to be a settlement area or 'zone'. If they do not overlap, this gap is usually referred to as a 'negotiating gap'.

Strategy

The strategy used by each side will partly reflect the strength of their position. Negotiators will need to decide their strategy in the light of their objectives and the degree of knowledge they have gained in preparation for the negotiations. This may be supplemented in the opening stages where the parties 'sound out' each others cases. There is a range of strategies that may attempt to change the balance of power, trade off concessions or link various issues.

Tactics

There are many tactics that negotiators use to achieve short-term advantage or further their objectives. These are far too numerous to list here, but we give a few examples below to provide a flavour of the type of thing we mean.

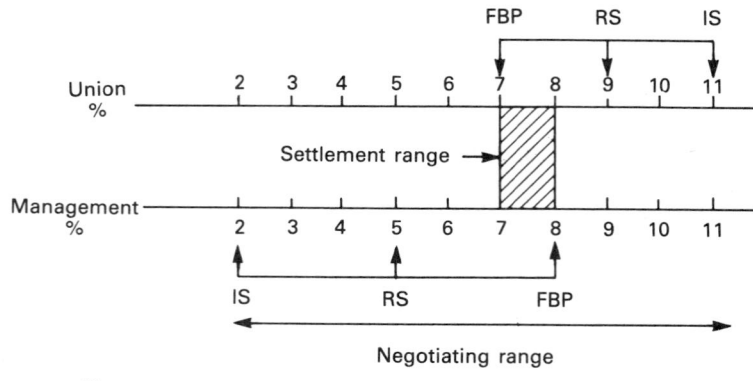

Fig. 26.2 Pay negotiation showing negotiating and settlement range

Offensive

☐ 'Final first offer' — as the name implies, an initial firm stance
☐ Obstinacy/threats
☐ Making opponent appear unreasonable

Defensive

☐ Silence — sometimes successful in producing movement in opponent's case
☐ Pretended misunderstanding — may provide time to gather thoughts or ideas
☐ Questioning accuracy of 'facts'

Settlement

When to 'close' negotiations is, again, a matter of judgement. Experience will often help to sense when the claim and offer are getting close. The management side may decide to make a 'final offer' and refuse to negotiate further. Alternatively, they may trade off various concessions and suggest this as a basis of agreement. There are, of course, various other ways of reaching the final settlement, but it is important that negotiations are not concluded too quickly, as this may create a sense of frustration that could lead to a hardening of attitudes by the other side.

As referred to earlier, negotiating is something that requires a great deal of skill and experience. Whether the responsibility rests with a line manager or the personnel manager the negotiator will require these attributes as well as a thorough knowledge of industrial relations procedures and agreements with unions.

THE CLOSED SHOP AND 'NEW STYLE' AGREEMENTS

The union membership agreement, or 'closed shop' as it is better known, has been a major form of controversy over the past 25 years or so. It has been attacked by various pieces of legislation, from attempts to ban it to various attempts to control its influence. More recently, legislation has only allowed the formation or continuation of the closed shop with the overwhelming support of those concerned by such arrangements. The Employment Act 1988 has now effectively ended the enforceable closed shop.

It is often difficult to identify a closed shop situation in an organization as often they are not formally enforced. However, with this proviso it would appear that the number of employees covered by 'closed shop' has declined during the 1980s with the Workplace IR Survey of 1984 [3] showing a figure of 3.5 million workers covered. This is still a considerable number of people, and although opponents of the closed shop claim that it infringes human rights, those in favour, both managers and trade unionists, state that it leads to stability in industrial relations (further discussion of dismissal and the closed shop may be found on page 329).

Not all closed shop agreements are restricted to one union, but a more recent entry into the UK industrial relations scene is the 'single union' or 'new style' agreement often referred to as a 'no strike agreement', even though this is considered strictly incorrect.

One of the unions most forthrightly in favour of this type of agreement has been the electricians' union, the EETPU. Their agreement with Japanese employers in the UK, as well as a range of smaller British companies, have been widely reported [9] and have also led to their expulsion from the TUC. in 1988. The EETPU would claim that this type of agreement reflects a 'new realism' in British industrial relations, whereas other unions would claim that it is contrary to their principles of the use of legitimate sanctions.

So what is a 'new style' agreement? The generally accepted ingredients are as follows:

☐ *Sole recognition* of a single union (although not necessarily a closed shop).
☐ *Single status* terms and conditions of employment for all staff.
☐ *Employee consultation* and participation in decision making through a recognized form, such as an 'advisory board'.

☐ *Flexibility* of working practices.
☐ *Binding arbitration*, usually 'pendulum' or 'flip-flop'.

There is nothing particularly novel about any single one of these points with exception, perhaps, of 'pendulum' arbitration. Here, the arbitrator has to decide in favour of either the employer's case or the union's. He cannot reach a compromise position as is common in normal arbitration. It is claimed that this leads to responsible negotiation whereby the parties do not maintain extreme positions in the expectation that the arbitrator will 'split the difference'.

Although this type of agreement could not be termed common in the UK, various features are being considered by an increasing number of employers and unions.

REFERENCES

1. Flanders, A. (1965). *Industrial Relations. What is Wrong with the System?* Faber & Faber.
2. Lord Donovan (1968). *Report of the Royal Commission on Trade Unions and Employers' Associations* HMSO.
3. *Workplace Industrial Relations in Britain* (1986). HMSO.
4. National Board for Prices and Incomes. (1967). *Report No. 36*. HMSO.
5. Flanders, A. (1964). *The Fawley Productivity Agreements*. Faber & Faber.
6. Fox, A. (1968). 'Donovan Commission Research Paper No. 3'. HMSO.
7. In Kessler, S. and Weekes, B. (Eds.) (1971). *Conflict at Work*, Chapter 4. BBC Publications.
8. Scott, W.P. (1981). *The Skills of Negotiating*. Gower.
9. Gregory, M. (1986). 'The no-strike deal in action', *Personnel Management*, December.

27
Consultation and participation

JOINT CONSULTATION

Joint consultation, as its name implies, generally refers to the discussion between management and workers on matters of joint concern, often limited to matters that are not the subject of collective bargaining with trade unions. In non-unionized organizations, joint consultation may, of course, be the only channel of collective communication concerning matters of employment. Consultation usually takes place through a Joint Consultative Committee on which representatives of management and employees serve. The employee representatives are usually elected or appointed on a departmental or sectional basis.

The development of joint consultation was boosted considerably by the recommendations of the Whitley Committee of 1916. However, few of the committees set up survived the inter-war years. The Second World War brought the next development when several major industries such as engineering, coal mining and shipbuilding set up 'Joint Production Committees'. Once again, many of these ceased after the end of the war, but during the late 1940s the government made a further effort to encourage joint consultation, and provision was made for the setting up of consultative committees in the various Nationalization Acts.

The present position is that joint consultation is highly developed in the public sector, but in the private sector, companies having consultative machinery are in the minority. So what are the benefits and problems attributed to joint consultation? From management's point of view, the following are some of the suggested benefits:

- [ ] it acts as a safety valve for grievances
- [ ] it enables workers to 'have a say' concerning their welfare
- [ ] it provides an opportunity for workers to suggest improvements to working methods and productivity
- [ ] it encourages loyalty and morale
- [ ] it improves communication
- [ ] it stimulates management and workforce to solve problems on a joint basis.

These advantages will of course depend upon the attitudes of both management and the unions as well as the scope of the committee's terms of reference. If it does not have the overt commitment of top management it is likely to become impotent. Likewise, if it is boycotted by union representatives in favour of collective bargaining it may become irrelevant. If the matters on which it is allowed to make a decision are trivial, it will probably become discredited in the eyes of the workforce.

Whereas, traditionally, joint consultation and collective bargaining have operated through separate machinery and dealt with different topics, this separation is considered by many to be artificial. In many organizations the scope of collective bargaining is being increased to cover items traditionally the reserve of joint consultation. Many trade unionists consider that joint consultation is paradoxical, in that subjects such as new machinery and work methods that management reserve as their prerogative and would not discuss in collective bargaining, are included in joint consultation on the grounds that they are areas where the interests of the two sides converge rather than conflict. The Joint DE/PSI/SSRC survey of industrial relations [1] indicated a substantial growth in joint consultative committees in the late 1970s, alongside established trade union representation. Many of these discussed topics of substance concerning pay and conditions of employment. This pattern is in marked contrast to the traditional British industrial relations system where certain topics have been the preserve of collective bargaining. Although this movement has not reached the level of Works Councils in Europe, it is nonetheless interesting.

INDUSTRIAL DEMOCRACY/PARTICIPATION

What is industrial democracy?

Industrial democracy, also referred to as 'workers' participation' and 'co-determination', has become a fashionable topic of discussion in recent years. But what is it? Some would suggest that it is about workers' participation in decision making. Others might consider that it is about power and control. The most recent debates have concerned worker directors and board structures although this is only one aspect to which we shall return. Walker [2] suggsts that there are four main forms of industrial democracy:

1 Democratization of *ownership* — through issue of shares to employees, etc.
2 Democratization of *government* of the enterprise — through participation at board level.

3 Democratization of *terms of employment* — through collective bargaining, etc.
4 Democratization of *management* — through formal and informal participation.

Walker considers that 1 and 2 above have little direct impact upon the individual worker and that the key issue in industrial democracy is the 'democratization of management'.

How can it be achieved?

Some different levels of democratization have been referred to above. But how can worker participation be achieved in practice? Until recently, most trade unionists would have taken a view that collective bargaining is the only effective way to influence the individual's working life. In fact, this view is probably still held by many today. In recent years, the distinction between collective bargaining and joint consultation has become less clear, and bargaining nowadays covers a wide range of topics apart from basic working conditions. In Europe, the Works Council system is widely used to enable workers to discuss and influence a wide range of decisions.

Some organizations consider that true participation can only be achieved by providing for employees to share in the ownership of the enterprise. But share ownership schemes have met with varying degrees of success. In some larger organizations employees have shown little interest in holding shares. In others, such as the John Lewis Partnership and the Scott Bader organization, the system is claimed to be successful. It would appear that the more successful schemes combine ownership with participation in decision making.

Many managers would agree with Walker that participation is more meaningful when integrated into the day-to-day work situation. Methods might include looking at actual job design and content. Various systems of 'job extension' and 'job enrichment' as suggested by Herzberg might be tried at the individual level. Organizations such as Saab Scania and Volvo have developed the semi-autonomous work-group method of extending the worker's ability to influence the way in which he carries out the work. Simple techniques, such as 'Flexitime', can also provide freedom of choice for the employee. Quality circles have been introduced successfully by various UK organizations (for further discussion of these areas see Chapter 5).

Participation at board level

Britain's accession to the European Economic Community (EEC) turned attention to worker participation at board level. The EEC issued the 'Fifth Directive' in 1972 which suggested the harmonization of company law within member countries. Its proposals included the adoption of a 'two-tier' board structure for larger companies, similar to that already operated in Germany and Holland. The 'supervisory' board would include workers' representation, whereas the 'management' board would be appointed by the supervisory board to manage the company on a day-to-day basis. By 1974, every member of the EEC except Britain had some form of legislation providing for worker directors and/or a system of works councils.

Attitudes in this country to the provisions of the Fifth Directive have varied. Employers' organizations considered that worker-directors would not have the necessary expertise and would jeopardize the shareholders' control of a company. The TUC accepted the main recommendations with certain qualifications, including the fact that worker-directors should be elected through trade union machinery. It was also stressed that the board structure should supplement, and not supplant, the traditional system of collective bargaining.

The Bullock report

Owing largely to the progress of a private members' bill, the government set up a Committee of Enquiry on Industrial Democracy under the chairmanship of Lord Bullock in 1975. Its terms of reference implied that the enquiry should concentrate on means of implementing representation at board level rather than a consideration of industrial democracy generally. The committee which was made up of industrialists, trade unionists and academics reported in January 1977 [3], after considering the European situation and taking a great deal of evidence.

A unanimous report was not possible and it finally consisted of:

1   The majority report — 7 members including the chairman, being the trade unionists, the academics, with a note of dissent by Mr N. S. Wilson, a solicitor
2   The minority report — 3 industrialists

The majority report rejected the two-tier board system on the grounds that it was incompatible with UK law and traditions. They opted instead for a unitary board based on a $2x + y$ formula, where the $2x$ is an equal number of shareholder and union representatives who jointly agree upon the y group, which would consist of an odd number of 'independents'. The system would apply initially to all companies employing more than 2 000 persons, provided the workforce agreed by secret ballot. The ballot could only be initiated by a 'recognized' trade union representing 20% or more of the company's employees. Only nominees of the trade unions represented within the company would be eligible for election, and nominations would be made by a new joint union committee designated a Joint Representation Committee. Mr Wilson dissented in respect of the $2x + y$ formula, considering that it would be divisive and advocated that 'worker-directors' should remain in a minority.

The minority report advocated a two-tier system with worker representation on the upper 'supervisory board'. They also recommended the European Works Council system and considered that any representatives should be elected by *all* employees, whether or not union members.

It is apparent from reaction to the Bullock Report that it tried to introduce too much too quickly. Various problems were cited concerning the $2x + y$ formula and the problems of legal powers and liabilities of the newly appointed directors. Support for the proposals was by no means universal within the trade union movement, and it was certainly non-existent amongst employers. It was obvious that any legislation would have to take these views into consideration.

White paper

In May 1978 the government published its white paper entitled 'Industrial Democracy' [4]. As expected, it was a considerable compromise, and the paper refers to the desirability of voluntary extensions to industrial democracy. Where suitable machinery for consultation is not established, a statutory fall-back right is established whereby companies would be 'required' to discuss strategy via a Joint Representative Committee referred to in Bullock. After a period of 3 – 4 years it is proposed that a statutory right to elect representatives at board level should come into operation, significantly under a two-tier system.

European initiatives

By early 1985, the EEC Fifth Directive, with its controversial proposals concerning board-level worker representation, had reached the final stage of the law-making process. It now needed only the Council of Ministers' approval to become law throughout the EEC, although this is recognized as a difficult hurdle. Although the provisions for employee representation are now more flexible than originally proposed, the implications of this law are significant for personnel practitioners in larger organizations.

A directive that has reached a similar stage of the EEC process is the Vredeling Directive (1980), which relates to 'procedures for informing and consulting employees'. This requires companies with at least 1000 workers employed in the EEC to:

☐ provide annual information from the parent company about the economic and financial situation of the business
☐ give advance notice of decisions of the parent company liable to

have serious consequences for the interests of the employees of
EEC subsidiaries
☐ consult employees on plans for which advance notice had been
given

Although there are safeguards on 'secret' information, this directive is
being forcibly opposed by UK employers.

Whether or not directives and laws are the best means of encouraging
worker participation is open to debate. However, they undoubtedly
reflect views held within society, and will no doubt stimulate activity in
this area.

It is clear that there is strong pressure from many quarters for
industrial democracy to be encouraged and developed. Authority is
tending to be challenged within society generally, and there is no reason
to believe that this will be left behind at the factory gate. Whether
participation is achieved through board level representation, an
extension of collective bargaining or a less formal process of change in
management style will depend on the circumstances of individual
organizations. Much discussion is taking place at present concerning
technological change caused by micro-electronics. It could be that social
change within industry will be even more important. Many of our EEC
partners are concerned with the concept of 'social space', i.e., giving
people a say in the affairs of their company. With 1992 not far away, we
may need to do more [5].

Inducements and assistance

Under the Employment Act 1982, all companies employing more than
250 persons must include a statement in the annual Director's Report
that sets out what, if any, steps have been taken during the preceding
year to develop arrangements to increase employee 'involvement' in the
company's affairs. The matters to be covered should include:

☐ supply of *information* to employees on matters of concern to them
☐ *consultation* on decisions affecting employees
☐ *involvement* of employees through share ownership or other means
☐ *awareness* by employees of economic factors affecting the performance of the company

Although the obligation only requires details of arrangements, if any,
rather than actual steps taken, this may act as an inducement to
organizations to give more consideration to employee participation.

The Institute of Personnel Management and the Industrial Participation Association have issued joint documents on Employee Involvement
and Participation [6]. One is in effect a code of practice, the other an

action guide. They offer practical help and guidance to those wishing to formulate policy and take action in this area.

REFERENCES

1. DE/PSI/SSRC. (1983). *Workplace Industrial Relations in Britain*. HMSO.
2. Walker, K. (1970). *Industrial Democracy*. Times Publication Department.
3. Cmnd. 6706. (1977). HMSO.
4. Cmnd. 7231. (1978). HMSO.
5. Tuckman, F. (1988). 'Social space', *Administrator*, October.
6. IPA/IPM. (1983). *Employee Involvement and Participation*.

28
Strikes and other industrial actions

STRIKES

When a group of workers or a trade union are in dispute with an employer, the employees or their representatives may take some form of industrial action. This may occur after a recognized disputes procedure has been exhausted or earlier, depending on the circumstances. The types of industrial action that might be taken could include overtime bans, working-to-rule, go-slows, and the 'blacking' of certain goods or materials. However, although these methods are widely used, they rarely receive as much attention as all-out strikes.

What is a strike?

The answer to this question is not as straightforward as would at first appear. According to Hyman [1] a strike is:

A temporary stoppage of work by a group of employees in order to express a grievance or enforce a demand.

From an official point of view, strikes are measured in accordance with pre-determined criteria and statistics are generally based upon reports from employers. Official figures exclude strikes involving fewer than 10 workers or lasting less than 1 day, unless the total number of working days lost exceeds 100. The accuracy of the statistics is subject to the information supplied, and varies from industry to industry. Thus it is generally thought that official figures are unreliable, but are useful as an indicator of trends.

Official or unofficial?

An *official* strike could be described as a strike that is recognized or authorized by the Executive Committee of a union or other appropriate body and for which strike benefit will normally be paid by the union. Most British strikes are both unofficial and unconstitutional. An *unofficial* strike is, of course, the opposite of an official strike described above, whereas an *unconstitutional* strike is conducted in breach of an agreed disputes procedure.

It is estimated that about 95% of strikes in Britain are unofficial. In fact, they will usually be over before the union headquarters becomes aware of them. Studies of the motor industry have shown that many strikes consist of short stoppages confined to a single section or department. The fact that a strike is 'unofficial' does not necessarily mean that the union would disapprove of it, and some are given retrospective recognition. Although unofficial strikes are often directed by shop stewards, they are sometimes initiated by the workforce against the advice of the shop steward.

Nature and purpose

Apart from the official/unofficial distinction, strikes may vary according to the purpose for which they are used. They may be:

☐ a demonstration of indignation concerning a management decision or action

☐ a gesture of defiance or frustration concerning a long-standing grievance

☐ part of a strategy to improve terms and conditions of employment

The strike may be aggressive or defensive in nature, although management is likely to view most as falling within the former category. In the past, particularly during the 1920s and 1930s, the 'trial of strength' strike was not uncommon. These often lasted for many weeks and became bitter struggles between employees attempting to establish rights and employers who jealously defended their prerogatives. Many, in fact, took the form of 'lock-outs' rather than strikes as such. Although this type of strike still occurs from time to time, the shorter strike, mounted for various reasons, is much more common nowadays.

Whatever the purpose of a strike, it must be remembered that to be lawful it must comply with the more narrow definition laid down in the Employment Act 1982. This restricts action to workers in dispute with their own employers and wholly or mainly concerned with matters such as their pay, jobs and terms and conditions of employment.

Trends

It is not possible to make a detailed analysis of strike statistics here, and further reading is recommended [2]. However, it may prove useful to review certain trends in the incidence of strikes.

On an historical basis it is suggested that strike activity in Britain can be divided into five main phases:

1 *Phase 1* (end of 19th Century to World War I): despite low union membership, high loss of days due largely to relatively small number of workers on strike for long periods

2 *Phase 2* (World War I to middle 1930s): starting with unrest, the general strike and some other widespread stoppages, followed by a stable low level of activity

3 *Phase 3* (middle 1930s to early 1960s): pattern of increasing number of strikes, but shorter and smaller than previously

4 *Phase 4* (mid-1960s to 1970s): increase in the frequency and severity of strikes

5 *Phase 5* The 1980s have generally experienced low levels of strike activity, although the 1984 miners' strike was a major event against this trend.

These trends are illustrated in Fig. 28.1.

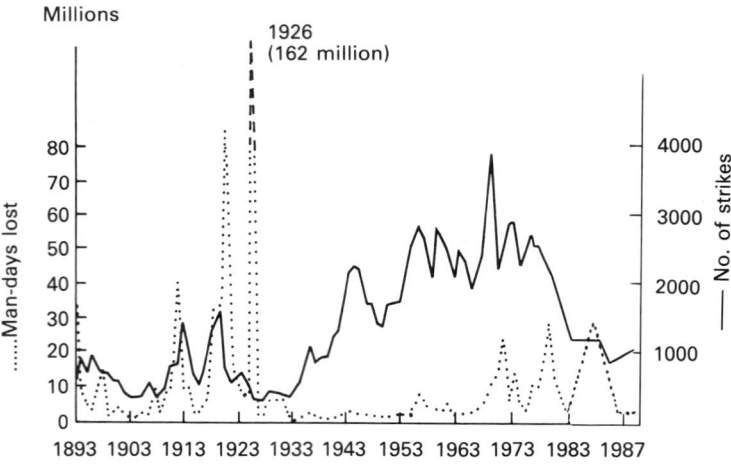

Fig.28.1 Strike trends in the UK, 1893–1987 (Source: Department of Employment Gazette)

Reasons for fluctuations in the historical incidence of strikes are difficult to analyse. However, it would appear that the statistics are sensitive to economic activity and the frequency of strikes tends to increase in boom years. They do, however, tend to be short compared to the larger and less frequent strikes that occur during a recession. It is suggested that in periods of prosperity workers are more ready to strike and employers to concede in the belief that costs will be easily recovered. Prices and incomes policies have tended to upset this pattern to some extent and strikes may then be in response to government policy rather than against the employer.

International comparisons are difficult, owing to differences in definitions of a strike and the efficiency of data collection (as stated, Britain's statistics appear to severely understate the incidence of strikes). However, subject to this proviso, it can be seen from Table 28.1 that Britain's strike record is by no means the worst. Selected industries, those that account for a high proportion of strikes, have been chosen, as this partially reduces the effect of variations in industrial mix when comparing all stoppages. Comparisons on an industrial or occupational basis are possible, although reasons for variations may be more difficult to find.

As might be expected, strikes appear to be most common in industries which employ large numbers of male manual workers and where unionisation levels are high (this was confirmed in the 1983 DE/PSI/SSRC survey). Certain industries, such as coalmining have a tradition of strike proneness. Table 28.2 gives official figures of numbers of stoppages and days lost in respect of the main industrial sectors.

Causes

When discussing the 'causes' of strikes, it is necessary to distinguish between the immediate causes of individual strikes and general theories as to why strikes take place. At the 'immediate' level, there are further difficulties of interpretation as the issue giving rise to the strike may not be the fundamental cause.

Pay is a commonly stated cause of strikes, although it often masks other deep-rooted grievenaces. Given this caveat, pay still accounts for approximately half of the industrial stoppages recorded. Other causes include manning and work allocation, disciplinary matters, negotiating rights and protests against management plans.

Many theories have been postulated in order to explain why strikes occur, particularly within certain industries. The well known research by Joan Woodward [3] looked into the 'socio-technical' aspects of industry, and concluded that certain industrial processes produce much higher levels of dissatisfaction amongst employees. The geographical isolation of some working communities, such as coalminers has also been suggested by Kerr and Siegel [4] as leading to greater solidarity during periods of dispute. Neither of these theories, however, explain variations between similar industries in different countries.

Poor human relations have been used as an explanation of strike-proneness, but most theories do not provide an adequate rationale for differences between different industries. Some studies have suggested that the larger the size of the work group or the greater the span of

Table 28.1 Industrial disputes: working days lost per 1000 employees* in all industries and services 1977–86

	1977	1978	1979	1980	1981	1982	1983	1984	1985	1986	Average† 1977–81	Average† 1982–86	Average† 1977–86
UK	450	410	1270	520	200	250	180	1280	300	90	580	420	500
Australia	330	420	780	630	780	370	310	240	230	240	590	280	430
Austria	–	–	–	10	–	–	–	–	10	–	–	–	–
Belgium	220	330	200	70	–	–	–	–	–	–	(200)	–	–
Canada	380	830	840	930	890	610	460	390	310	690	780	490	630
Denmark**	120	70	80	90	320	50	40	60	1060	40	140	260	200
Finland	1310	70	130	840	340	100	360	750	80	1320	540	530	530
France**	210	130	210	100	80	130	80	80	50	60	140	80	110
Germany (FR)	–	200	20	10	–	–	–	260	–	–	(50)	(70)	(50)
Greece	810	630	1040	1740	480	840	320	320	620	700	940	560	750
Ireland	570	770	1750	480	500	500	380	470	520	..	810	(470)	(660)
Italy	1170	720	1920	1140	730	1280	980	610	270	390	1140	700	920
Japan	40	40	20	30	10	10	10	10	10	10	30	10	20
Netherlands	60	–	70	10	10	50	30	10	20	10	30	20	30
New Zealand**	410	360	350	350	360	300	340	380	660	1110	360	570	470
Norway	20	40	–	60	20	170	–	60	40	560	30	170	100
Portugal	130	..	200	200	330	170	230	100	100	140	(220)	150	(180)
Spain	1940	1380	2310	790	670	360	580	880	440	300	1440	510	990
Sweden	20	10	10	1150	50	–	10	10	130	170	250	60	160
Switzerland**‡	–	–	–	–	–	–	–	–	–	–	–	–	–
United States**‡	260	270	230	230	190	100	190	90	70	120	230	110	170

Sources:
Working days lost: International Labour Office (ILO), Yearbook of Labour Statistics, 1980 and 1986 (Geneva: 1980; 1987).
Employees in employment: ILO and OECD publications.
( )Brackets indicate averages based on incomplete data.
.. Not available.
– Less than five days lost per 1,000 employees.
* Employees in employment: some figures have been estimated.
† Annual averages for those years within each period for which data are available, weighted for employment.
** Note the coverage differences mentioned in the text under the heading 'significant differences'.
‡ Figures for all years reflect the threshold of more than 1000 workers involved which was introduced in 1981.
Reproduced from Employment Gazette, June 1988.

Table 28.2 Stoppages in progress, by industry, 1987

UK

Industry group (SIC 1980)	Class	Working days lost (thousands)	Workers involved (thousands)	Stoppages
All industries and services:		3546	887.4	1016
Energy and Water (Div.1)		*226*	*99.3*	*302*
Manufacturing (Divs 2 to 4)		*595*	*202.2*	*340*
Services (Divs 6 to 9)		*2703*	*582.1*	*354*
Agriculture, forestry and fishing	01–03	—	—	—
Coal extraction	11	217	97.7	296
Extraction and processing of coke, mineral oil and natural gas	12–14	—	—	—
Electricity, gas, other energy and water	15–17	9	1.5	6
Metal processing and manufacture	21,22	11	2.3	7
Mineral processing and manufacture	23,24	14	2.0	10
Chemicals and manmade fibres	25,26	10	1.9	8
Metal goods not elsewhere specified	31	25	2.7	11
Mechanical engineering	32	160	23.7	62
Electrical engineering and equipment	33,34	34	14.5	17
Instrument engineering	37	3	0.1	1
Motor vehicles	35	158	97.0	100
Other transport equipment	36	67	38.7	29
Food, drink and tobacco	41,42	40	8.4	34
Textiles	43	18	1.9	5
Footwear and clothing	45	32	5.0	23
Timber and wooden furniture	46	1	0.2	2
Paper, printing and publishing	47	18	2.3	18
Other manufacturing industries	44,48,49	6	1.6	16
Construction	50	22	3.8	24
Distribution, hotels and catering, repairs	61–67	3	0.6	11
Railways	71	2	1.5	16
Other inland transport	72	90	30.2	44
Sea transport	74	3	0.5	6
Other transport and communication	75,79	1596	170.1	100
Supporting and miscellaneous transport services	76,77	14	4.6	25
Banking, finance, insurance, business services and leasing	81–85	1	1.0	7
Public administration, sanitary services and education	91–94	939	361.0	99
Medical and health services	95	6	4.0	24
Other services	96–99	49	8.7	23

– Means nil or negiligible (less than half the final digit shown).
Note: 1 The figures for working days lost and workers have been rounded and consequently the sums of constituent items may not agree precisely with the totals.
2 Some stoppages involved workers in more than one of the above industry groups, but have each been counted as only one stoppage in the totals for all industries and services.
Source: Department of Employment.

control of the supervisor, the more likelihood there is of industrial action. Other studies have failed to discover such a correlation, but government statistics have tended to show that in the manufacturing industry small enterprises appear much less strike-prone than large ones.

It is evident from the information available that no theory has yet satisfactorily explained which factors indicate strike-proneness. Every country, industry and firm operates within a complex system of different characteristics and circumstances that cannot be simply analysed or compared.

STRIKE BALLOTS

Ballots are a traditional part of trade union activity, but strike ballots have gained wide publicity in recent years due largely to legislative provisions. In earlier years ballots were often conducted by show of hands at factory gates or by slips completed at the workplace. The government, as part of its claimed objective of greater union democracy, has attempted to enforce 'secret' and postal ballots. The Employment Act 1980 even made government funds available for the conduct of approved secret ballots.

The most significant changes were introduced by the Trade Union Act 1984, which removed trade unions' immunity from legal action where they do not hold an 'approved' ballot prior to authorizing and endorsing strike action. The Act went on to specify how the ballot should be conducted as regards the timing of the ballot, who should be balloted and the form and distribution of the ballot paper (an implied condemnation of 'show of hands' ballots).

We have discussed earlier the spontaneous and short-lived nature of many strikes whereby a ballot by the union would not be possible even if it was aware of the situation. However, most unions and the TUC have accepted that the secret ballot has become a normal part of the way of life. Despite the apparent wide-spread compliance with the requirements of the 1984 Act, the government continues to tighten the requirements for ballots to remain lawful. The Employment Act 1988 has introduced even more regulations concerning the coverage of ballots where employees are based at different sites as well as a need to point out on the ballot slip that by going on strike the employee could be in breach of his contract of employment.

PICKETING

The use of large-scale picketing during various industrial disputes over the past decade or so has highlighted this aspect of industrial action. It has become an emotive topic, particularly as a result of the 1984 miner's strike. The legislation and case law developed over the years makes this a technically difficult and complex subject. Further reading is recommended for those interested, but we shall endeavour to outline some of the issues involved.

The right to picket

There is no legal 'right to picket' as such, but peaceful picketing has long been recognized as a lawful practice. Under TULRA Section 15 (as amended by the Employment Act 1980) picketing is declared lawful:

1 if undertaken in contemplation or furtherance of a trade dispute
2 by a person attending at or near his own place of work (unless a relevant TU official)
3 for peacefully obtaining and communicating information, and
4 peacefully persuading a person to work or not to work

'Secondary' picketing

The Employment Act 1980 specifically outlaws 'secondary' picketing, i.e., picketing away from the pickets' place of work. It does allow 'secondary' picketing in restricted cases where there is no direct dispute with an employer. This essentially amounts to legitimate picketing of the supply of goods and services between the pickets' own employer and another employer who is in dispute with the union. They must not, however, blockade their own employer against *all* goods and services leaving or entering the premises.

Penalties for unlawful picketing

Civil liability

Under the Employment Acts 1980 and 1982 employers have statutory rights to sue for injunction and seek damages for unlawful industrial action, including unlawful picketing. The 1982 Act broadens liability from individuals to the trade union itself where unlawful action is authorized by the executive or senior officials of the union. Upper limits are set on damages, but these go up to £250 000 for larger unions.

Criminal liability

It has always been the case that pickets are as liable as anyone else regarding criminal action. The law in respect of assault, nuisance, breach of the peace and obstruction of the highway will be enforced by the police in the normal manner.

Practical considerations

Apart from the legal considerations, the organization of effective picketing requires sensible planning and control. A Code of Practice was issued in 1980 under the authority of the Employment Act 1980 and outlines both the legal provisions and the practical aspects of lawful picketing. These cover such things as numbers of pickets, picket organizers, armbands, positioning of the picket, etc. Picketing is an integral and traditional part of industrial relations action in this country which has received a bad press owing to particular and well-publicized examples. Many less emotive situations are, however, picketed in an effective and lawful manner.

OTHER FORMS OF INDUSTRIAL ACTION

As stated, strikes appear to attract much more publicity than other forms of industrial action. Also, the imperfections of recording strikes are insignificant when compared to the difficulties of measuring other techniques that are used to express discontent or enforce demands. Apart from the more organized techniques referred to above, such as overtime bans, go-slows and work-to-rules, action may take place on a less organized basis. Dissatisfaction may be expressed through absenteeism, lateness, output restriction, sabotage and general lack of co-operation. Ironically, some industries that have experienced a reduction in actual strikes in recent years have witnessed a compensating increase in absenteeism and turnover.

From the evidence available, it is clear that the absence of strikes does not imply industrial peace and harmony. In times of economic difficulty and unemployment, workers may prefer to express their grievances by other means.

REFERENCES

1. Hyman, R. (1972). *Strikes*. Fontana.
2. See, for example, Department of Employment *Gazette*, Special Reports, etc.
3. Woodward, J. (1965). *Industrial Organisation: Theory and Practice*. Oxford University Press.
4. Kerr, C. and Siegel, A. (1954). 'Inter-industry propensity to strike', in Kornhauser *et al. Industrial Conflict*, Chapter 4, McGraw-Hill.

29
Third party intervention and legislation

THIRD PARTY INTERVENTION

Apart from direct intervention by the government, which is discussed below, other bodies have been set up from time to time for various purposes. Based upon the Conciliation Act 1896 and the industrial Court Act 1919, machinery has existed for many years for third parties to try to keep the peace of industrial relations through the traditional methods of 'Conciliation, Arbitration and Inquiry'.

More recently, third party intervention has developed for reasons other than peace-keeping. These have included incomes policy, trade union recognition, research, education and reform. These bodies have been set up by governments of both complexions with contrasting motivation and varying degrees of neutrality and commitment. Some have also been relatively independent of government interference.

Two of the more substantial bodies, which have since been disbanded, were committed to the reform of industrial relations and the changing of attitudes rather than a purely judicial role. These were the *National Board for Prices and Incomes* (NBPI) and the *Commission on Industrial Relations* (CIR).

The NBPI was set up with the agreement of the TUC and the CBI in 1965 and consisted of 'independents' from both sides of industry and the academic world. It is possibly best known for its judicial role in connection with the prevailing Incomes Policy. However, with the aid of many specialists it carried out several in-depth enquiries that went far beyond the Board's judicial role. Through the publication of its findings it sought to educate both the parties concerned and the wider public concerning any implications and to change attitudes accordingly. It was also in a position to provide independent consultancy for companies with particular problems. Although the NBPI was abolished in 1970, it made a lasting contribution to questions of productivity, pay and collective bargaining in many industries, as well as to the methodology of third party intervention.

The CIR was set up in 1969 on the recommendation of the Donovan

Commission. It was to concentrate on industrial relations institutions and procedures as opposed to substantive reform, but its methodology followed the example set by the NBPI. Like the NBPI, it was originally formed with the agreement of both sides of industry, although the TUC withdrew its support (and some commissioners resigned) as a result of the 1971 Industrial Relations Act, which was introduced by the Conservative government. The CIR had no powers of enforcement, but set out to investigate and assist organizations with problems. Where there were problems of union recognition or procedural processes, particularly at plant level, the Commission would interview employees and management and put forward proposals in an attempt to persuade the parties to agree upon a particular remedy. The Commission continued until 1974, and contributed towards increased knowledge and understanding, better procedures and extension of trade union recognition, particularly in the white collar sector.

ACAS

The 1975 Employment Protection Act introduced a new 'third party' known as ACAS — the Advisory, Conciliation and Arbitration Service. It is an independent body governed by a council of nine members drawn equally from trade unions, employers and independent sources, and chaired by a full-time chairman. ACAS deals with most of the functions provided by one or other of its predecessors, three of which are contained in its title.

ACAS officers are willing to conciliate when requested by parties to an industrial dispute, subject to any agreed procedures. Where the parties require an independent third party to make recommendations for a settlement, this is usually described as mediation rather than conciliation, and ACAS will also appoint a mediator when requested. Conciliation is available in individual cases where an alleged infringement of statutory rights is alleged such as unfair dismissal. Arbitration arranged by ACAS can be by a single arbitrator, a board of arbitration or through the standing Central Arbitration Committee (CAC). The advisory function takes various forms, from relatively straightforward advice to meetings, visits and special courses. Longer-term investigations are also made into various aspects of industrial relations within certain industries or organizations.

Finally, ACAS issues Codes of Practice from time to time on various aspects of industrial relations. They carry no statutory authority, but could obviously be quoted in any dispute where practice was being queried by either side.

To date, ACAS appears to be concentrating on the traditional conciliation arbitration and enquiry methods of third party intervention, with little emphasis upon the reforming role of some of its predecessors. Its statutory ties have kept it busy with a great deal of detailed work. It will be interesting to see whether it continues to concentrate upon this, or to endeavour to influence industrial relations practices in other ways.

INDUSTRIAL RELATIONS LEGISLATION

It is probably fair to say that employment legislation dealing with 'collective' matters has varied significantly over the years according to the prevailing political climate and the government in power. Some of the earlier legislation, such as the Trades Disputes Act 1906, established fundamental trade union rights, often in the face of High Court decisions. In more recent years these rights and activities have been restricted, re-established and again restricted.

Before the 1970 General Election, the Labour Government had published a white paper entitled 'In Place of Strife'. This incorporated many of the Donovan Commission proposals concerning the 'formalization' of trade unions and their activities. It also proposed compulsory 'conciliation pauses' for unconstitutional strikes, but, as a result of union pressures, these were dropped from the Bill, which was in any case overtaken by events when the Conservative Government was returned.

The Conservative government's answer to the problems of union power was the controversial and ill-fated Industrial Relations Act 1971. This attempted to give trade unions new legal status through a registration procedure and to control their activities through a new National Industrial Relations Court. Various activities were considered 'unfair industrial practices' and were penalized accordingly. These provisions were far too rigid and restrictive in the view of the unions, and massive protest and non-cooperation brought the Act to its knees within a year of enactment. The Act and the court dragged on for a further two years until they too became victims of a General Election in 1974.

There has been so much legislation in the last decade or so that it would be impossible to deal with it in any detail here. We shall, however, endeavour to summarize the main provisions of the legislation dealing with *collective* issues over recent years.

Trade Union and Labour Relations Acts 1974 and 1976

☐ Repealed Industrial Relations Act 1971 (but not IR Code of Practice)
☐ Re-established immunity from actions in tort in furtherance of 'trade dispute'
☐ Re-established right of 'peaceful picketing'
☐ Allowed 'fair' dismissal in closed shop situations ('religious

grounds' only acceptable reason for failing to join or remain in Union)

Employment Protection Act 1975

- ☐ Established ACAS and CAC
- ☐ Set up union recognition procedure (through ACAS)
- ☐ Established right of trade unions to obtain disclosure of information for collective bargaining purposes
- ☐ Extended scope and powers of Wages Councils
- ☐ Created consultation and notification requirements for employers contemplating redundancies.

Employment Act 1980

- ☐ Government funds available for secret ballots
- ☐ Secretary of State for Employment empowered to issue Codes of Practice on industrial relations matters
- ☐ 'Lawful' picketing restated and 'secondary' picketing outlawed
- ☐ New closed shop agreements prohibited without secret ballot
- ☐ Protection against unfair dismissal in connection with closed shops extended
- ☐ Repealed statutory provisions concerning application for union recognition to ACAS (Employment Protection Act, 1975)

Employment Act 1982

- ☐ Provides for retrospective compensation for closed shop dismissals
- ☐ Increases in compensation for dismissal in connection with 'trade union activities'
- ☐ 'Union labour only' contracts made null and void
- ☐ Removal of wider trade union immunities from actions in tort where authorised by executive of union. Union liable to damages (subject to maxima)
- ☐ 'Trade dispute' redefined and restricted to workers and their *own* employer and related *wholly or mainly* to specified subject matter
- ☐ Prevents claims for unfair dismissal, where *all* on strike are dismissed

Trade Union Act 1984

- ☐ Requirement for members of union executive committee to be re-elected by secret ballot of members.
- ☐ Secret ballots required before industrial action in order to maintain immunity from legal action
- ☐ Expenditure on political activities to be approved by members in secret ballot
- ☐ Restrictions on use and transfer of political funds where political activities not approved by members

Employment Act 1988

- ☐ Trade union members given right to restrain industrial action where this has not been authorized by secret ballot.
- ☐ Union members have the right not to be 'unjustifiably disciplined' by their union for not taking part in industrial action.
- ☐ Industrial action to enforce a closed shop is unlawful.
- ☐ Dismissal for non-membership of a closed shop is unlawful.
- ☐ Postal ballots must be held at regular intervals for the election or re-election of *all* union executive committee members.
- ☐ Strike ballots to contain specific information and to be aggregated in accordance with new rules where different sites balloted.
- ☐ Members have rights to inspect unions' financial records and to take legal action to prevent the unlawful use of funds.

THE LEGISLATIVE INFLUENCE

For many years it was considered that legislation was not an effective way of regulating industrial relations in the UK. The ill-fated Industrial Relations Act of 1971 was viewed as a classic example of a 'transplant' rejected by the voluntary 'body' of industrial relations. It was certainly a case of 'too much too soon'.

However, the Conservative government's Acts of 1980, 1982, 1984 and 1988 have constituted a rather more gradualist approach to the use of legislation as a controlling mechanism. These 'Queensberry Rules' of trade union and employer behaviour, as they have been called [1], have proved effective in terms of their stated aims of 'trade union democracy'. The membership ballot has been at the centre of much of the recent legislation as part of a procedural code which must be complied with.

Bystanders might point to the strike record of the past few years and suggest that the legislation has curbed the excesses of the trade unions. Others may be concerned that legislative excesses could undermine a delicate relationship of many years' standing.

REFERENCE

Mackie, K.J. (1988). 'One more time: how do we democratize organizations?', *Industrial Relations Journal*. January.

PART 7: **FURTHER RECOMMENDED READING**

Towers, B. (1987). *A Handbook of Industrial Relations Practice*. Kogan Page.
Farnham, D. and Pimlott, J. (1986). *Understanding Industrial Relations*, 3rd Edn. Cassell.
Fox, A. (1966). *Industrial Sociology and Industrial Relations*. Royal Commission Research Paper No. 3. HMSO.
Flanders, A. (1970). *Management and Unions: The Theory and Reform of Industrial Relations*. Faber & Faber.
Batstone, E., Boraston, I. and Frenkel, S. (1977). *Shop Stewards in Action*. Blackwell.
Marsh, A. (1982). *Employee Relations Policy and Decision Making*. Gower.
Palmer, G. (1983). *British Industrial Relations*. George Allen & Unwin.
Wallace Bell, D. (1979). *Industrial Participation*. Pitman.
Cronin, J.E. (1979). *Industrial Conflict in Modern Britain*. Croom Helm.

PART 7: **SAMPLE EXAMINATION QUESTIONS**

By what means or mechanisms does the State attempt to secure order in industrial relations? IPM

How would you set about assessing the prospects for successful productivity bargaining within your organization (or one well known to you)? IPM

The strike is one form of behaviour utilized by employees when they are in conflict with management. Distinguish between different types of strike action. Many people believe the law should be used in the regulation or prevention of strike activity. How might this be achieved? CACA

Assuming that senior management agree that employees should be more involved in the decision-making process, by what means might this policy be implemented? CACA

Describe and comment on the role of trade unions within the relationship between employer and employee. CACA

Two contrasting management attitudes towards industrial relations are commonly described as 'unitary' and 'pluralistic'. Outline and comment on these two differing approaches. CACA

(a) Explain the difference between collective bargaining and joint consultation.

(b) Compare procedural and substantive agreements. CBSI

(a) What are the functions of staff associations and trade unions in a building society?

(b) How can an employer make the most effective use of such means of employee representation?

(c) What are the objectives of an industrial relations policy for a national building society?

(d) What items should be included in that policy? CBSI

Identify the essential elements of a grievance procedure. Why is it necessary to have a formal procedure? CBSI

Evaluate the merits of the arguments frequently advanced in favour of participation by lower-level employees in the management of the enterprise. Quoting specific instances where you can — ideally from your own experience — show how participation can bring benefits *for management*, and discuss the 'price' which management has to pay for these benefits. ICSA

Outline the various negotiating strategies and tactics available to managements when dealing with a trade union, and dicuss the circumstances in which the use of any given strategy might be considered appropriate. ICSA

How far would it be correct to argue that the incidence of industrial conflict is dependent on the presence of a positive legal framework designed principally to regulate the actions of employers and trade unions? ICSA

What is collective bargaining?

Explain the reasons for the development of collective bargaining in banking in recent years. CIB

(a) Distinguish between 'disciplinary' and 'grievance' procedures.
(b) What guidelines would you lay down for the conduct of:
    (i) Disciplinary procedures?
    (ii) Grievance procedures? IAM

What, in the context of industrial relations, is meant by the term 'sanction'? Describe some sanctions that may be utilized:
(i) By the employer;
(ii) By a trade union. IAM

What factors affect the industrial relations climate of a business? What are the major influences currently affecting the industrial relations climate in banking? Do you expect more or less conflict in the immediate future? Give reasons for your answer. CIB

Review and comment on any evidence you are aware of that trade union ideologies and/or trade union objectives are currently undergoing modification. IPM

What aspects of employee relations would you recommend should be controlled by procedures agreed with worker or trade union representatives? Why? IPM

What role does the first-line union representative (e.g., shop steward or office representative) play in (a) the management of conflict, and (b) the containment of conflict, in the workplace? IPM

Part 8
Termination of employment

30
Dismissals

A contract of employment may be terminated by either employer or employee giving proper notice. The period of notice may be determined by provisions of the contract, trade custom or statute.

PERIOD OF NOTICE

The Employment Protection (Consolidation) Act 1978 establishes minimum periods of notice for full-time employees. These are:

Period of service	*Period of notice*
1 month	Not less than 1 week
2 years	2 weeks
more than 2 years	An additional week for each year of service up to a maximum of 12 weeks

An employee is required to give only 1 week's notice after one month's continuous service unless otherwise provided.

It should be noted that the periods prescribed by the Act are minima and may be extended by a contract of employment or trade custom. In the absence of agreement, an employee is entitled to 'reasonable notice'. This may be rather longer than anticipated. In determining what is 'reasonable' considerations would appear to include the employee's status and responsibility, his length of service, whether he is paid on a weekly, monthly or annual basis and the period which a person in his position normally receives in the trade or industry concerned. Thus, for example, in 1971, when statute required a rather shorter period of notice, the Court of Appeal held that an engineer aged 61 who had been employed for over 30 years should have received between 6 and 12 months notice [1].

WRONGFUL AND SUMMARY DISMISSAL

Normally an employer must give proper notice. There may, however, occur circumstances when the conduct of an employee is such that it undermines the contractual relationship between employer and employee. Given such circumstances, it may be possible to dismiss an employee without notice. Examples might be gross negligence, dishonesty, violence, drunkenness or immorality. However, while such may provide grounds for instant dismissal, they may not provide grounds for dismissal at all since in each case the determining factor must be the extent to which conduct destroyed the contractual basis. An incautious summary dismissal may thus give rise to a claim of wrongful dismissal or alternatively unfair dismissal.

The more common course of action for an employee is to claim unfair dismissal; this is discussed in detail below. Under certain circumstances, however, an employee may not be eligible to make such a claim or may feel that he is entitled to greater compensation than industrial tribunals are authorized to award. In such cases an employee may choose to claim wrongful dismissal and sue his former employer in a County or High Court.

UNFAIR DISMISSAL

Prior to the Industrial Relations Act 1971, statute placed little constraint on the power of an employer to dismiss staff. The Contracts of Employment Act 1963 imposed minimum periods of notice and many staff were already party to contracts or agreements encompassing arrangements for termination of employment. However, so long as an employer gave the agreed or statutory period of notice, he was virtually free to hire and fire at will, however spurious his reasons.

The Employment Protection (Consolidation) Act 1978 re-enacted a right originally created by the Industrial Relations Act 1971 — the right not to be 'unfairly' dismissed. An employee who fulfils certain preconditions (see below) can bring a claim to an industrial tribunal. If the tribunal considers that the dismissal was unfair in the prevailing circumstances it may award compensation or order re-instatement of the employee (see 'Remedies' below). Prior to 1980 the onus was on the employer to prove that the dismissal was fair, but the Employment Act 1980 has created regulations whereby tribunals take a more neutral approach to this aspect of evidence. They are also required to take into account the size and administrative resources of the employer's undertaking when forming a view of his actions.

Unfair dismissal has become extremely complex and much case law has developed since the intitial legislation. Various amendments and additions have also been introduced by the Employment Act 1980 and 1982. One concept which has developed over the years is that of 'constructive dismissal'.

Constructive dismissal

What is meant by constructive dismissal? Interpretation of the provision has changed significantly since its inception. To begin with, tribunals interpreted it as meaning any situation in which an employee was not dismissed but rather felt bound to resign because of his employer. Thus an employer who by various means made life generally miserable for an employee in the hope perhaps that the employee would resign could find that the resignation would be considered not a voluntary termination of employment, but rather a constructive and probably unfair dismissal. Considerable use was made of this provision. It now appears, however, that the provision was interpreted too widely. In 1978 a Court of Appeal decision [2] suggested that constructive dismissal should be determined strictly in accordance with the law of contract and not simply by applying a test of reasonableness or otherwise to an employer's conduct. The test now appears to be: to what extent did the employer's behaviour amount to a breach of contract which entitled the employee to resign?

Pre-conditions of claim for unfair dismissal

An employee must satisfy certain conditions before he is eligible to bring a claim for unfair dismissal under the law. In summary, the conditions are:

1. That the applicant was employed by the respondent (employer) under a contract of employment.
2. That he was dismissed (this is not always as clear-cut as it would appear).
3. *That he was employed for the qualifying period* — normally 2 years' service. (See also the exclusion of qualifying period for trade union-related dismissals referred to below and race and sex discrimination while there is no qualifying period.)

Certain employees are excluded from the statutory right not to be unfairly dismissed. These include:

1. Registered dock-workers.
2. Fishermen sharing in the profits or earnings of the vessel.
3. Employees normally working outside Great Britain.
4. Part-time employees. (Hours for qualifications as a full-time employee to be determined by the Secretary of State for Employment from time to time. At present, this is 16 hours or more per week; 8 hours per week for staff wiith more than 5 years' service.)
5. Employees above retirement age.
6. Fixed term contracts of one year or more in relation to which the employee has agreed in writing to forgo his right to any claim.

ACCEPTABLE REASONS FOR DISMISSAL

It would be a misapprehension to assume that statute only describes circumstances likely to be considered unfair. The 1978 Act indicates a number of situations when dismissal will normally be acceptable. These are when an employee is dismissed:

1. for reasons of ability or qualifications,
2. for reasons of conduct,
3. for reasons of redundancy,
4. for reasons such that an employee cannot continue in work without causing either the employer or himself to contravene a legal duty or restriction, e.g. an alien without a work permit,
5. for some other substantial reason which is such as to justify dismissal.

So far as an employer is concerned it is important to demonstrate that the reason cited is one of those listed above; failure so to do will mean that the tribunal *must* find the dismissal unfair.

Nevertheless, even having established one of these reasons, unfair dismissal may still be substantiated. In each case the tribunal will wish to consider the particular circumstances, including the nature of the employing organization and to what extent the employer acted reasonably in treating the reason as just cause for dismissal.

Throughout any hearing considerable emphasis will be placed on the question of reasonable behaviour. 'What would a reasonable employer have done in the circumstances?' It can be seen, therefore, that there is no possible clear or guaranteed division of reason for dismissal into fair or unfair categories. The decision must always, to some degree, be a subjective one. It is this absence of rigid categorization that sometimes appears to produce conflicting decisions in reported cases. Given that no guaranteed rules may be preferred, are there any obvious traps to avoid? Under what circumstances is a normally fair reason potentially unfair?

1. *An employee is dismissed for reasons of ability or qualifications*

To prove reasonable cause becomes more difficult the longer an employee remains employed. Since a complaint of unfair dismissal may only be made by an employee with (in most cases) more than 2 year's service, it would seem prudent in order to avoid difficulty that an employer should do two things. First, a thorough review of personnel procedures should be conducted, in particular to ensure the adequacy of selection procedures and arrangements made for the monitoring of initial training. Second, consideration should be given to employing all new staff on a probation basis. Within this period unsatisfactory staff can be identified and employment terminated. Note that notice must be given within and not at the end of the 2-year period.

A particularly important consideration is that of the employee whose job capability is affected by pregnancy. To dismiss an employee simply because she is pregnant will normally be unfair unless, by reason of her pregnancy, she is incapable of adequately fulfilling her duties or for her to continue would involve breaking the law. In either case, before dismissal, she must be offered any suitable alternative vacant job within the organization.

Such a procedure is indeed to be recommended in any case of proposed dismissal on grounds of ability. Evidence that an employer has attempted to place an employee in a suitable alternative post will do much to enhance the former's case in any examination of the extent to which the employer has acted in a reasonable fashion.

The same could be said in respect of employees whose lack of capability is due to ill-health. These cases require careful handling and the member of staff should be consulted before any action is taken. It is almost certainly advisable for the employer to arrange a medical examination by a doctor nominated by him. The doctor's comments on the employee's condition in the light of the latter's job requirements should help the employer to reach a decision.

2. *An employee is dismissed for reasons of conduct*

Where an offence is well known to provide grounds for dismissal by its publication in a rule book or similar document, then the employer may be in a relatively strong position so long as it can be shown that in dealing with the offence a reasonable procedure was adopted.

But again, as throughout this section, note carefully the word 'reasonable' in the sentence above. Thus a minor breach of even a well-known rule might not be a good enough reason for dismissal. In each case the conduct of both employee and employer will be scrutinized. What was the gravity of the offence? What was its effect on the perpetuation of the employment contract? What was the nature of the employer's previous employment and conduct record?

Dress, swearing, fighting, conduct outside work, sexual behaviour, drunkenness, dishonesty, insubordination, breach of safety rules, absenteeism and sundry other offences have all been considered at one time or another by tribunals, often with apparently conflicting results. The practical implications of such uncertainty will be considered later.

3. *An employee is dismissed for reasons of redundancy*

Provisions relating to redundancy generally are dealt with in the next chapter. Here we will deal only with those aspects which may result in a claim for unfair dismissal.

While redundancy normally provides perfectly reasonable grounds for terminating employment, a mishandled redundancy may give rise to an unfair dismissal claim.

Such claims generally arise from circumstances which suggest discrimination in selecting an individual for redundancy or where the selection was made in contravention of a customary arrangement or agreed procedure and there were no good reasons for departing from it (see below – 'Dismissals deemed to be unfair'). A claim, however, may also succeed if there is evidence that good industrial relations practice has not been observed.

Again in such instances, case law points to the importance of reasonable employer behaviour. The basis of what might be considered reasonable has been spelt out by ACAS in its Code of Practice of dismissal and in case judgements. A number of principles may be drawn from these sources. These are:

☐ that as much warning of redundancy as is possible should be given,
☐ that there should be full consultation with any trade unions involved,
☐ that selection criteria should be capable of being objectively measured,
☐ that selection criteria should be properly applied,
☐ that any alternative employment should be offered.

4. *An employee is dismissed for reasons to do with a statutory duty or restriction*

Such cases tend to be relatively clear-cut, though even here problems may occur. Dismissal may, for example, be unfair if alternative employment is feasible, but not considered; or if the problem is not of long duration and may be overcome in some other way. Discrimination may again give rise to a claim, for example where one employee fails to meet a statutory requirement and is dismissed, while others, equally deficient, continue in employment.

5. *An employee is dismissed for some other substantial reason*

An employer who cannot rely on any of the four first reasons for dismissal discussed already may nevertheless still succeed if he can show some other substantial reason. It should not, however, be assumed that this presents an easy escape route for the employer. Decisions on cases brought under the provision show clearly the weight placed by tribunals on the word 'substantial'. What seems to be required is evidence that a conduct or situation rendered it impossible to continue the relationship as a result of which the only reasonable course of action was to dismiss the employee.

Examples of reasons which have been accepted by tribunals include economy — the cost of transporting two employees to work was almost equal to their weekly wage; and protection of business interests — where an employee refused to sign a reasonable restrictive covenant.

DISMISSALS DEEMED TO BE UNFAIR

Union-related dismissals

Dismissal will automatically be considered unfair where the main reason for it was that the employee

☐ was or proposed to become a member of an independent trade union (i.e., a union certified as independent by the Certification Officer), or

☐ had taken, or proposed to take, part at a reasonable time (i.e., either outside working hours or within working hours at a time permitted by the employer) in the activities of an independent trade union, or

☐ had refused to join or remain a member of a trade union or a specific trade union (NB: this includes cases involving a refusal to join a closed shop, see Chapter 25),

☐ was a member of a group of employees affected by redundancy, but was singled out for redundancy for a trade union related reason as described above, or was selected in contravention of an agreed redundancy selection procedure (see below).

It should be noted that the pre-condition of 2 years' service does not apply in the above cases or, indeed, where dismissal was on grounds of sex or race discrimination.

Dismissal on grounds of pregnancy

Where the principal reason for dismissal is an employee's pregnancy she will be deemed to have been unfairly dismissed unless she is incapable of carrying out her duties due to her condition or to employ her would constitute a contravention of statute.

Unfair selection for redundancy

Where an individual has been selected from amongst a group of workers for redundancy despite similar circumstances, his dismissal will be considered unfair where

☐ his selection was contrary to an agreed procedure or customary arrangement and there were no special reasons for departing from these arrangements, or

☐ the reason for his selection was 'union-related' (see 'Union related dismissals' above).

DISMISSAL DURING LOCK-OUT OR STRIKE

Legislation culminating in the Employment Act 1982 has limited the ability of an industrial tribunal to accept claims for unfair dismissal where employees are dismissed or not re-engaged as a result of a lock-out or strike. Currently no claim can be entertained, i.e., dismissal is automatically 'fair', unless it can be shown that either

☐ *all* relevant employees have *not* been dismissed, or
☐ other employees in the group have been offered re-engagement within 3 months of the date of dismissal.

WRITTEN STATEMENT OF REASONS FOR DISMISSAL

The EPCA provides that an employee with 6 months' continuous service may require his employer to provide a written statement of reasons for dismissal. Such a statement must be supplied within 14 days of the request and may be used in evidence before a tribunal.

If an employer refuses, or the reasons stated are considered untrue, an employee has right of appeal to an industrial tribunal which if satisfied will require the employer to pay the employee two weeks wages. At the same time, the tribunal may declare what it considers were the employer's reasons for the dismissal.

EMPLOYEE RIGHTS IN CASES OF ALLEGED UNFAIR DISMISSAL

The 1971, 1974, 1975 and 1978 Acts all give an employee the right of appeal to an industrial tribunal. Both the 1971 and 1974 Acts give tribunals the power to *recommend* re-instatement or re-employment, or to make an order for compensation. The 1975 and 1978 Acts impose on a tribunal the duty to *seek* re-instatement or re-employment wherever possible. At the same time, they increase the cost for an employer who is unable or chooses not to accept such a recommendation.

PROCEDURE FOR DEALING WITH COMPLAINTS

Having received notice of dismissal or having left employment where no notice was given, an employee who considers himself unfairly dismissed must register his complaint at the regional tribunal office *within 3 months* of the effective date of termination of employment.

Notice of a complaint will be served on the employer concerned and a Conciliation Officer attached to ACAS. The conciliation officer has a duty to consider whether his intervention in the matter is likely to promote a settlement of the complaint without the need for a tribunal hearing. (In practice, a large proportion of cases are either withdrawn or settled by conciliation.)

If not withdrawn or settled by conciliation, the cases are set down to be considered by a tribunal. In deciding whether or not an employee was unfairly dismissed, a tribunal will seek to discover:

- ☐ the reason for the dismissal,
- ☐ the extent to which the reason for and manner of dismissal were reasonable under the circumstances.

Evidence is under oath and tribunals may call for documents supporting any allegation. It is vital, therefore, that adequate records be kept of events leading up to the dismissal and action taken. It should be noted that not only will a tribunal be interested in the facts but also the procedure adopted in dealing with the matter and the extent to which any collective agreement was followed. In the absence of such an agreement it will be to the employer's advantage to show that he has adhered to the guidelines contained in the ACAS Code of Practice No. 1, Disciplinary Practice and Procedures in Employment. The significance of this code will be discussed later.

REMEDIES FOR UNFAIR DISMISSAL

Re-instatement or Re-employment

If dismissal is found to be unfair, a tribunal must explain to an employee the remedies available to him and in particular must determine whether he wishes to be re-instated to his old job or re-engaged in a comparable post with the same or an associated employer.

A tribunal may issue an order for re-instatement or re-engagement. In deciding whether to issue such an order, it must take into account:

1. the employee's wishes,
2. whether it is practicable for the employer to comply with an order,
3. the extent to which the employee caused or contributed to his own dismissal.

A tribunal is not required to take account of any permanent replacement employed unless an employer can show that the work could not be done without one, or that the dismissed employee had not within a reasonable time indicated a wish to be re-instated or re-employed. For an employer this may present serious difficulty. A dismissed employee has three months in which to make a complaint and during this time an employer may either have to make arrangements for the job to be carried out on a 'stop gap' basis or accept the risk of incurring a financial penalty by employing a permanent replacement.

If an order for re-instatement or re-employment is made, all rights, privileges, including seniority and pension rights, arrears of pay and any other benefit must be restored or paid as determined by the tribunal. Should the terms of such an order not be complied with, a tribunal may make a further award taking into account any loss sustained by the employee.

Compensation

Where re-instatement or re-engagement is not desired, practicable or acceptable, compensation will be considered. This may consist of four parts:

1. basic award,
2. compensatory award,
3. higher award,
4. special award.

Basic Award

This is essentially a redundancy payment. An employee is entitled to compensation subject to a maximum weekly wage to be determined by the Secretary of State for Employment from time to time. The award is calculated according to the normal redundancy payment formula, i.e.:

$\frac{1}{2}$ weeks' pay for each year of employment between the ages of 18 and 21,

1 week's pay for each year of employment between the ages of 22 and 40,

$1\frac{1}{2}$ weeks' pay for each year of employment between the ages of 41 and 64 (or 59 for women).

In calculating an award, account is taken of the last 20 years of employment only. Under certain circumstances, e.g. where an employee refuses alternative employment in a redundancy situation, an award may be limited to two weeks' pay. Where dismissal is because of trade union membership or non-membership, a higher basic award may be payable. Account is also taken of any redundancy payment made and the extent to which the employee contributed to his own dismissal.

Compensatory Award

In addition to a basic award, an employee may be entitled to a compensatory award which shall be 'such amount as the tribunal considers just and equitable in all the circumstances', subject to a statutory maximum which is set each year. In computing the award a tribunal will wish to assess any expenses incurred as a result of the dismissal together with any loss of benefit which the employee might reasonably have expected had the dismissal not occurred. Again, a tribunal will consider the extent to which an employee contributed to his own dismissal together with the extent to which he has sought to mitigate his loss.

Additional Award

If a re-instatement or re-employment order is made but not complied with, an employer must satisfy the tribunal that it is not practicable to comply. Failing this, the tribunal may make an additional award of between 13 and 26 weeks pay. (Again subject to the maximum determined by the Secretary of State.) Similary, if the reason for dismissal is unfair since it concerns membership of an independent trade union, or is unlawful on race or sex grounds, an additional award may be made, though this time of between 26 and 52 weeks' pay.

Special Award

The Employment Act 1982 replaces the additional award with a 'special award' for those dismissed on grounds of union membership, union activity or refusal to join a non-independent trade union where re-instatement or re-engagement cannot be arranged. As in other cases above, such an award may take into account any behaviour on the part of the employee which has prevented re-instatement or re-engagement. However, the limits of the special award are higher than the additional award with a maximum, at present, of 156 weeks' pay with no ceiling on a 'week's pay'.

Interim Relief Pending Determination of Complaint
An employee who considers that his dismissal results from trade union membership or activity or proposed membership may apply to a tribunal for interim relief. Such an application must be made within seven days of the dismissal and must be supported by a certificate signed by an authorized officer of an independent trade union, stating:

1. that on the date of dismissal the employee was or had proposed to become a member of the union, and
2. that reasonable grounds exist for supposing that the reason for dismissal has to do with union membership or activity.

If, having heard the application, it appears likely to a tribunal that union membership or activity was the principal reason, it may require the employer to re-instate or re-employ the employee. Should the employer refuse, the tribunal may make an order for the continuation of the contract of employment until the full hearing is completed.

Compensation may also be awarded if considered just and equitable in view of loss suffered by the employee.

APPEALS FROM INDUSTRIAL TRIBUNALS

An appeal from the decision of the industrial tribunal is heard by the Employment Appeal Tribunal (EAT). This consists of judges and lay members with 'special knowledge or experience of industrial relations either as representatives of employers or as representatives of workers'. However, appeals can only be brought on a point of law and legal advice should be sought before making an appeal.

As well as dealing with appeals regarding unfair dismissal cases, the EAT hears appeals arising from:

1. the Employment Protection (Consolidation) Act 1978,
2. the Equal Pay Act 1970,
3. the Sex Discrimination Act 1975,
4. the Employment Protection Act 1975,
5. the Race Relations Act 1976,
6. the Employment Act 1980,
7. the Employment Act 1982,

and other legislative provisions.

A further right of appeal may be granted to the Court of Appeal.

CONSEQUENCES OF UNFAIR DISMISSAL PROVISIONS

The provisions described earlier, perhaps not surprisingly, have from time to time been interpreted as making it virtually impossible to dismiss an employee without fear of dire financial consequences.

However, an examination of dismissal statistics over the last five years indicates that any such interpretation is exaggerated. Of the approximately 30,000 or so cases of unfair dismissal registered in an average year, nearly two-thirds are withdrawn or settled by conciliation. Of those cases considered by tribunals, around one-third are found in favour of employees.

Compensation in such instances is rarely the maximum permitted. Although it has increased significantly in recent years, the median award is currently approximately £1800 [3].

Such conclusions have naturally led to demands for review of the system for dealing with complaints. Certainly it appears that tribunals are not, as has often been argued, heavily biased in favour of employees. However, at the same time, it does appear that for many employers the cost of implementing and monitoring legislation and defending claims made is often very much greater than compensation finally awarded. The problem is naturally more acute for small employers.

Although originally intended to provide a means whereby employers and employees could present their cases without legal representation, a whole new area of case law has been generated encouraging what Lord Justice Lawson has described as 'excellent displays of legal learning'. Such displays tend to be expensive, and while nearly a half of employers are legally represented compared with a third of employees, for many it is often easier and cheaper to make an 'out of court' financial settlement rather than defend a case. Certainly there are few other areas of law where so much expensive litigation is committed to recovering such small compensation.

Pre-hearing assessments

In an attempt to simplify and reduce the cost of tribunal hearings, new rules were introduced in 1980.

Under the 1980 Industrial Tribunal Regulations either side may request a pre-hearing assessment (PHA). Such assessments provide tribunals with an outline of the case to be heard so that frivolous or hopeless applications may be identified. They may also allow the opportunity for a particular point on which the whole of the application rests, e.g. whether a time limit was met, to be considered in isolation. Where as a result of a PHA a tribunal feels that a full hearing is not desirable it may issue a warning to the party concerned that if he proceeds with a full hearing and loses he may be liable for the other party's costs.

DISMISSAL AND COMPANY POLICY

The combined effect of the various provisions discussed above is to make it necessary for employers to at least consider that in dismissing employees they risk a potentially expensive unfair dismissal claim. What can an employer do to minimize the problem?

Several practical aspects have already been discussed under the various reasons for dismissal outlined above. Policies and procedures will have to be prepared to deal with many of these areas. In summary, the following steps need to be taken:

☐ Consult with staff and unions on acceptable standards of performance and conduct.

☐ Publicize agreed policies, rules and procedures.

☐ Ensure that all managers and others in authority adhere to and operate procedures based upon agreed equitable standards and recommendations of ACAS Code No. 1 (see below).

ACAS Code of Practice No. 1: Disciplinary Practice and Procedures in Employment: 1977

This code replaced the Code of Industrial Relations Practice which was attached to the 1971 Act and subsequently to the TULRA 1974. It should be noted that while the Code is in no way legally binding, an employer's failure to comply with it, or adhere to its recommendations is 'admissable in evidence, and if any provision of such a Code appears to the tribunal or Committee to be relevant to any question arising in the proceedings it shall be taken into account in determining that question'.

Whereas the 1971 Code of Practice accepted that in very small establishments a formal procedure might not be necesary, the 1977 Code suggests that even these might adopt its provisions and incorporate them into a simple procedure. The 1977 Code therefore provides an essential basis for the formulation of disciplinary policy and practice in all organizations irrespective of size.

Employee Participation and Information

Paragraph 7 of the Code recommends that all employees be made aware of rules, and procedures likely to be implemented if such rules are broken. In practical terms this means publishing rules on notice-boards and in handbooks issued to all new employees. In addition, a further explanation should form part of any induction course and indeed may be reinforced during subsequent training sessions. The EPA reinforces this by requiring that employees must, in any contract of employment, receive the following information:

- ☐ Details of any disciplinary rules and procedures.
- ☐ The identity of a person to whom the employee may appeal if dissatisfied with any disciplinary procedure relating to him.

The Code further urges the need for consultation and participation in the development of new procedures. While inevitably the need for negative discipline, i.e. discipline carrying a threat of punishment, will occur, the most useful *form* of discipline is undoubtedly positive or self-discipline. To a considerable extent it is management's responsibility to create an atmosphere in which staff are ready and willing to discipline themselves. Nevertheless, when the need for formal discipline arises, its application will be all the easier if accepted by those subject to it. It is with this in mind that the Code recommends management to involve staff at all levels when determining new rules and procedures.

Essential Features of Disciplinary Procedures

The ACAS Code recommends that procedures should be in writing and make provision for prompt settlement of matters. They should:

☐ specify who has authority to take various forms of disciplinary action;

☐ not allow a supervisor to dismiss an immediate subordinate without reference to senior management;

☐ ensure that an employee is always given the opportunity to be accompanied by a friend or representative, hear complaints made against him and state his case before any action is taken;

☐ ensure that no employee is dismissed for a first offence except in the case of gross misconduct;

☐ ensure than an alleged offence is always fully investigated before any action is taken;

☐ ensure that an explanation of any action taken is given together with details of any appeals procedure.

Outline disciplinary procedure

Whatever procedure is adopted, justice must not only be done — it must be seen to be done. In many minor cases, an informal supervisor's reprimand is all that is required to ensure that an incident does not re-occur. In serious cases, an employee may be suspended while the matter is investigated. Normally, however, the procedure might be as follows:

1. On the first offence, the employee should be given a formal warning which should be recorded. However, only in serious cases should it be necessary to confirm the warning in writing at this stage. Nevertheless, the employee should be given the opportunity to be accompanied by a friend or representative and should be advised that the interview constitutes the first formal stage of the organization's disciplinary procedure. He should also be advised of the possible consequences of further misconduct and any right of appeal. Arrangements should be made for details of the offence and interview to be removed from the employee's file after a fixed period.

2. Further misconduct will require a formal interview normally conducted by a senior manager together with the immediate supervisor. At this stage the employee should be encouraged to be accompanied or represented. A final warning should be issued and confirmed in writing. This should contain a statement indicating the likely consequences of any re-occurrence and any right of appeal available. Arrangements should again be made for details to be removed from the employee's record after a fixed period.

3. If further misconduct occurs, another formal interview should take place following which disciplinary action should be taken. The employee should again be accompanied and advised of any appeals procedure. Details should be confirmed in writing. In

determining the disciplinary action to be taken it is important to bear in mind the test of reasonableness. This will involve consideration of the employee's past record and the nature of the offence or offences committed. It is also important that any penalty is consistent and not too severe when compared with previous cases with the organization.

4. A right of appeal should exist at the end of the procedure or indeed at any other stage. This might be to a senior manager, board of senior managers or often to a joint disciplinary committee consisting of both management and employee representatives. Alternatively, on exhaustion of the procedure, right of appeal may exist to an independent body in accordance with an agreed grievance procedure [4].

It is of vital importance that at all stages of the procedure, proper records are kept of the nature of alleged offences, action taken and subsequent development.

Disciplinary action and union representatives

A particular problem may occur in relation to offences committed by union representatives or officials. The fact that an employee is also a union official cannot exempt him from disciplinary action. However, it is likely that action against such an employee might be interpreted as victimization and so lead to industrial action by fellow union members. For this reason it is normal practice to delay disciplinary action until the case has been discussed with a full-time official of the union concerned.

DISMISSAL — THE FINAL SANCTION

Dismissal should be the ultimate sanction. It is, after all, proof that a manager or supervisor despairs or is incapable of dealing with a recalcitrant subordinate. In any case, it may be too severe for the offence, some other alternative (e.g. suspension, demotion, or a fine) being more appropriate.

Legislation makes it more difficult and expensive to dismiss staff. However, even without statutory provisions dismissal can be a costly process. A reputation for 'hiring and firing' may severely affect recruitment costs and possibly wage costs. Industrial action in response to dismissal is a common occurrence. Together with the direct cost of consequent disruption, account must be taken of possible effects on relationships between employer, other employees, customers and the community at large. Frequent dismissals will inevitably contribute to a lowering of morale manifested in a host of negative forms. Finally, costs associated with labour turnover, albeit self-inflicted, must be considered (see Chapter 7).

REFERENCES

1. Hill v Parsons (1971).
2. Western Excavating (ECC) Ltd v Sharp (1978).
3. Source: Central Office of Industrial Tribunals.
4. Upton, R. (1987). 'What makes a disciplinary procedure appealing?', *Personnel Management*, December, pp. 46–49. For an excellent guide to disciplinary procedures and practice the reader is referred to the ACAS advisory handbook, *Discipline at Work*, 1987.

31
Redundancy

Before 1965, a redundant employee was not entitled to compensation unless it could be shown that a breach of contract of employment by his employer had occurred in which case an action for damages might be possible. Government statistics show that in 1963, 1.75 million workers were protected by 371 redundancy agreements. By present-day standards, very few of those agreements would be considered generous. For example, when the British Motor Corporation made 6000 workers redundant in June 1956, workers with 3 to 10 years' service received compensation of only one week's wages, those with more than 10 years service received 2 weeks' wages. The Redundancy Payments Act 1965 (RPA) amended by the Employment Protection Act 1975 (EPA) radically changed this situation by providing that any employee who is dismissed by reason of redundancy shall normally be automatically entitled to compensation. These and other provisions now form part of the Employment Protection (Consolidation) Act 1978 (EPCA).

WHEN IS AN EMPLOYEE REDUNDANT?

Section 81 of the EPCA 1978 states that a dismissal shall be for reason of redundancy if it is wholly or mainly attributable to:

- [ ] an employer ceasing or proposing to cease to carry on the business for the purpose of which the employee was employed or,
- [ ] an employer ceasing or proposing to cease to carry on that business in the place where the employee was employed or,
- [ ] the requirements of that business for employees to carry out work of a particular kind, or for them to carry out that work in the place where they are so employed, have ceased or diminished or are expected to cease or diminish.

LAYOFFS AND SHORT-TIME WORKING

A claim for redundancy payments may also arise as a result of layoffs or short-time working. Both may occur if an employer finds that temporarily he has inadequate work to keep staff fully occupied. (For the purposes of the EPCA, short-time working is defined as being where less than a half the normal week's pay is earned.)

If the period of layoff or short-time working lasts for more than 4 consecutive weeks, or more than 6 weeks in any 13, an employee may give written notice to his employer that he intends to claim redundancy pay. An employer may either accept such notice or serve a counter notice indicating that he anticipates being able to provide at least 13 uninterrupted weeks work without further layoffs or short-time working. If neither claim nor counter-claim are withdrawn, the matter may be referred to an industrial tribunal.

WORKERS NOT PROTECTED BY STATUTE

Certain groups of workers are not protected by statutory redundancy provisions. These are:

☐ registered dockworkers
☐ share fishermen
☐ employees normally working outside Great Britain
☐ part-time employees (hours for qualification as a full-time employee to be determined by the Secretary of State for Employment from time to time)
☐ domestic servants employed by close relatives
☐ employees who have been offered suitable alternative employment and have unreasonably refused it (see below)
☐ crown servants
☐ employees above normal statutory retirement age
☐ employees on fixed-term contracts of two years or more if they have agreed in writing to forgo any rights to a claim
☐ employees covered by redundancy agreements negotiated by independent trade unions and approved by the Secretary of State
☐ employees with less than 2 years continuous employment with the employer against whom the claim is made

COMPENSATION

The EPCA 1978 provides that an employee who is dismissed for reason of redundancy and has been employed for at least 2 years by his current employer is entitled to redundancy pay at the following rates:

$\frac{1}{2}$ week's pay for each year of employment between the ages of 18 and 21

1 week's pay for each year of employment between the ages of 22 and
40
$1\frac{1}{2}$ weeks' pay for each year of employment between the ages of 41
and 64 (or 59 for women)

When calculating redundancy pay, account is taken of the last 20 years of
employment only and a maximum weekly wage to be determined by the
Secretary of State from time to time.

An employer with less than 10 employees who makes a redundancy
payment is entitled to a rebate from a National Redundancy Fund.
Rebates are available so long as an employer is liable to pay and has paid
redunduncy compensation. Payments on an *ex gratia* basis, in excess of
statutory requirements, or payments for some reason other than a
redundancy as described by Section 81 of the EPCA 1978 or payments by
larger employers, do not attract a rebate.

Section 106 of the EPCA provides that where an employer is
insolvent and an employee is unable to obtain a redundancy payment,
then that payment may be claimed in full from the National
Redundancy Fund.

Any dispute regarding entitlement to or the amount of any
redundancy payment or rebate may be referred to an industrial tribunal
for determination.

ALTERNATIVE EMPLOYMENT

The EPCA provides that where a redundant employee is offered
suitable alternative employment by his employer and either accepts or
unreasonably refuses the offer, he will not be entitled to redundancy
pay.

In determining what is a 'suitable alternative', account must be taken
of the extent to which the terms and conditions of the new job differ
from those of the old, together with the nature of the work and the
qualifications and experience of the employee concerned. If suitability
is disputed, the matter may be referred to a tribunal. When considering
such cases, tribunals have tended not only to consider the criteria
indicated above, but also the possible effect on the domestic and social
life of the employee.

If an employee accepts alternative employment, he has a right to 4
weeks' trial period in the new job, though a longer period may be
agreed in writing. During the trial period, either employer or employee
may terminate the new contract, in which case the employee will
normally be considered redundant, and thus entitled to redundancy
payments as if the trial period had never occurred. However, if during
the trial period an employee unreasonably terminates his new contract

or is fairly dismissed for reasons not connected with his new job, e.g., misbehaviour, then he may forfeit his rights to redundancy compensation.

REDUNDANCY PROCEDURES

The RPA 1965 is principally concerned with ensuring financial compensation for redundant employees and does not indicate any procedure for dealing with redundancies. The EPA 1975 seeks to remedy this.

Notification of redundancies to the Department of Employment

Employers intending to declare more than 10 employees redundant are required to give appropriate notice to the Department of Employment. If more than 10 are to be dismissed as redundant in one establishment over a period of 30 days or less, at least 30 days' notice must be given. If 100 or more are involved over a period of 90 days or less, at least 90 days' notice must be given.

If as a result of special circumstances, it is not reasonably practicable for an employer to comply fully with the required periods of notice, he must do all that he can to comply and be ready to explain why full compliance was not possible.

Details of the circumstances surrounding the redundancy must also be provided together with information regarding trade union consultation. Failure to give proper notice may result in a fine.

Consultation with independent trade unions

An employer is also required to consult with union officials if an independent trade union is recognized in respect of the group or category of employees concerned. Consultation must begin at the earliest opportunity, but if 10 or more employees are likely to be made redundant, then it must take place in accordance with the minimum periods of notice required to be given to the Department of Employment (see above).

The duty to consult applies whether or not the employee concerned is a member of a trade union. The determining factor is whether the employee is a member of a work group or category in respect of which an independent union has negotiating rights. Where no union exists, or no union is recognized, there is no statutory duty to consult, though Section 45 of the Code of Practice 1972 nevertheless recommends that consultation should in all cases take place with employees or their representatives.

In order that meaningful consultation may occur, an employer is required to disclose in writing full information about his plans. In particular, he must state:

- [ ] the reasons for his proposals
- [ ] the number and description of employees he proposes to dismiss as redundant
- [ ] the total number of employees of each description employed at that establishment
- [ ] the proposed method of selecting the employees who may be made redundant
- [ ] the proposed timing and method of carrying out the dismissals, taking account of any agreed procedures

Consultation, however, does not begin and end with the provision of this information. An employer is further required to consider and reply to any trade union representations, and if any are rejected to state his reasons. It is important to note that the duty is to consult. It is not required that agreement be reached, though there are obvious practical advantages in doing so. Nevertheless, an employer must at all times proceed with caution, bearing constantly in mind his possible liability for unfair dismissal claims arising from redundancy.

Failure to consult

If an employer fails to consult as requried by statute, an independent recognized trade union may complain to a tribunal. The complaint will initially be referred to a conciliation officer attached to ACAS, who will consider whether he is able to help resolve the matter without the need for a formal hearing. If not settled by conciliation, the case will be considered by a tribunal.

An employer may again offer the defence that it was not practicable for him to comply fully with statutory requirements. If however, the tribunal finds a complaint justified, it may make a protective award safeguarding the pay of employees who have already been declared redundant or it is proposed to make redundant. The duration of the protective award must not exceed the statutory consultative periods, though where less than 10 employees are involved, a protected period of up to 28 days may be granted. During the protected period, all employees to whom it relates are entitled to normal pay, whether still employed or not. Any employee who fails to receive pay in accordance with an award may apply to a tribunal, which may order payment.

TIME OFF TO LOOK FOR WORK

An employee with 2 year's service is also entitled to time off with pay in order to find other work or to arrange training. If an employer refuses time off or pay, the employee may complain to an industrial tribunal.

EFFECTS OF REDUNDANCY LEGISLATION

In order to assess the effects of the redundancy legislation outlined above, it is necessary to examine its objectives. The RPA 1965 was the result of two principal forces:

☐ an increasing social awareness, and in particular a growing acceptance of management's social responsibilities
☐ a perception of the need for manpower planning not only at corporate but also national level. Originally part of a statutory package that also included the Contracts of Employment and Industrial Training Acts, it was intended to form part of an overall national manpower policy encouraging standardized terms of employment, industrial training and mobility of labour

By making a lump-sum severance payment it was intended to compensate employees for the loss of employment while at the same time reducing resistance to job change and encouraging mobility of labour; workers moving from overmanned sectors of industry to those with a labour shortage. This 'cash solution' has been the subject of considerable controversy.

Advocates of the scheme have argued that it provides job security by encouraging redundancy avoidance and thus adequate manpower planning and that workers are encouraged to spend more time considering alternative employment, a possible move of house or retraining, unfettered by financial concern. Others have argued that cash payments act as a disincentive to find other work and indeed have contributed to Britain's long-term unemployment problem. Further, that its provisions are unfair, since both the long-term unemployed and workers who find other work immediately are treated alike. It has also been suggested that workers and employers conspire together to make fraudulent claims, that expanding industries are subsidizing declining ones via the levy – rebate system, and that employers are unable to afford redundancy payments, thereby inhibiting mobility of labour.

Studies of the behaviour of redundant workers show a high level of consistency. A study carried out by Standard Telephones and Cables Ltd in 1974 of employees made redundant by the Company in 1972 showed that 59% found new work within four weeks — 78% within three months. This is consistent with earlier studies carried out by

Daniel [1] of works closures in South East London. Of the workers involved in the closures, a third had new jobs even before being dismissed. Similarly, a government survey in 1971 [2] found that 60% were re-employed within a month.

Such examples were, of course, in a period of relatively full employment. However, whether in circumstances of high employment or unemployment, it would seem that the average worker attempts to find re-employment as quickly as possible, irrespective of the size of any redundancy payment.

Evidence in a time of unemployment casts doubt indeed on whether transfer of manpower could ever be as potentially free as originally anticipated. A study published by the MSC in 1980 [3] suggested that almost three quarters of the long-term unemployed had previously been manual workers generally in semi-skilled or unskilled jobs. To what extent, irrespective of redundancy compensation, it is ever likely that such workers might find regular employment in a rapidly and relentlessly re-structuring workforce is a matter of conjecture. However, whether in productive or service industries, it is surely the case that new technologies will require skills and aptitudes foreign to such individuals, and those opportunities that do arise for re-training are most likely to be made available to either the young or those who through some skill or other show at least some element of transferable aptitude.

A further point of consensus is noteworthy. Although many of those displaced, in the examples above, suffered little hardship before finding new employment, a minority experienced extreme difficulty, even in a time of full employment. Kahn [4], Daniel [1] and MacKay and Reid [5] all identify age as a critical factor in determining the period of time taken to find another job and the standards of job found, workers aged 55+ having the greatest difficulty. Indeed, Daniel [6] suggests that age is more important than skill, occupational level or even level of local unemployment as a determining factor.

Again, an examination of current unemployment statistics reinforces the point. Unemployment is highest among the young, particularly in the immediate post-school years, and among those who are aged 60 and over. The problem is not, however, peculiarly British. Similar problems have been identified in both France and Germany. However, in both of these countries, specific steps have been taken to protect the older worker. In France, government officials are empowered to require alterations to lists of employees selected for redundancy, on the grounds that an employee may have more than normal disadvantages in finding alternative employment. Similarly, permission to make an employee over the age of 60 redundant may be withheld unless placement in another job or special financial arrangements have been made. In Germany, both statute and collective agreements such as that within the German metals industry emphasise the priority to be given to retaining or re-employing older workers [7].

In our first edition of this book, we proposed that future government policies must surely abandon altogether the pre-occupation with direct cash solutions, and instead set about creating a co-ordinated national situation where workers are ready and willing to change jobs as necessary in the knowledge that they are secure not in a particular job, but in a sequence of jobs. Regrettably, such a situation now appears a fond pipe-dream. For employees at all levels, in all types of organization, redundancy is now a potential reality with no promise for the future. A willingness to move or change jobs is in many cases an irrelevance.

COMPANY POLICY

To a considerable degree, legislation providing rights for redundant workers was demanded by the general lack of manpower planning existing in many organizations. This lack of foresight tended to encourage a policy of hiring and firing in sympathy with organizational requirements. Such policies, although convenient in their flexibility, were and are often expensive for both employer and employees. Many of the problems evident in industry — restrictive practices, demarcation, overmanning, antagonism to productivity schemes and to work study and new techniques, are based on a conscious or sometimes subconscious fear of redundancy — fear of 'the dole'. Security, as you have already seen, has been described as one of man's primary, or basic needs.

In modern society, for most of us, this means a secure job. If an employer is to instil into his staff a sense of loyalty towards him, he must reciprocate. For all these reasons, redundancy and its avoidance are of particular importance to the personnel manager [21]. How then may an employer minimize the need to make staff redundant?

The most obvious starting point is, of course, efficient and adequate manpower planning. By assessing manpower requirements accurately, by examining and developing manpower resources, by recruiting appropriate numbers of staff, we may enjoy the relatively problem-free state of affairs that exists when manpower supply matches demand precisely. However, such an idyllic state of affairs is unlikely to continue forever, even in the best ordered organization. Given an economically and politically free society, no employer can guarantee absolute job security. However, an employer facing a redundancy problem can, and should, take every step to avoid the declaration of redundancies, or at least to minimize the number of staff affected. It is vital therefore that two plans exist and are communicated to both management and staff. First, a plan to avoid redundancy: second, a plan of action should redundancy prove inevitable.

Redundancy avoidance

Several courses of action are available:

- ☐ restrictions on or freezing recruitment: allowing manpower to be reduced by natural wastage. Although such a policy has much to commend it, being relatively painless, over a long term it may lead to a weakening of the organizational structure. It may further cause staff to fear for their future and so leave, the most able and employable often being the first to go
- ☐ early retirement: as an alternative to redundancy, its introduction usually on a voluntary basis may prove an attractive proposition for many older staff. Its feasibility however, is largely dependent on the generosity of the employer or company pension scheme
- ☐ reduction or elimination of overtime
- ☐ retirement of employees past normal retirement age
- ☐ retraining and transfer of staff to other work in the organization
- ☐ reduction or elimination of part-time work and use of sub-contractors
- ☐ selling surplus capacity and taking on sub-contract work from other organizations
- ☐ producing for future demand. Although this will create obvious financial difficulties, these may be less difficult than having to meet redundancy payments
- ☐ short-time working
- ☐ short-term layoffs

In some industries, particularly those subject to regular seasonal fluctuations, e.g., hotels, management-induced redundancy has tended to be seen as an unavoidable fact of life. If such fluctuations are facts of life, they may be exceedingly expensive, and increasingly therefore attention has been given to techniques of employment stabilization. Much of this is based on a well planned, well organized personnel policy and good personnel procedures, e.g., adequate manpower planning and efficient, perhaps centralized, recruitment and training in order to increase flexibility and interchangeability. It should be remembered that cyclical trade is not just uneconomic and undesirable in relation to personnel resources, but rather all resources used by an organization. For this reason, many employers have investigated the adoption of more stable production schedules, stimulating out-of-season sales and diversification to produce a flatter pattern of production.

A plan for redundancy

Section 45 of the 1972 Code of Practice states that:

A policy for dealing with reductions in the work force, if they become necessary, should be worked out in advance so far as practicable and should form part of the undertakings employment policies. As far as is consistent with operational efficiency and the success of the undertaking, management should, in consultation with employee representatives seek to avoid redundancies.

The Code also recommends that:

If redundancy becomes necessary, management in consultation, as appropriate, with employees or their representatives, should:
1 give as much warning as practicable to the employees concerned and to the Department of Employment
2 consider introducing schemes for voluntary redundancy, retirement, transfer to other establishments within the undertaking, and a phased rundown of employment
3 establish which employees are to be made redundant and the order of discharge
4 offer help to employees in finding other work in co-operation, where appropriate with the Department of Employment, and allow them reasonable time off for the purpose
5 decide how and when to make the facts public, ensuring that no announcement is made before the employees and their representatives and trade unions have been informed

Much of this is now obligatory in accordance with the EPCA. Minimum periods of notice are laid down that must be given and during which time consultation should occur. Notice of intended redundancies must be given to the Department of Employment. Time off must be given to enable redundant workers to obtain other work. Other points are not yet subject to statutory control, and it is therefore valuable, in an attempt to defuse a potentially explosive situation bred from uncertainty and fear, that management does not merely rely on statutory requirements and arrangements, but rather consults with, and communicates to, staff a written policy to which it will adhere should redundancy become necessary.

It will be recalled that although redundancy is usually acknowledged as a fair reason for termination of employment, a redundant employee may nevertheless claim unfair dismissal if staff are selected for redundancy in a discriminatory fashion or if an agreed procedure is not used. A basis for selection of staff for redundancy should therefore be agreed and stated in advance. Usually the basis will be seniority or efficiency. Generally, where unions are recognized, they will seek to negotiate a policy based on seniority, i.e., 'last in, first out' (LIFO). Although this is perhaps a fair basis, it in no way guarantees efficiency, since workers to be made redundant are not selected for adequacy or inadequacy of performance. Management might therefore prefer an efficiency basis. How to measure efficiency is no easy task, and indeed in the light of recent legislation and tribunal decisions, reliance on the comparative performance of workers as a basis for selection seems increasingly fraught with difficulty. Seniority recognizes service and loyalty. It recognizes that an older man is less likely to gain employment having been made redundant. It does not perhaps, however, recognize the often more considerable financial and other responsibilities of a younger person [21].

Kahn [4] suggests that although most workers initially express a preference for LIFO, this is little more than a surface veneer, most actually admitting the importance of efficiency, timekeeping, skill, etc. Indeed, many employers do successfully apply a combination of factors.

In selecting staff for redundancy, the problem of treatment of union officials must receive consideration. That a man is a union official is no reason for him not to be considered for redundancy. At the same time, if he is considered, a claim of victimization may well be made. It is therefore often prudent to exclude union officials from redundancy plans so long as they hold office, or at least until the matter has been thoroughly discussed with union officials at district level.

Non-statutory responsibility

Statute has made it increasingly difficult and increasingly expensive to make staff redundant. Statute has placed several duties on the employer. However, all of those duties currently cease when the employer has complied with time and money, and the employee has left. It is widely accepted that an employer has responsibilities over and above those imposed by Act of Parliament. Redundancy is a traumatic experience, at least in the short term for most workers. Some may welcome it, some may recover very rapidly. But for most it is an emotional jolt that may present a serious threat to the individual's self-esteem and promote attitudes that make future employment all the more unlikely [8]. With his image and reputation exposed, the employer must wherever possible help the redundant worker through this difficult time. How?

In a time of full employment, ideally the employer should attempt to re-locate staff with other employers or at least actively recruit the assistance of the Department of Employment. In less favourable times much can still be done. Staff should be counselled: advised of alternative opportunities, re-training facilities, how to enhance their re-employment prospects, agencies existing to help, their rights in relation to social security benefit, advice on managing any redundancy payments, etc. A Hardship Committee may be established, as at Delta Metals, providing not only a counselling service but also perhaps financial assistance in cases of particular hardship.

IPM CODE OF PRACTICE

In 1984 both statutory and non-statutory duties were brought together in convenient form in the IPM Redundancy Code [9]. The purpose of the code was 'to contribute to (the) improvement of current practice in relation to avoidance of redundancy, its implementation on a fair basis and the assistance given to employees'. It was intended to reflect 'minimum standards of good practice'.

Clearly, such a code has no legal implication, though it does encompass statutory provisions. It is, nevertheless, valuable for what it is; a professional code of practice with which personnel professionals ought to comply. As well as dealing with legal aspects, the code goes on to consider methods for the avoidance of compulsory redundancy, the drafting of redundancy agreements, procedures for implementing redundancies and assisting redundant employees. At first sight, it at times appears to state the obvious. However, shortly following its publication, the Group Manpower Manager of Cadbury Schweppes, in welcoming its introduction, referred to 'a steady stream of shock/horror stories . . .' displaying 'an ineptitude and crass lack of sensitivity' on the part of at least some UK personnel practitioners indicating that a lot of learning had still to be done [10]. Let us, therefore, examine the extent to which the policies outlined in the Code and earlier in this book are commonly implemented.

COMPANY PRACTICE

According to a survey of 350 companies carried out for the British Institute of Management in 1974 [11], approximately 60% had some form of redundancy policy, of which 75% had been introduced since 1965. Not surprisingly, most of these were larger companies with specialist personnel staff. Despite the obvious disadvantages regarding flexibility, most of those who had a comprehensive written policy considered that these were outweighed by the advantages to employees of knowing 'where they stood'. Over 80% of those companies already consulted unions and complied, more or less, with the terms of the EPCA. Most had schemes for providing counselling and re-training, and 80% gave notice and compensation in excess of the statutory minimum. A few (9%) also gave financial help to ex-employees unable to find other employment. Most restricted recruitment, took measures to re-train or transfer staff if redundancy appeared possible. Most gave financial assistance to ease difficulties arising from a change of job type or location within the organization. In selecting employees for redundancy, the most usual order of priority was:

☐   those over normal retiring age

☐ voluntary redundancy
☐ last in, first out

Seven years later, an extensive survey conducted by Alan Anderson of the Institute of Manpower Studies revealed a more chequered picture [12]. Faced with a need for a rapid shake-out of manpower during the late 1970s, employers at first responded by generous redundancy terms which produced a rapid and favourable employee response. The process was expensive, but relatively painless for all concerned. After a while, however, employers realized that the same results could be achieved at less cost.

Increasingly, the tendency was towards less generous terms, often indeed the absolute legal minimum. In his study of over 2000 employers who had recently made staff redundant, Anderson found that only one in three redundants received an extra-statutory pay, 35% of employees received nothing, 15% received less than £500 and only 4% received more than £5000. Apart from pensions, continuing payments were rarely made. So far as non-financial provision was concerned, less than 2% were given enhancement training, re-training in new skills or job sampling. Although almost 10% were given job-finding training, generally this lasted only half a day. Ninety per cent received no training at all. Less than 10% of employers informed employees about MSC re-training schemes or attempted to place employees in other jobs.

Such worrying statistics may, of course to some extent be explained by employees not requiring assistance or employers being simply unable to afford such facilities. Nevertheless, it does appear that employers' undertakings 'to do everything possible' often seem to fall short of really effective assistance. From the studies of employers' attempts to deal with redundancy through all or some of the measures mentioned, one finding stands out above all others. Namely, that if an employer's efforts are to have more than a marginal effect, a substantial commitment of resources, personal and above all, time is required. In a time of financial difficulty, such resources are often inevitably absent.

Having looked at an employer's responsibilities and policies, it may be appropriate to consider briefly his problems. The announcement of redundancies will often trigger industrial relations problems that could have repercussions throughout the workforce and aggravate the original situation. Redundancy may arise at a time of economic difficulty for the company and, as stated, a great deal of resources will be required to administer the problem, apart from any redundancy payments. In such circumstances, management may well be confronted by a common dilemma — a shrinking order book and diminishing cash-flow, accompanied by the inability to cut back on manpower owing to the costs of compensation.

REDUNDANCY AND THE WORKER

There have been many studies concerning the effects of redundancy upon the individual worker in recent years, most of them from a socio-economic point of view. To examine them all would provide material for a book in itself, and the following can only therefore be a brief summary perhaps tempting you to further reading.

The redundancy process may for convenience be divided into four stages:
1   a period of planning
2   a period following the announcement of redundancies
3   a period following the layoffs, during which the worker starts to seek other work
4   a period of settlement into a new job, jobs or long-term unemployment

Period 1 appears to have received little or no attention, though some insight is available from the 'Milton Plan' [13]. Period 2 similarly has produced little important research, apart from various attitude surveys. Many of these suggest the obvious fact that redundancy affects different people in different ways, the major determinant being their expectation of finding other work [14]. Peter Packard [15] proposes that the trauma felt by many is added to by a feeling of alienation as redundant staff become 'unclean'. Management avoids them, wishing to stay out of the firing line 'for redundant staff are likely to be hostile and slavering to bite the hand which once fed them', and prudent and ambitious colleagues put as much distance as possible between themselves and their 'failed' colleagues.

Periods 3 and 4 have received considerable attention. Reference has already been made to studies revealing the particular problems of the 55+ age group. Other studies have examined the various job finding methods used by different worker groups [1] and the criteria adopted by them in accepting or refusing alternative employment. MacKay and Reid [16], for example, distinguish between 'stickers' who look for work with comparable characteristics to their previous jobs, and 'snatchers' who take any job they can, while continuing to look for better employment, perhaps changing several times. Daniel's study also examined skill and job satisfaction and differences between old and new jobs. He found, for example, that 25% accepted a down-grading in skill level and that older workers, supervisors and men with specialist skills found least satisfaction in their new jobs. The same study also identified the problem of 'Galloping redundancy' and suggests that a worker, once made redundant, is at the top of a slippery slope leading to further redundancies with ever-decreasing compensation and job opportunities. Several recent studies have revealed further problems in finding new work, showing that even if employers are not overtly biased against the redundant worker, most are at least cautious when recruiting staff.

A considerable amount is known, therefore, about the practical economic aspects of worker behaviour during the period of unemployment, and in particular how, when and where they set about finding new jobs. Rather less is known about the psychological consequences of redundancy. For most the financial penalties seem to be not, at least in the short-term, too severe. However, Daniel [6] suggests that even for these 'the main costs are the less tangible ones involved in enduring a period of uncertainty, insecurity and fears associated with having one of the foundations of their lives threatened by decisions outside their control'. For some, this produces surprisingly positive responses [14]. However, generally as indicated above, writers, including Triffany et al. [17], Hartmann [18] and Hayes [8], refer to a reduction of self-esteem, which may promote attitudes that prevent an easy return to normal working life. Such a reaction, together with other factors, tends to lead to stress, which further reduces the ability to cope with problems, causing further loss of esteem, further stress and potentially ever onwards into a downward spiral [19]. Such consequences clearly have implications, not only for redundant employees but also, we would suggest, impose a moral duty on the employer making staff redundant to take steps, wherever possible, to minimize such negative reaction. Parkes [20], suggesting that redundancy can be expected to have all the normal consequences of profound emotional loss, argues that society should become more sensitive to such consequences. For managers this implies handling redundancy in such a way as to minimize damage to employees' self-esteem and by providing support and counselling as well as practical help in finding new work.

Redundancy is a fact of life in a free, modern society, and it may well be that current levels of unemployment will become the norm or increase still further as methods of production and new technology change the nation's manpower needs. It is, in our opinion, of critical importance, not only that more attention is given to investigating redundancy's psychological consequences, but also that more attention be given at shop-floor level to identifying and implementing means of helping individuals to cope more effectively.

REFERENCES

1. Daniel, W.W. (1972). *Whatever Happened to the Workers in Woolwich: A Survey of Redundancy in SE London.* PEP.
2. Parker, S.R. (1971). *Effects of the Redundancy Payments Act.* HMSO.
3. MSC (1980). *A Study of the Long-term Unemployed.* Manpower Services Commission.
4. Kahn, H.R. (1964). *Repercussions of Redundancy.* George Allen & Unwin.
5. MacKay, D.I. and Reid, G.L. (1971). *Men Leaving Steel.* British Steel Corporation.

6. Daniel, W.W. (1976). 'The high price of redundancy payments', *Personnel Management*, September.
7. Mukherjee, S. (1973). *Through No Fault of Their Own*. MacDonald.
8. Hayes, J. (1982). 'Changing the individual as a strategy for ameliorating the effects of unemployment', *Personnel Review*, Vol. 11, No. 3, pp. 26–32.
9. IPM (1984). *The Redundancy Code*. IPM.
10. Vaughan-Griffiths, C. (1984). 'Codifying practice on redundancy', *Personnel Management*, March, p. 3.
11. Smith, C.M. (1974). *Redundancy Policies*. BIM.
12. Anderson, A. (1981). 'Redundancy provisions', *Employment Gazette*, August, pp. 350–352.
13. Fox, A. (1975). *The Milton Plan*. IPM.
14. Pyne, R. and Arroba, T. (1980). 'Reactions to redundancy: a first test of a response typology', *Personnel Review*, Vol. 9, No. 3, Summer, pp. 22–26.
15. Packard, P. (1984). 'Redundancy: training staff to face the future', *Personnel Executive*, July, pp. 42–43.
16. MacKay, D.I. and Reid, G.L. (1972). 'Redundancy, unemployment and manpower policy', *The Economic Journal*, Vol. 82, No. 328, December.
17. Tiffany, D.W. *et al.* (1970). *The Unemployed: A Socio-Psychological Portrait*. Prentice-Hall.
18. Hartmann, P. (1972). 'A study of attitudes in industrial rehabilitation', *Occupational Psychology*, Vol. 46, No. 2, pp. 87–97.
19. Fineman, S. (1979). 'A psychological model of stress and the application to managerial unemployment', *Human Relations*, Vol. 32, pp. 323–345.
20. Parkes, C.M. (1971). 'Psycho-social transitions: a field for study', *Social Science and Medicine*, pp. 101–115.
21. ACAS (1986). *Redundancy Arrangements*. ACAS.

PART 8: FURTHER RECOMMENDED READING

Selwyn, N.M. (1982). *Law of Employment*. Butterworths.
Whincup, M. (1983). *Modern Employment Law*. Heinemann.
Slade, E.A. (1983). *Tolley's Employment Handbook*. Tolley.

PART 8: SAMPLE EXAMINATION QUESTIONS

(a) Outline the current law relating to redundancy.
(b) Discuss the implications of this legislation for the building society personnel manager at a time when the number of mergers between societies has increased considerably. CBSI

Douglas McGregor used the 'red hot stove' rule as a way of explaining good disciplinary practice because of four features involved when someone touches a red hot stove:

(a) The burn is immediate. There is no question of cause and effect.
(b) There was warning. Everyone know what will happen if they touch a red hot stove.
(c) The discipline is consistent. Everyone who touches the stove is burned.
(d) The discipline is impersonal. A person is burned not because of who he is, but because he touched the stove.

How adequate do you regard that analogy as a model for disciplinary procedure? IPM

Why is it necessary to have a disciplinary procedure? Draft a model procedure. CBSI

Indicate the advice you would give to your top management if asked to submit your views on the criteria that should govern the formulation of a policy with regard to redundancies and methods for the implementation of redundancies. ICSA

Describe the disciplinary procedure and practice in an organization (or section of an organization) with which you are familiar and explain how and why you feel it needs to be altered. IPM

On what grounds will dismissal generally be fair? What measures can a Personnel Manager take to ensure as far as possible that unfair dismissal is avoided? CBSI

In what ways may an organization plan to avoid unnecessary redundancies, and ease those which are inevitable? IAM

The introduction of new technology is beginning to cause overmanning in the region of the bank in which you are a personnel officer. It is thought that it should be possible to reduce the total number of employees in the region by 33 per cent over a 3-year period. Clerical and administrative staff will be most affected.

It has been agreed that the reduction will be met by:

  (i) the cessation of all recruitment of clerical workers and administrative staff for the foreseeable future;
  (ii) normal wastage (currently 4 per cent per annum in these groups);
 (iii) transfer of staff between branches;
 (iv) a re-training programme; and
  (v) voluntary early retirement (this should account for about 2 per cent per annum in the appropriate grades).

Your regional manager asks you to outline a programme of communication and consultation. What would you propose?   CIB

Evaluate the role of each in industrial conflict.   CIB

How would you improve the operation of the disciplinary procedure in your organization? Indicate why you think your proposal might be an improvement.
                    IPM

(a) Distinguish between 'disciplinary' and 'grievance' procedures.
(b) What guidelines would you lay down for the conduct of:
  (i) disciplinary procedures?
  (ii) grievance procedures?   IAM

Outline the steps involved in a formal disciplinary procedure (for an organization with unionized employees) and show how the procedure would operate in a case of:

(a) persistent absenteeism, and
(b) theft of envelopes from the organization's offices.   ICSA

Part 9
Change

32
The management of change

Change is inevitable. It may be dictated by events outside an organization or generated internally. In an ever-changing environment, more resourceful managements endeavour to prepare for and initiate change rather than react to events as they occur. In order to do this, their staff must be adaptable and imaginative and encouraged to face up to the challenge of change rather than ignore it. Changes in technology receive much publicity, but they cannot succeed without a workforce that possesses the right attitudes and abilities. This requires much more than training; a total climate has to be created in which individuals will not feel threatened by change.

If is often stated that the 'pace of life' is quickening and that individuals are subjected to greater stress both at work and in their private lives. This section aims to consider the effects of change on the individual and the workgroup, and how management might help to ease this burden. People generally are suspicious of change and might feel insecure or threatened. If management attempts to impose change in an autocratic manner, these emotions may be followed by strong resistance. The personnel manager will need to use his knowledge of human relations in advising management on methods of introducing change.

RESISTANCE TO CHANGE

It is usually assumed that change is both logical and desirable. In what circumstances, therefore, is resistance to change likely to be encountered? The following are suggested for consideration:

1 *When psychological and social needs are insufficiently understood and met.*
Personality and attitudes are developed through childhood over many years. These are extremely difficult to change over a short period, but may be responsive to different styles of leadership and management. An intellectual assessment of a situation may not agree with an employee's emotional view. The reasons behind these

emotions must be probed in order to understand them. Imagined threats of change, e.g. redundancy, may be countered with various 'defence mechanisms' such as aggression, withdrawal or lack of co-operation.

More rational considerations concerning employees might also be appropriate. Management might ask questions that are undoubtedly going through the minds of individuals. These could include: what incentive is there for individual change? any rewards? any loss of present rewards?; any compensation for losses?; is he/she equipped to deal with change?. Social habits and relationships cannot be overlooked either, and where groups have established methods of working it may be difficult to get them to change.

2   *When technological needs are insufficiently taken into consideration.*
Change may hold fears of technical inadequacy for individuals and it is essential that the effects upon skill requirements be communicated and remedied through training where necessary. The 'socio-technical' systems must also be taken account of (see Chapter 3) in order that teamwork may be used to the full.

Despite the implicit common sense of the above points, much empirical research has found that often management does not take these considerations into account when change occurs or is introduced. Ronken and Lawrence [1] found that changes in the social situation are as important as technical change.

In an electronics factory in which they were researching, a new engineer was appointed whose duties included the supervision of female operators. His brusque manner contrasted with that of his predecessor, and it was observed that certain operators reacted to this and did not co-operate as well as previously. This resistance to social change is not uncommon, but is often undetected owing to 'blind spots' of busy managers.

A classic study of resistance to change was carried out by Coch and French [2] in a clothing factory. A change in work method was introduced to four separate work groups. The methods of introduction were, however, controlled by the researchers. The change was imposed upon the first group allowing no participation by group members. Slightly more participation was allowed in the second and third groups, and the fourth group was allowed total participation in the planned change. After the change, the output of the first group was reduced by one third, there was aggression and lack of co-operation and some staff left. The fourth group, however, experienced a lower initial drop in output than the others, a speedy recovery and virtually no hostility from the staff.

Participation in change is only one aspect that will be pursued later. It is important to remember, however, that resistance to change is inevitable if it is not managed properly, and any cosmetic consultation will be quickly seen for what it is. Account must be taken of the social climate within the organization if change is to be beneficial rather than a cause of confrontation and unrest.

DEALING WITH CHANGE

How can organizations best face up to the challenge? It is possible merely to react to changes as they occur — a kind of 'management by crisis'. When an established market is suddenly lost or a major item of equipment breaks down, it is management's job to deal with the problem, and it could be stated that this is part of day-to-day task of management. Although this is perfectly true it might be pertinent to question whether or not an organization is receiving too many 'surprises', and whether the staff is capable of handling the situation. Is the management endeavouring to anticipate problems, both technical and social, before they arise and are staff being involved in this process?

It is a question of creating a climate within which change can be both accommodated and initiated without undue stress or disruption. In recent years, many organizations have introduced initiatives with the object of ensuring that management and staff are both able to cope with the problems of change, and recognize the opportunities that change might offer. These are usually known by the title of 'Organization Development'.

ORGANIZATION DEVELOPMENT (OD)

Organization development has been described by Bennis [3] as

'an educational strategy adopted to bring about a planned organizational change'

whereas French and Bell [4] refer to it as

'a long-range effort to improve an organization's problem-solving capability and its ability to cope with change . . . with the help of an external consultant'.

It will be seen from the above definitions that they both agree on one thing — helping the organization to be able to cope with change. The actual way in which OD is approached will vary depending on the situation and, of course, the individual consultant or manager responsible. It embraces many areas and techniques and doesn't really have any defined boundaries [5]. Various theories have been introduced regarding organizations and change. They lead to various techniques that are, however, basically directed towards similar goals. It may be helpful to outline some of these goals as described by Bennis [3] who has worked with many organizations as a consultant 'change agent'. Those most commonly sought are:

- ☐ improvement in interpersonl competence
- ☐ a shift in values so that human factors are considered legitimate
- ☐ development of increased understanding between and within working groups in order to reduce tensions
- ☐ development of more effective 'team management'
- ☐ development of better methods of conflict resolution — more rational and open methods
- ☐ development of 'organic' rather than 'mechanical' organizations

Organizations may ask external 'change agents' to analyse problems and act as a catalyst in developing an improved climate. Larger companies may employ full time OD specialists, and General Motors of America is reputed to have well over 100 specialists working in different parts of the world. Given that OD is attempting to solve practical problems using behavioural expertise, how do the specialists set about introducing an OD 'programme' and what techniques do they use? It may be useful to describe briefly some of the situations that may indicate a need for OD, and outline some of the strategies and activities that take place as part of OD.

Indications of need

1 Rapid and unexpected change — particularly technological change — may overwhelm an inflexible and bureaucratic organization
2 Rapid growth — despite improvements in communication systems; large organizations often operate well below their real potential and the pace of growth may outstrip the level of human resources
3 Diversification — in both industrial activity and occupations
4 Changes in attitudes — both middle management and other employees have new values and aspirations and different attitudes to auhority from those of their predecessors

Activities

The above situations may give rise to various problems for an individual or a work group. After careful analysis of the organization, some of the more common techniques used by OD specialists are discussed below.

Team development

This activity often forms an early part of a programme, and will concentrate on both the relationships and the tasks of the group in question. The specialist may conduct individual interviews and group sessions, and the usual pattern will be, collection of information, feedback to the team, discussion and action planning. These sessions often throw up serious misconceptions of the roles and personalities of different members of the group.

Intergroup relationships

Most people can think of examples of individual or group conflict in an organization. It is one of the most common problems and expends a great deal of energy in wasteful competition. Again the OD specialist will spend time with each of the groups, endeavouring to analyse their attitudes and problems. He will then bring the groups together in order to reduce tension and encourage discussion of problems. Several techniques have been developed for dealing with this common problem, which is often based upon simple misunderstandings that have become emotionally charged.

Goal-setting and planning

Goal-setting at individual, group or organizational level often forms a major part of an OD programme. Although the setting of targets might be considered an obvious aspect of running a business, OD orientated programmes concentrate particularly on commitment and involvement at all levels. Where an organization is experiencing particular problems of stress, such as a recent change in top management or a major product diversification, a technique known as a 'confrontation meeting' is sometimes used. This will probably involve the whole of the management staff, including top management. In essence, the meeting is intended to encourage open and frank discussion about problems, and it is essential that those participating are assured that no recriminations will take place. A dynamic action programme must follow the main confrontation session if it is to be put to positive use.

Survey feedback

A great deal of OD work involves the exchange and feedback of information. Surveys are conducted on a formal basis by some practitioners, but others favour a more flexible system. The responses obtained are analysed and used to encourage a more open and realistic climate, one of the key principles of OD theory.

T-group sessions

A great many OD specialists employ 'T-group training', or 'sensitivity training' as it is sometimes called. Essentially, this is a small group effort designed to make its participants more aware of themselves and the group process. It is essential that these sessions are carried out under the guidance of a competent behavioural scientist, as they can become stressful for persons of a sensitive disposition. These 'laboratory' sessions have caused some controversy, despite the beneficial effects claimed by advocates of the technique, and they are discussed further under Training and Development.

Criticisms

OD is not without its critics. Apart from the criticisms of some of the methodology, such as T-group training, which is referred to elsewhere, other weaknesses are cited. Many OD programmes are considered to be too ambitious and expensive. A Blake and Mouton grid programme (see Chapter 5) may, for instance, last for up to 5 years. It is also suggested that they pay insufficient attention to technical and structural problems while concentrating on the human and social aspects of organizations. OD programmes have also been accused of being too ready to adopt an 'ideal' model and of failing to find permanent answers to organizational problems. These criticisms obviously contain some substance, although many of them would be refuted by proponents of OD. There are undoubtedly cases of success and failure. The fact remains that many organizations are employing OD techniques for the development of their staff. They realize that developing managers and other staff as individuals may not be enough. People cannot work in isolation, and development of groups and inter-group cooperation is of equal importance for coping with change.

OD and the personnel manager

Where an outside consultant is not employed, it may rest with the personnel manager to take on the role of 'change agent'. He is, in any case, likely to be well involved in any OD programme. Either way, it will be necessary to ensure that his diagnostic and behavioural skills are well developed. He will then be in a position to take part in the analysis of the organization and its problems as well as helping to solve some of them. It will also be necessary to identify with the objectives of the organization and show clearly that the personnel manager has a real contribution to make to their successful attainment. Thakur *et al.* [6] illustrate how OD can be developed through the personnel function, and they also include some case studies.

PRACTICAL CONSIDERATIONS

Many managers consider that OD and other similar approaches are too theoretical and probably only apply to the USA. These views are understandable and have some validity, as we have already indicated above. However, there are many examples of successful change management in the UK from which we can all learn practical lessons.

The Work Research Unit (WRU) of the Department of Employment recently undertook a series of studies of the implementation of change, particularly new technology, and its effects upon organizations and workers [7]. These studies included the introduction of computer-based information systems at Lloyds Register of Shipping, the move of 2500 National Westminster Bank employees to the new 600 ft headquarters tower in the City and the construction of a new computer-controlled brewery by Courage.

As a result of the many examples of success and difficulty, the WRU was able to isolate certain key factors both as prerequisites for successful change and influencing the change process.

Some of the conditions favouring successful change were:

☐ senior management commitment
☐ early consultation with trade unions and/or employees
☐ adequate funding (to avoid skimping on facilities, training, etc).
☐ effective communication throughout the process
☐ an external facilitator can often help
☐ shared economic motives — the competitiveness and success of the business is recognized by staff as legitimate, provided their security is also considered
☐ patience — few major changes can be achieved without it

Further factors that were considered to be vital to the success of managing change included:

☐ remembering that technical decisions affect employees
☐ genuine involvement and participation by employees generates ideas and the willingness to learn and adapt. (It was recognized that a participative approach goes against traditional management style and threatens trade union conventions in some organizations. These difficulties must be allowed for, but should not obscure the benefits of this approach)
☐ regular progress reviews, with revision of objectives if necessary

Much of the above appears almost obvious when simply listed in this way. Mistakes are still made, however, and problems will always be present. Change also presents opportunities for the economic performance of the organization and the job security and satisfaction of the workforce. These opportunities will only be fully realized if the change is technically feasible, properly financed and carried out by management that recognizes and understands the factors for success.

TECHNOLOGY AGREEMENTS

Many larger employers have negotiated agreements with trade unions concerning the introduction of new technology. These would obviously vary in detail, but areas covered might include:

1 A statement of the type of technology to be introduced and the *advantages* to the organization.
2 The effects of technology upon *employment* and terms and conditions of work, e.g., regarding de-skilling, redeployment, redundancy.
3 Facilities to enable the union to *monitor* the effects of technology on such things as work flow, working conditions, health and safety.
4 Provisions for *training* and retraining of staff.
5 Safeguards and facilities for dealing with *health and safety* matters, e.g., eye strain, noise levels, ventilation, radiation.

REFERENCES

1. Ronken, H. and Lawrence, P.R. (1952). *Administering Changes: A Case Study of Human Relations in a Factory*. Harvard University Press.
2. Coch, L. and French, J.R.P. (1948). 'Overcoming resistance to change', *Human Relations*.
3. Bennis, W.G. (1969). *Organisation Development: Its Nature, Origin and Prospects*. Addison-Wesley.
4. French, W.L. and Bell, C.H. (1978). *Organisation Development*, 2nd Edn. Prentice-Hall.
5. For a review of these approaches see Pritchard, W. (1984). 'What's new in organisation development', *Personnel Management*, July.
6. Thakur, M., Bristow, J. and Corby, K. (1978). *Personnel in Change*. IPM.
7. Department of Employment (1982). *Meeting the Challenge of Change*.

PART 9: FURTHER RECOMMENDED READING

French, W.L. and Bell, C.H. (1973). *Organisational Development: Behavioural Science Interventions for Organisation Improvement.* Prentice-Hall.

Lawrence, P.R. and Lorsch, J.W. (1969). *Developing Organisation: Diagnosis and Action.* Addison-Wesley.

Beckhard, R. and Harris, R.T. (1977). *Organisational Transitions: Managing Complex Change.* Addison-Wesley.

Faucheaux, C., Amado, G. and Laurant, A. (1982). 'Organisation development and change', *Annual Review of Psychology.* Vol. 33.

Tichy, N. (1983). *Managing Strategic Change — Technical, Political and Cultural Dynamics.* Wiley.

PART 9: SAMPLE EXAMINATION QUESTIONS

What problems do management face in adapting to new work technologies?
                                                                    CACA
What are the managerial and organizational implications for the banks of current technological and economic change?   CIB

Why do people sometimes resist change in organizations? What can be done to reduce resistance?   CIB

Diversification and deregulation are subjects of current debate in the building society industry. What organizational and human problems do you anticipate they will create, and what techniques can the personnel manager use to alleviate these?   CBSI

Introducing change within an organization is often difficult. Why do staff often resent change and how can management ensure it is more readily received?
                                                                    CBSI

(a) Why do most people resent change?
(b) Is employee resistance to change always detrimental to an organization?
                                                                    IAM
(a) Discuss some objectives that the management of an organization may seek to achieve when introducing new technology.
(b) Suggest, if possible with examples, how management may seek to minimize some of the possible consequences of technological change with regard to
    (i) employment
    (ii) job design   IAM

In recent years the larger banking groups have introduced a wide range of new products/services and entered new markets. Giving examples of some of the main innovations which have taken place, discuss the implications of these changes for the management of the banks.   CIB

What administrative, organizational and behavioural problems of implementation may be experienced by an enterprise which is designing and installing a new computer-based management information system?   CACA

'Technical change is still often seen as a technical matter, with no established role or function for personnel management.' Why are personnel specialists so often excluded from the planning and introduction of technical change? What can they do to increase their involvement?   ICSA

Examine the behavioural implications of the widespread introduction of computers and information technology in either office environment or a factory.
IPM

Describe an example of some organizational change (e.g., a relocation, introduction of new technology) with which you are familiar either through your reading or through personal experience. Comment on the way the change was managed, with particular reference to any techniques that you consider could have been helpful, or mistakes made that could have been avoided.   IPM

Author Index

Tuckman, F. 302
Turner, H.A. 273
Tyson, S. 15

Ulrich, L. 138
Ungerson, B. 139, 168
Upton, R. 339

Vaughan-Griffiths 351
Vroom, V.H. 56, 61, 75, 207

Walker, K. 298
Watson, T. 17
Weitz, J. 119
Whitehill, A.M. 56
Whyte, W.F. 208
Woodward, J. 307

Subject Index